Architecture NATA

Part-B (MCQ-Paper)

Latest Edition
Practice Kit

10 Tests
10 Mock Test

Based On Real Exam Pattern

✓ Thoroughly Revised and Updated

✓ Detailed Analysis of all MCQs

Title	: Architecture NATA Part-B (MCQ-Paper)
Author Name	: Mr. Rohit Manglik
Published By	: EduGorilla Community Pvt. Ltd.
Publishers Address	: 12/651, First Floor Opp. Arvindo Park, Near Jama Masjid, Indira Nagar, Lucknow, Uttar Pradesh-226016, India

Copyright EduGorilla

ISBN : 978-93-90239-86-3

Second Edition

Disclaimer EduGorilla

Compiled and created by EduGorilla Community Pvt. Ltd

Printed By EduGorilla Community Pvt. Ltd.

ROHIT MANGLIK
CEO, EduGorilla

Dear Applicants,

People say *"Success comes to those who work hard."* But I've seen people working hard for their exams day in and day out for marginal success. While others succeed in their examinations by putting in just half the work. So are they God Gifted? No! I believe that it's because they work *smart* and not just *hard*. Similarly, for your exams, you should strategize your preparation so as to increase the likelihood of success. Well with EduGorilla get ready to increase your *chances of selection* in your exam by *16x*.

EduGorilla helps you in not only working *hard* but also working in a *smart and strategic* manner. With EduGorilla's preparation package, you get a chance to make your exam preparation easy, and a fun learning path towards selection. Finding the right path to your preparations can be difficult if you don't know in which direction to head. Don't worry, we have you covered! EduGorilla will be your guide to success in your journey. With our Preparation Package, you can prepare strategically and beat the exam in just one attempt.

EduGorilla's Preparation Package includes-

• **Test Series**   • **Books**

Our preparation package is handcrafted as per the latest changes, expert opinions, and students' discretion. Thus, enabling you to get through each stage of the selection process for your exam.

Our Books are designed by the teachers and experts of the respective exam with a combined 150+ years of experience; to provide you with easy, efficient, and effective learning. Our books are smart, in the sense that not only do they give you the answers to the questions but also provide similar questions for practice.

EduGorilla's competent Test Series gives you real-time experience and confidence through which you can clear your offline or online exam in just one attempt. We currently host 83,000+ mock tests for 1,440+ competitive and academic exams.

Thus, EduGorilla misses no chance to assist you in your preparation and covers all stages of the exam, so that you don't have to look anywhere else.

We provide complete preparation packages for defense, banking, teaching, and other National & State-Level exams. Hence, it doesn't matter which exam you aspire to because you will reach your success.

ALL THE BEST !

Let EduGorilla be your Guide to Success.

Rohit Manglik,
Founder and CEO, EduGorilla

INTRODUCTION

EduGorilla focuses on guiding students to succeed in their examinations. With that in mind, our book, titled "Architecture NATA : Part-B (MCQ-Paper)", has been drafted through the collective efforts of our distinguished experts with 150+ years of combined experience. This book consists of questions that are created following the latest changes in the syllabus and exam pattern. We compiled the book on the basis of questions that are most likely to appear in the NATA. Through EduGorilla's "Architecture NATA : Part-B (MCQ-Paper)" your chances of success will increase 16x.

EduGorilla does this through our Complete Preparation Package. This package consists of well-conceptualized and structured content in the form of questions that are tailor-made according to your needs and will help you practice for exams in a smart way by pinpointing all the necessary information. It also provides hints and solutions, along with a smart answer sheet for your self-evaluation. You can assess your shortcomings and work accordingly on areas that may require more of your attention.

EduGorilla promises to help you succeed in your examination and accomplish your dream goals. We believe in our aspirants and see them at the top of the merit list. And the first step towards the top is to start preparing with us. EduGorilla's "Architecture NATA : Part-B (MCQ-Paper)" includes the following attributes.

➤ Well-Researched Content

➤ Top-Notch Quality

➤ Detailed Answers and Analysis

➤ Smart Answer Sheet

➤ Exam Relevant Questions

Therefore, EduGorilla fortifies your preparation and makes it durable enough to help you stand tall and beat the examination.

NATA

Scan QR code for Eligibility, Exam Pattern, Syllabus and more.

Book ID: 0166

TABLE OF CONTENTS

Mock Test 01

Mathematics

Q.1 If f is a function of real variable x satisfying f (x + 4) − f (x + 2) +f(x) = 0, then f is a periodic functionwith period:

A. 6   **B.** 8   **C.** 10   **D.** 12

Q.2 The number of integral values of m for which the equation, (1 + m2) x2 − 2(1 + 3m) x + (1 + 8m) = 0, has no real root, is:

A. 1   **B.** 2
C. 3   **D.** infinitely many

Q.3 If $\tan\frac{\alpha}{3} = \frac{1}{2}$, then the value of $\tan\alpha + \cot\alpha$ is:

A. $\frac{11}{23}$ **B.** $\frac{12}{23}$ **C.** $\frac{121}{46}$ **D.** $\frac{125}{22}$

Q.4 In a single throw of two dice, find the probability of the first dice always occur odd number and sum of two dice is greater than 5.

A. $\frac{1}{4}$ **B.** $\frac{2}{3}$ **C.** $\frac{3}{4}$ **D.** $\frac{1}{3}$

Q.5 For acute angle θ, find value of sec²θ−tan²θ

A. 1   **B.** 2   **C.** 3   **D.** 0

Q.6 If the system of linear equations :

x+ 3y +7z = 0

-x + 4y +7z = 0

(sin3θ)x+ (cos2 θ)y +2z = 0 has a non-trivial solution, then the number of values of θ lying in the interval [0, π], is-

A. one   **B.** two
C. three   **D.** more then three

Q.7 A box contains 5 black and 4 white balls. A ball is drawn at random and its colour is noted. The ball is then put back in the box along with two additional balls of its opposite colour. If a ball is drawn again from the box, then the probability that the ball drawn now is black, is

A. $\frac{7}{11}$ **B.** $\frac{5}{11}$ **C.** $\frac{53}{99}$ **D.** $\frac{48}{99}$

Q.8 For a positive integer n, if the mean of the binomial coefficient in the expansion of
(a + b)²ⁿ⁻³ is 16, then n is equal to-

A. 4   **B.** 5   **C.** 7   **D.** 9

Q.9 A code word of length 4 consists of two distinct consonants in the English alphabet followed by two digits from 1 to 9, with repetition allowed in digits. If the number of code words so formed ending with an even digit is 432 k, then k is equal to :

A. 7   **B.** 5   **C.** 49   **D.** 35

Q.10 Let a, b, c, d and e be distinct positive numbers. If a, b, c and 1/c, 1/d, 1/e both are in A.P. and b, c, d are in G.P. then

A. a, c, e are in G.P.   **B.** a, b, e are in G.P.
C. a, b ,e are in A.P.   **D.** a, c, e are in A.P.

Q.11 Six bells commencing tolling together toll at intervals of 2, 4, 6, 8,10 and 12 seconds respectively.In 30 minutes how many times do they toll together?

A. 12   **B.** 16   **C.** 18   **D.** 15

Q.12 The ratio of the two numbers is 5 : 7 and their LCM is 105. If X is the ratio of the sum of the numbers and the difference of the numbers. What is the value of X?

A. 18   **B.** 21   **C.** 6   **D.** 12

Q.13 A gardener had a number of shrubs to plant in rows . At first he tried to plant 8, then 12 and then 16 in a row but he always had 3 shrubs left with him . On trying 7 shrubs he was left with none.Find the total number of shrubs.

A. 149   **B.** 159   **C.** 156   **D.** 147

Q.14 One of the two events, A and B must occur. If $P(A) = \left(\frac{2}{3}\right) P(B)$, the odds in favour of B are:

A. $1:2$ **B.** $3:2$ **C.** $2:3$ **D.** $3:5$

Q.15 Find the least number of five digits which is exactly divisible by 12, 15 and 18.

A. 1080   **B.** 10080   **C.** 10025   **D.** 11080

Q.16 The order of the matrix $\begin{bmatrix} 1 & 2 \\ 3 & 4 \end{bmatrix}$ is:

A. 2 × 2   **B.** 4 × 1
C. 1 × 4   **D.** None of these

Q.17 The average weight of 45 passenger on board an aircraft is 50 kg. If the weight of 5 members of the crew is added, the average is reduced by half kilogram . What is the average weight of the crew members?

A. 45 kg   **B.** 48kg   **C.** 58kg   **D.** 68kg

Q.18 A man spends Rs 1,800 per month on an average for the first four mouths and Rs 2,000 per month for the nest 8 months and saves Rs 5,600 a year. What is his average monthly income ?

A. Rs 5,400   **B.** Rs 3,500   **C.** Rs 4,400   **D.** Rs 2,400

Q.19 The average of 5 numbers is 9 and the average of the last three numbers is 5.Find the average of the first two numbers.

A. 45   **B.** 15   **C.** 25   **D.** 35

Q.20 Monica's average expenses for 4 days is Rs 6.0. She spent Rs 7.70 on first day, Rs 6.30 on second day. If she spent 10 on third day , How much did she spend on the 4th day?

A. Rs 2   **B.** Rs 3   **C.** Rs 4   **D.** Rs 0

General Aptitude

Q.21 Direction: Which answer figure will complete the pattern in the Problem figure?

Problem Figure

Answer Figure

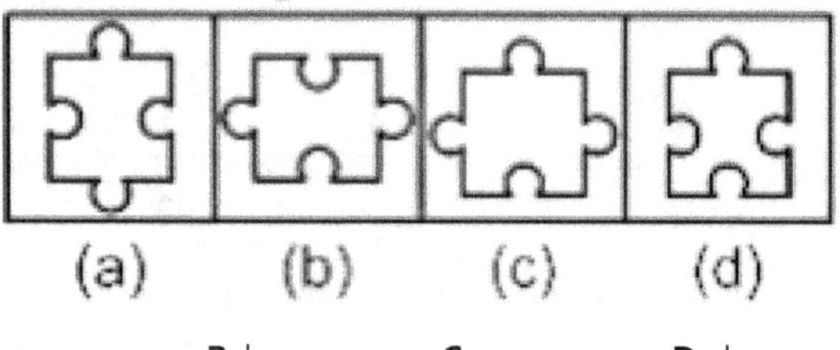

A. a   **B.** b   **C.** c   **D.** d

Q.22 The drawing represents a flat piece of sheet. The dotted lines show where the sheet has to be folded. Find the object that can be made by folding the sheet.

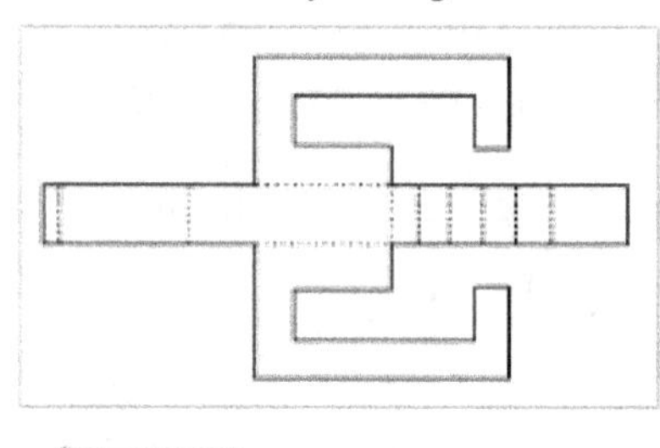

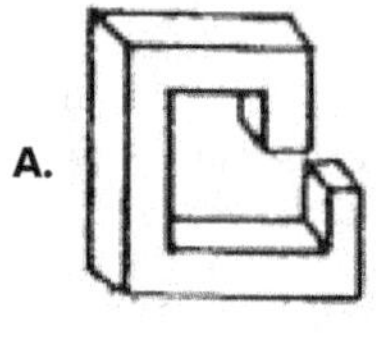

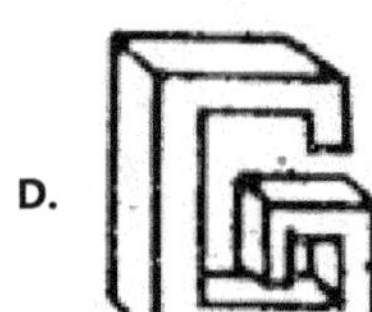

Q.23 Select the figure which when placed in the blank space of the figure marked 'X' would complete the pattern.

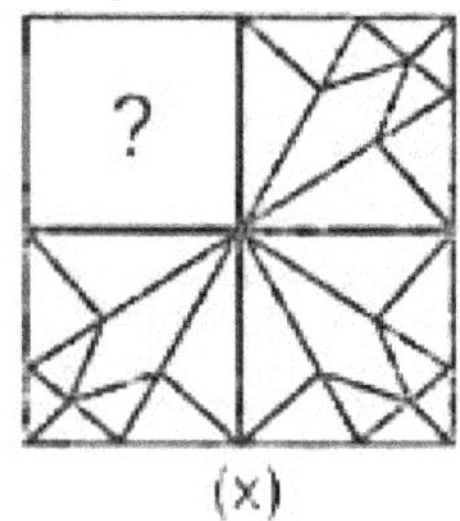

(X)

A.

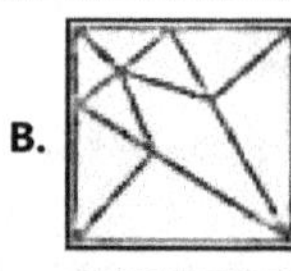

B.

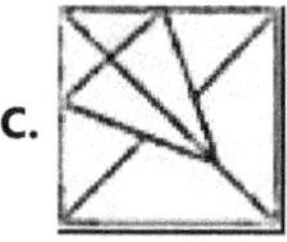

C.

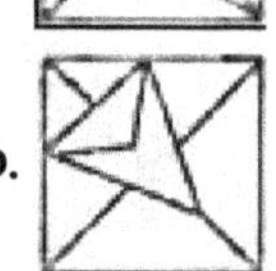

D.

Q.24 Complete the given number series by stating the value in place of ?-

1, 2, 5, 16, 65, ?

A. 326   **B.** 324   **C.** 330   **D.** 340

Q.25 Arrange the objects given the question figure, according to the stated manner and choose the correct composite figure.

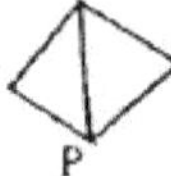

P

Q

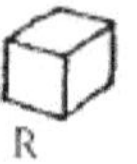

R

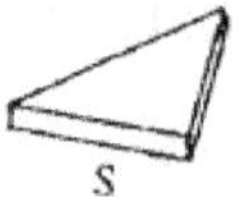

S

Q touching P only, P between R & Q only, S touching R only

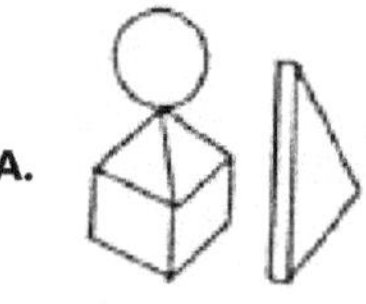

A.

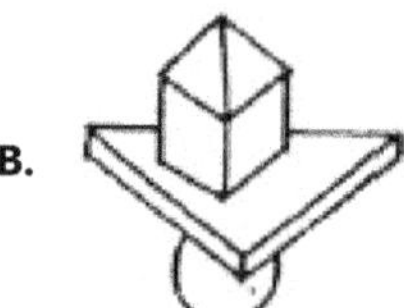

B.

C.

D.

Q.26 In the numeric series given below, a term is missing. Find that missing term from the options-

121, 225, 361, ?

A. 529   **B.** 729   **C.** 185   **D.** 400

Q.27 Out of the given figures, four are similar in a certain way, one is not. Which figure does not belong to the group?

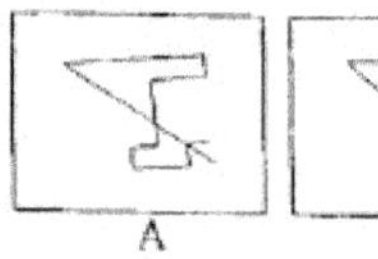

A

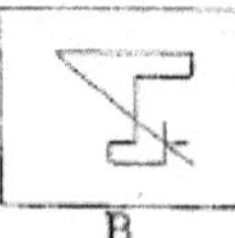

B

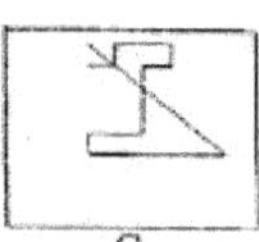

C

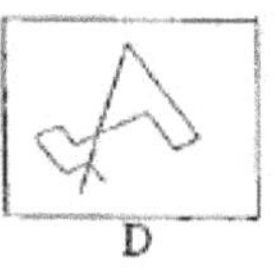

D

A. a   **B.** b   **C.** c   **D.** d

Q.28 Out of the four figures given in each question. Three are similar in a certain way. However, one figure is not like the other three. Trace the number of that figure which is different from the rest.

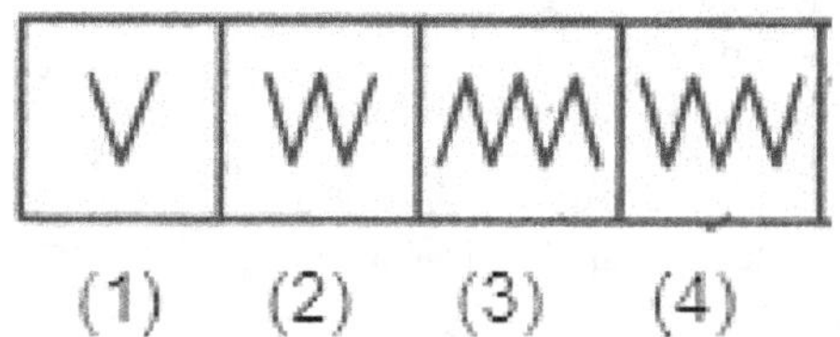

(1)   (2)   (3)   (4)

A. 1   **B.** 2   **C.** 3   **D.** 4

Q.29 The problem figure in the box on the left has one identical figure from amongst A, B, C and D on the right. Find the figure

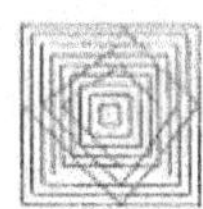 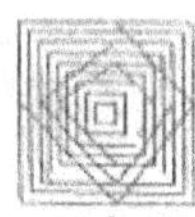 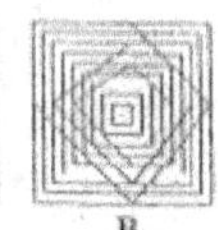 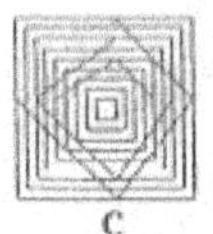 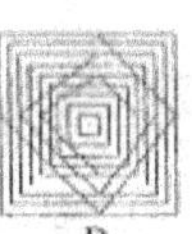

A. a   **B.** b   **C.** c   **D.** d

Q.30 The problem figure in the box on the left has one identical figure from amongst A, B, C and D on the right. Find the figure

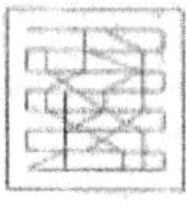 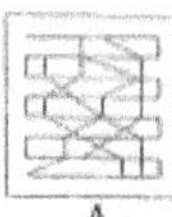 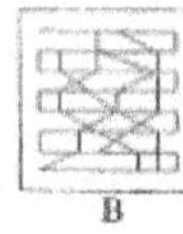 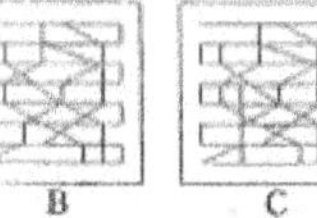 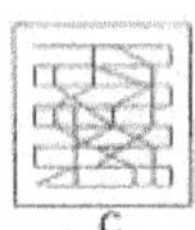 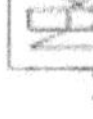

A. a   **B.** b   **C.** c   **D.** d

Q.31 Select from the alternatives, the dice that can be formed by folding the open dice given below-

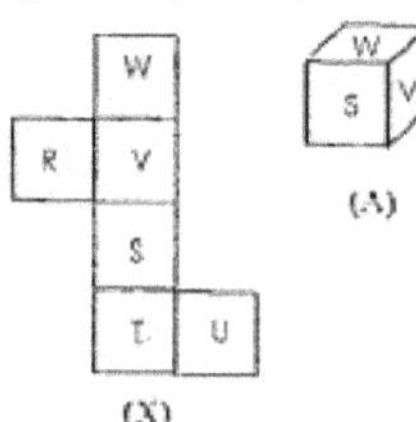

A. Only A   **B.** Only B
C. Only A and C   **D.** All of these

Q.32 If a mirror is placed on line AB, then which of the answer figures is the right image of the given figure?

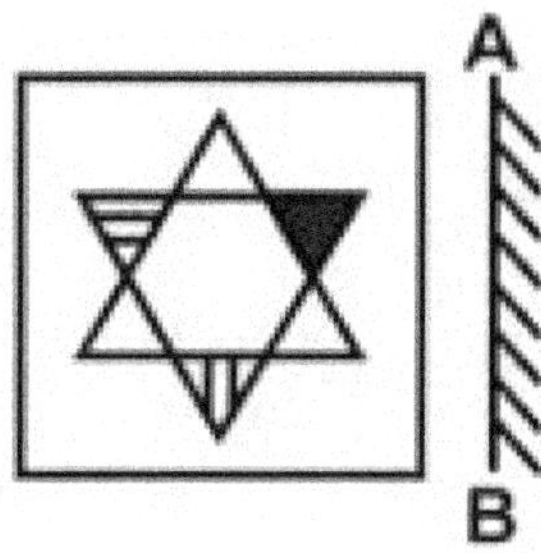

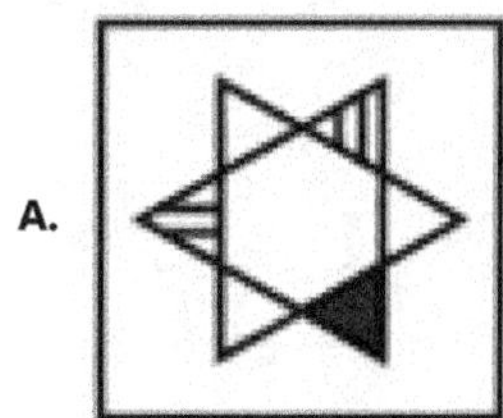 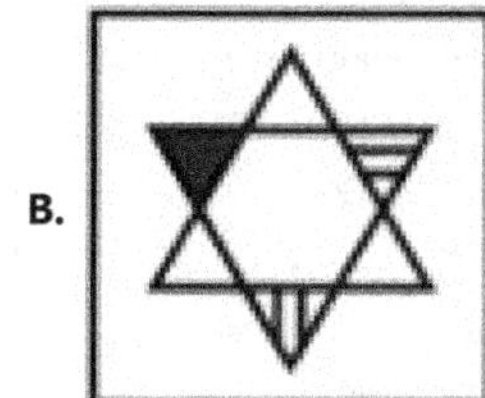

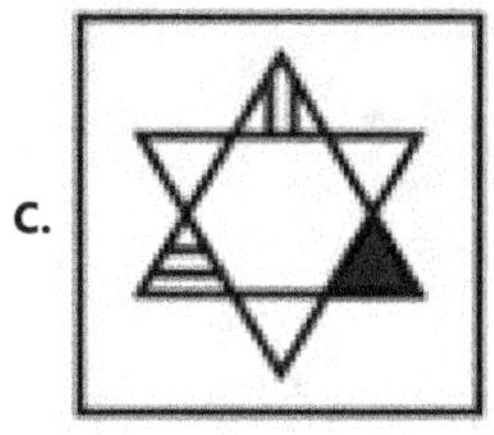 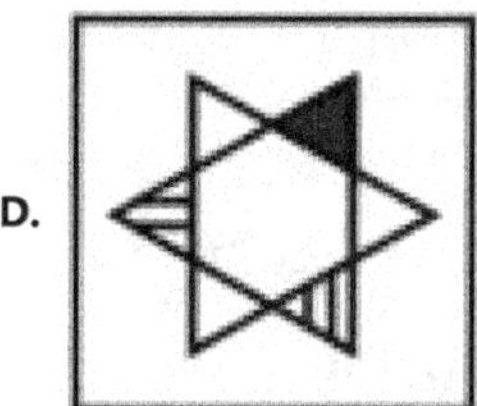

A. B. C. D.

Q.33 Complete the number series given below by stating the number that will come in place of ?

1, 8, 9, 64, 25, ?

A. 216   **B.** 343   **C.** 125   **D.** 49

Q.34 Which of the option is the correct mirror image of the following figure if the mirror is placed on line AB?

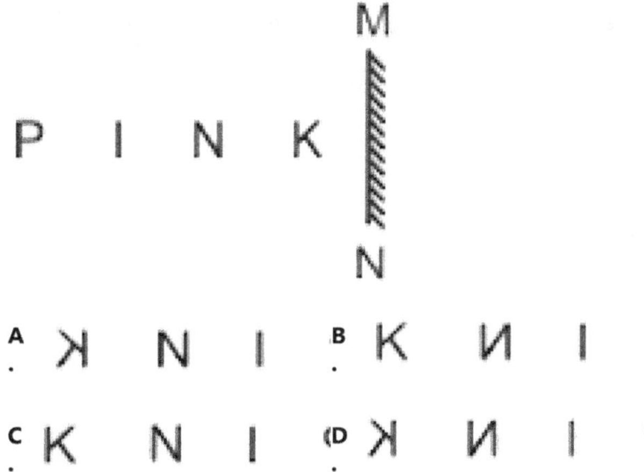

A. B. C. D.

Q.35 Direction: What should come at the place of question mark (?) in the following question?

$$\sqrt{?}\% \text{ of } 160 = 64 \div 2$$

A. 40   **B.** 400   **C.** 20   **D.** 30

Q.36 Which one of the following is not built in red sandstone?
A. Agra Fort   **B.** Red Fort
C. Golconda Fort   **D.** Fatehpur Sikri

Q.37 According to the 2011, census, which of the following Indian State has the highest slum population?
A. Andhra Pradesh   **B.** Maharashtra
C. Bihar   **D.** Uttar Pradesh

Q.38 The indentation on the top of a brick is called
A. Fracture   **B.** Bed   **C.** Bat   **D.** Frog

Q.39 "Every great architect necessarily - a great poet. He must be an original interpreter of his time, his day, his age." Was quoted by which famous architect ?
A. Frank Gehry   **B.** Frank L. Wright
C. Ayn Rand   **D.** Alvar Alto

Q.40 Bibi ka maqbara' bears a striking resemblance to which famous monument?
A. Humayun's Tomb
B. Taj Mahal
C. Diwan-i-khas, Fatehpur Sikri
D. Hindola Mahal

Q.41 _________is the ancient science of construction / architecture.
A. Vaastu Shastra   **B.** Shilpa Shastra
C. Neeti Shastra   **D.** Artha Shastra

Q.42 __________is generally used as re-enforcement in RCC.
A. Platinum   **B.** Potassium
C. Steel   **D.** Brass

Q.43 __________is the architect of 'Bharat Bhavan' in Bhopal.
A. B. V. Doshi   **B.** Anant Raje
C. Hafez Contractor   **D.** Charles Correa

Q.44 Find the number of triangles in the given figure.

A. 5   **B.** 8   **C.** 10   **D.** 7

Q.45 The famous Empire State building is in which of the following cities?
A. Tokyo   **B.** Melbourne
C. New York   **D.** Barcelona

Q.46 Identify the building in the given image

A. Income Tax Headquarters
B. Indian Habitat Centre
C. United Nations South- Asian Headquarters
D. LIC Headquarter

Q.47 Identify the building from the given image

A. Burj Khalifa, Dubai
B. Taipei 101,Taipei
C. Willis Tower, Chicago
D. CN Tower, Toronto

Q.48 How many triangles are there in the following figure?

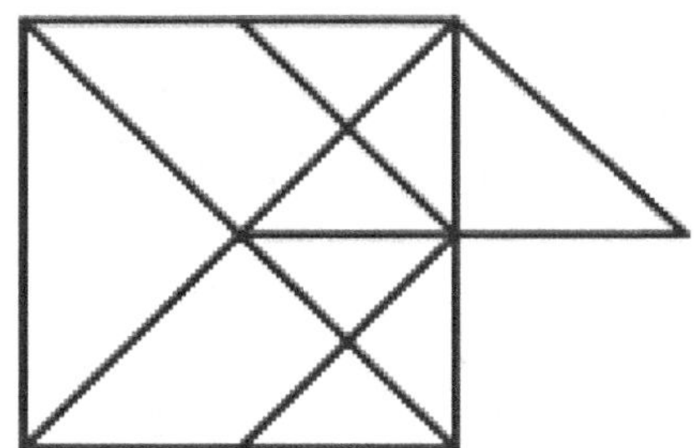

A. 18   **B.** 21   **C.** 20   **D.** 22

Q.49 Find the odd one out from the given series.
3, 5, 11, 14, 17, 21
A. 21   **B.** 17   **C.** 14   **D.** 3

Q.50 Find the odd one out.
8, 27, 64, 100, 125, 216, 343
A. 27   **B.** 100   **C.** 125   **D.** 343

Q.51 Find the odd one out.
10, 25, 45, 54, 60, 75, 80
A. 10   **B.** 45   **C.** 54   **D.** 75

Q.52 Find the odd one out.
396, 462, 572, 427, 671, 264
A. 396   **B.** 427   **C.** 671   **D.** 264

Q.53 Find the odd one out.
6, 9, 15, 21, 24, 28, 30
A. 28   **B.** 21   **C.** 24   **D.** 30

Q.54 Insert the missing number.
16, 33, 65, 131, 261, (....)
A. 523   **B.** 521   **C.** 613   **D.** 721

Q.55 Insert the missing number.
10, 5, 13, 10, 16, 20, 19, (....)

A. 22   **B.** 40   **C.** 38   **D.** 23

Q.56 Insert the missing number.

1, 4, 9, 16, 25, 36, 49, (....)

A. 54   **B.** 56   **C.** 64   **D.** 81

Q.57 Choose the correct alternative that will continue the same pattern and replace the question mark in the given series.

120, 99, 80, 63, 48, ?

A. 35   **B.** 38   **C.** 39   **D.** 40

Q.58 Choose the correct alternative that will continue the same pattern and replace the question mark in the given series.

6,12,21,?,48

A. 33   **B.** 38   **C.** 40   **D.** 45

Q.59 Choose the correct alternative that will continue the same pattern and replace the question mark in the given series

3, 10, 101,?

A. 10101   **B.** 10201   **C.** 10202   **D.** 11012

Q.60 Choose the correct alternative that will continue the same pattern and replace the question mark in the given series.

In the series 2, 6, 18, 54, ... what will be the 8th term ?

A. 4370   **B.** 4374   **C.** 7443   **D.** 7434

// Smart Answer Sheet //

Correct Percentage of students who answered correctly. **Skipped** Percentage of students who skipped.

Q.	Ans.	Correct / Skipped	Q.	Ans.	Correct / Skipped	Q.	Ans.	Correct / Skipped	Q.	Ans.	Correct / Skipped	Q.	Ans.	Correct / Skipped
1	D	10.46 % / 30.68 %	13	D	18.66 % / 33.64 %	25	D	54.25 % / 24.82 %	37	B	29.51 % / 20.38 %	49	C	44.14 % / 24.23 %
2	D	25.59 % / 34.03 %	14	B	17.4 % / 36.45 %	26	A	44.31 % / 24.33 %	38	D	30.82 % / 24.25 %	50	B	40.57 % / 19.35 %
3	D	20.06 % / 34.87 %	15	B	30.2 % / 35.42 %	27	B	46.7 % / 21.75 %	39	B	42.99 % / 22.84 %	51	C	58.6 % / 21.79 %
4	D	12.36 % / 40.68 %	16	A	42.56 % / 31.64 %	28	C	51.47 % / 25.54 %	40	B	45.13 % / 14.82 %	52	B	29.55 % / 24.69 %
5	A	34.91 % / 34.8 %	17	A	23.17 % / 37.93 %	29	D	37.46 % / 24.24 %	41	A	58.78 % / 16.05 %	53	A	53.71 % / 18.26 %
6	D	12.37 % / 38.66 %	18	D	18.27 % / 40.34 %	30	C	52.94 % / 25.76 %	42	C	54.94 % / 18.32 %	54	A	34.29 % / 21.1 %
7	C	15.29 % / 38.18 %	19	B	36.25 % / 29.18 %	31	B	47.81 % / 21.81 %	43	D	30.38 % / 20.72 %	55	B	26.5 % / 26.26 %
8	B	16.09 % / 39.91 %	20	D	37.01 % / 26.66 %	32	B	66.1 % / 19.58 %	44	C	26.58 % / 20.23 %	56	C	57.69 % / 21.1 %
9	D	9.49 % / 41.0 %	21	B	48.44 % / 17.7 %	33	A	29.4 % / 22.37 %	45	C	48.15 % / 24.5 %	57	A	43.24 % / 24.39 %
10	A	15.17 % / 39.17 %	22	B	30.06 % / 17.57 %	34	D	56.78 % / 18.09 %	46	D	26.44 % / 25.55 %	58	A	38.33 % / 27.55 %
11	B	18.31 % / 36.42 %	23	B	60.14 % / 20.12 %	35	B	25.11 % / 23.37 %	47	A	67.62 % / 18.87 %	59	C	21.52 % / 26.47 %
12	C	20.84 % / 38.08 %	24	A	31.93 % / 19.65 %	36	C	46.19 % / 17.34 %	48	C	47.0 % / 18.02 %	60	B	38.12 % / 29.17 %

//Hints and Solutions//

1. We have , f(x+4)-f(x+2)+f(x)=0 for all x .

Replacing x by x +2, we get

f(x+6)-f(x+4)+f(x+2)=0 for all x

Adding (i) and (ii) ,we get

f(x+6)+f(x)=0   ....(iii)

Replacing x by x+6 , we get

f(x+12)+f(x+6)=0   ....(iv)

From (iii) and (iv), we obtain

f(x+12)=f(x) for all x

Therefore, f(x) is periodic with period 12.

Hence, the correct option is (D).

2. $(1 + m^2)x^2 - 2(1 + 3m)x + (1 + 8m) = 0$

for no real roots $D < 0$

$$\Rightarrow 4(1 + 3m)^2 - 4(1 + m^2)(1 + 8m) < 0$$

$$\Rightarrow 1 + 9m^2 + 6m - (m^2 + 6m^3 + 1 + 6m) < 0$$

$$\Rightarrow 1 + 9m^2 + 6m - m - 8m^3 - 1 - 8m < 0$$

$$\Rightarrow 8m^3 - 8m^2 + 2m > 0$$

$$\Rightarrow 2m(4m^2 - 4m + 1) > 0$$

$$\Rightarrow 2m(2m - 1)^2 > 0m > 0$$

$\Rightarrow$ Infinite integral values of m

3. Given:

$$\tan\frac{\alpha}{3} = \frac{1}{2}$$

We know that,

$$\tan 3A = \frac{3\tan A - \tan^3 A}{1 - 3\tan^2 A}$$

Here,

$$\alpha = 3A$$

$$\Rightarrow A = \frac{\alpha}{3}$$

$$\tan\alpha = \frac{3\tan\left(\frac{\alpha}{3}\right) - \tan^3\left(\frac{\alpha}{3}\right)}{1 - 3\tan^2\left(\frac{\alpha}{3}\right)}$$

$$= \frac{3\times\left(\frac{1}{2}\right) - \left(\frac{1}{2}\right)^3}{1 - 3\left(\frac{1}{2}\right)^2}$$

$$= \frac{\frac{3}{2} - \frac{1}{8}}{\frac{1}{4}}$$

$$= \frac{11}{2}$$

To find $\cot\alpha$,

We use $\cot\alpha = \dfrac{1}{\tan\alpha} = \dfrac{1}{\frac{11}{2}} = \dfrac{2}{11}$

$$\tan\alpha + \cot\alpha = \frac{11}{2} + \frac{2}{11}$$

$$= \frac{121+4}{22}$$

$$= \frac{125}{22}$$

Hence, the correct option is (D).

4. We know that in a single throw of two dice, the total number of possible outcomes is (6 × 6) = 36

Let S be the sample space. Then, n(S) = 36

Let E = first dice always occur odd number and sum of two dice is greater than 5. Then,

E = {(1,5), (1, 6), (3, 3), (3, 4), (3, 5), (3, 6), (5,1), (5, 2), (5, 3), (5, 4), (5, 5), (5, 6)}

$\therefore$ n(E) = 12

So, the probability that first dice always occur odd number and sum of two dice is greater than 5 $= P(E) = \dfrac{n(E)}{n(S)} = \dfrac{12}{36} = \dfrac{1}{3}$

Hence, the correct option is (D).

5.

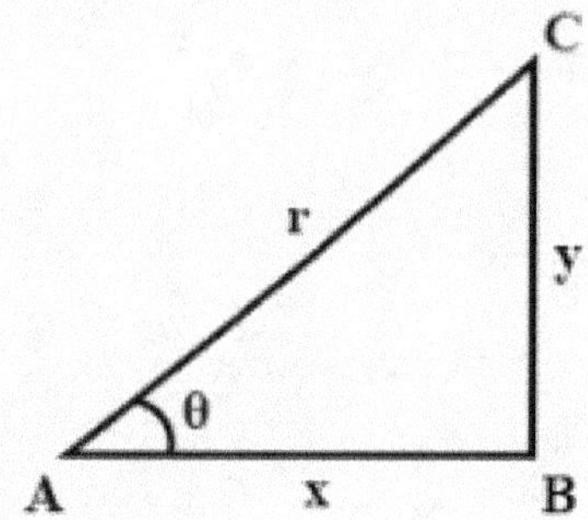

Consider right angle $\triangle ABC, \angle B = 90°, \angle A = \theta$

Also, $AB = x, BC = y$ and $AC = r$

By Pythagoras theorem, $x^2 + y^2 = r^2$

$$\sec^2\theta - \tan^2\theta = \left(\frac{r}{z}\right)^2 = \left(\frac{y}{x}\right)^2 = \frac{r^2}{x^2} - \frac{y^2}{x^2} = \frac{r^2-y^2}{x^2}$$
$$= \frac{x^2}{x^2} = 1$$

$So, 1$ is correct.

6. $\begin{vmatrix} 1 & 3 & 7 \\ -1 & 4 & 7 \\ \sin 3\theta & \cos\theta & 2 \end{vmatrix} = 0$

$1(8 - 7\cos 2\theta) - 3(-2 - 7\sin 3\theta) + 7(-\cos 2\theta = -4\sin 3\theta) = 0$

$8 - 7\cos2\theta + 6 + 21\sin3\theta - 7\cos2\theta - 28\sin3\theta = 0$

$-7\sin3\theta - 14\cos2\theta + 14 = 0$

$\sin3\theta + 2\cos2\theta - 2 = 0$

$3\sin\theta - 4\sin3\theta + 2(1 - 2\sin2\theta) - 2 = 0$

$3\sin\theta - 4\sin3\theta + 2 - 4\sin2\theta - 2 = 0$

$-\sin\theta(4\sin2\theta + 4\sin\theta - 3) = 0$

$-\sin\theta(4\sin2\theta + 6\sin\theta - 2\sin\theta - 3) = 0$

$-\sin\theta(2\sin\theta - 1)(2\sin\theta + 3) = 0$

$\sin\theta = 0, \sin\theta = \dfrac{1}{2}$

\\(\theta=0, \pi, \frac{\pi}{6}, \frac{5 x}{6}\\)

Hence, the correct option is (D).

7.

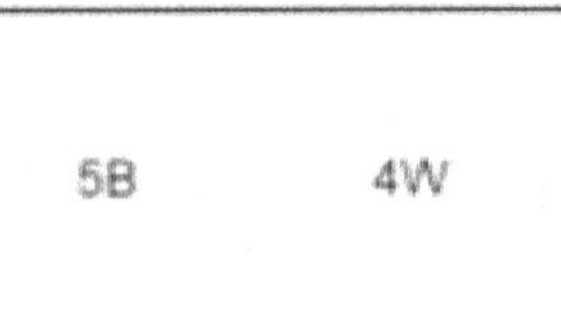

$$P(B) = \frac{5}{9} \cdot \frac{5}{11} + \frac{4}{9} - \frac{7}{11} = \frac{53}{99}$$

Hence, the correct option is (C).

8. $\dfrac{x^2 c_0 + {}^2 - 3c_1 + \dots {}^{2n+3}c_{n-3}}{2a-2} = 16$

$2^{2n-3} = 32(n - 1) \Rightarrow n = 5$ (by observation)

Hence, the correct option is (B).

9. Number of consonants = 21

Number of given digits = 9

so total number formed = 21 × 20 × 9 × 4 = 432k

$\Rightarrow$ k = 35

Hence, the correct option is (D).

10. Let common ratio of b, c, d is r

then $b = \dfrac{c}{r}, d =$ or

$a = \dfrac{x}{t} - c$

$e = \dfrac{c^2 r}{2c - cr}$

Now $ae = c^2$

$\Rightarrow a, c, e$ are in $G.P$

Hence, the correct option is (A).

11. 1. L.C.M of 2, 4, 6, 8, 10 and 12 is 120.

so, the bells will toll together after 120 seconds i.e. 2 minutes .

In 30 minutes the bells toll together 30/2 + 1 = 16 times.

Hence, the correct option is (B).

12. Given:

$LCM = 105$

Let the two numbers be $5x$ and $7x$ respectively.

LCM of $5x$ and $7x$ is $35x$.

$35x = 105$

$\Rightarrow x = \dfrac{105}{35}$

$\Rightarrow x = 3$

The sum of the two numbers $= 5 \times 3 + 7 \times 3 = 15 + 21 = 36$

Difference of the two numbers $= 21 - 15 = 6$

The ratio of the sum and difference of both the numbers $X = \dfrac{36}{6} = 6$

Hence, the correct option is (C).

13. L.C.M of 8,12,16 = 48

Now, 48 x 1 + 3 = 51 -not divisible by 7

48 x 2 + 3 = 99 - not divisible by 7

48 x 3 + 3 = 147 - not divisible by 7

Required number = 147

Hence, the correct option is (D).

14. Given: One of the two events A and B must occur,

So: $P(A) + P(B) = 1$

$\Rightarrow \left(\dfrac{2}{3}\right) P(B) + P(B) = 1$

$\therefore P(B) = \dfrac{3}{5}$

Now, $P\left(\bar{B}\right) = 1 - P(B) = 1 - \dfrac{3}{5} = \dfrac{2}{5}$

Odds in favour of $B = \dfrac{P(B)}{P\left(\bar{B}\right)} = \dfrac{\frac{3}{5}}{\frac{2}{5}} = \dfrac{3}{2}$

Hence, the correct option is (B).

15. The least number of 5 digits is 10000.

L.C.M. of 12, 15 and 18 is 180 .

On dividing 10000 is 100.

=> 10000 + 180- 100 = 10080

10080 is divisible by 180.

Hence, the correct option is (B).

16. If a matrix has m rows and n columns then its order is $m \times n$. Clearly, in the given matrix, the number of rows and columns are each 2. So, its order is 2×2.

Hence, the correct option is (A).

17. Total weight of 45 passenger = 45 x 50 = 2250 kg

Total weight of 45 passenger and 5 crews = 50 x 49.5 = 2475 kg

Total weight of 5 crews = 2475-2250 = 225kg

Average weight of 5 crews = 225/5 = 45kg.

Hence, the correct option is (A).

18. Total expenditure during first four months = 1,800 x 4 = Rs 7,200

Total expenditure during the next 8 months = 2,000 x 8 = Rs 16,000 Saving = Rs 5,600

Total of expenditure and saving (equal to income the year) = 7,200+ 16,000 + 5,600=Rs 28,800

Average monthly income = $\dfrac{28,000}{12}$ = Rs 2,400

Hence, the correct option is (D).

19. Sum of 5 numbers = 9 x 5 = 45

Sum of last three numbers = 15

The average of 1st two numbers = 45-15/2 = 30/2 = 15.

Hence, the correct option is (B).

20. Required Amount = 24 - (7.70 + 6.30 + 10)
= 24 - 24 = 0

Hence, the correct option is (D).

21. Answer figure b will complete the pattern in the Problem figure.

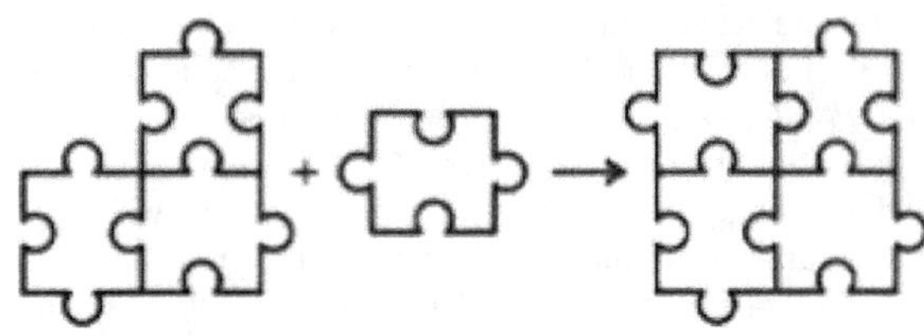

Hence, the correct option is (B).

22.

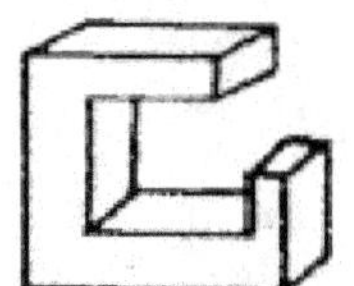

23. After placing the figure given in option (B) in the blank space of the figure marked 'X' the complete pattern is:

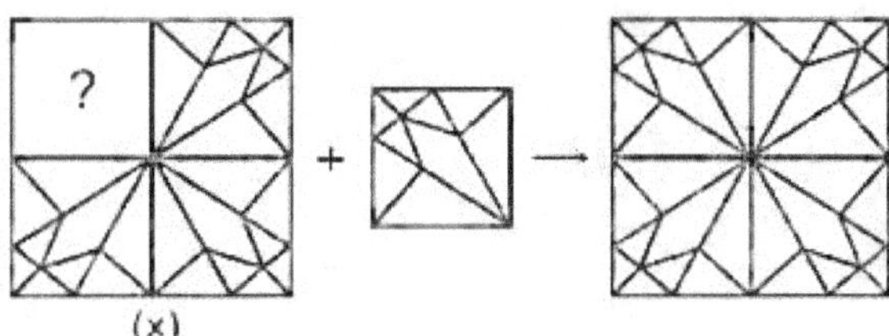

Hence, the correct option is (B).

24. The number series given is-

1, 2, 5, 16, 65, ?

The pattern is-

$$(1 \times 1) + 1 = 2$$
$$(2 \times 2) + 1 = 5$$
$$(5 \times 3) + 1 = 16$$
$$(16 \times 4) + 1 = 65$$

On following the same pattern,

$$? = (65 \times 5) + 1 = 326$$

326 will come in place of ?.

Hence, the correct option is (A).

25. By observation, we get,

Hence, the correct option is (D).

26. The numeric series given is-

121, 225, 361, ?

The logic followed is- $11^2, 15^2, 19^2$ (Squares of odd numbers starting from 11 and having a gap of 4).

On applying the same logic, we have- $23^2 = 529$ in place of ?.

Hence, the correct option is (A).

27.

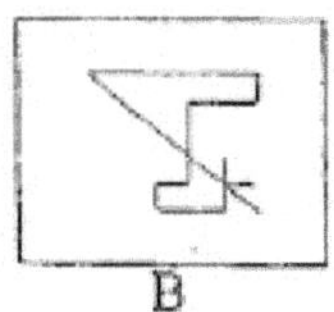

Hence, the correct option is (B).

28. Fig. (3) is formed by a combination of A-shaped elements while all other figures are formed by a combination of V-shaped elements.

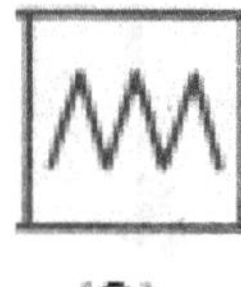

(3)

Hence, the correct option is (C).

29.

Hence, the correct option is (D).

30.

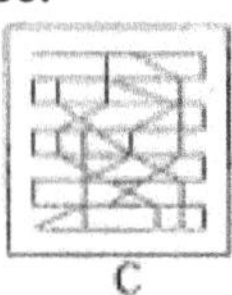

Hence, the correct option is (C).

31. From the open dice, we can conclude that-

W and S are opposites of each other

V and T are opposites of each other

R and U are opposites of each other

On the basis of these conclusions, only the second dice-

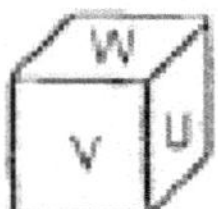

can be formed.

Hence, the correct option is (B).

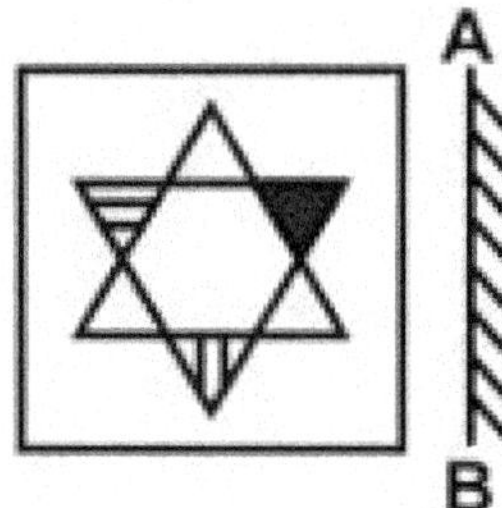

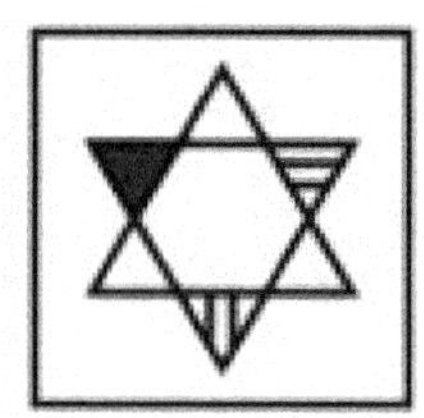

32.

Hence, the correct option is (B).

33. The number series given is-

1, 8, 9, 64, 25, ?

The pattern followed is- $1^2, 2^3, 3^2, 4^3, 5^2, ?$

Square and cube of consecutive numbers starting from 1 are taken to generate the series.

On following the same pattern,

$$? = 6^3 = 216$$

Hence, the correct option is (A).

34. If the mirror is placed on line AB then the correct mirror image of the given figure will be:

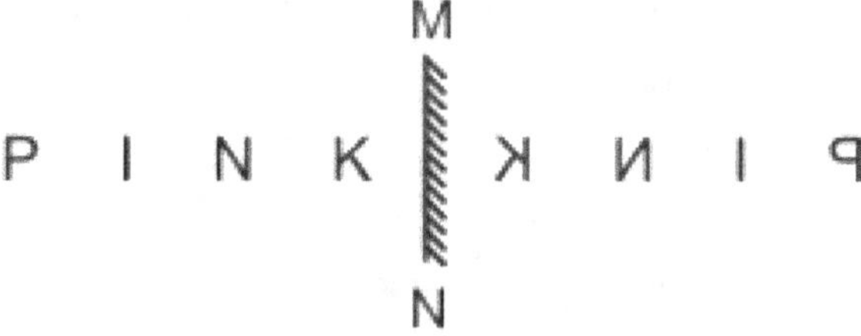

Hence, the correct option is (D).

35. $\sqrt{?}\%$ of $160 = 64 \div 2$

$$\Rightarrow \frac{160 \times \sqrt{?}}{100} = 32$$

$$\Rightarrow \sqrt{?} = \frac{32 \times 100}{160}$$

$$\Rightarrow \sqrt{?} = 20$$

$$\Rightarrow ? = 400$$

Hence, the correct option is (B).

36. Golconda, also known as Golconda, is a citadel and fort in Southern India and was the capital of the medieval sultanate of

the Qutb Shahi dynasty (c.1512–1687), is situated 11 km (6.8 mi) west of Hyderabad. Golconda Fort was first built by the Kakatiyas as part of

their western defenses along the lines of the Kondapalli Fort. The city and the fortress were built on a granite hill.

Hence, the correct option is (C).

37. Maharashtra accounted for 11.8 million slum population which is 18.1% of the total slum population of the country. It was followed by Andhra Pradesh (10.2 million), West Bengal (6.4 million) and Uttar Pradesh (6.2 million). The 21st century has witnessed a rapid growth of urban population coupled with incommensurate development of social facilities which has resulted in the creation of slums and associated problems of an alarming magnitude.

Hence, the correct option is (B).

38. The depression provided in the face of brick during its manufacturing is known as frog of bricks. Depth of the brick is 10mm to 20mm. If the bricks are laid according to British standards, the frog should be laid upward and filled with mortar. When the frog is laid upwards, the load is evenly spread throughout the width of the brick all the way down to the foundations. If the frog is laid down, the load is forced to the outsides of the brick.

Hence, the correct option is (D).

39. Frank Lloyd Wright (June 8, 1867 – April 9, 1959) was an American architect, interior designer, writer, and educator, who designed more than 1,000 structures, 532 of which were completed. Wright believed in designing structures that were in harmony with humanity and its environment, a philosophy he called organic architecture. This philosophy was best exemplified by Fallingwater (1935), which has been called "the best all-time work of American architecture".

Hence, the correct option is (B).

40. The Bibi ka Maqbara is a tomb located in Aurangabad, Maharashtra, India. It was built by Mughal emperor Aurangzeb's son Azam Shah in the memory of his mother. It bears a striking resemblance to the famous Taj Mahal, the mausoleum of wife of Shah Jahan. He had built the Badshahi Mosque at Lahore one of the largest Mosques in the world and the largest one at that time, as well as the small, but elegant, Pearl Mosque at Delhi.

Hence, the correct option is (B).

41. Vastu shastra is a traditional Hindu system of architecture which literally translates to "science of architecture." These are texts found on the Indian subcontinent that describe principles of design, layout, measurements, ground preparation, space arrangement, and spatial geometry.Vastu Shastras incorporate traditional Hindu and in some cases Buddhist beliefs.

Hence, the correct option is (A).

42. Reinforced Cement Concrete (R.C.C.) is the combination of ordinary concrete with the reinforcement to increase its compressive and tensile strength to a great extent. Concrete is a versatile material for modern construction which is prepared by mixing well proportioned quantities of cement, sand, crushed rock orgravel and water.

It has been used from foundations to the rooftop of the buildings, in the construction of highways, roads traffic etc.

Hence, the correct option is (C).

43. Charles Correa widely known for his works in contemporary architecture, played an important and vital role in the development of architecture in India after Independence. His principles of designing icludes prevailing resources, energy and climatic aspects to create and determine order of space. His works include the Chapalimaud Foudation Centre in Lisbon, also famous by the name "Project to the Unknown", the Sabarmati Ashram in Ahmedabad and the Madhya Pradesh Legislative Assembly in Bhopal. Craft Museum, New Delhi, Bharat Bhavan, Bhopal, Jawahar Kala Kendra in Jaipur are some other examples of his intellectual knowledge.

Hence, the correct option is (D).

44. Given Figure:

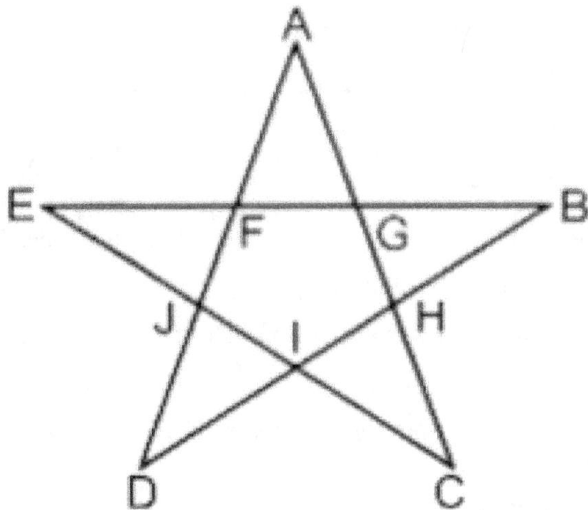

Triangles: AFG, BGH, CHI, DIJ, EJF, DAH, CEG, BDF, ACJ, EBI

Thus, total of ten triangles are there in the given figure.

Hence, the correct option is (C).

45. The Empire State Building is a skyscraper in New York City, United States. It is 381 meters (1,250 feet) tall and has 102 floors, and the height to its pinnacle is 1,454 feet.

Hence, the correct option is (C).

46. LIC of India Head Office Address: LIC of India Company Limited Registered Office, Jeevan Bima Marg, Nariman Point, Mumbai, Maharashtra

Hence, the correct option is (D).

47. The Burj Khalifa, known as the Burj Dubai prior to its inauguration in 2010, is a skyscraper in Dubai, United Arab Emirates. With a total height of 829.8 m and a roof height of 828 m, the Burj Khalifa has been the tallest structure and building in the world since its topping out in 2009.

Hence, the correct option is (A).

48. The number of triangles in the given figure is:

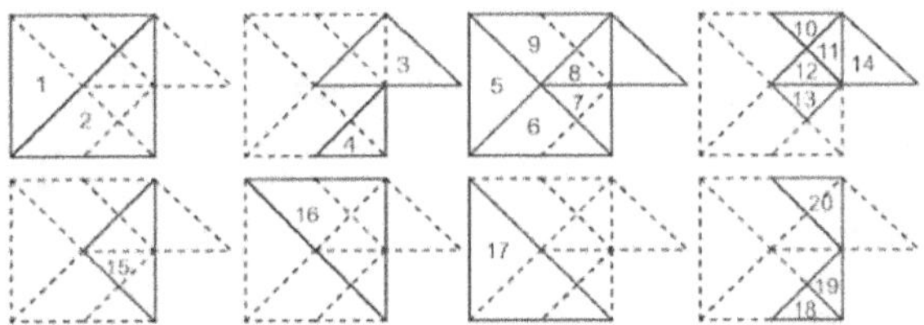

Therefore, "20" is the correct answer.

Hence, the correct option is (C).

49. Each of the numbers except 14 is an odd number.

The number '14' is the only even number.

Hence, the correct option is (C).

50. $2 \times 2 \times 2 = 8$

$3 \times 3 \times 3 = 27$

$4 \times 4 \times 4 = 64$

$5 \times 5 \times 5 = 125$

$6 \times 6 \times 6 = 216$

$7 \times 7 \times 7 = 343$

The pattern is 2^{32}, 3^3, 4^3, 5^3, 6^3, 7^3. But, 100 is not a perfect cube.

Hence, the correct option is (B).

51. Each of the numbers except 54 is multiple of 5.

Hence, the correct option is (C).

52. In each number except 427, the middle digit is the sum of other two.

Hence, the correct option is (B).

53. Each of the numbers except 28, is a multiple of 3.

Hence, the correct option is (A).

54. Each number is twice the preceding one with 1 added or subtracted alternatively.

The pattern followed is:

16×2=32+1=33

⇒ 33×2=66-1=65

⇒ 65×2=130+1=131

⇒ 131×2=262-1=261

⇒ 261×2=522+1=523

Hence, the correct option is (A).

55. There are two series .One is

10+3=13

13+3=16

16+3=19

Second is-

5 ×2=10

10 ×2=20

20 ×2=**40**

Hence, the correct option is (B).

56. Numbers are 1^2, 2^2, 3^2, 4^2, 5^2, 6^2, 7^2.

So, the next number is $8^2 = 64$.

Hence, the correct option is (C).

57. The pattern is - 21, - 19, - 17, - 15,.....

120-21=99

99-19=80

80-17=63

63-15=48

So, missing term = 48 - 13 = 35.

Hence, the correct option is (A).

58. 6,12,21,?,48
The given series is +6,+9,+12,+15....
Thus, each term is added with a number increased by 3 from the previous added number.

6+6=12

11+9=21

21+12=**33**

33+15=48

Missing term = 33

Hence, the correct option is (A).

59. Each term in the series is obtained by adding 1 to the square of the preceding term.

3 ×3+1=10

10 ×10+1=101

So, missing term = (101)2 + 1 = **10202.**

Hence, the correct option is (A).

60. Clearly,

2 x 3 = 6

6 x 3 = 18

18 x 3 = 54

So, the series is a G.P. in which a = 2, r = 3.

Therefore 8th term = ar^{8-1} = ar^7 = 2×3^7 = (2 x 2187) = 4374.

Hence, the correct option is (B).

Mathematics

Q.1 The length of the diameter of the circle which touches the x-axis at the point (1, 0) and passes through the point (2, 3) is

A. $\frac{6}{5}$ **B.** $\frac{5}{3}$ **C.** $\frac{10}{3}$ **D.** $\frac{3}{5}$

Q.2 LCM of two numbers is 16 times their HCF. The sum of LCM and HCF is 850. If one number is 50, then what is the other number ?

A. 800   **B.** 1200   **C.** 1600   **D.** 2400

Q.3 The value of i^i is :

A. ω **B.** $-\omega^2$ **C.** $\frac{\pi}{2}$ **D.** $e^{-\frac{\pi}{2}}$

Q.4 If two vertices of a triangle are (5, -1), (-2, 3) and the orthocentre of the triangle lies at the origin, then the third vertex is

A. (4, 7)   **B.** (-4, -7)   **C.** (4, -7)   **D.** (-4, 7)

Q.5 Find the sum of the series : $C_0 - 3C_1 + 5C_2 + ... + (-1)^n (2n + 1) C_n$ for n > 1

A. 1   **B.** 2   **C.** 3   **D.** 0

Q.6 There are unlimited number of identical balls of four different colours. How many arrangements of at most 8 balls in row can be made by using them?

A. 97380   **B.** 87380   **C.** 87370   **D.** 87480

Q.7 If $\frac{dy}{dx} = \frac{1}{x} + 3x^2$ then $y =$

A. ln x+(x³/2)+c   **B.** ln x+3x³+c
C. ln x+(x³/3)+c   **D.** ln x+x³+c

Q.8 If a < 0, the function f(x) = $e^{ax} + e^{-ax}$ is a monotonically decreasing function for values of x given by :

A. x > 0   **B.** x < 0   **C.** x > 1   **D.** x < 1

Q.9 How many three-digit numbers can be formed without using the digits 0, 2, 3, 4, 5 and 6 ?

A. 64   **B.** 63   **C.** 62   **D.** 60

Q.10 For what value of 'a' is the area bounded by the curve $y = a^2x^2 + ax + 1$ and the straight line y = 0, x = 0 & x = 1 the least ?

A. $-\left(\frac{3}{4}\right)$ **B.** $-\left(\frac{3}{5}\right)$
C. $-\left(\frac{3}{2}\right)$ **D.** None of these

Q.11 The 4 th term from the end in the expansion of $\left(\frac{x^3}{2} - \frac{2}{x^2}\right)^7$ is

A. 35X   **B.** 50X   **C.** 25X   **D.** 70X

Q.12 If $a_1, a_2, a_3, ...a_{20}$ are AMs between 13 and 67, then the maximum value of product $a_1 a_2 a_3 ....a_{20}$ is.

A. $(20)^{20}$ **B.** $(60)^{20}$ **C.** $(80)^{20}$ **D.** $(40)^{20}$

Q.13 A (3, 2, 0), B (5, 3, 2) and C (-9, 6, -3) are three points forming a triangle and AD is bisector of the angle BAC . AD meets BC at the point :

A. $\left(\frac{19}{8}, \frac{57}{16}, \frac{17}{16}\right)$ **B.** $\left(-\frac{19}{8}, \frac{57}{16}, \frac{17}{16}\right)$
C. $\left(\frac{19}{8}, -\frac{57}{16}, \frac{17}{16}\right)$ **D.** None of these

Q.14 A number when divided by the sum of 555 and 445 gives two times their difference as quotient and 30 as remainder. The number is

A. 220030   **B.** 22030   **C.** 1220   **D.** 1250

Q.15 If $^{16}C_r = {}^{16}C_{r+2}$, then find $^rC_4$.

A. 35   **B.** 45   **C.** 20   **D.** 40

Q.16 How many five digit numbers can be formed by using the digits 1,2,3,4,5 without repetition of digits?

A. 120   **B.** 240   **C.** 150   **D.** 160

Q.17 From a group of persons the number of ways of selecting 5 persons is equal to that of 8 persons. The number of persons in the group is

A. 13   **B.** 40   **C.** 18   **D.** 21

Q.18 If $A = \begin{vmatrix} 2 & 3 \\ 6 & 9 \end{vmatrix}$ then $|A| =$

A. 0   **B.** 1   **C.** 2   **D.** 3

Q.19 If A=[1], then the order of the matrix is

A. 1x1   **B.** 2x1
C. 1x2   **D.** None of these

Q.20 Evaluate $\cos^{-1}\left(\cos\left(\frac{\pi}{4}\right)\right)$

A. $\frac{\pi}{4}$ **B.** $\frac{3\pi}{4}$ **C.** $-\frac{3\pi}{4}$ **D.** $-\frac{\pi}{4}$

General Aptitude

Q.21 Red, Yellow and _______ form a primary colour scheme

A. Purple   **B.** Blue   **C.** Black   **D.** White

Q.22 Identify the structure

A. Rashtrapati Bhavan **B.** Parliament House
C. Red Fort **D.** Taj mahal

Q.23 What is the finish of sanitary fittings?
A. Glossy & Rough **B.** Glossy & Smooth
C. Matte & Rough **D.** Matte & Smooth

Q.24 A 3-D problem figure is given below. Identify the correct front view from the options

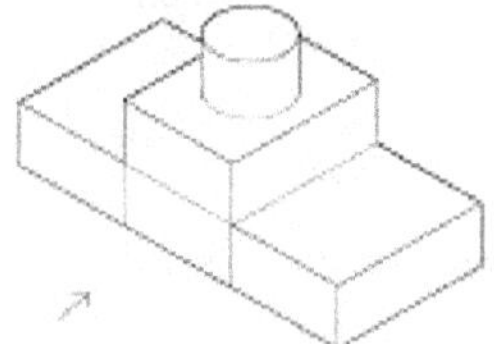

A.
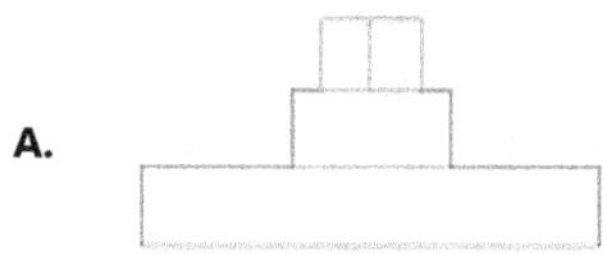

B.

C.
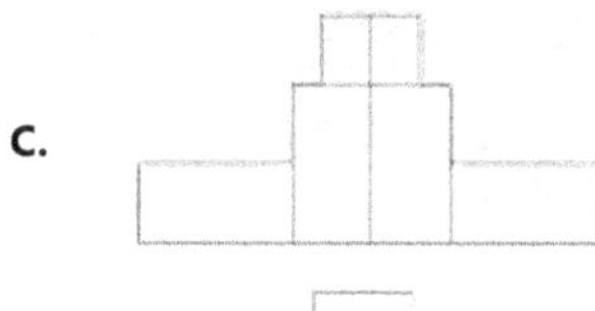

D.

Q.25 A 3-D problem figure is given below. Identify the correct top view from the options

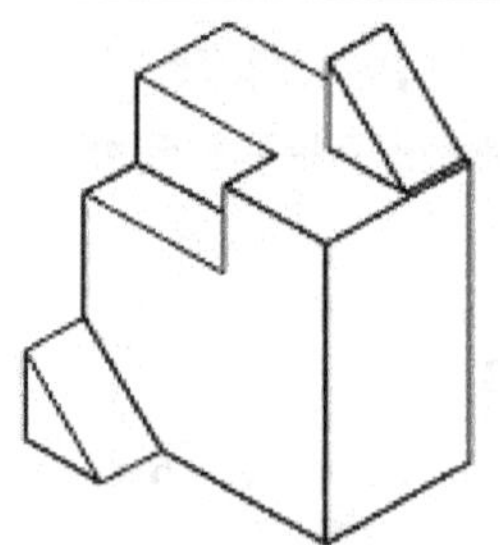

A.

B.
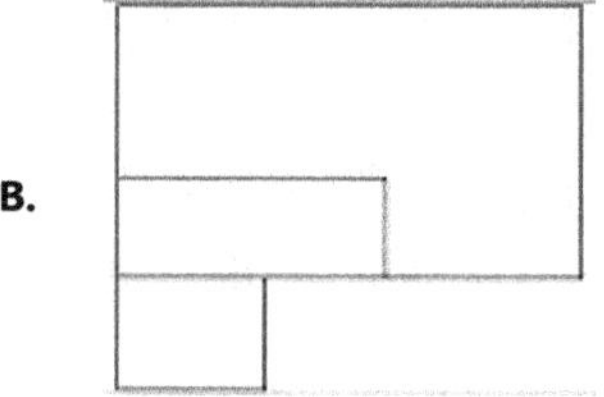

C.
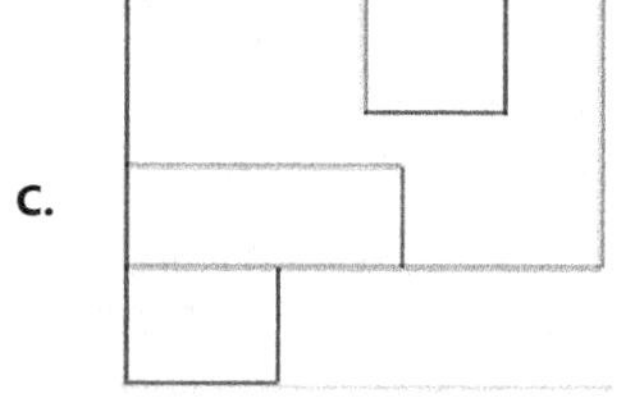

D.
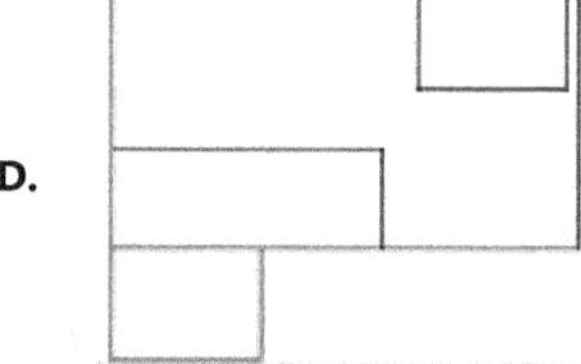

Q.26 Identify the structure

A. Colossus of Rhodes
B. Statue of liberty
C. Pharos of Alexandria
D. Tower of Piza

Q.27 If a colour is made darker by adding black, the result is called a _________.

A. Shade **B.** Chroma **C.** Tone **D.** Tint

Q.28 Complete the series of the problem figures by choosing the correct answer from the options given below

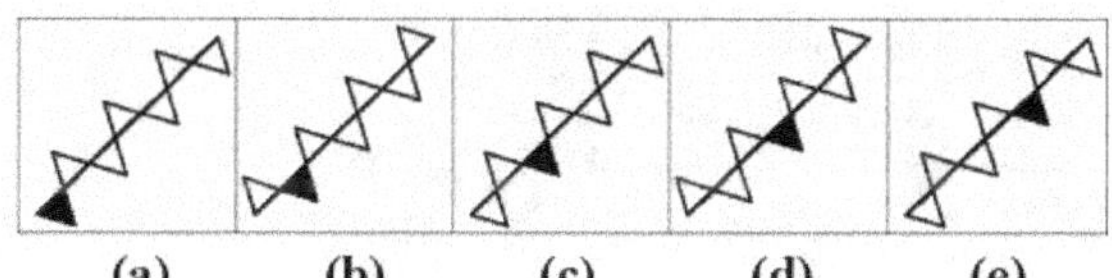

   (a)   **(b)**   **(c)**   **(d)**   **(e)**

A. 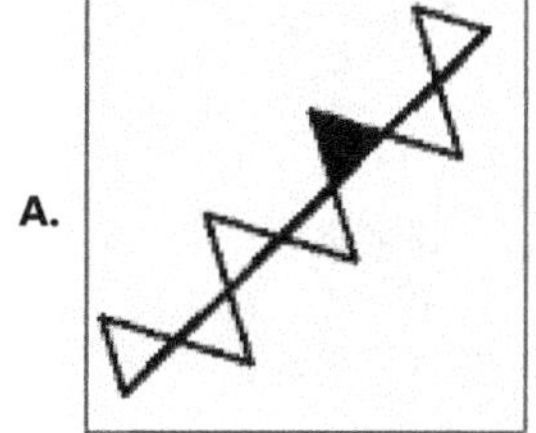 **B.** 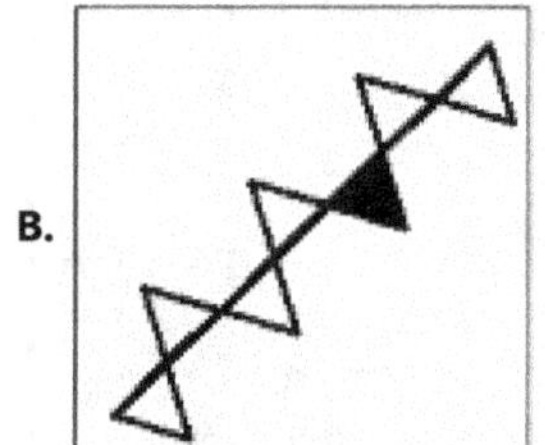

C. 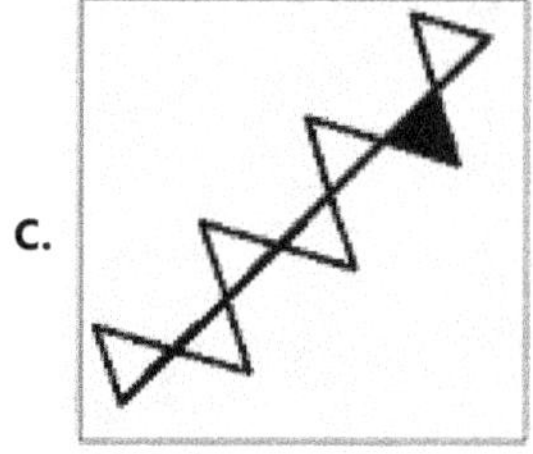 **D.** 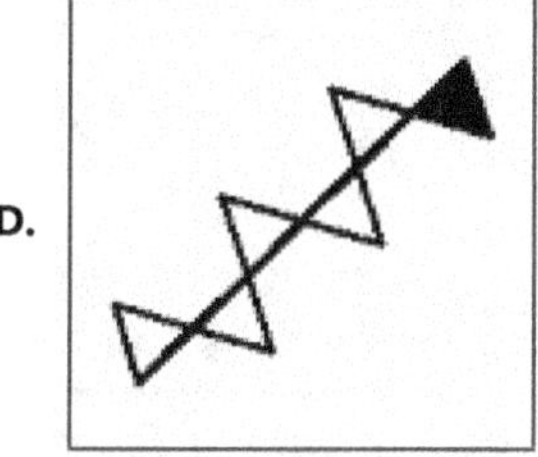

Q.29 CN Tower is also known as-

A. Canadian National Tower
B. Canada Nations Tower
C. Canada Nationalist Tower
D. Canadian Nations Tower

Q.30 Higher the purity of a colour, higher the ______.

A. Saturation **B.** Value
C. Chroma **D.** Luminance

Q.31 Identify the building

A. Lic building
B. Air India Building
C. Kanchanjunga Apartments
D. None of the above

Q.32 Find the correct 3-D figure from the options, which has the same front view as given in the problem figure, looking in the direction of the arrow

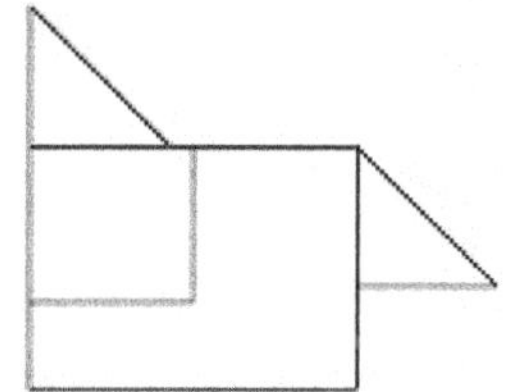

A. 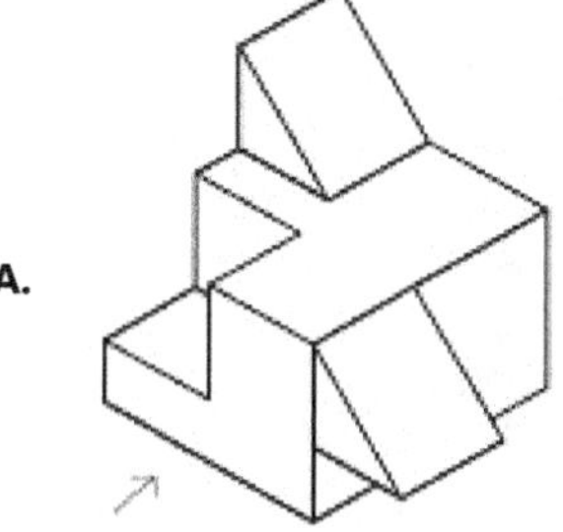

B. 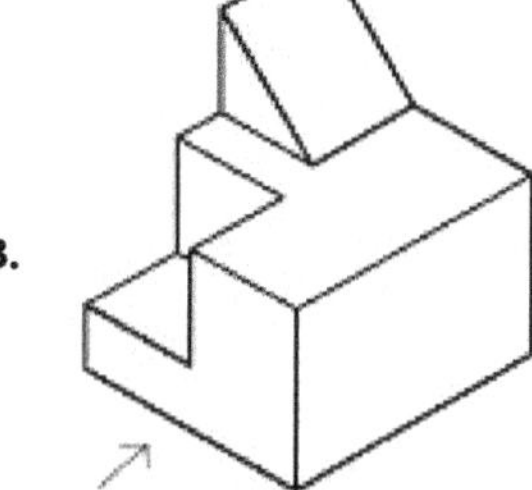

C. 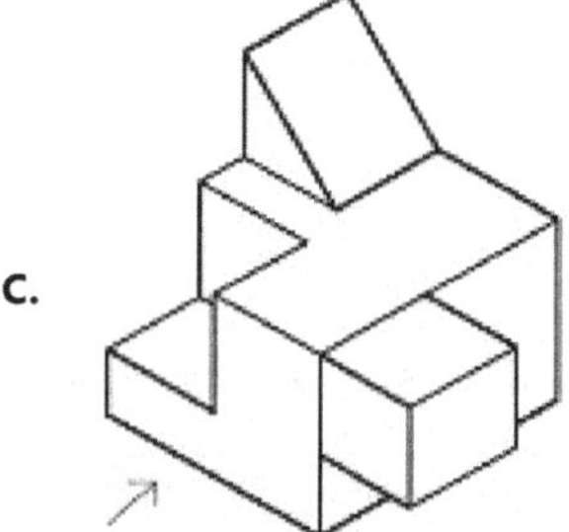

D. 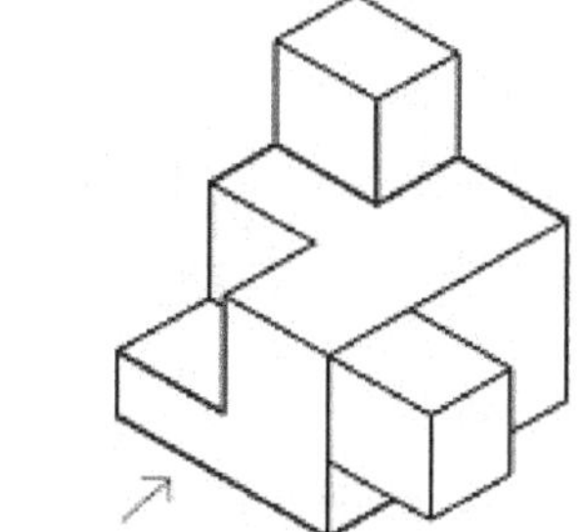

Q.33 Identify the building

A. CN Tower   **B.** Sky Tower
C. Petronas Towers   **D.** Sydney Tower

Q.34 In the given problem figure, find out the total number of surfaces of objects

A. 12   **B.** 13   **C.** 16   **D.** 15

Q.35 TEOTIHUACAN is famous for __________
A. Egyptian Pyramids
B. Mesoamerican Pyramids
C. Ziggurats
D. Mastabas

Q.36 A sheet of paper is folded & cut in the given steps. Select the correct answer from the options given below which resembles the pattern paper acquires when it is unfolded

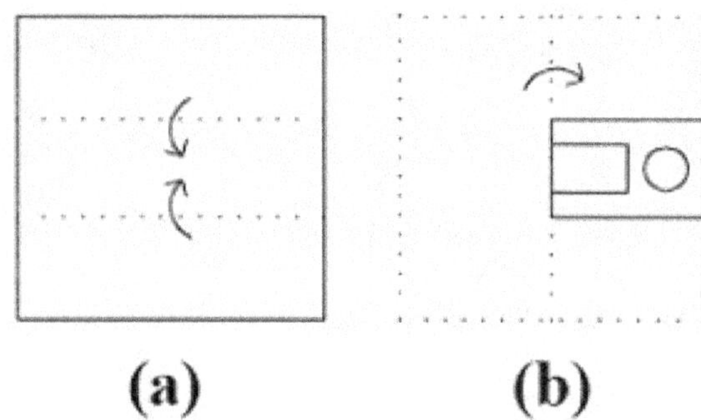

A. 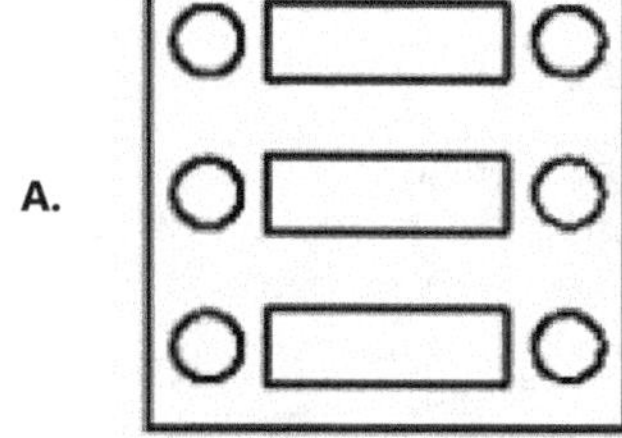

B. 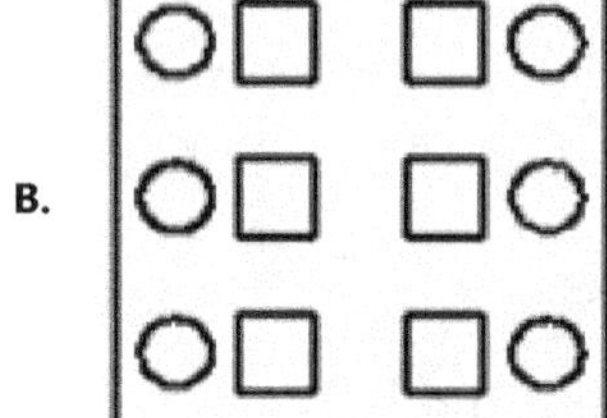

C. 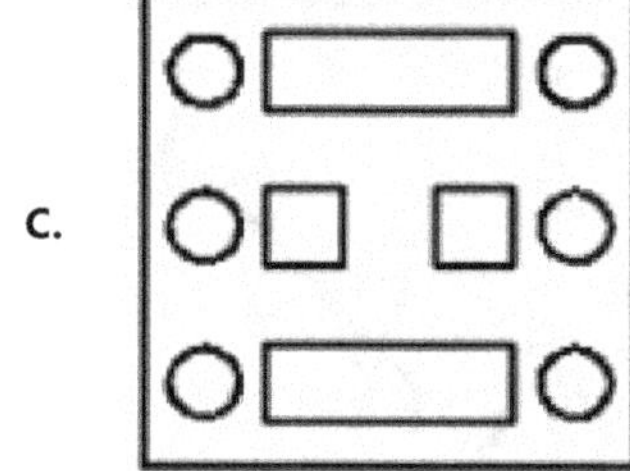

D. 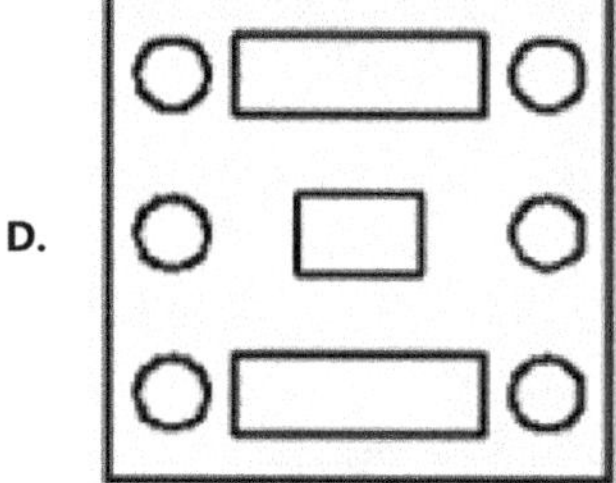

Q.37 Why India Gate was built ?
A. To pay homage to British Soldiers who died during World War I
B. To commemorate India's freedom
C. To celebrate shifting of capital to New Delhi by Britishers
D. As a gift from Britishers to India

Q.38 Identify the structure

A. Gebel Barkal
B. Louvre pyramid
C. Transamerica Pyramid
D. Pyramid of Cestius

Q.39 Why was Statue Of Liberty Built?

A. It was a gift from France to celebrate America's freedom

B. None

C. After the end of 1812 war

D. After the end of civil war

Q.40 Which of the following dices is identical to the unfolded figure shown below

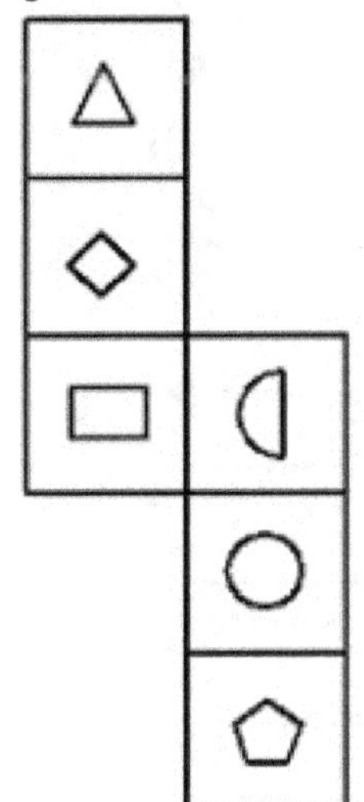

A. 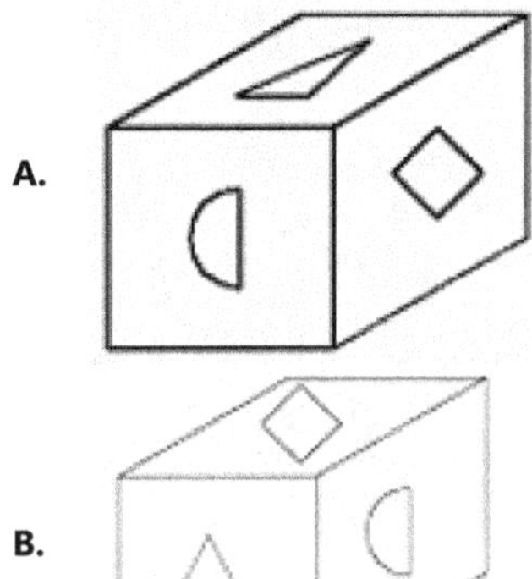

B.

C.

D. 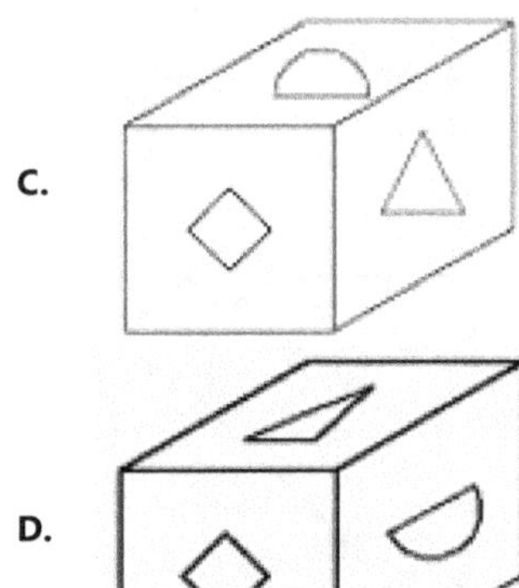

Q.41 Why is Statue Of Liberty green in colour ?

A. Because it is decaying

B. Weathering of Copper

C. Oxidation Effects

D. Because of Fungus

Q.42 Understand the relationship between a & b. Choose the missing figure from the options given such that a similar relationship is established between c & d

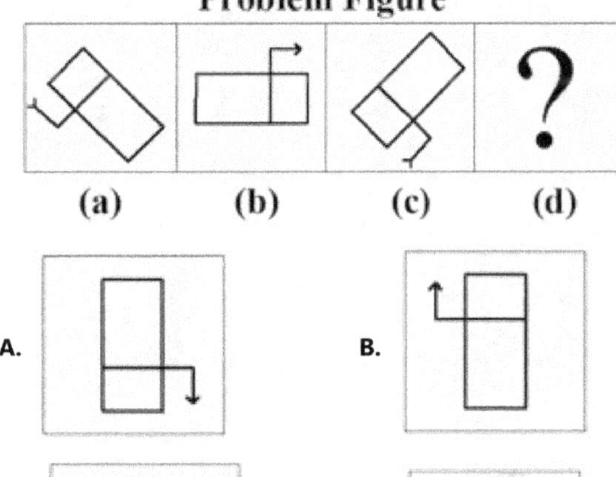

Problem Figure

(a)   **(b)**   **(c)**   **(d)**

A. 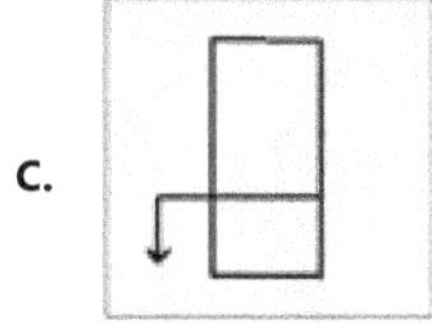

B. 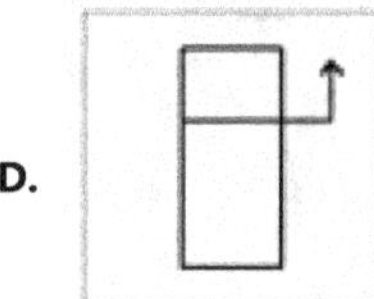

C. 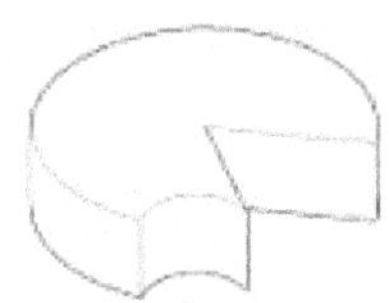

D.

Q.43 In the given problem figure, find out the total number of surfaces of objects

A. 8   **B.** 7   **C.** 5   **D.** 6

Q.44 Identify the structure

A. Taj Mahal   **B.** Humayun's Tomb

C. Red Fort   **D.** Fatehpur Sikri

Q.45 __________ is a tint of red.

A. Orange   **B.** Pink   **C.** Maroon   **D.** Brown

Q.46 Who is the designer of the "Statue of Unity"?
A. Herbert Baker
B. Edwin Lutyens
C. Henry Irwin
D. Michael Graves

Q.47 A sheet of paper is folded & cut in the given steps. Select the correct answer from the options given below which resembles the pattern paper acquires when it is unfolded

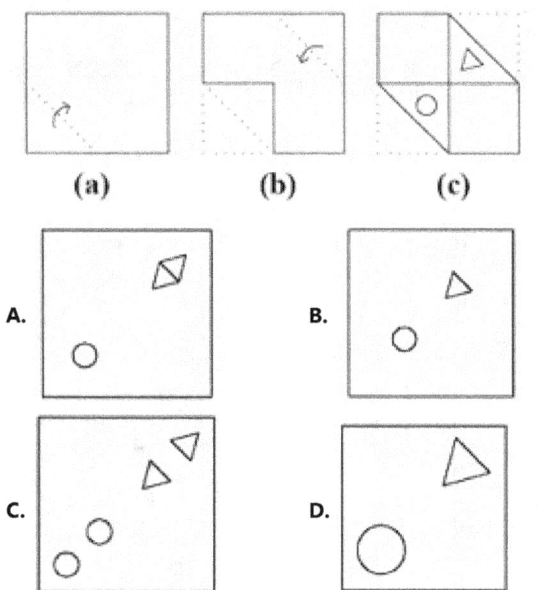

Q.48 Understand the relationship between a & b. Choose the missing figure from the options given such that a similar relationship is established between c & d

Problem Figure

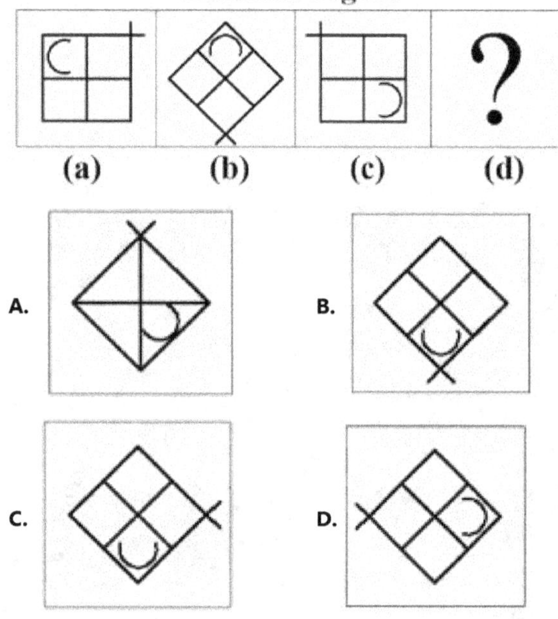

Q.49 If Orange : Juice, then Mango : _______
A. Shake
B. Pulp
C. Pie
D. None

Q.50 Understand the relationship between a & b. Choose the missing figure from the options given such that a similar relationship is established between c & d

Problem Figure

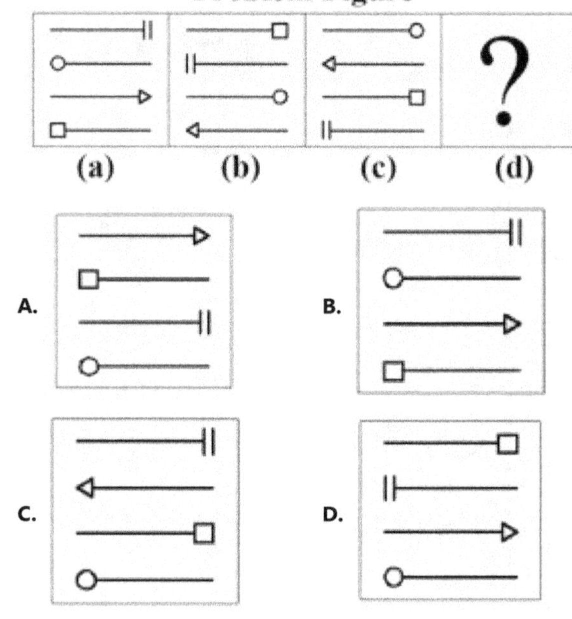

Q.51 Violet, indigo, blue, green, yellow, orange, red form the _________.
A. Prang Colour Wheel
B. Munsell Colour System
C. Warm Colour Wheel
D. Visible Spectrum

Q.52 Assuming the question figure to be a transparent sheet with a given pattern. Find out the correct figure from the options which would appear when the problem figure is folded along the dotted line

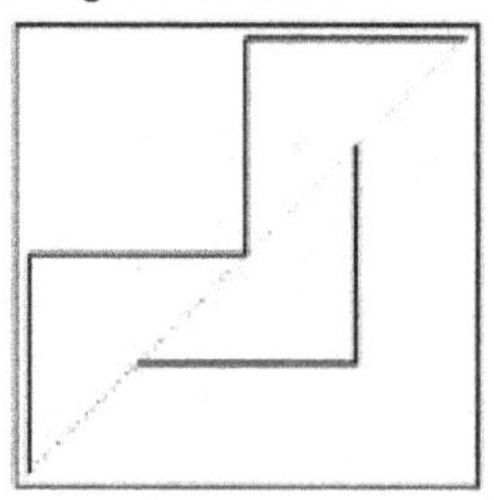

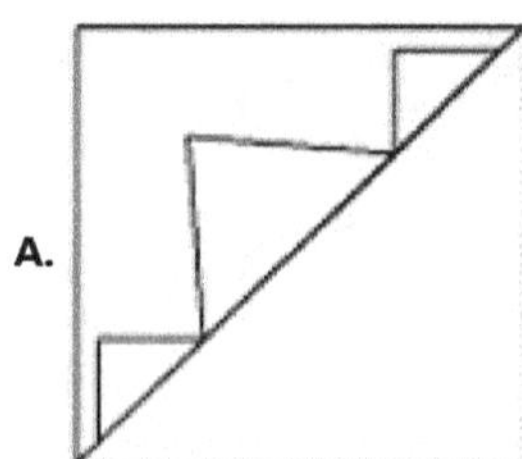

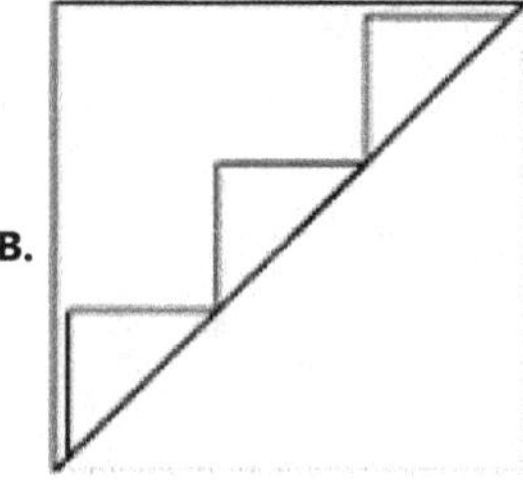

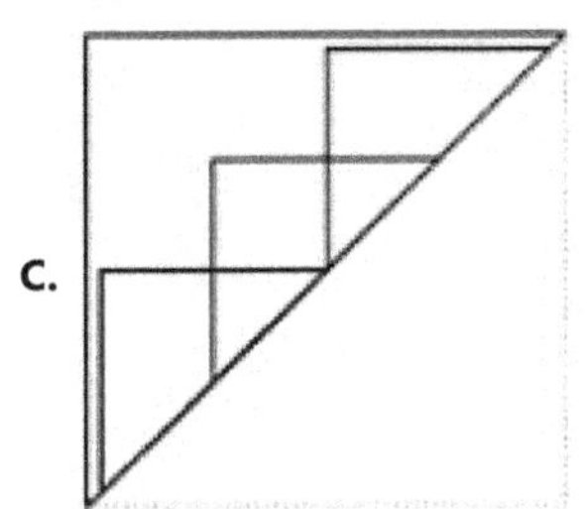

C.

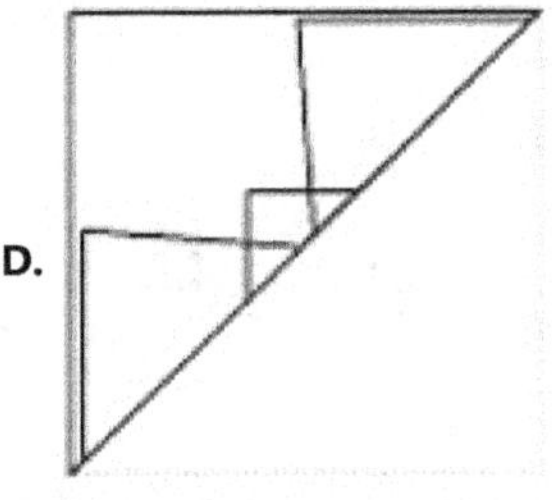

D.

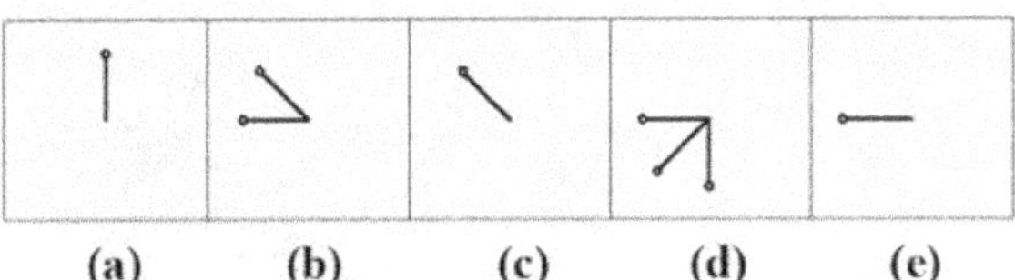

(a)   (b)   (c)   (d)   (e)

Q.53 A 3-D problem figure is given below. Identify the correct front view from the options.

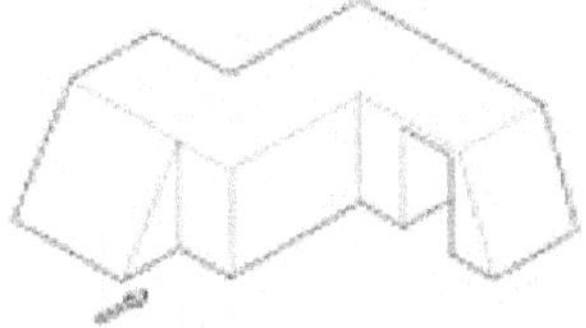

A.

A.

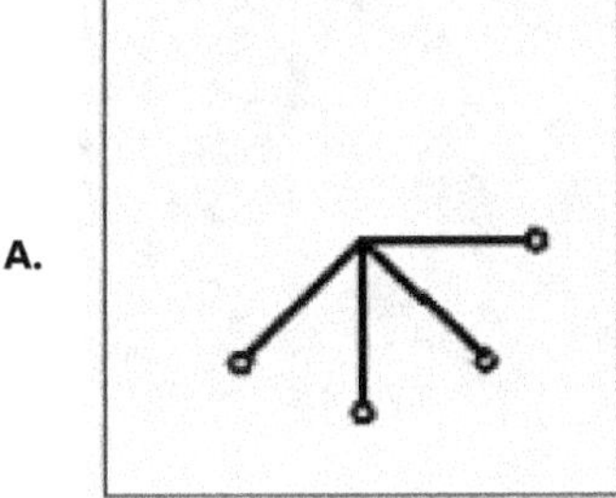

B.

B.

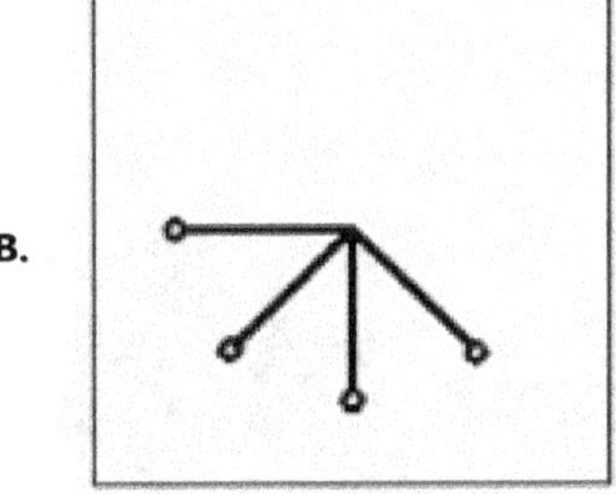

C.

C.

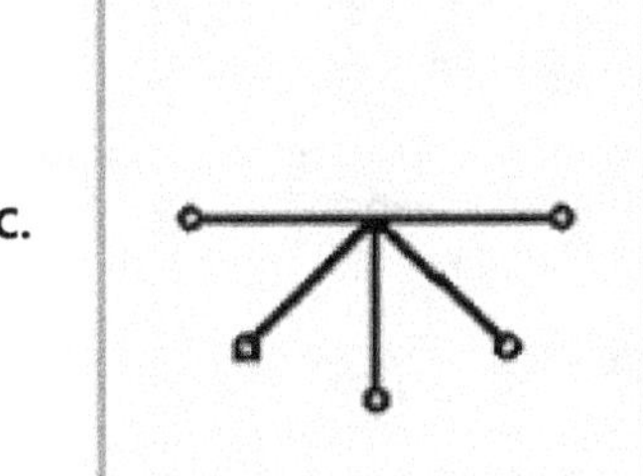

D.

Q.54 In the given problem figure, find out the total number of surfaces of objects

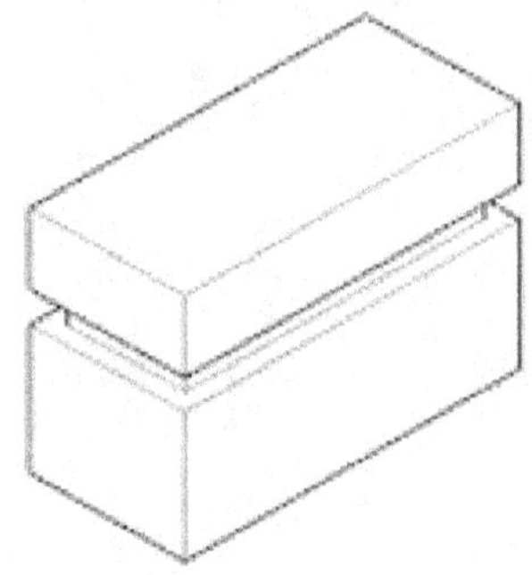

D.

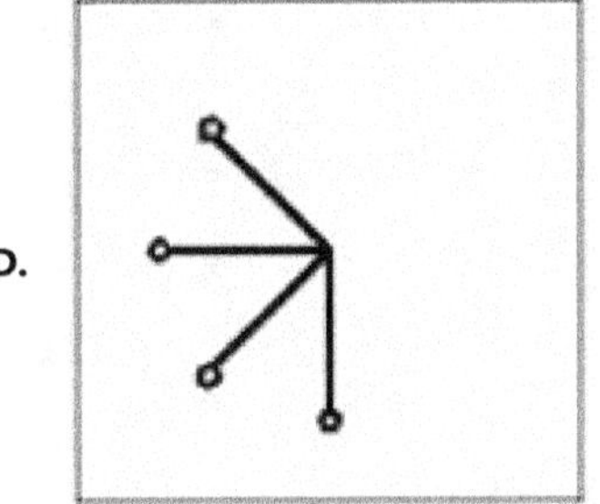

Q.56 Identify the architect of the structure

A. 13   **B.** 14   **C.** 16   **D.** 15

Q.55 Complete the series of the problem figures by choosing the correct answer from the options given below

A. Robert Fellows Chisholm
B. Edwin Lutyens
C. Herbert Baker
D. Henry Irwin

Q.57 Identify the location of the structure

A. Calcutta
B. Ahmedabad
C. Banglore
D. Indore

Q.58 Complete the series of the problem figures by choosing the correct answer from the options given below

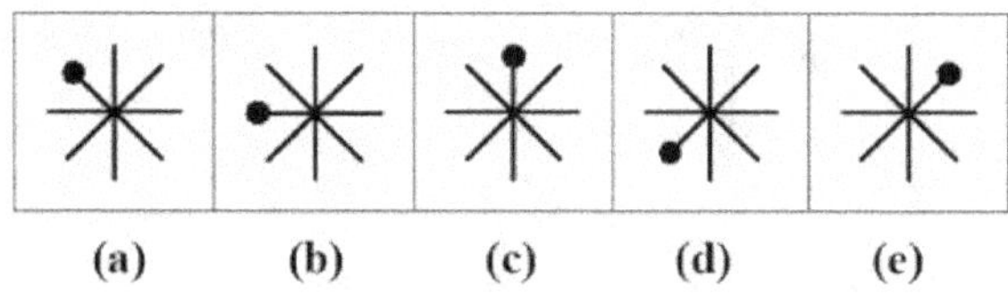

(a)   (b)   (c)   (d)   (e)

A.
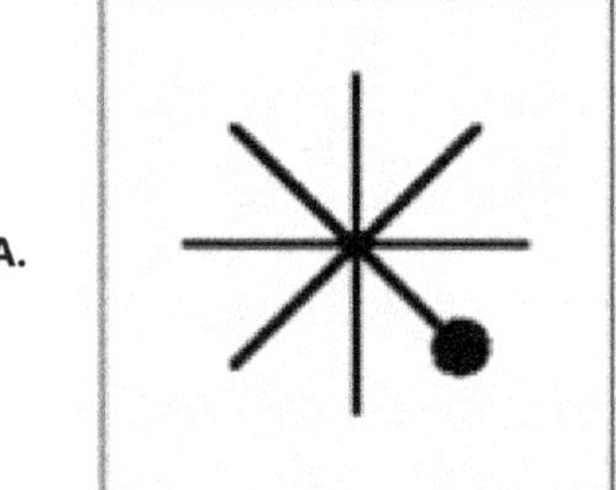

B.
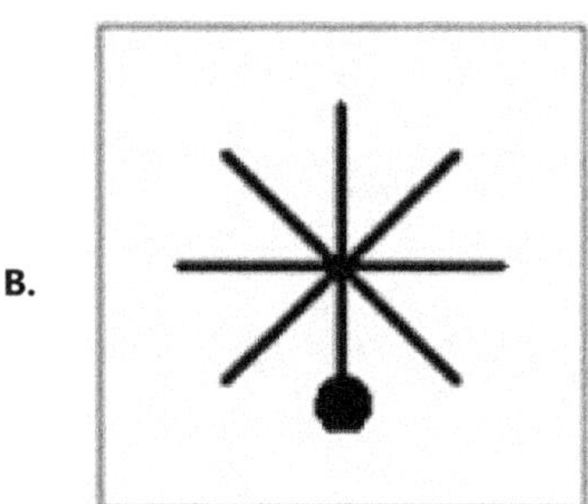

C.
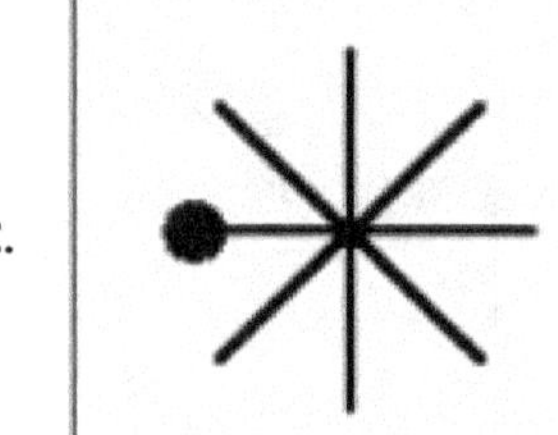

D.
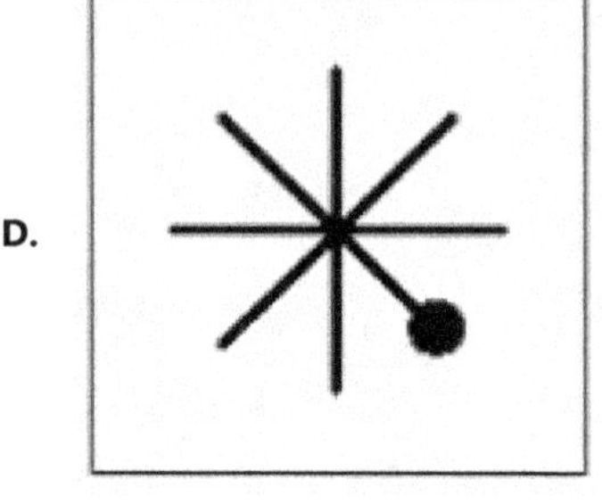

Ques (59-60):(Directions): Study the following information carefully and answer the questions follows:

Eight people Pawan, Qureshi, Rashid, Sonam, Tarikh, Veer, Wasim and Yogesh like eight different fruits – Papaya, Grapes, Mango, Pomegranate, Guava, Banana, Cherry and Watermelon but not necessarily in same order. They also like different cars namely Audi, BMW, Mercedes, Honda, Swift, Maruti, Ertiga and Xylo but not necessarily in the same order.

Rashid doesn't like Xylo car but likes Banana. Pawan and Tarikh don't like Mercedes car. Pawan doesn't like Papaya. Yogesh doesn't like Watermelon, but likes Honda car. Qureshi's favourite car is Ertiga. Veer likes Pomegranate. Sonam likes Mango and his favourite car is Maruti. The one who likes Grapes has Mercedes. The one who has swift likes Papaya. The one who like Guava likes Audi car.

Q.59 Which of the following combination is true for given people?
A. Yogesh-Mango-Honda
B. Veer-Cherry-Xylo
C. Pawan-Guava-Audi
D. Tarikh-Papaya-BMW

Q.60 Which person likes Xylo?
A. Qureshi   B. Veer   C. Yogesh   D. Rashid

// Smart Answer Sheet //

Correct Percentage of students who answered correctly.   **Skipped** Percentage of students who skipped.

Q.	Ans.	Correct / Skipped	Q.	Ans.	Correct / Skipped	Q.	Ans.	Correct / Skipped	Q.	Ans.	Correct / Skipped	Q.	Ans.	Correct / Skipped
1	C	14.63 % / 31.1 %	13	A	16.46 % / 35.37 %	25	D	80.49 % / 12.8 %	37	A	48.17 % / 12.81 %	49	B	41.46 % / 12.81 %
2	A	15.24 % / 31.1 %	14	A	29.88 % / 32.32 %	26	B	85.37 % / 13.41 %	38	B	62.8 % / 15.86 %	50	B	50.61 % / 14.63 %
3	D	22.56 % / 31.71 %	15	A	14.02 % / 33.54 %	27	A	69.51 % / 13.42 %	39	A	69.51 % / 14.03 %	51	D	68.29 % / 14.03 %
4	B	21.34 % / 37.81 %	16	A	50.61 % / 27.44 %	28	C	55.49 % / 14.63 %	40	D	30.49 % / 17.68 %	52	C	82.32 % / 14.63 %
5	D	18.29 % / 35.98 %	17	A	24.39 % / 35.98 %	29	A	66.46 % / 15.86 %	41	B	49.39 % / 12.2 %	53	A	84.15 % / 11.58 %
6	B	23.78 % / 37.2 %	18	A	53.05 % / 36.58 %	30	C	20.73 % / 15.86 %	42	B	68.29 % / 14.64 %	54	C	57.32 % / 13.41 %
7	D	31.1 % / 35.97 %	19	A	68.29 % / 21.34 %	31	A	70.73 % / 15.25 %	43	D	73.78 % / 14.63 %	55	A	55.49 % / 17.07 %
8	B	21.95 % / 39.03 %	20	A	41.46 % / 31.1 %	32	A	83.54 % / 13.41 %	44	A	89.02 % / 10.98 %	56	B	53.05 % / 13.41 %
9	A	37.2 % / 31.09 %	21	B	82.32 % / 10.97 %	33	C	73.17 % / 12.2 %	45	B	57.32 % / 14.02 %	57	B	59.76 % / 13.41 %
10	A	17.07 % / 39.03 %	22	A	68.9 % / 10.98 %	34	A	77.44 % / 13.41 %	46	D	21.95 % / 13.42 %	58	B	57.93 % / 16.46 %
11	D	12.2 % / 38.41 %	23	B	57.93 % / 15.85 %	35	B	39.63 % / 20.13 %	47	C	78.05 % / 15.24 %	59	C	44.51 % / 25.0 %
12	D	13.41 % / 36.59 %	24	B	86.59 % / 11.58 %	36	A	79.27 % / 15.85 %	48	C	47.56 % / 13.42 %	60	B	52.44 % / 25.61 %

//Hints and Solutions//

1. Let the equation of the circle is $(x-1)^2 + (y-k)^2 = k^2$

It passes through (2, 3)

$\Rightarrow$ (2-1)² + (3-k)² = k²

$\Rightarrow$ 1+9+k²-6k=k²

$\Rightarrow$ 10-6k=0

$\Rightarrow$ k=- $\dfrac{10}{6}$

$\Rightarrow$ k = 5/3 $\Rightarrow$ diameter = $\dfrac{10}{3}$

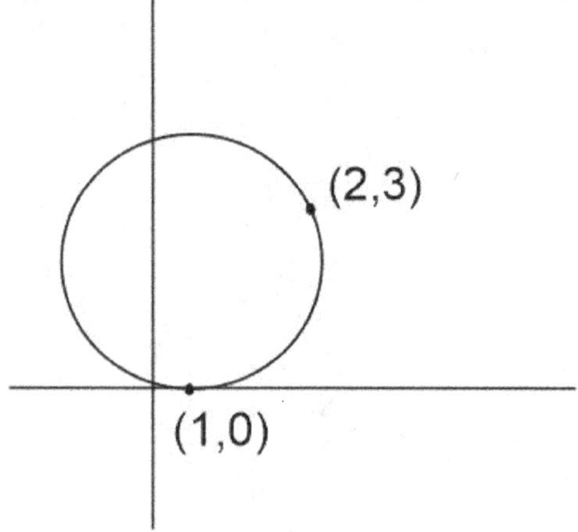

Hence, the correct option is (C).

2. Let first number $= x$, second number $= y$

$\therefore \quad LCM \times HCF =$ Product of numbers $= x \times y$

Also, LCM $= 16HCF, LCM + HCF = 850$ and $x = 50$

$\therefore \quad 17HCF = 850$

$\Rightarrow HCF = 50$

Now, LCM $= 16 \times 50 = 800$

$\therefore \quad 800 \times 50 = 50 \times y$

$\therefore \quad y = 800$

Hence, the correct option is (A).

3. Let A=i^i

$\Rightarrow$ log A = i log i

$\because$ e$^{i\theta}$ = cos θ + i sin θ

$\therefore$ e$^{i\frac{\pi}{2}}$ = i

$\therefore$ i . $\dfrac{\pi}{2}$ = log i

$\therefore$ log A = i · i $\dfrac{\pi}{2}$ = - $\dfrac{\pi}{2}$

$\Rightarrow$ A = e$^{-\frac{\pi}{2}}$

Hence, the correct option is (D).

4. Let the third vertex C be (x₁ , y₁) since O(0, 0) is the orthocenter

m$_{CO}$ × m$_{AB}$ = $-$ 1

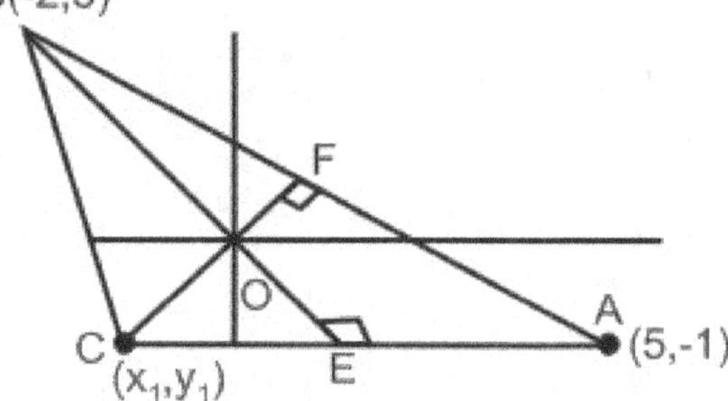

$\Rightarrow$ y 1 - 0 x 1 - 0 · 3 - 1 - 2 - 5 = - 1

$\Rightarrow$ y 1 x 1 · 4 7 = 1 $\Rightarrow$ 7 x 1 = 4 y 1

Also   mBO × mAC = $-$ 1

$\Rightarrow$ 3 - 2 × y 1 + 1 x 1 - 5 = - 1 $\Rightarrow$ 3 y 1 + 3 = 2 x 1 - 1 0

$\Rightarrow$ 3 × 7 4 x 1 + 3 = 2 x 1 - 1 0

$\Rightarrow$ x₁ = $-$ 4

y₁ = $-$ 7

Hence, the third vertex is

($-$ 4, $-$ 7)

Hence, the correct option is (B).

5. We have

$$(1-x)^n = C_0 - C_1 x + C_2 x^2 - \cdots + C_n(-1)^n x^n$$

(i)

Replacing x by x^2 in equation (i), we have

$$(1-x^2)^n = C_0 - C_1 x^2 + C_2 x^4 - \cdots + C_n(-1)^n x^{2n}$$

Multiplying throughout by x, we have

$x1 - x2n - c0x - C1 \times 3 + C2 \times 5 - \ldots + Cn - 1nx$

$2n + 1$

Differentiating equation (iii) wretx, we have

$$(1-x^2)^n - 2nx^2(1-x^2)^{n-1} = C_0 - 3C_1 x^2 + 5C_2 x^4 - \cdots + (-1)^n(2n+1)C_n x^{2n}$$

(iv)

Putting $x - 1$ in equation (iv), we have

$$C_0 - 3C_1 + 5C_2 - \cdots + (-1)^n(2n + 1)C_n = 0$$

Hence, the correct option is (D).

6. The number of arrangements of one ball $= 4$ because there are only four different balls. The number of arrangements of two balls

$$-4 \times 4 - 4^2, \text{ etc}$$

∴ the required number of arrangements

$$= 4 + 4^2 + 4^3 + \cdots + 4^8 = \frac{4(4^8 - 1)}{4 - 1}$$
$$= 4348 - 1 = 43 \times 65535 = 4 \times 21845$$

$$= 87380$$

Hence, the correct option is (B).

7. $\frac{dy}{dx} = \frac{1}{x} + 3x^2$

$$\Rightarrow dy = \left(\frac{1}{x} + 3x^2\right) dx$$

$$\Rightarrow \int dy = \int \left(\frac{1}{x} + 3x^2\right) dx, \text{ integrate both sides}$$

$$\Rightarrow y = \ln x + 3 \cdot \frac{x^3}{3} + c = \ln x + x^3 + c$$

Hence, the correct option is (D).

8. f(x) = eax + e- ax

But a < 0

∴ e ax - e - ax > 0 ⇒ e ax > e - ax

⇒ ax > - ax ⇒ 2 ax > 0

∴ ax > 0, then   x < 0   (∵ a < 0)

Hence, the correct option is (B).

9. Three-digit numbers are to be formed by using the digits 1, 7, 8 and 9.

To form a number of three digits, we are to fill up three places : the hundred's, the ten's and the unit's. The hundred's place can be filled in 4 different ways because anyone of 1, 7, 8 and 9 can fill up this place.

Similarly, ten's and unit's places can also be filled in 4 different ways each.

Accordingly, by FPC,

the no. of three-digit numbers = 4 × 4 × 4 = 64

Hence, the correct option is (A).

10.

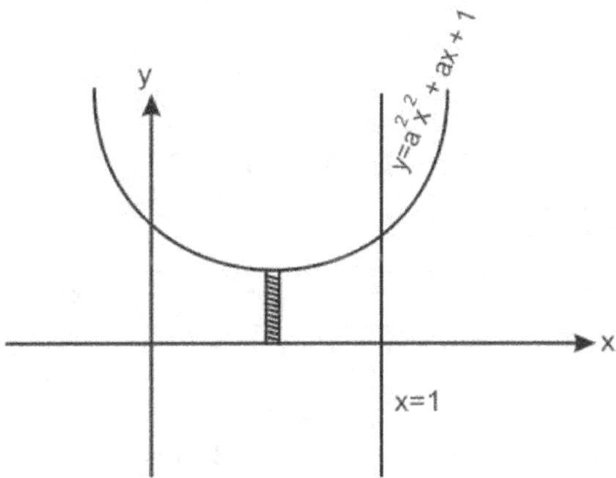

$$y = a^2x^2 + ax + 1$$
$$\left(x + \frac{1}{2a}\right)^2 = \frac{1}{a^2}\left(y - \frac{3}{4}\right) \text{ upward parabola with vertex}$$
$$\left(\frac{-1}{2a}, \frac{3}{4}\right)$$

Required area $= f(a) = \int_0^1 (a^2x^2 + ax + 1)\, dx$

$\Rightarrow fa = a23 + a2 + 1$

for $f(a)$ to be least

$\$f$

$$\frac{2a}{3} + \frac{1}{2} = 0$$

$$a = -\left(\frac{3}{4}\right)$$

Hence, the correct option is (A).

11. For the above question $T_{r+1} = {}^7C_r x^{21-5r} 2^{2-7}$

For the fourth term, from the end $r = 4$

$$T_{5+1} = {}^7C_4 x^1 2$$
$$= (35)(2)x$$
$$= 70x$$

Hence, the correct option is (D).

12. because $13, a_1, a_2, a_3, \quad a_{20}, 67$ are in AP

$$\therefore a_1 + a_2 + a_3 + \cdots + a_{20} = 20\left(\frac{13+67}{2}\right) = 800$$

Now. $AM \geq GM$

$$because \frac{a_1 + a_2 + a_3 + \cdots a_{20}}{20} \geq (a_1 a_2 a_3 \ldots a_{20})^{1/20}$$

$$\Rightarrow \left(\frac{800}{20}\right) \geq (a_1 a_2 a_3 - a_{20})^{1/20}$$

$$a_1 a_2 a_3 - a_{20} \leq (40)^{20}$$

∴ Maximum value of $a_1 a_2 a_3 \ldots a_{20}$ is $(40)^{20}$

Hence, the correct option is (D).

13. The bisector of BAC ie. AD divides the side BC in the ratio $AB:AC$

ie. $\dfrac{BD}{CD} = \dfrac{AB}{AC}$

Now. $AB - 3 - 52 + 2 - 32 + 0 - 22$

$= \sqrt{4 + 1 + 4} = 3$

$AC = \sqrt{(-9 - 3)^3 + (6 - 2)^2 + (-3 - 0)^2}$
$= \sqrt{144 + 16 + 9} = 13$

Let co-ordinates of $D(x, y, z)$

$x = 3x - 9 + 13 \times 53 + 13 = 3816 = 198$

$y = 3 \times 6 + 3 \times 133 + 13 = 5716$

$z = -3 \times 3 + 13 \times 23 + 13 = 1716$

$\therefore D\left(\dfrac{19}{8}\,\dfrac{57}{16}\,\dfrac{17}{16}\right)$

Hence, the correct option is (A).

14. Divisor $= 555 + 445 = 1000$

Quotient $= 2 \times (555 - 445) = 220$

Remainder $= 30$

$\therefore$ Dividend $=$ Divisor $\times Q$ uotient $+$ Remainder

$= 1000 \times 220 + 30 = 220030$

Hence, the correct option is (A).

15. $^{16}C_r = ^{16}C_{r+2}$

Use the formular $^mC_x = ^nC_y \Rightarrow x + y = n$

$r + r + 2 = 16$

$2r + 2 = 16$

$r = 7$

$^rC_4 = ^7C_4 = \dfrac{71}{4^{191}} = \dfrac{765}{321} = 35$

Thus, the value is 35

Hence, the correct option is (A).

16. 1,2,3,4,5

Number of given digits $= 5$ Number of Digited number to be formed $= 5$ Number of such numbers $^5P_3$

$= \dfrac{5!}{0!}$

$= 5!$

$= 120$

Number of such numbers $= 120$

17. we know, number of ways of selecting r persons from n persons $= {}^nC_r$

i.e. $^nC_n = ^nC_B$

but, $^nC_r = ^nC_{n-r}$

$\Rightarrow n = r + (n - r)$

$\Rightarrow n = 5 + 8$

$\Rightarrow n = 13$

Hence, the correct option is (A).

18. Finding determinant of the give matrix $=|A|$

$=2$ times $9-6$times $3=18-18=0$

Hence, the correct option is (A).

19. Since, given matrix contain a single element means it contain one row and one column.

$\therefore$ Order of matrix A is 1×1

Hence, the correct option is (A).

20. As for $\cos^{-1}(\cos\theta) = \theta \in [0, \pi]$

$\cos^{-1}\left(\cos\left(\dfrac{\pi}{4}\right)\right) = \dfrac{\pi}{4}$

Hence, the correct option is (A).

21. Any of a group of colours from which all other colours can be obtained by mixing.

Red, Yellow and Blue form a primary colour scheme

Hence, the correct option is (B).

22. The Rashtrapati Bhavan is the official home of the President of India located at the Western end of Rajpath in New Delhi, India.

HENCE, THE CORRECT OPTION IS (A).

23. One of the most distinguishing features of all **sanitary** tube **fittings** is the surface **finish**, most commonly referred to as Roughness Average (Ra). At a microscopic level, stainless steel has peaks and valleys that can harbor bacteria throughout the production cycle.

Hence, the correct option is (B).

24.

Hence, the correct option is (B).

25.

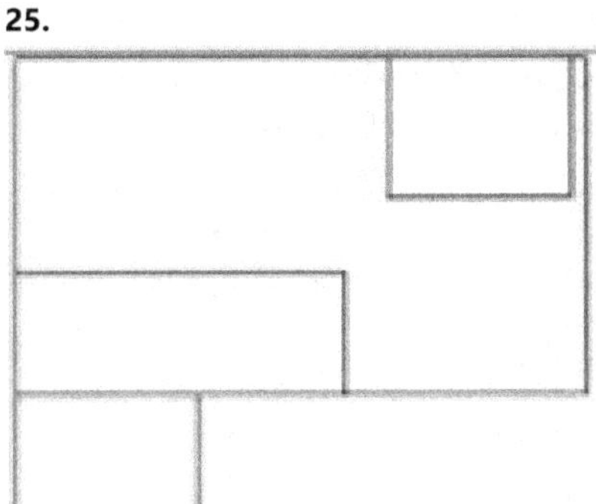

Hence, the correct option is (D).

26. The Statue of Liberty is a colossal neoclassical sculpture on Liberty Island in New York Harbor in New York, in the United States.

The copper statue, a gift from the people of France to the people of the United States, was designed by French sculptor Frédéric Auguste Bartholdi and its metal framework was built by Gustave Eiffel. The statue was dedicated on October 28, 1886.

Hence, the correct option is (A).

27. The important thing to remember is how the color varies from its original hue. If white is added to a color, the lighter version is called a "tint". If the color is made darker by adding black, the result is called a "shade". And if gray is added, each gradation gives you a different "tone.

Hence, the correct option is (A).

28.

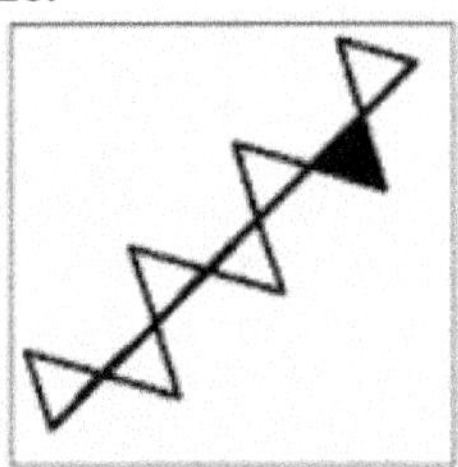

Hence, the correct option is (C).

29. Its name "CN" originally referred to Canadian National, the railway company that built the tower. Following the railway's decision to divest non-core freight railway assets prior to the company's privatization in 1995, it transferred the tower to the Canada Lands Company, a federal Crown corporation responsible for real estate development.

Hence, the correct option is (A).

30. The difference is in the dimension of **chrome** by which the degree of **color** strength or intensity is measured. The stronger the hue, the **greater** the saturation or intensity. ... INTENSITY is the strength or **purity of a color**.

Hence, the correct option is (C).

31. LIC Building is a 15-storied building in Chennai, India, serving as the southern regional headquarters of the Life Insurance Corporation of India

Hence, the correct option is (A).

32.

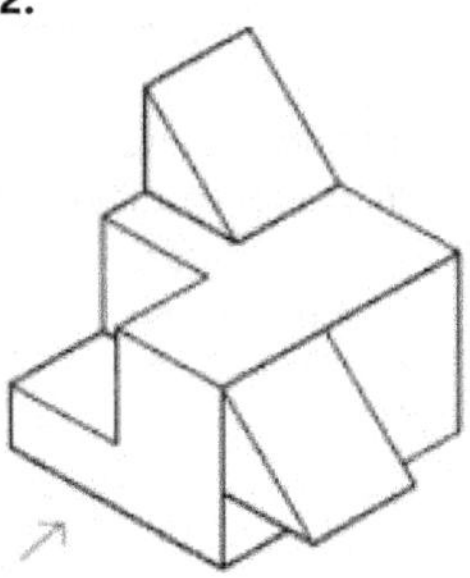

Hence, the correct option is (A).

33. The Petronas Towers, also known as the Petronas Twin Towers, are twin skyscrapers. According to the Council on Tall Buildings and Urban Habitat (CTBUH)'s official definition and ranking, they were the tallest buildings in the world from 1998 to 2004 and remain the tallest twin towers in the world.

Hence, the correct option is (C).

34.

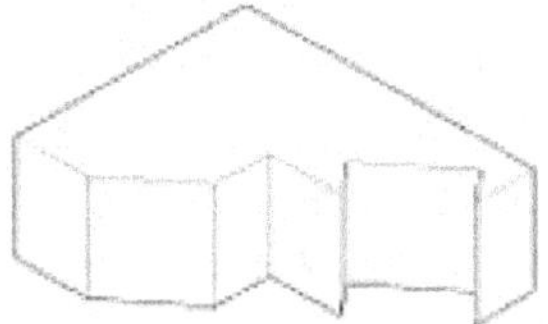

12 number of surfaces of objects.Hence, the correct option is (A).

35. TEOTIHUACAN is an ancient Mesoamerican city located in a sub-valley of the Valley of Mexico, located in the State of Mexico 40 kilometres (25 mi) northeast of modern-day Mexico City, known today as the site of many of the most architecturally significant Mesoamerican pyramids built in the pre-Columbian Americas.

Hence, the correct option is (B).

36.

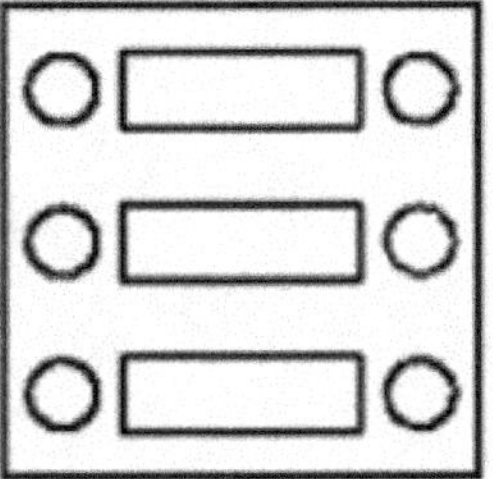

Hence, the correct option is (A).

37. This monument is regarded as the heritage of India and is located on Raj Path in New Delhi. India Gate was designed by Sir Edwin Lutyens and was built in 1931 and initially named as 'All India War Memorial'. ... India Gate was built to honor these soldiers.

Hence, the correct option is (A).

38. The Louvre Pyramid is a large glass and metal pyramid designed by Chinese-American architect I. M. Pei, surrounded by three smaller pyramids, in the main courtyard) of the Louvre Palace in Paris.

Hence, the correct option is (B).

39. 1865 - 1886. In 1865, a French political intellectual and anti-slavery activist named Edouard de Laboulaye proposed that a statue representing liberty be built for the United States. This monument would honor the United States' centennial of independence and the friendship with France.

Hence, the correct option is (A).

40.

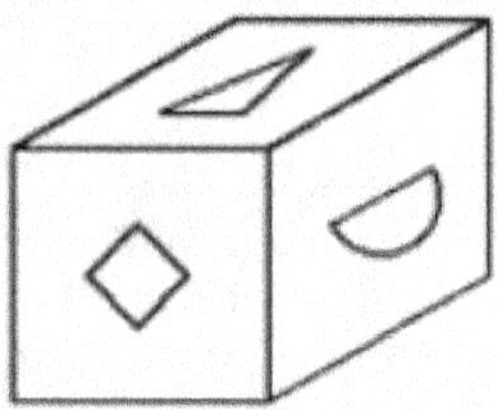

Hence, the correct option is (D).

41. When the Statue was unveiled in 1886, it was a shiny brown color, like a penny. By 1906, the color had changed to green. The reason the Statue of Liberty changed colors is that the outer surface is covered with hundreds of thin copper sheets. Copper reacts with the air to form a patina or verdigris.

Hence, the correct option is (B).

42.

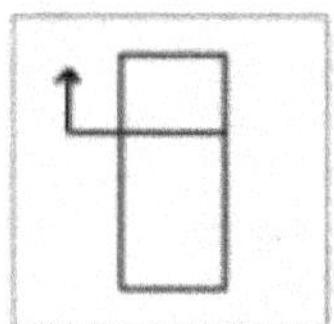

Hence, the correct option is (B).

43.

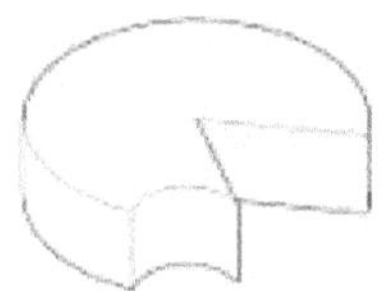

Ther are 6 object in a image.

Hence, the correct option is (D).

44. The Taj Mahal meaning "Crown of the Palaces" is an ivory-white marble mausoleum on the south bank of the Yamuna river in the Indian city of Agra

Hence, the correct option is (A).

45. Pink is a tint of red.The lightness or darkness of a color is called its value. ... **Tints** are light values that are made by mixing a color with white. For example, **pink is a tint of red**, and light blue is a **tint** of blue. Shades are dark values that are made by mixing a color with black.

Hence, the correct option is (B).

46. Michael Graves is the designer of the "Statue of Unity", Gujarat, India, now boasts the tallest statue in the world.

The nearly 600-foot-tall Statue of Unity, completed on November 1, is a bronze duplicate of India's first deputy prime minister Sardar Vallabhbhai Patel. It was designed and master-planned by Michael Graves Architecture & Design (MGA) and is intended to anchor what will eventually become a resort.

Hence, the correct option is (D).

47.

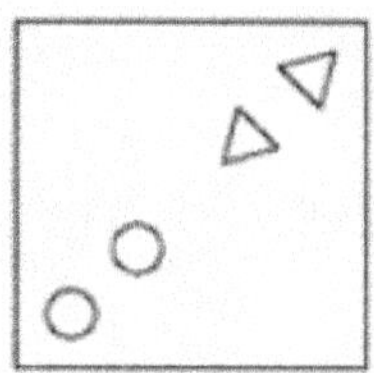

Hence, the correct option is (C).

48.

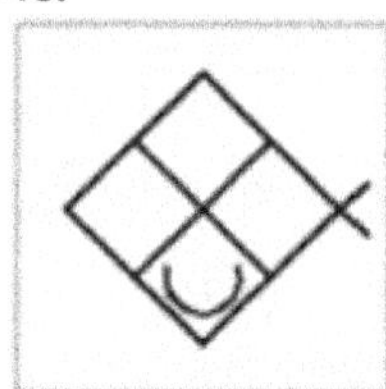

Hence, the correct option is (C).

49. Orange makes juice is in the same way that Mango makes pulp.

Hence, the correct option is (B).

50.

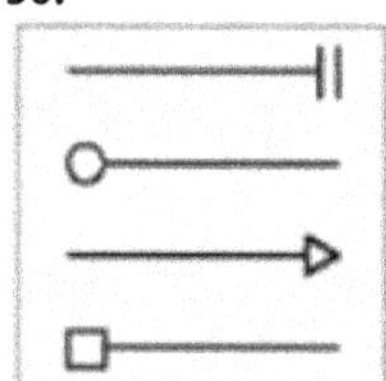

Hence, the correct option is (B).

51. There are seven wavelength ranges within the visible spectrum that each correspond to a different color. The colors fall in an order commonly referred to with the acronym ROYGBIV. ROYGBIV can aid in remembering the order of the colors: red, orange, yellow, green, blue, indigo, and violet.

Hence, the correct option is (D).

52.

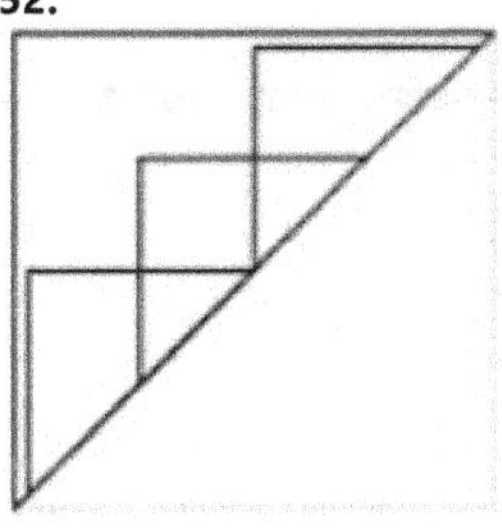

Hence, the correct option is (C).

53.

Hence, the correct option is (A).

54.

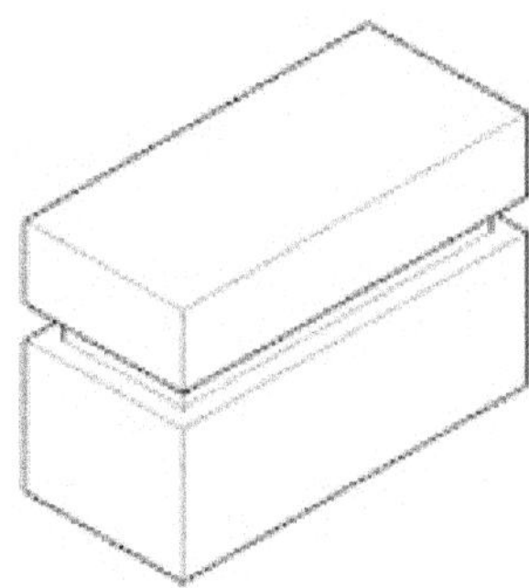

In the given figure 16 surfaces of objects.

Hence, the correct option is (C).

55.

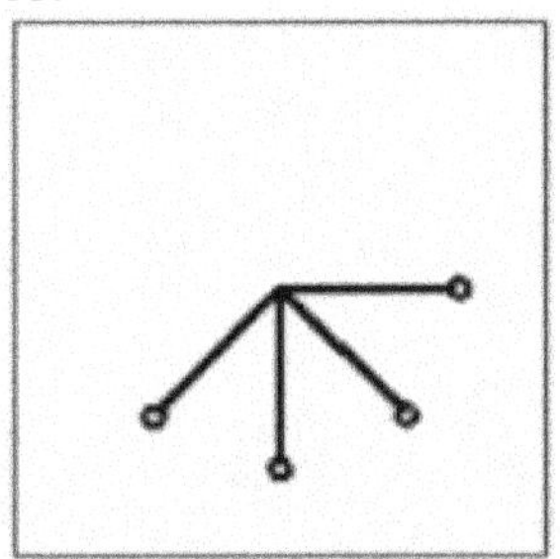

Hence, the correct option is (A).

56. Edwin Lutyens played an instrumental role in designing and building New Delhi, which would later on serve as the seat of the Government of India. In recognition of his contribution, New Delhi is also known as "Lutyens' Delhi". In collaboration with Sir Herbert Baker, he was also the main architect of several monuments in New Delhi such as the India Gate; he also designed Viceroy's House, which is now known as the Rashtrapati Bhavan.

Hence, the correct option is (B).

57. Ahmedabad is the largest city and former capital of the Indian state of Gujarat. It is the administrative headquarter of the Ahmadabad district and the seat of the Gujarat High Court.

Hence, the correct option is (B).

58.

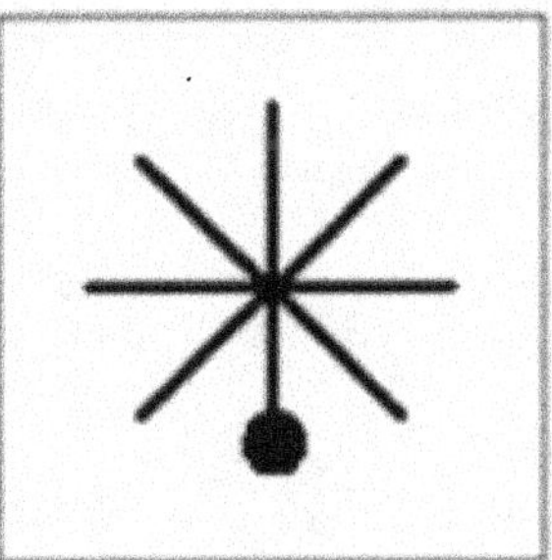

Hence, the correct option is (B).

59. Pawan – Guava – Audi is the true arrangement.

Hence, the correct option is (C).

60. Veer likes Xylo.Hence, the correct option is (B).

Mathematics

Q.1 Find the middle term in the expansion of

$$\left(\frac{2}{3}x - \frac{3}{2x}\right)^{20}$$

A. $^{20}C_{10}x^{10}y^{10}$ **B.** $^{20}C_{11}x^{11}y^{11}$

C. $^{20}C_9x^{11}y^{10}$ **D.** $^{20}C_9x^9y^{10}$

Q.2 The area bounded by the curves $x + 2|y| = 1$ and $x = 0$ is:

A. $\frac{1}{3}$ **B.** $\frac{1}{2}$ **C.** 2   **D.** 3

Q.3 $(x-1)^2 + (y-2)^2 = 3\left(\frac{x+y-3}{\sqrt{2}}\right)^2$

A. $\frac{9}{2}$ **B.** 0   **C.** 3   **D.** $\frac{3}{2}$

Q.4 Sum of n terms of series 12 + 16 + 24 + 40 + ... will be

A. $2(2^n - 1) + 8n$ **B.** $2(2^n - 1) + 6n$

C. $3(2^n - 1) + 8n$ **D.** $4(2^n - 1) + 8n$

Q.5 $\sin[\cot^{-1}\{\cos(\tan^{-1}x)\}] =$

A. $\sqrt{\frac{1+x^2}{2+x^2}}$ **B.** $\sqrt{\frac{1-x^2}{2+x^2}}$ **C.** $\sqrt{\frac{1+x^2}{2-x^2}}$ **D.** $\sqrt{\frac{2+x^2}{1+x^2}}$

Q.6 Let $A = \begin{bmatrix} \sin\alpha & \sin\alpha\sin\beta \\ -\sin\alpha & 0 & \cos\alpha\cos\beta \\ -\sin\alpha\sin\beta & -\cos\alpha\cos\beta & 0 \end{bmatrix}$, then

A. $|A|$ is independent of α and β

B. A^{-1} depends only on α

C. A^{-1} depends only on β

D. $|A|$ is dependent of α

Q.7 The value of $\lim\limits_{x \to 0} \frac{5\sin x - 7\sin 2x + 3\sin 3x}{x^2 \sin x}$ is

A. -5   **B.** -7   **C.** 5   **D.** 7

Q.8 From the bottom of pole of height h, the angle of elevation of the top of a tower is α. The pole subtends an angle β at the top of the tower. Then the height of the tower is:

A. $h\sin\alpha\cos\beta\cos(\alpha - \beta)$

B. $h\sin\alpha\csc\beta\cos(\alpha - \beta)$

C. $h\csc\alpha\sin\beta\cos(\alpha - \beta)$

D. none of these

Q.9 The length of the longer diagonal of the parallelogram constructed on $5\vec{a} + 2\vec{b}$ and $\vec{a} - 3\vec{b}$, if it is given that $|\vec{a}| = 2\sqrt{2}, |\vec{b}| = 3$ and angle between $\vec{a}\,\&\,\vec{b}$ is $\frac{\pi}{4}$

A. 15   **B.** $\sqrt{113}$ **C.** $\sqrt{593}$ **D.** $\sqrt{369}$

Q.10 Suppose a, b, c are in AP and a^2, b^2, c^2 are in GP. If $a < b < c$ & $a+b+c = \frac{3}{2}$, then the value of a is-

A. $\frac{1}{2} - \frac{1}{\sqrt{2}}$ **B.** $\frac{1}{2} + \frac{1}{\sqrt{2}}$

C. $\frac{1}{2}$ **D.** None of these

Q.11 The function $f(x) = \frac{\log_e(\pi + x)}{\log_e(e + x)}$ is

A. Increasing on $(0, \infty)$

B. Decreasing on $(0, \infty)$

C. Increasing on $\left(0, \frac{\pi}{e}\right)$, decreasing on $\left(\frac{\pi}{e}, \infty\right)$

D. none of these

Q.12 If $\log_2(4^{x+1} + 4)\log_2(4^x + 1) = \log_2 8 \cdot$ then x equals

A. -1   **B.** 0   **C.** 16   **D.** 64

Q.13

Let $f(x) = e^{(x-1)} - 2x^2 + b$ & $g(x) = \begin{cases} e^{x-1} & \text{for } x \le 1 \\ x^2 + 1 & \text{for } x > 1 \end{cases}$ with $f'(1) = 2$.

The values of a and b for which the function $h(x) = f(x) \cdot g[x]$, is differentiable at x = 1, are respectively

A. $-\left(\frac{1}{2}\right), -\left(\frac{3}{2}\right)$ **B.** $-\left(\frac{1}{2}\right), \left(\frac{3}{2}\right)$

C. $-\left(\frac{1}{2}\right), -2$ **D.** none of these

Q.14 If $'M'$ and σ^2 are mean and variance of random variable X, whose distribution is given by -

$X = x$	0	1	2	3	4	5
$P(X) = x$	$\frac{1}{4}$	0	$\frac{1}{4}$	0	$\frac{1}{2}$	0

then,

A. $M = 1, \sigma^2 = 2$ **B.** $M = \frac{5}{2}, \sigma^2 = \frac{9}{4}$

C. $M = \frac{5}{2}, \sigma^2 = \frac{11}{4}$ **D.** $M = 1, \sigma^2 = \frac{9}{4}$

Q.15 If $\vec{a}.\vec{b}.\vec{c}$ are three unit vectors such that $\vec{a} \times \left(\vec{b} \times \vec{c}\right) = \frac{1}{2}\vec{b}$ and b is not parallel to c. then the angle between a and c is

A. $\frac{\pi}{6}$ **B.** $\frac{\pi}{4}$ **C.** $\frac{\pi}{3}$ **D.** $\frac{\pi}{2}$

Q.16 The equation $|z - \omega|^2 + |z - \omega^2|^2 = \lambda.$ represents the equation of a circle with ω, ω^2 as extremities of a diameter, then λ, is. (where ω, ω^2 are cube roots of unity)

A. $\sqrt{2}$ **B.** 2   **C.** 3   **D.** 4

Q.17 If $\sin^{-1}x + \sin^{-1}y + \sin^{-1}z = \pi/2$ then $x^2 + y^2 + z^2 + 2xyz$ is equal to -

A. -1 **B.** 0 **C.** 1 **D.** $\frac{1}{2}$

Q.18 If $b^2 \geq 4ac$ for the equation $ax^4 + bx^2 + c = 0$, then all the roots of the equation will be real if-

A. b>0, a<0, c>0 **B.** b<0, a>0, c>0
C. b>0, a>0, c>0 **D.** b>0, a>0, c<0

Q.19 If $x = a(\theta - \sin\theta)\ \&\ y = a(1 - \cos\theta)$, then the value of

A. $\frac{d^2y}{dx^2}$ at $\theta = \frac{\pi}{2}$ equals $-\frac{1}{a}$

B. $\frac{d^2y}{dx^2}$ at $\theta = \frac{\pi}{2}$ equals

C. $\frac{d^2y}{dx^2}$ at $\theta = \frac{\pi}{3}$ equals $-\frac{1}{a}$

D. none of these

Q.20 The value of the definite integral $\int_0^1 \frac{dx}{(x^2+2x\cos\alpha+1)}$ for $0 < \alpha < \pi$, equal to-

A. $\sin\ \alpha$ **B.** $\tan^{-1}(\sin\ \alpha)$
C. $\alpha\sin\ \alpha$ **D.** $\frac{\alpha}{2\sin\alpha}$

General Aptitude

Q.21 The below question consists of problem figures and followed by four answer figures (A), (B), (C) and (D). Find out the figure from the answer figures which will continue the given series.

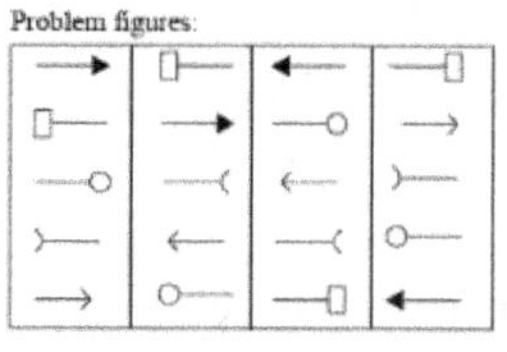 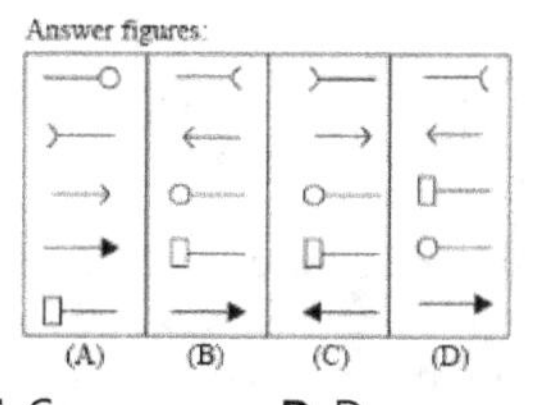

A. A **B.** B **C.** C **D.** D

Q.22 The below question consists of problem figures and followed by four answer figures (A), (B), (C) and (D). Find out the figure from the answer figures which will continue the given series.

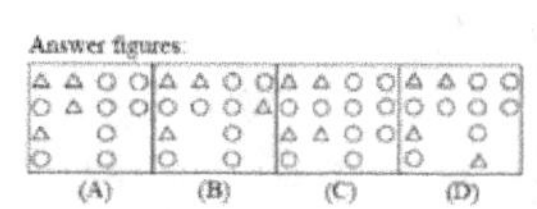

A. A **B.** B **C.** C **D.** D

Q.23 The below question consists of a set of four figures K, L, M and N showing a sequence of folding of a piece of paper. Figure N shows the manner in which the folded paper has been cut. These four figures are followed by another four figures (1), (2), (3) and (4) from which you have to choose a figure which would most closely resemble the unfolded form of figure N.

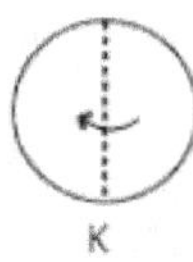 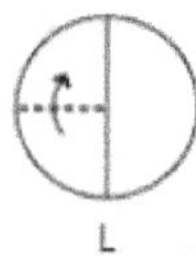 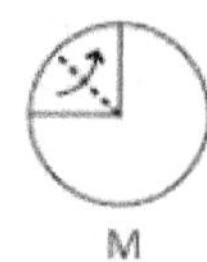 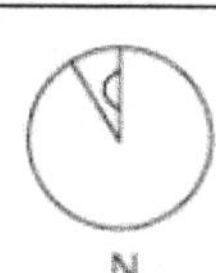

K   L   M   N

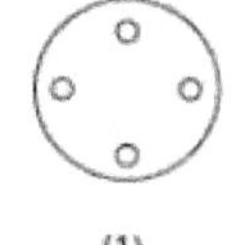 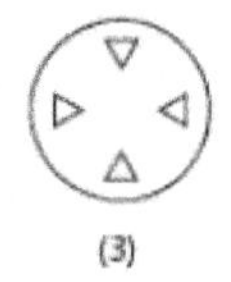 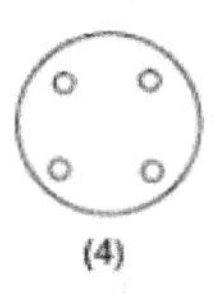

(1)   (2)   (3)   (4)

A. 1 **B.** 2 **C.** 3 **D.** 4

Q.24 Find out which of the figures (a), (b), (c) and (d) can be formed from the pieces given in figure (X).

(X)   (a)   (b)   (c)   (d)

A. a **B.** b **C.** c **D.** d

Q.25 The below question consists of four figures a, b, c and d and followed by answer figures marked as (A), (B), (C) and (D) each consisting of two figures marked a and d. Select a figure from the answer sets which suitable in the problem figure such that c is related to figure d and in the same way figure a is related to figure b.

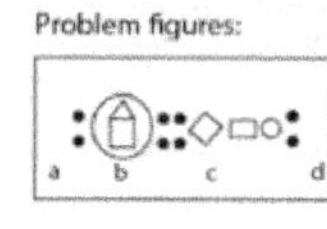

Problem figures: Answer figures:

A. A **B.** B **C.** C **D.** D

Q.26 In the below question, element (b) is related to element (a) in a particular way in three pairs of figures out of the given four. Find out the pair of figures in which the element (b) is not related to element (a).

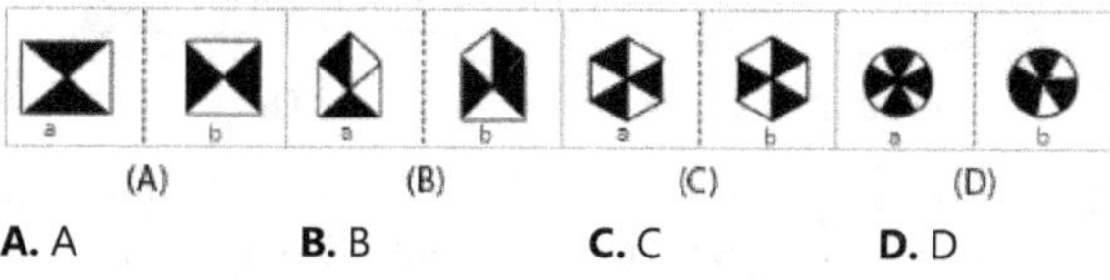

(A)   (B)   (C)   (D)

A. A **B.** B **C.** C **D.** D

Q.27 The below question consists of a question figure and followed by four figures (a), (b), (c) and (d), which show the possible water images of the question figure. Choose one out of these four figures which shows the correct water image of the question figure.

B n 6 K M X h

(a) B ᴜ 9 K W X ᴘ   (c) B ᴜ ǝ K W X ᴘ

(b) ᙠ ᴜ 9 K W X ᴅ   (d) B ᴜ ǝ ʞ W X ᴘ

A. a **B.** b **C.** c **D.** d

Q.28 The below question consists of a question figure and followed by four figures (a), (b), (c) and (d). Choose one out of

these four figures that can replace '?' to complete the question figure.

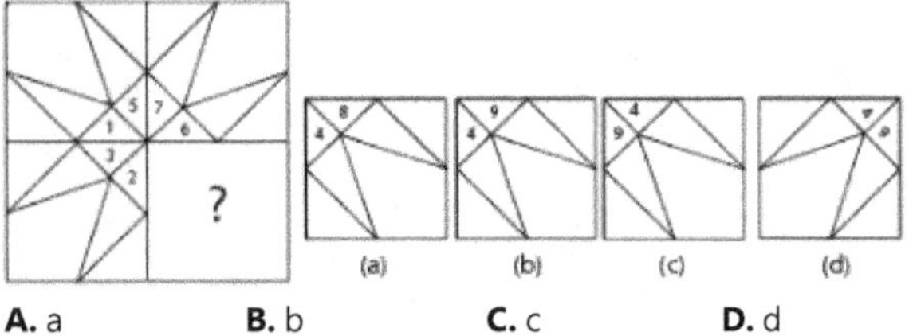

A. a   **B.** b   **C.** c   **D.** d

Q.29 In the below question, one or more dots are placed in the problem figure (X) followed by four alternatives (a), (b), (c) and (d). One out of these four alternatives contain region(s) common to the circle, square, triangle and rectangle similar to that marked by the dot in figure (X).

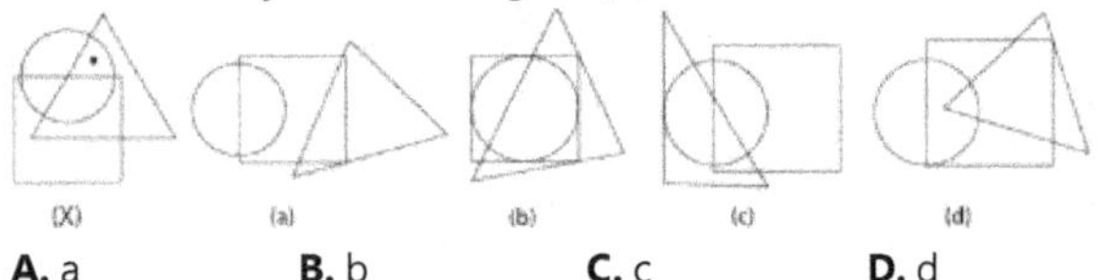

A. a   **B.** b   **C.** c   **D.** d

Q.30 Three-position of a cube are shown below. Which number will be opposite to the face containing 5?

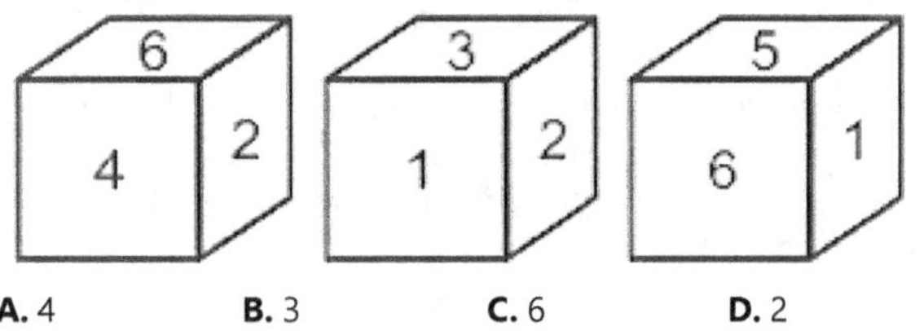

A. 4   **B.** 3   **C.** 6   **D.** 2

Q.31 The below question consists of figure (Y) and followed by four alternatives (1), (2), (3) and (4). Choose the correct alternative among the four alternatives such that the pattern would appear like when the figure (Y) is folded at the dotted line.

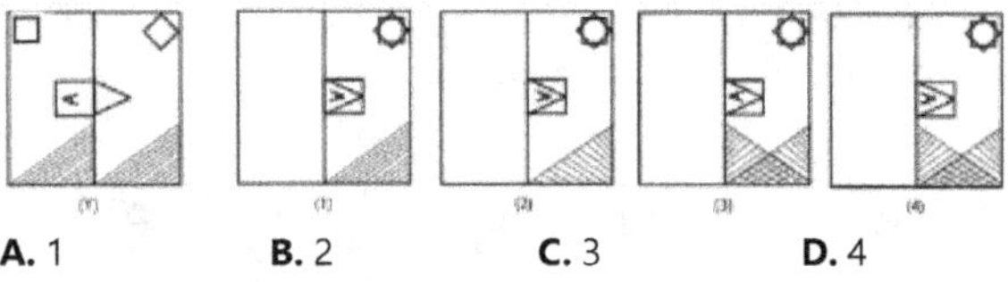

A. 1   **B.** 2   **C.** 3   **D.** 4

Q.32 Choose the correct mirror image for the given figure among the four alternatives (1), (2), (3) and (4). The mirror is represented by a line AB.

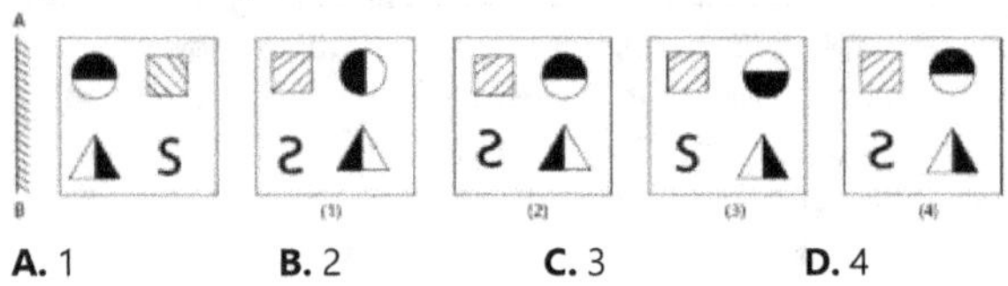

A. 1   **B.** 2   **C.** 3   **D.** 4

Q.33 Find the number of triangles in the given figure

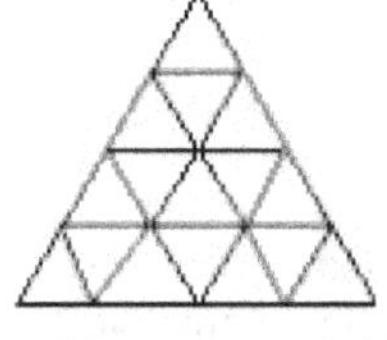

A. 23   **B.** 26   **C.** 28   **D.** 27

Q.34 The below question consists of a problem figure (X) followed by four other alternative figures marked (a), (b), (c) and (d). Select a figure from the alternative figures which exactly fit into figure(X) to form a complete hexagon.

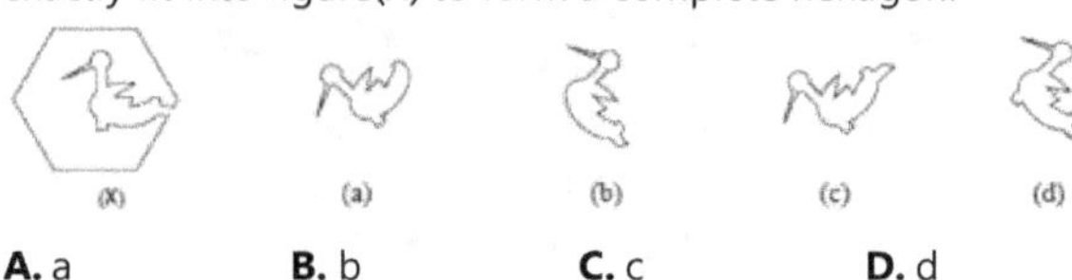

A. a   **B.** b   **C.** c   **D.** d

Q.35

Group the given figures into three classes using each figure only once.

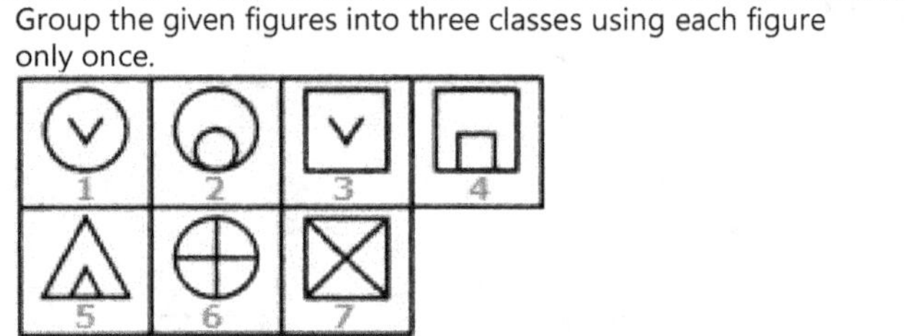

A. 1,2,6 ; 3,4,7 ; 5   **B.** 1,3 ; 2,6 ; 4,5,7

C. 1,2,6,7 ; 3 ; 4,5   **D.** 1,3 ; 2,4,5 ; 6,7

Q.36 The below question consists of a four figures. Three are similar in a certain way and so form a group. Find out which one of the figures does not belong to that group.

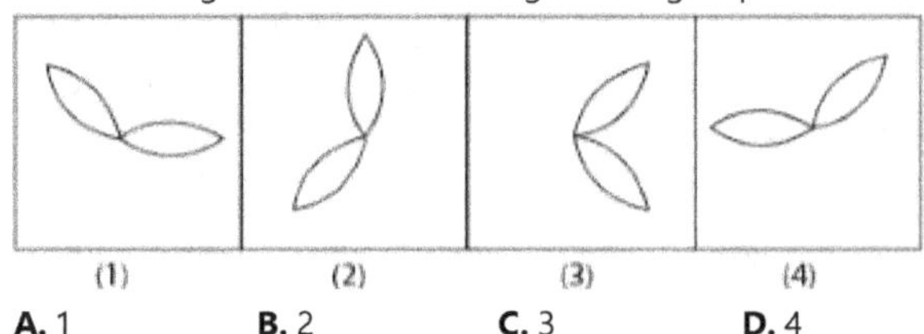

A. 1   **B.** 2   **C.** 3   **D.** 4

Q.37 The below question consists of a four figures. Three are similar in a certain way and so form a group. Find out which one of the figures does not belong to that group.

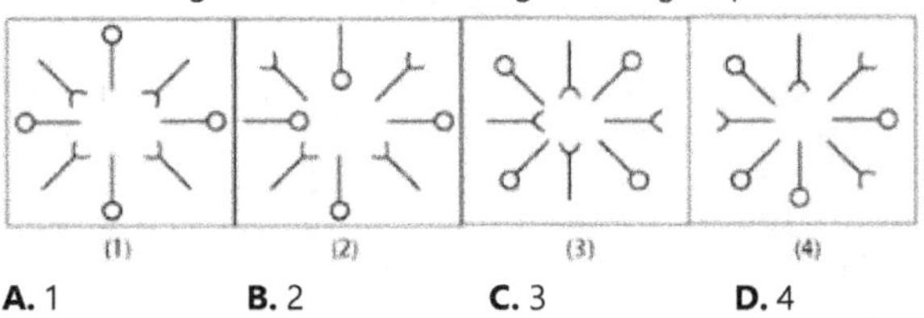

A. 1   **B.** 2   **C.** 3   **D.** 4

Q.38 Choose the correct alternative which contains figure (X) as its part.

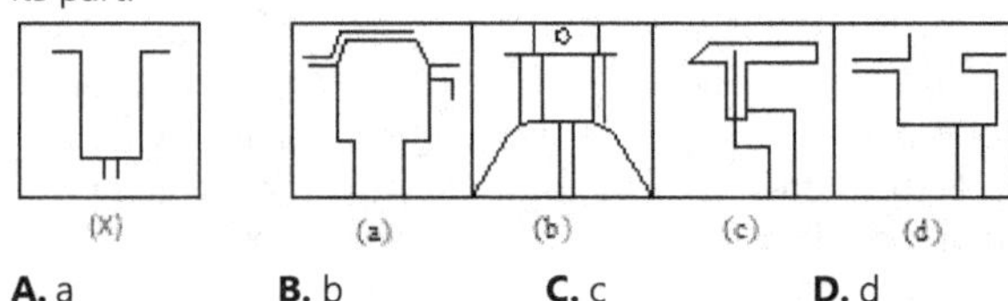

A. a   **B.** b   **C.** c   **D.** d

Q.39 Group the given figures into three classes using each figure only once.

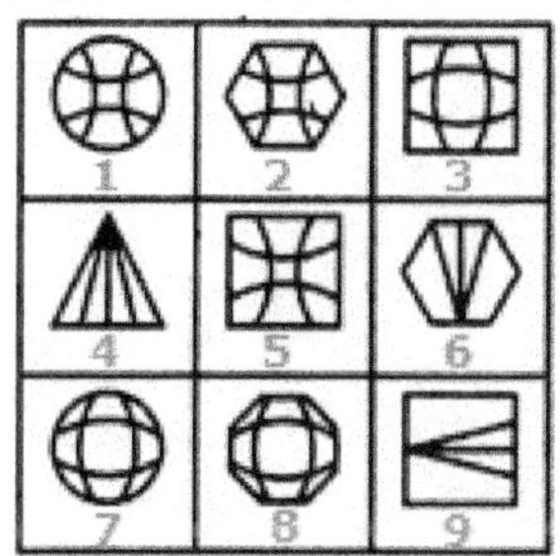

A. 1,2,5 ; 3,7,8 ; 4,6,9   **B.** 1,7,2 ; 3,9,6 ; 4,5,8
C. 2,3,8 ; 4,6,9 ; 1,5,7   **D.** (147), (258), (369)

Q.40 The below question consists of a five figures. Four are similar in a certain way and so form a group. Find out which one of the figures does not belong to that group.

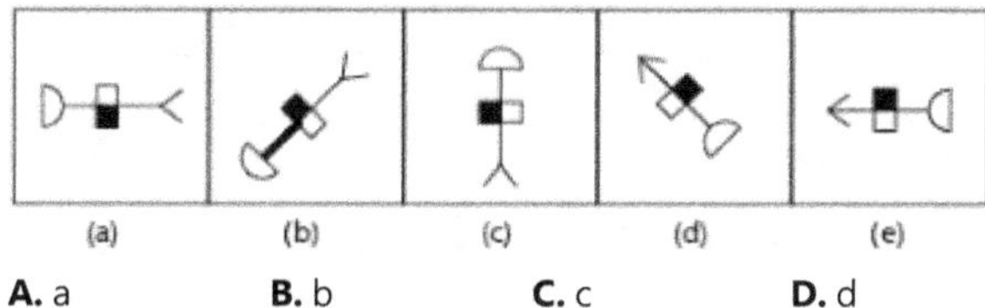

A. a   **B.** b   **C.** c   **D.** d

Q.41 Identify the given image

A. Minaret of Medan's Grand Mosque
B. Minaret of Great Mosque of Kairouan
C. Minaret of National Mosque of Malaysia
D. The Ghawanima Minaret

Q.42 Every one of the following questions consists of a related pair of words, followed by four pairs of words. Choose the pair that best represents a similar relationship to the one expressed in the original pair of words.
DIVISION : SECTION
A. layer : tier   **B.** tether : bundle
C. chapter : verse   **D.** riser : stage

Q.43 Every one of the following questions consists of a related pair of words, followed by four pairs of words. Choose the pair that best represents a similar relationship to the one expressed in the original pair of words.
DEPRESSED : SAD
A. neat : considerate
B. towering : cringing
C. progressive : regressive
D. exhausted : tired

Q.44 Every one of the following questions consists of a related pair of words, followed by four pairs of words. Choose the pair that best represents a similar relationship to the one expressed in the original pair of words.
BRISTLE : BRUSH
A. arm : leg   **B.** stage : curtain
C. recline : chair   **D.** key : piano

Q.45 Every one of the following questions consists of a related pair of words, followed by four pairs of words. Choose the pair that best represents a similar relationship to the one expressed in the original pair of words.
RAIN : DRIZZLE
A. swim :dive   **B.** hop : shuffle
C. juggle : bounce   **D.** run :jog

Q.46 The depression in the brick is called as

A. bin   **B.** frog   **C.** duct   **D.** smug

Q.47 Quick lime (or caustic lime)
A. is obtained by the calcination of pure lime stone
B. has great affinity to moisture
C. is amorphous
D. All the above.

Q.48 Pick up the correct statement from the following:
A. soft stones are required for carving
B. light stones are required for arches
C. hard stones are required to stand high pressure
D. All the above.

Q.49 Name the type of cement from the following for canal linings :
A. sulphate resisting cement
B. rapid hardening cement
C. quick setting cement
D. pozzuolana cement.

Q.50 Mastic asphalt is generally used for-
A. damp proof course   **B.** water proof layer
C. partition walls   **D.** both (a) and (b).

Q.51 The headquarters of the National Power Training institute is located in-
A. Pune   **B.** Bhopal
C. Faridabad   **D.** Lucknow

Q.52 The Dr. Babasaheb Ambedkar Marathwada University is at which of the following places?
A. Aurangabad   **B.** Nanded
C. Parbhani   **D.** Nagpur

Q.53 The Indian Institute of Science is located at-

A. Kerala	**B.** Madras
C. Bangalore	**D.** New Delhi

Q.54 'Bagh', a village in Gwalior is famous for-

A. Sculptures	**B.** Architecture
C. Cave Painting	**D.** All of the above

Q.55 Which city is known as 'Electronic City of India'?

A. Mumbai	**B.** Hyderabad
C. Guragon	**D.** Bangalore

Q.56 Indian School of Mines is located in-

A. Dhanbad	**B.** Asansol
C. Tatanagar	**D.** Rourkela

Q.57 Which of the following place is famous for its gigantic rock-cut statue of Buddha?

A. Bamiyan	**B.** Borobudur
C. Anuradhapuram	**D.** Angor Vat

Q.58 Siachen is a

A. desert frontier zone between India and Pakistan

B. frontier zone between China and India

C. frontier zone between India and Myanmar

D. glacier frontier zone between India and Pakistan

Q.59 Golden Temple is situated in-

A. New Delhi	**B.** Agra
C. Amritsar	**D.** Mumbai

Q.60 Where is the headquarters of Oil and Natural Gas Commission?

A. Dehradun	**B.** Vadodara
C. Digboi	**D.** Mumbai

// Smart Answer Sheet //

Correct — Percentage of students who answered correctly.   **Skipped** — Percentage of students who skipped.

Q.	Ans.	Correct / Skipped	Q.	Ans.	Correct / Skipped	Q.	Ans.	Correct / Skipped	Q.	Ans.	Correct / Skipped	Q.	Ans.	Correct / Skipped
1	A	20.47 % / 42.52 %	13	D	5.51 % / 45.67 %	25	C	31.5 % / 20.47 %	37	D	38.58 % / 11.03 %	49	A	29.13 % / 14.96 %
2	B	31.5 % / 40.15 %	14	C	14.96 % / 44.88 %	26	D	40.16 % / 14.96 %	38	B	70.87 % / 15.74 %	50	D	55.12 % / 11.81 %
3	B	19.69 % / 44.88 %	15	C	14.17 % / 44.1 %	27	C	66.93 % / 10.24 %	39	B	38.58 % / 14.18 %	51	C	34.65 % / 13.38 %
4	D	18.9 % / 40.94 %	16	C	7.09 % / 44.88 %	28	A	74.02 % / 12.59 %	40	B	56.69 % / 9.45 %	52	A	51.97 % / 12.6 %
5	C	11.81 % / 43.31 %	17	C	25.98 % / 40.95 %	29	C	48.03 % / 14.96 %	41	B	36.22 % / 13.39 %	53	C	51.18 % / 10.24 %
6	A	20.47 % / 44.88 %	18	B	18.11 % / 44.88 %	30	D	30.71 % / 15.75 %	42	A	31.5 % / 12.59 %	54	C	31.5 % / 8.66 %
7	A	9.45 % / 44.88 %	19	A	11.81 % / 40.16 %	31	D	59.84 % / 12.6 %	43	D	74.02 % / 12.59 %	55	D	55.91 % / 11.02 %
8	B	22.05 % / 46.45 %	20	D	7.09 % / 42.52 %	32	B	73.23 % / 9.45 %	44	D	46.46 % / 11.81 %	56	A	44.88 % / 14.18 %
9	C	12.6 % / 46.46 %	21	A	37.01 % / 17.32 %	33	D	22.83 % / 11.03 %	45	D	54.33 % / 14.96 %	57	A	39.37 % / 12.6 %
10	A	9.45 % / 42.52 %	22	C	39.37 % / 11.02 %	34	D	59.84 % / 8.66 %	46	B	68.5 % / 11.81 %	58	D	35.43 % / 14.96 %
11	B	18.11 % / 44.88 %	23	A	73.23 % / 11.81 %	35	C	44.88 % / 15.75 %	47	D	56.69 % / 10.24 %	59	C	85.04 % / 10.24 %
12	B	21.26 % / 44.09 %	24	B	68.5 % / 11.03 %	36	C	77.17 % / 10.23 %	48	D	64.57 % / 10.23 %	60	A	38.58 % / 13.39 %

//Hints and Solutions//

1. Given that, $\left(\frac{2x}{3} - \frac{3y}{2}\right)^{20}$

$n = 20 \Rightarrow$ even

For even values of n, middle term is $\left(\frac{n}{2} + 1\right)$ th

$\Rightarrow$ middle term $= \left(\frac{20}{2} + 1\right)$ th $= 11$ th

Now use the formula $T_{r+1} = {}^nC_r(a)^{n-r}(b)^r$

Here, $r = 10, a = \frac{2x}{3}, b = \frac{3y}{2}$

$T_{11} = T_{10+1} = {}^{20}C_{10}\left(\frac{2x}{3}\right)^{2-10}\left(\frac{3y}{2}\right)^{10}$

$T_{11} = {}^{20}C_{10}\left(\frac{2x}{3}\right)^{10}\left(\frac{3y}{x}\right)^{10}$

$T_{11} = {}^{20}C_{10}x^{10}y^{10}$

Hence, the correct option is (A).

2. $x + 2|y| = 1 \Rightarrow x + 2y = 1, x - 2y = 1$

$\Rightarrow \frac{x}{1} + \frac{y}{(1/2)} = 1$ and $\frac{x}{1} + \frac{y}{(-1/2)} = 1$

Clearly $BC = \frac{1}{2} + \frac{1}{2} = 1, OA = 1$

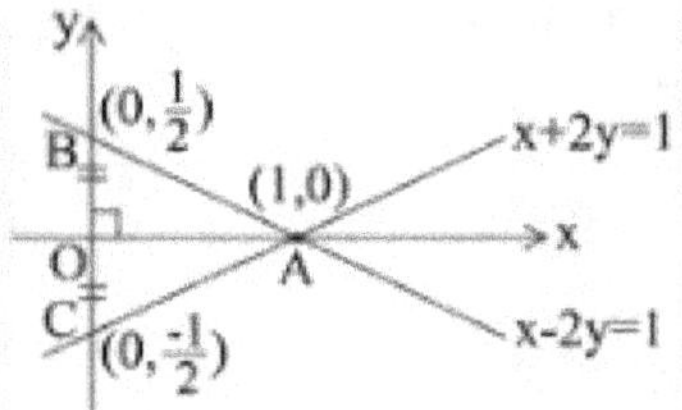

Area of $ABC = \frac{OA \cdot BC}{2} = \frac{1 \times 1}{2} = \frac{1}{2}$

Hence, the correct option is (B).

3. Consider the given equation,

$(x - 1)^2 + (y - 2)^2 = 3\left(\frac{x+y-3}{\sqrt{2}}\right)^2$

$x^2 + 1^2 - 2x + y^2 + 2^2 - 2y = \frac{3(x+y-3)^2}{2}$

$x^2 + 1 - 2x + y^2 + 4 - 2y = \frac{3(x^2+y^2+(-3)^2+2xy+2y(-3)+2(-3)x)}{2}$

$x^2 + y^2 - 2x - 2y + 5 = \frac{3(x^2+y^2+9+2xy-6y-6x)}{2}$

$\frac{1}{2}x^2 + \frac{1}{2}y^2 + 3xy - 7x - 7y + \frac{17}{2} = 0$

Hence, the correct option is (B).

4. $S_n = 12 + 16 + 24 + 40 + \cdots \ldots \ldots + t_n$

$S_n = 0 + 12 + 16 + 24 + \cdots \ldots \ldots t_{n-1} + t_n$

On Subtracting. $0 = 12 + 4 + 8 + 16 + \cdots +$

$(t_n - t_{n-1}) - t_n$

Or $t_n = 12 + [4 + 8 + 16 + \cdots (n-1) \text{ terms }]$

$= 12 + \frac{4(2^{n-1}-1)}{2-1}$

$= 12 + 2^{n-1+2} - 4$ or, $t_n = 8 + 2^{n+1} = 8 + 2.2^n$

$S_n = \sum_{n=1}^{n} t_n = \sum_{n=1}^{n}(8 + 2.2^n) = 8n +$

$2\left[\frac{2\cdot(2^n-1)}{2-1}\right]$

$= 8n + 4(2^n - 1)$ as $\sum 2.2^n = 2\sum 2^n =$

$2(2 + 2^2 + 2^3 + \cdots)$

Hence, the correct option is (D).

5. Let $\tan^{-1}x = \alpha \Rightarrow \tan\alpha = x$

So $\cos\alpha = \frac{1}{\sqrt{1+x^2}}$

$\therefore \sin[\cot^{-1}\{\cos(\tan^{-1}x)\}] = \sin\left(\cot^{-1}\frac{1}{\sqrt{1+x^2}}\right)$

Let $\cot^{-1}\frac{1}{\sqrt{1+x^2}} = \beta \Rightarrow \cot\beta = \frac{1}{\sqrt{1+x^2}}$

$\therefore \sin\beta = \frac{\sqrt{1+x^2}}{\sqrt{2+x^2}}$

$\therefore \sin\beta = \sin[\cot^{-1}\{\cos(\tan^{-1}x)\}] = \sqrt{\frac{1+x^2}{2+x^2}}$

Hence, the correct option is (C).

6. $|A| = -\sin\alpha(\sin\alpha\sin\beta\cos\alpha\cos\beta) + \sin\alpha\sin\beta$

$(\sin\alpha\cos\alpha\cos\beta)$

$= -\sin^2\alpha\sin\beta\cos\alpha\cos\beta + \sin^2\alpha\sin\beta\cos\alpha\cos\beta$

$= 0$

$\because |A| = 0 \Rightarrow A^{-1}$ does not exists.

Hence, the correct option is (A).

7. $\lim\limits_{x\to 0} \frac{5\sin x - 14\sin x\cdot\cos x + 3(3\sin x - 4\sin^3 x)}{x^2\sin}$

$= \lim\limits_{x\to 0} \frac{5 - 14\cos x + 9 - 12\sin^2 x}{x^2}$

$= \lim\limits_{x\to 0} \left(\frac{14(1-\cos x)}{x^2} - 12\frac{\sin^2 x}{x^2}\right)$

$= \lim\limits_{x\to 0} \frac{28\sin^2\frac{x}{2}}{\left(\frac{x}{2}\right)^2\times 2^2} - 12\lim\limits_{x\to 0}\left(\frac{\sin x}{x}\right)^2 = \frac{28}{4} - 12 = -5$

Hence, the correct option is (A).

8.

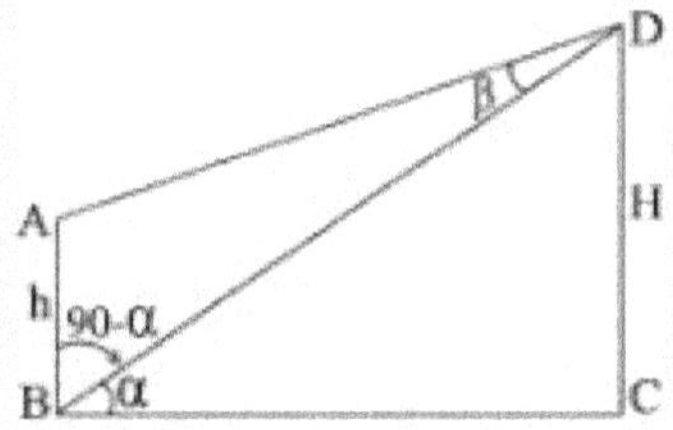

Let AB be the pole and CD be the tower. Then as given in the question. $AB = h \angle DBC = \alpha \cdot \angle ADB = \beta$

Let $CD = H$

$$\ln \Delta BCD \cdot \sin\alpha = \frac{H}{BD}$$

$$\Rightarrow BD = \frac{H}{\sin\alpha} = H\csc\alpha$$

$$\angle ABD = 90° - \alpha$$

$$\angle BAD = 180° - (90° - \alpha + \beta) = 90° + \alpha - \beta$$

in $\triangle ABD$ applying sine Rule, we have

$$\frac{\sin\beta}{h} = \frac{\sin(\angle BAD)}{BD}$$

$$\Rightarrow \frac{\sin\beta}{h} = \frac{\sin(90°+\alpha-\beta)}{H\csc\alpha} \Rightarrow \frac{\sin\beta}{h} = \frac{\cos(\alpha-\beta)}{H\csc\alpha}$$

$$\Rightarrow H = \frac{h\cos(\alpha-\beta)}{\sin\beta\csc\alpha}$$

$$\Rightarrow H = h\csc\beta\sin\alpha\cos(\alpha - \beta)$$

Hence, the correct option is (B).

9. $\alpha = p + q, p - q = \beta$

where $p = 5a + 2b, q = a - 3b$, then $\alpha = p + q = 6a - b$

$$\alpha^2 = (6a - b)^2 = 36a^2 + b^2 - 12a \cdot b$$

$$= 36(8) + 9 - 12(2\sqrt{2})(3)\cos\left(\frac{\pi}{4}\right) = (15)^2$$

$$\beta^2 = \left(\vec{p} - \vec{q}\right)^2 = \left(4\vec{a} + 5\vec{b}\right)^2 = 16a^2 + 25b^2 + 40\vec{a} \cdot \vec{b}$$

$$= 16(8) + 25(9) + 40(2\sqrt{2})(3)\cos\left(\frac{\pi}{4}\right) = 593$$

$$\therefore \alpha = 15, \beta = \sqrt{593}, \beta > \alpha$$

$$\therefore \beta = \sqrt{593} \text{ is required length. } (c)$$

Hence, the correct option is (C).

10. a, b, c are in $AP \Rightarrow 2b = a + c$

Also, $a + b + c = 3/2 \Rightarrow 3b = 3/2$

$$\Rightarrow b = 1/2$$

$$\Rightarrow a^+ C - 1$$

Next, a^2, b^2, c^2 are in GP

$$\Rightarrow b^2 = \sqrt{a^2 c^2} \Rightarrow b^2 = \pm ac$$

$$\Rightarrow ac - 1/4 \quad (2)$$

Or

$$ac = -1/4$$

From (1)$\&$(2) a $\&$c are roots of a quadratic $x^2 - (a + c)x + ac = 0$

$$\Rightarrow x^2 - x + (1/4) = 0$$

$$\Rightarrow \left(x - \frac{1}{2}\right)^2 = 0$$

Thus, the equation has roots $a = c = \frac{1}{2}$

since, acbsc. the above results are not satisfied

If we consider $ac = -1/4$, then

$$x^2 - x - (1/4) = 0$$

$$x = \frac{1 \pm \sqrt{2}}{2}$$

$$= \frac{1}{2} \pm \frac{1}{\sqrt{2}}$$

since the $a = \frac{1}{2} - \frac{1}{\sqrt{2}}$

and

$$c = \frac{1}{2} + \frac{1}{\sqrt{2}}$$

Hence, the correct option is (A).

11. $f(x) = \frac{\ln(\pi+x)}{\ln(e+x)}$

$$f'(x) = \left[\frac{\ln(e+x)}{(\pi+x)} - \frac{\ln(\pi+x)}{(e+x)}\right] \times \frac{1}{(\ln(e+x))^2}$$

$$= \frac{(e+x)\ln(e+x)-(\pi+x)\ln(\pi+x)}{(\pi+x)(e+x)(\ln(e+x))^2}$$

But $e < \pi$

$$\Rightarrow (e + x) < (\pi + x)\forall x \in R$$

$$\Rightarrow \ln(e + x) < \ln(\pi + x), \text{ provided } e + x > 0 \& \pi + x > 0$$

$$\Rightarrow (e + x)\ln(e + x) < (\pi + x)\ln(\pi + x) \text{ for } x \in (-e, \infty)$$

$$\Rightarrow (e + x)\ln(e + x) - (\pi + x)\ln(\pi + x) < 0 \text{ for } x \in (-e, \infty)$$

$$\Rightarrow f'(x) < 0\forall x \in (-e, \infty)$$

$$\Rightarrow f'(x) < 0\forall x \in (0, \infty)$$

Hence, the correct option is (B).

12. $\log_2(4^{x+1} + 4)\log_2(4^x + 1) = \log_2 8$

$$\Rightarrow \log_2 4(4^x + 1)\log_2(4^x + 1) = \log_2 8$$

$$\Rightarrow \left(\log_2 4 + \log_2(4^x + 1)\right)\log_2(4^x + 1) = \log_2 8$$

$$\Rightarrow (\log_2 2^2 + y) = \log_2 2^3 \Rightarrow (2 + y)(y) = 3$$

$$\Rightarrow y^2 + 2y - 3 = 0 \Rightarrow y = 1, -3 \Rightarrow \log_2(4^x + 1) = 1, -3$$

$$\Rightarrow 4^x + 1 = 2^1 \text{ or } 4^x + 1 = 2^{-3}$$

$$\Rightarrow 4^x = 1 \text{ or } 4^x = \frac{1}{8} - 1 = -\frac{7}{8}$$

$\Rightarrow x = 0$ or $x \in \phi, \{as_4 x$ is always positive $\}$

$\Rightarrow x = 0$

Hence, the correct option is (B).

13. $f(x) = e^{(x-1)} - ax^2 + b$

$\Rightarrow f'(x) = e^{(x-1)} - 2ax$

$\Rightarrow f'(1) = e^0 - 2a = 1 - 2a$

$\therefore f'(1) = 2 \Rightarrow 1 - 2a = 2 \Rightarrow a = -\frac{1}{2}$

$\cdots (x) = e^{(x-1)} + \frac{x^2}{2} + b$

$h(x) = f(x) \cdot g(x) \Rightarrow h(x) = \left(e^{(x-1)} + \frac{x^2}{2} + b\right)$

$e^{(x-1)}, x \leq 1$

$= \left(e^{(x-1)} + \frac{x^2}{2} + b\right)(x^2 + 1), x > 1$

For $h(x)$ to be differentiable at $x = 1$ it must be continuous

at $x = 1$

$\lim_{h \to 0} h(1 - h) = \lim_{h \to 0} h(1 + h) = h(1)$

$\lim_{h \to 0} h(1 - h) = \lim_{h \to 0} h(1 + h) = h(1)$

$\Rightarrow \left(e^0 + \frac{1}{2} + b\right) e^0 = \left(e^0 + \frac{1}{2} + b\right)(2) =$

$\left(e^0 + \frac{1}{2} + b\right) e^0$

$\Rightarrow b + \frac{3}{2} = 2\left(b + \frac{3}{2}\right) \Rightarrow b + \frac{3}{2} = 0 \Rightarrow b = -\frac{3}{2}$

$\therefore h(x) = \left(e^{x-1} + \frac{x^2}{2} - \frac{3}{2}\right) e^{x-1}, x \leq 1$

$= \left(e^{x-1} + \frac{x^2}{2} - \frac{3}{2}\right)(x^2 + 1), x > 1$

$h'(x) = \left(e^{x-1} + \frac{x^2}{2} - \frac{3}{2}\right) e^{(x-1)} + e^{(x-1)}\left(e^{x-1} + x\right)$

$, x < 1$

$h'(x) = \left(e^{x-1} + \frac{x^2}{2} - \frac{3}{2}\right) 2x + (x^2 + 1)\left(e^{x-1} + x\right)$

$, x > 1$

$\because h'(1-) = 2 \& h'(1+) = 4$ therefore $h'(1) = \varphi$

Hence there are no value of a $\& b$ for which $h(x)$ is

differentiable at $x = 1$

Hence, the correct option is (D).

14. The mean of a probability distribution is given as

$M = \Sigma P$

$\left(x_1 = \left(\frac{1}{4} \times 0\right) + (0 \times 1) + \left(\frac{1}{4} \times 2\right) + (0 \times 3) + \left(\frac{1}{2}\right.\right.$

$\times 4) + (0 \times 5) = \frac{5}{2}$

$\sigma^2 = \Sigma P_1 (M - x_1)^2$

$= \frac{1}{4}\left(\frac{5}{2} - 0\right)^2 + \frac{1}{4}\left(\frac{5}{2} - 2\right)^2 + \frac{1}{2}\left(\frac{5}{2} - 4\right)^2$

$= \frac{1}{4}\left(\frac{25}{4}\right) + \frac{1}{4} \cdot \frac{1}{4} + \frac{1}{2}\left(\frac{9}{4}\right)$

$= \frac{25 + 1 + 18}{16}$

$= \frac{11}{4}$

Hence, the correct option is (C).

15. $\vec{a} \times \left(\vec{b} \times \vec{c}\right) = \frac{1}{2}\vec{b}$

$\Rightarrow \left(\vec{a} \cdot \vec{c}\right)\vec{b} - \left(\vec{a} \cdot \vec{b}\right)\vec{c} = \frac{1}{2}\vec{b}$

Comparing on both sides of the equation $\vec{a} \cdot \vec{c} = \frac{1}{2}$

$\Rightarrow ac\cos\theta = \frac{1}{2}$ (θ is the angle between a and c)

$\Rightarrow \cos\theta = \frac{1}{2}$ since a,b,c have unit magnitude

$\Rightarrow \theta = \frac{\pi}{3}$

Hence, the correct option is (C).

16. If $P(z)$ lies on a circle whose diametrically opposite points

are $A(z_1) \& B(z_2)$ then

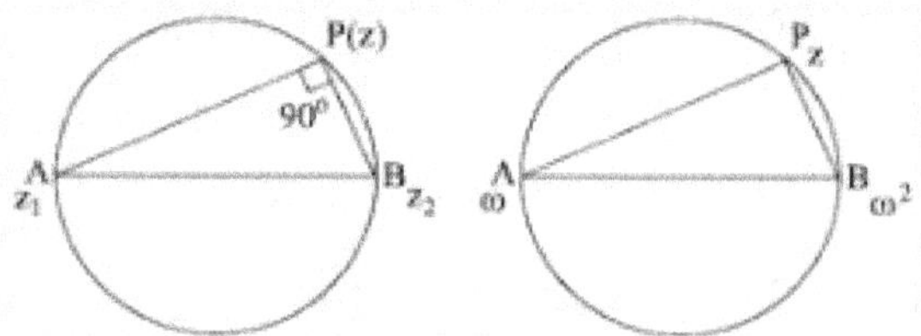

$PA^2 + PB^2 = AB^2$

$\Rightarrow |z - z_1|^2 + |z - z_2|^2 = |z_1 - z_2|^2$

$\Rightarrow |z - w|^2 + |z - w^2|^2 = |w - w^2|^2$

$\Rightarrow |z - w|^2 + |z - w^2|^2 = |w(1 - w|^2 =$

$|w|^2 |1 - w|^2$

$\Rightarrow |z - w|^2 + |z - w^2|^2 = \left|1 - e^{i\frac{2\pi}{3}}\right|^2$

$|, (\because |w| = 1)$

$\Rightarrow |z - w|^2 + |z - w^2|^2 = \left|1 - \left(-\frac{1}{2} + i\frac{\sqrt{3}}{2}\right)\right|^2$

$\Rightarrow |z - w|^2 + |z - w^2|^2 = \left|\frac{3}{2} - i\frac{\sqrt{3}}{2}\right|^2$

$\Rightarrow |z - \omega|^2 + |z - \omega^2|^2 = \left(\frac{3}{2}\right)^2 + \left(\frac{\sqrt{3}}{2}\right)^2$

$\Rightarrow |z - \omega|^2 + |z - \omega^2|^2 = 3$

Hence, the correct option is (C).

17. Given $\sin^{-1}x + \sin^{-1}y + \sin^{-1}z = \frac{\pi}{2}$

$\Rightarrow \sin^{-1}x + \sin^{-1}y = \frac{\pi}{2} - \sin^{-1}z$

taking cos on both side,

$\cos(\sin^{-1}x + \sin^{-1}y) = \cos\left(\frac{\pi}{2} - \sin^{-1}z\right)$

$$\Rightarrow \cos\left(\sin^{-1}x\right)\cos\left(\sin^{-1}y\right) - \sin\left(\sin^{-1}x\right)\sin\left(\sin^{-1}y\right) = \cos\left(\frac{\pi}{2} - \sin^{-1}z\right)$$

$$\Rightarrow \left(\sqrt{1-x^2}\right)\left(\sqrt{1-y^2}\right) - xy = \sin(\sin^{-1}z)$$

$$\Rightarrow \left(\sqrt{1-x^2}\right)\left(\sqrt{1-y^2}\right) = xy + z$$

$$\Rightarrow (1-x^2)(1-y^2) = (xy+z)^2$$

$$\Rightarrow x^2 + y^2 + z^2 + 2xyz = 1$$

Hence, the correct option is (C).

18. Substituting $x^2 = t$ $ax^4 + bx^2 + c = 0 \Rightarrow at^2 + bt + c = 0$

Clearly, if all the roots of $ax^4 + bx^2 + c = 0$ are real, then the equation $at^2 + bt + c = 0$ must have both the roots positive. But $at^2 + bt + c = 0 \Rightarrow t^2 + \frac{b}{a}t + \frac{c}{a} = 0$, which is a quadratic with positive coefficient of t^2. Hence for both the roots to be positive:

$$f(0) > 0 \;\&\; -\frac{b}{2a} > 0$$

$$\Rightarrow \frac{c}{a} > 0 \;\&\; -\frac{b/a}{2\times 1} > 0 \Rightarrow \frac{c}{a} > 0 \;\&\; \frac{b}{a} < 0$$

$\Rightarrow a \,\&\, c$ are of same sign and a $\& b$ are of opposite sign

$$\Rightarrow (a > 0, c > 0 \;\&\; b < 0) \text{ or } (a < 0, c < 0 \;\&\; b > 0)$$

Hence, the correct option is (B).

19. $\dfrac{dy}{dx} = \dfrac{dy/d\theta}{dx/d\theta} = \dfrac{a(0+\sin\theta)}{a(1-\cos\theta)} = \dfrac{\sin\theta}{1-\cos\theta}$

$$\frac{d^2y}{dx^2} = \frac{d}{dx}\left(\frac{dy}{dx}\right) = \frac{d}{dx}\left(\frac{\sin\theta}{1-\cos\theta}\right)$$

$$= \frac{d}{d\theta}\left(\frac{\sin\theta}{1-\cos\theta}\right)\frac{d\theta}{dx} = \frac{d}{d\theta}\left(\frac{\sin\theta}{1-\cos\theta}\right)\left[\frac{1}{dx/d\theta}\right]$$

$$= \frac{(1-\cos\theta)(\cos\theta)-\sin\theta(\sin\theta)}{(1-\cos\theta)^2}\;\frac{1}{a(1-\cos\theta)} =$$

$$\frac{\cos\theta - \cos^2\theta - \sin^2\theta}{a(1-\cos\theta)^3}$$

$$= \frac{\cos\theta - 1}{a(1-\cos\theta)^3} = -\frac{1}{a(1-\cos\theta)^2}$$

$$\left.\frac{d^2y}{dx^2}\right|_{at}\;\theta = \frac{\pi}{2} = -\frac{1}{a\left(1-\cos\frac{\pi}{2}\right)^2} = -\frac{1}{a}$$

$$\left.\frac{d^2y}{dx^2}\right|_{at}\;\theta = \frac{\pi}{3} = -\frac{1}{a\left(1-\cos\frac{\pi}{3}\right)^2} = -\frac{4}{a}$$

Hence, the correct option is (A).

20. $I = \int_0^1 \dfrac{dx}{x^2+2x\cos\alpha+1} = \int_0^1 \dfrac{dx}{(x+\cos\alpha)^2+\sin^2\alpha}$

$$= \frac{1}{\sin\alpha}\left[\tan^{-}\left(\frac{x+\cos\alpha}{\sin\alpha}\right)\right]_0^1$$

$$= \frac{1}{\sin\alpha}\left[\tan^{-1}\left(\frac{1+\cos\alpha}{\sin\alpha}\right) - \tan^{-1}\left(\frac{\cos\alpha}{\sin\alpha}\right)\right]$$

$$= \frac{1}{\sin\alpha}\left[\tan^{-1}\cot\alpha/2 - \tan^{-1}\cot\alpha\right]$$

$$= \frac{1}{\sin\alpha}\left[\left(\frac{\pi}{2} - \frac{\alpha}{2}\right) - \left(\frac{\pi}{2} - \alpha\right)\right] = \frac{\alpha}{2\sin\alpha}$$

Hence, the correct option is (D).

21.

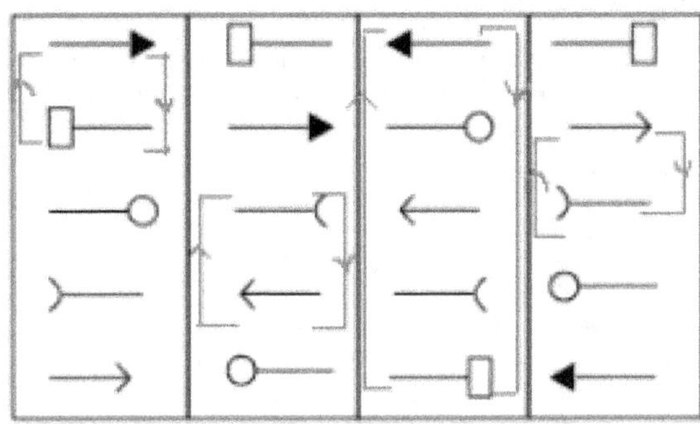

Get the next figure from the previous figure by swaping the elements as shown above and rotate the other elements through 180° and shift one place in anticlockwise direction.

Hence, the correct option is (A).

22.

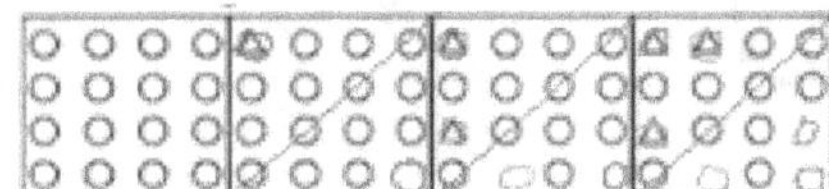

Hence, the correct option is (c).

23.

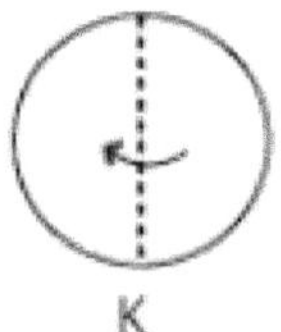

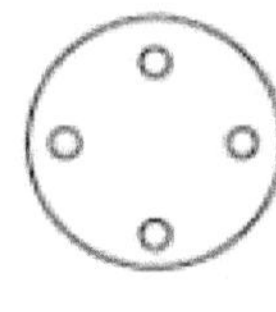

Hence, the correct option is (A).

24.

(b)

Hence, the correct option is (B).

25. From figure a to figure b: The first element encloses the other two elements, and the second element is mounted on the third element.

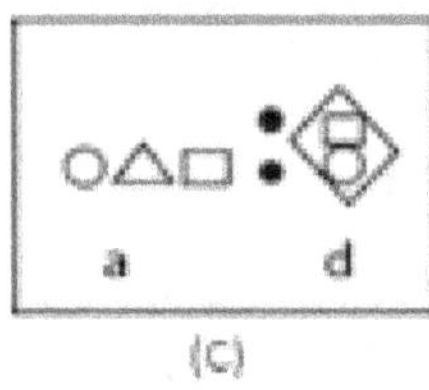

(C)

Hence, the correct option is (C).

26. In each option, on combining a and b gives a complete black block except in option D.

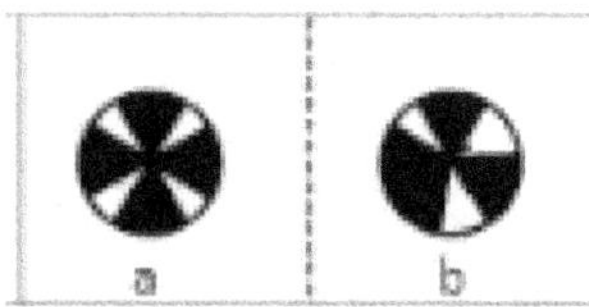

Hence, the correct option is (D).

27.

ABCDEFGHIJKLMNOPQRSTUVWXYZabcdefghijklmnopqrstuvwxyz0123456789

Hence, the correct option is (C).

28. The summation of opposite numbers = 9

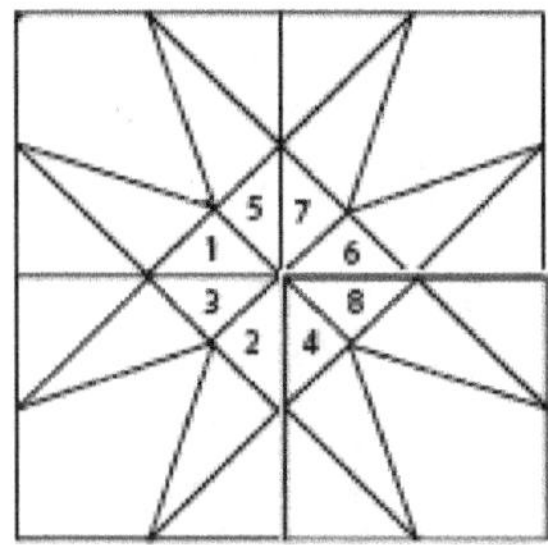

Hence, the correct option is (A).

29.

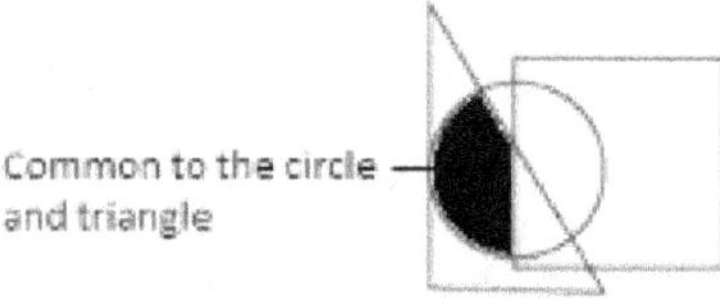

Hence, the correct option is (C).

30. According to the given information,

'3' will be opposite the face containing '6',

'1' will be opposite the face containing '4',

And,

'2' will be opposite to the face containing '5'.

Therefore, '2' is the correct answer.

Hence, the correct option is (D).

31.

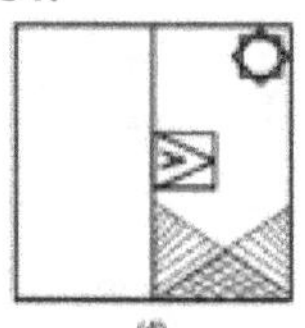

(4)

Hence, the correct option is (D).

32.

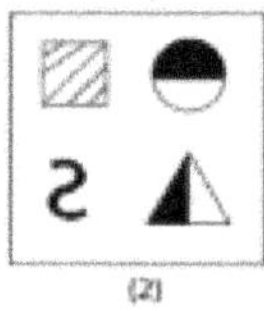

(2)

Hence, the correct option is (B).

33. 16 (triangles formed by single unit) + 7(triangles formed by four triangles) + 3(triangles formed by combining 9 triangles) + 1(big triangle) = 27

Hence, the correct option is (D).

34.

(d)

Hence, the correct option is (D).

35. 1, 3 contain a V-shaped element inside a geometrical figure.

2, 4, 5 contain two similar elements, one placed inside the other and touching it.

6, 7 contain geometrical figures which are divided into four equal parts by two mutually perpendicular straight lines.

Hence, the correct option is (C).

36.

In all figures, the angle between two leaves is 145° except in third figure.

Hence, the correct option is (C).

37.

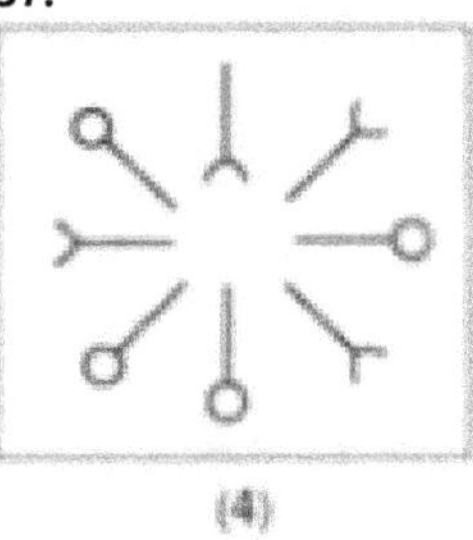

(4)

Clearly, we can say the first three figures are following some pattern. Hence, the correct option is (D).

38.

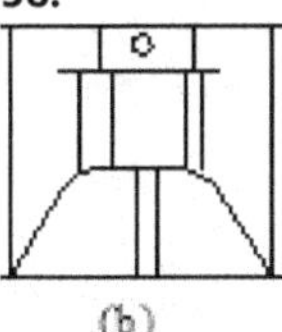

(b)

Hence, the correct option is (B).

39. 1, 2, 5 are figures that have patterns formed from four lines curved in a concave direction.

3, 7, 8 are figures that have patterns formed from four lines curved in a convex direction.

4, 6, 9 are figures that have patterns formed from these straight lines.

Hence, the correct option is (B).

40. If all the figures are rotated so that the semicircle lies on the top, then the shaded part of the rectangle lies on the LHS.

(b)

Hence, the correct option is (B).

41. The Great Mosque of Kairouan is one of the most impressive and largest Islamic monuments in North Africa; its perimeter is almost equal to 405 metres (1,328 feet). This space contains a hypostyle prayer hall, a marble-paved courtyard and a square minaret.

Hence, the correct option is (B).

42. Division and section are synonyms similarly layer and tier are synonym.Hence, the correct option is (A).

43. Depressed is an intensification of sad similarly exhausted is an intensification of tired.Hence, the correct option is (D).

44. A bristle is a part of a brush similarly a key is a part of a piano.Hence, the correct option is (D).

45. To drizzle is to rain slowly similarly to jog is to run slowly.Hence, the correct option is (D).

46. A frog is a depression in one bearing face of a molded or pressed brick. The frog reduces the weight of the brick and makes it easier to remove from the forms. ... This would make the brick wall only face-shell bedded, which produces less wall strength than full mortar bedding.

Hence, the correct option is (B).

47. Calcium oxide (CaO), commonly known as quicklime or burnt lime, is a widely used chemical compound. It is a white, caustic, alkaline, crystalline solid at room temperature. Calcium oxide that survives processing without reacting in building products such as cement is called free lime.

Hence, the correct option is (D).

48. 1.soft stones are required for carving

2.light stones are required for arches

3.hard stones are required to stand high pressure

Hence, the correct option is (D).

49. Sulfate resisting cement is used in construction exposed to severe sulfate action by water and soil in places like canals linings, culverts, retaining walls, siphons, etc.

Hence, the correct option is (A).

50. Mastic Asphalt is an ideal material for a whole range of construction applications, in both new build and refurbishment, where a smooth, seamless, durable surface is required. It offers total waterproofing integrity for roofing and tanking and acts as a tough working surface in flooring and paving.

Hence, the correct option is (D).

51. The corporate office of NPTI is at Faridabad, Haryana. NPTI operates on an all India basis through its units in different zones of the country.

Hence, the correct option is (C).

52. Dr. Babasaheb Ambedkar Marathwada University, formerly Marathwada University, is located in Aurangabad, Maharashtra, Republic of India. It is named after Bharat Ratna Dr. "Babasaheb" Ambedkar, an Indian jurist, political leader, academic and the chief architect of the Indian Constitution.

Hence, the correct option is (A).

53. Indian Institute of Science (IISc) is a public university for scientific research and higher education located in Bangalore, India. Established in 1909 with active support from Jamsetji Tata and H.H. Sir Krishnaraja Wodeyar IV, the Maharaja of Mysore. It is also locally known as the "Tata Institute".

Hence, the correct option is (C).

54. 'Bagh', a village in Gwalior is famous for. The Bagh Caves are a group of nine rock-cut monuments, situated among the southern slopes of the Vindhyas in Bagh town of Dhar district in

Madhya Pradesh state in central India. These monuments are located at a distance of 97 km from Dhar town.

Hence, the correct option is (C).

55. Electronic City is an information technology hub in Bangalore, India, located in Anekal taluk. It is one of India's largest electronic/IT industrial parks, spread over 800 acres (3.2 km²) in Konappana Agrahara and Doddathogur villages in Bangalore.

Hence, the correct option is (D).

56. The Indian Institute of Technology, Dhanbad is a public engineering and research institution located in Dhanbad, India. It was formerly known as Indian School of Mines and was a Central University before it was converted into an Indian Institute of Technology and an Institute of National Importance.

Hence, the correct option is (A).

57. Bamiyan famous for its gigantic rock-cut statue of Buddha.Hence, the correct option is (A).

58. The Siachen Glacier is a glacier located in the eastern Karakoram range in the Himalayas at about35.421226°N 77.109540°E, just northeast of the point NJ9842 where the Line of Control between India and Pakistan ends.

Hence, the correct option is (D).

59. The Golden Temple, respectfully known as "Darbar Sahib", is located in the city of Amritsar, Punjab. It is the holiest Shrine in Sikhism. It is also known as "harmandir" meaning "A Temple of God".

Hence, the correct option is (C).

60. Oil and Natural Gas Corporation (ONGC) is an Indian multinational oil and gas company earlier headquartered in Dehradun, Uttarakhand, India. As a Corporation, it's registered office is now at Deendayal Urja Bhavan, Vasant Kunj, New Delhi 110070 India.

Hence, the correct option is (A).

Mathematics

Q.1 The value of K, for which the equation $(K-2)x^2 + 8x + K + 4 = 0$ has both the roots real distinct and negative is:

A. 0   **B.** 2   **C.** 3   **D.** -4

Q.2 Which of the following statements is not correct?

A. $\log_{10} 10 = 1$

B. $\log (2 + 3) = \log (2 \times 3)$

C. $\log_{10} 1 = 0$

D. $\log (1 + 2 + 3) = \log 1 + \log 2 + \log 3$

Q.3 If A and B are two square matrices such that $B = -A^{-1} BA$, then $(A+B)^2$ is equal to-

A. 0   **B.** $A^2 + B^2$

C. $A^2 + 2AB + B^2$ **D.** A+B

Q.4 For

$$n \geq 2 \quad \text{the product} \ \{+a\}| + \alpha^2 \left\{1 + \alpha^{2^2}\right\}\right]$$
$$\left(1 + \alpha^{2^n}\right\}$$

where $\alpha = \left(\dfrac{1+i}{2}\right)$, is equal to:

A. $(1 + i)\left(1 - 2^{-2^n}\right)$

B. $(1 - 1)\left(1 - 2^{-2^{11}}\right)$

C. $(1 + i)\left(1 + 2^{-2^1}\right)$

D. none of these

Q.5 All the roots of $a_1 z^3 + a_2 z^2 + a_3 z + a_4 = 3$, where $|a_i| \leq 1 (i = 1,2,3,4)$

A. lie outside or on the circle $|z| = \frac{2}{3}$

B. lie on the circle $|z| = \frac{2}{3}$

C. lie inside or on the circle $|z| = \frac{2}{3}$

D. none of these

Q.6 The coefficient of the term independent of x in the

expansion of $(1 + x + 2x^3)\left(\dfrac{3}{2}x^2 - \dfrac{1}{3x}\right)^9$

A. $\frac{1}{3}$ **B.** $\frac{19}{54}$ **C.** $\frac{17}{54}$ **D.** $\frac{1}{4}$

Q.7 a, b, c are positive numbers and abc^2 has the greatest value $\dfrac{1}{64}$ Then

A. $a = b = (\frac{1}{4}), c=(\frac{1}{4})$ **B.** $a = b = (\frac{1}{4}), c=(\frac{1}{2})$

C. $a = b = c=(\frac{1}{3})$ **D.** None of these

Q.8 If $f(x) = x + \dfrac{1}{x} \forall x \in R - \{0\}$ then:-

A. $f^3(x) = f(x^3) + 3f\left(\frac{1}{x}\right)$

B. $f^3(x) = 3f(x^3) + f\left(\frac{1}{x}\right)$

C. $f^3(x) + f(x^3) + f(x)$

D. none of these

Q.9 The value of $\lim\limits_{x \to 1} \dfrac{3^{x+1} - 9}{4^{2x+1} - 64}$

A. $\dfrac{\ln 3}{128 \ln 4}$ **B.** $\dfrac{9 \ln 3}{128 \ln 4}$ **C.** $\dfrac{9 \ln 3}{\ln 4}$ **D.** $\dfrac{9 \ln 3}{64 \ln 4}$

Q.10 The altitude of a cone is 20cm and its semi-vertical angle is 30°. If the semi-vertical angle is increasing at the rate of 2° per second, then the radius of the base is increasing at the rate of-

A. $\dfrac{\pi}{27} cm/sec$ **B.** $\dfrac{8\pi}{27} cm/sec$

C. $\dfrac{8\pi}{9} cm/sec$ **D.** none of these

Q.11 The set of all values of the parameter a for which the points of minimum of the function $y = 1 + a^2 x - x^3$

Satisfy the inequality $\dfrac{x^2+x+2}{x^2+5x+6} \leq 0$ is

A. an empty set

B. $\left(-3\sqrt{3}, -2\sqrt{3}\right)$

C. $\left(2\sqrt{3}, 3\sqrt{3}\right)$

D. $\left(-3\sqrt{3}, -2\sqrt{3}\right) \cup \left(2\sqrt{3}, 3\sqrt{3}\right)$

Q.12 Let f(x) be a continuous function such that $f(a - x) + f(x) = 0$ for all $x \in [0,a]$. Then, the value of the integral

$\displaystyle\int_0^2 \dfrac{1}{1+e^{f(x)}} dx$ is equal to

A. a   **B.** $\frac{a}{2}$ **C.** fA.   **D.** $\frac{1}{2}$ fA.

Q.13 The function $f(x) = \int_0^x \log\left(t + \sqrt{1 + t^2}\right)$

A. an even function   **B.** an odd function

C. a periodic function   **D.** none of these

Q.14 The area bounded by curves y = f(x), the x-axis and the ordinates x = 1 and x = b is (b - 1) sin (3b + 4). Then f(x) is-

A. (x-1) cos (3x + 4)

B. sin (3x + 4)

C. sin (3x + 4) + 3 (x – 1) cos (3x + 4)

D. sin (3x + 4) + (x – 1) cos (3x + 4)

Q.15 If for a variable line $\dfrac{x}{a} + \dfrac{y}{b} = 1$, the condition $a^{-2} + b^{-2} = c^{-2}$ (c is a constant), is satisfied, then the locus of foot of the perpendicular drawn from origin to this is:

A. $x^2 + y^2 = \dfrac{c^2}{2}$ **B.** $x^2 + y^2 = 2c^2$

C. $x^2 + y^2 = c^2$ **D.** $x^2 - y^2 = c^2$

Q.16 The circles which can be drawn to pass through (1,0) & (3,0) and touching the y-axis, intersect at an angle θ. The value of cos θ is equal to

A. $\frac{1}{2}$ **B.** $\frac{1}{\sqrt{2}}$ **C.** $\frac{1}{4}$ **D.** $\frac{\sqrt{3}}{2}$

Q.17 The equation of the common tangent touching the circle $(x-3)^2 + y^2 = 9$ and the parabola $y^2 = 4x$ above the x-axis, is

A. $y\sqrt{3} = 3x + 1$ **B.** $y\sqrt{3} = -(x + 3)$

C. $y\sqrt{3} = x + 3$ **D.** $y\sqrt{3} = -(3x + 1)$

Q.18 A tangent having slope of $-\dfrac{4}{3}$ to the ellipse $\dfrac{x^2}{18} + \dfrac{y^2}{32} = 1$ intersects the major and minor axes in points A and B respectively. If C is the center of the ellipse then the area of the triangle ABC is:

A. 12 sq. units

B. 24 sq. units

C. 36 sq. units

D. 48 sq. units

Q.19 The eccentricity of the hyperbola whose latus rectum is half of its transverse axis, is:

A. $\sqrt{\dfrac{5}{2}}$

B. $\sqrt{\dfrac{7}{4}}$

C. $\sqrt{\dfrac{3}{2}}$

D. $\sqrt{\dfrac{5}{4}}$

Q.20 From a group of 7 men and 6 women, five persons are to be selected to form a committee so that at least 3 men are there on the committee. In how many ways can it be done?

A. 564   **B.** 645   **C.** 735   **D.** 756

General Aptitude

Q.21 Which one of the answer figures shows the correct view of the 3-D problem figure after the problem figure is opened up ?

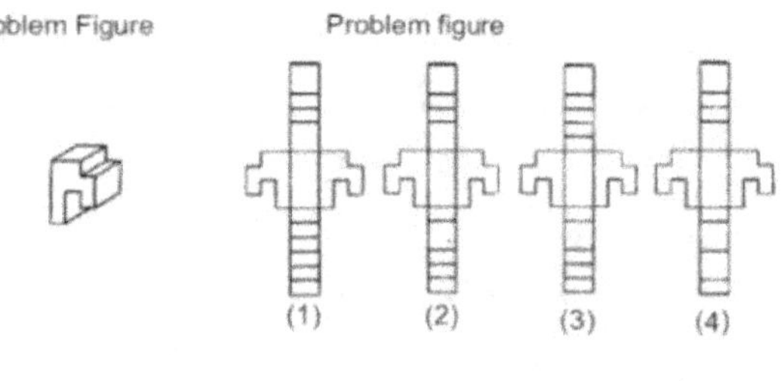

A. 1   **B.** 2   **C.** 3   **D.** 4

Q.22 Which one of the answer figures shows the correct view of the 3-D problem figure after the problem figure is opened up ?

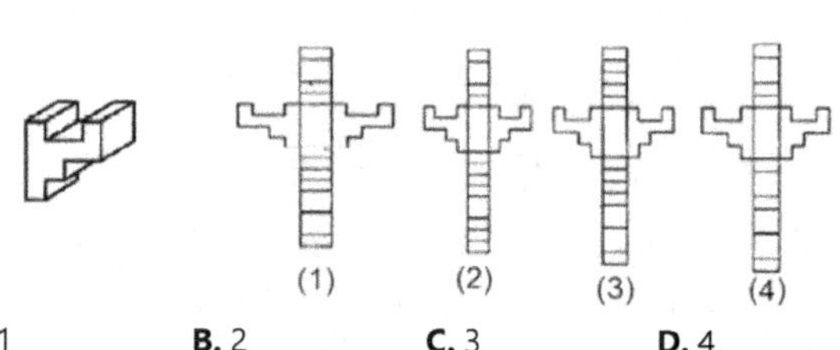

A. 1   **B.** 2   **C.** 3   **D.** 4

Q.23 Which one of the answer figures shows the correct view of the 3-D problem figure after the problem figure is opened up ?

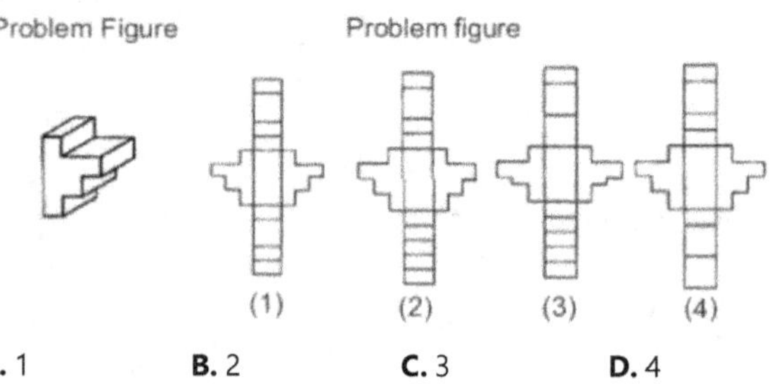

A. 1   **B.** 2   **C.** 3   **D.** 4

Q.24 Which one of the answer figures shows the correct view of the 3-D problem figure after the problem figure is opened up ?

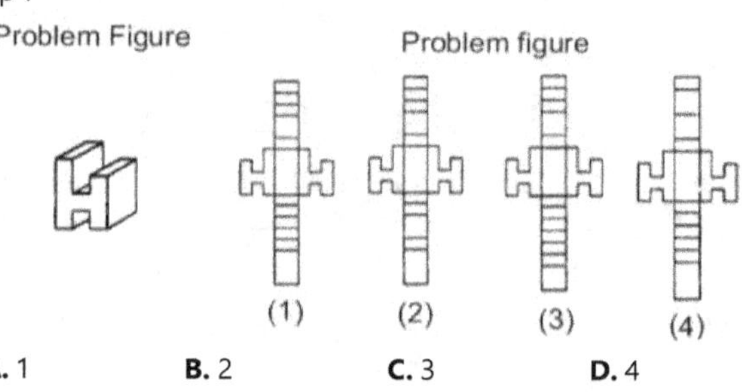

A. 1   **B.** 2   **C.** 3   **D.** 4

Q.25 Which one of the answer figures shows the correct view of the 3-D problem figure after the problem figure is opened up ?

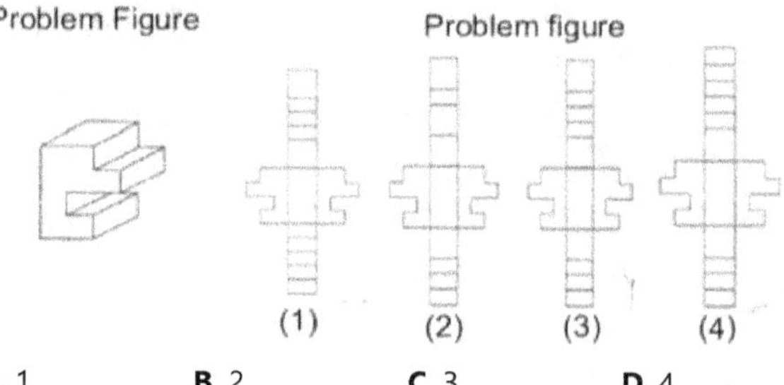

A. 1   **B.** 2   **C.** 3   **D.** 4

Q.26 What is the increased percentage rate of social media fraud in 2020?

A. 50%   **B.** 38%   **C.** 70%   **D.** 52%

Q.27 Which set of letters will come in place of '?' in the letter series given below?

AGM, BHN, CIO, ?

A. DJP   **B.** DPJ   **C.** EGP   **D.** EFG

Q.28 State what will come in place of ' ?' in the analogy given below-

$$7 : 48 :: 12 : ?$$

A. 143   **B.** 168   **C.** 51   **D.** 98

Q.29 State what will come in place of ' ?' in the analogy given below-

$$11 : 1330 :: 9 : ?$$

A. 728   **B.** 730   **C.** 81   **D.** 243

Q.30 One of the following answer figure is hidden in the problem figure in the same size and direction. Select the correct one.

A. 1   **B.** 2   **C.** 3   **D.** 4

Q.31 One of the following answer figure is hidden in the problem figure in the same size and direction. Select the correct one.

Problem Figure

Answer Figure

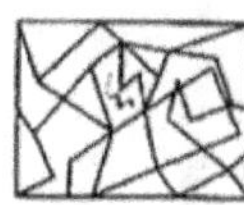   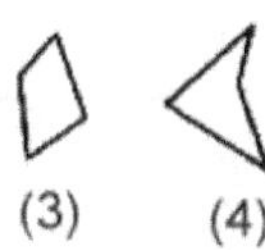

(1) (2) (3) (4)

A. 1 **B.** 2 **C.** 3 **D.** 4

Q.32 One of the following answer figure is hidden in the problem figure in the same size and direction. Select the correct one.

Problem Figure

Answer Figure

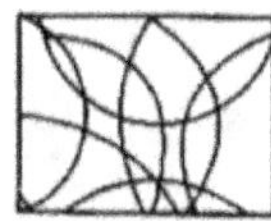   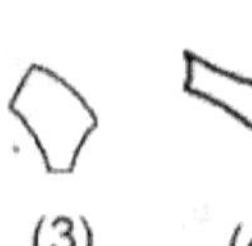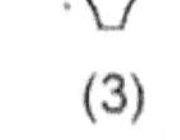

(1) (2) (3) (4)

A. 1 **B.** 2 **C.** 3 **D.** 4

Q.33 The problem figure shows the top view of objects. Looking in the direction of the arrow, identify the correct elevation, from amongst the answer figures.

Problem Figure

Answer Figure

(1) (2) (3) (4)

A. 1 **B.** 2 **C.** 3 **D.** 4

Q.34 The problem figure shows the top view of objects. Looking in the direction of the arrow, identify the correct elevation, from amongst the answer figures.

Problem Figure

Answer Figure

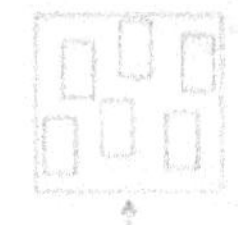 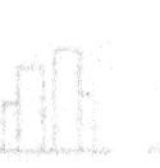 

(1) (2) (3) (4)

A. 1 **B.** 2 **C.** 3 **D.** 4

Q.35 The problem figure shows the top view of objects. Looking in the direction of the arrow, identify the correct elevation, from amongst the answer figures.

Problem Figure Answer Figure

 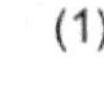

(1) (2) (3) (4)

A. 1 **B.** 2 **C.** 3 **D.** 4

Q.36 The 3-D problem figure shows the view of an objects. Identify the correct top view from amongst the answer figure.

Problem Figure Answer Figure

 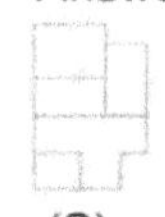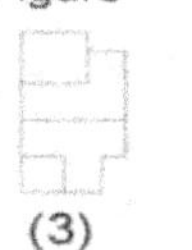

(1) (2) (3) (4)

A. 1 **B.** 2 **C.** 3 **D.** 4

Q.37 The 3-D problem figure shows the view of an objects. Identify the correct top view from amongst the answer figure.

Problem Figure Answer Figure

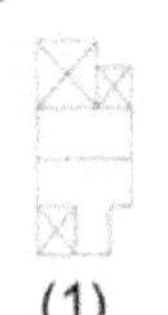 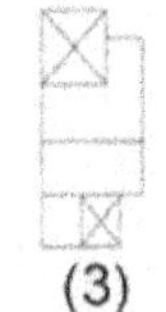

(1) (2) (3) (4)

A. 1 **B.** 2 **C.** 3 **D.** 4

Q.38 The 3-D problem figure shows the view of an objects. Identify the correct top view from amongst the answer figure.

Problem Figure Answer Figure

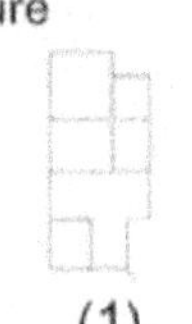 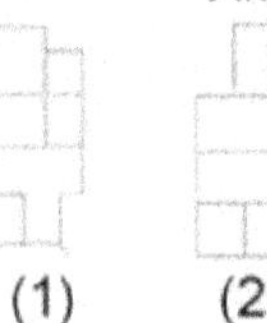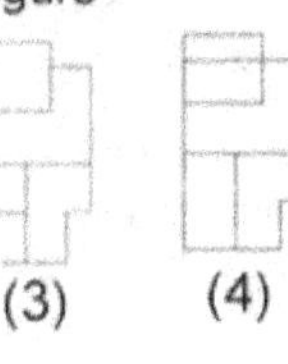

(1) (2) (3) (4)

A. 1 **B.** 2 **C.** 3 **D.** 4

Q.39 Which of the answer figures is the correct mirror image of the problem figure with respect to X-X ?

Problem Figure Answer Figure

 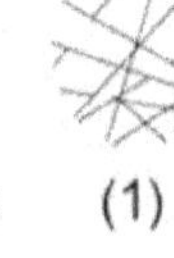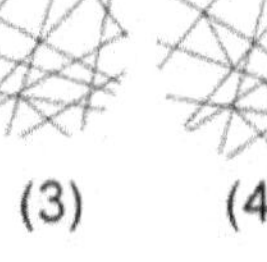

(1) (2) (3) (4)

A. 1 **B.** 2 **C.** 3 **D.** 4

Q.40 Which of the answer figures is the correct mirror image of the problem figure with respect to X-X ?

Problem Figure Answer Figure

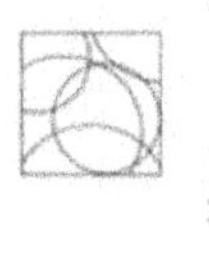 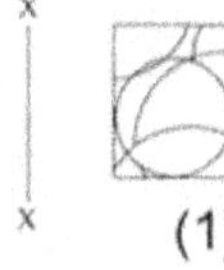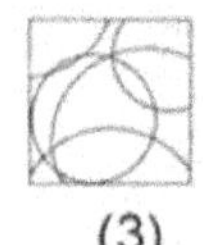

(1) (2) (3) (4)

A. 1 **B.** 2 **C.** 3 **D.** 4

Q.41 The Battle of Plassey was fought in-
A. 1757 **B.** 1782 **C.** 1748 **D.** 1764

Q.42 Famous akshardhan Temple is located at-
A. Mathura **B.** Ayodhya
C. Kathmandu **D.** Delhi

Q.43 Mohenjoaro and old Jaipur are planned on :
A. Radial **B.** Grid Iron pattern

C. Linear pattern   **D.** Organic pattern

Q.44 Which one is the oldest structure from amongst the following :
A. Panama canal
B. Ajanta caves
C. Pyramids of Egypt
D. Parthenon of Greece

Q.45 Identify the given material

A. Cement blocks   **B.** concrete bricks
C. Plastered clay tiles   **D.** fly ash bricks

Q.46 Ozone layer around the Earth prevents penetration of:
A. Ultra violet rays   **B.** Sound waves
C. Excessive heat   **D.** Infrared rays

Q.47 Red sand stone is not used in:
A. Red Fort   **B.** Fatehpur Sikri
C. Taj Mahal   **D.** Humayun's Tomb

Q.48 In the Northern Hemisphere, light entering from which side of opening in a room is more uniform throughout the day?
A. South   **B.** North   **C.** East   **D.** West

Q.49 Which place in India has French influence in Architecture?
A. Goa   **B.** Chandigarh
C. Pondicherry   **D.** Andaman

Q.50 Which amongst the following is more earthquake resistant structure ?
A. Brick in mud mortar
B. Brick in cement - sand mortar
C. Steel frame
D. Stone masonary

Q.51 What causes Tsunami in an ocean ?
A. Ocean Currents
B. Trade winds
C. Earthquake on sea bed
D. Ocean Tides

Q.52 Eiffel Tower is made of :
A. Bricks   **B.** Concrete   **C.** Steel   **D.** Stone

Q.53 Maximum amount of fresh water in our planet is trapped in :
A. Lake Eirie, U.S.A
B. Lake Victoria, Africa
C. Polar caps
D. Dead sea

Q.54 Burj Khalifa is located in :
A. Oman   **B.** Abhu Dhabi
C. Dubai   **D.** Saudi Arabia

Q.55 Which type of roof will provide maximum protection from heat radiation in a building ?
A. Painted aluminium sheeting
B. Concrete slab with plaster
C. Concrete slab with mud and brick tiles
D. Concrete slab water proofed and covered with a roof garden

Q.56 The Centre for Cellular and Molecular Biology is situated at:
A. Patna   **B.** Jaipur
C. Hyderabad   **D.** New Delhi

Q.57 Where is the Railway Staff College located?
A. Pune   **B.** Allahabad
C. Vadodara   **D.** Delhi

Q.58 The famous Dilwara Temples are situated in:
A. Uttar Pradesh   **B.** Rajasthan
C. Maharashtra   **D.** Madhya Pradesh

Q.59 Wadia Institute of Himalayan Geology is located at:
A. Delhi   **B.** Shimla
C. Dehradun   **D.** Kulu

Q.60 Identify the given image .

A. Jodhpur   **B.** Banaras
C. Rameshwaram   **D.** Allahabad

// Smart Answer Sheet //

Correct Percentage of students who answered correctly.　　**Skipped** Percentage of students who skipped.

Q.	Ans.	Correct / Skipped	Q.	Ans.	Correct / Skipped	Q.	Ans.	Correct / Skipped	Q.	Ans.	Correct / Skipped	Q.	Ans.	Correct / Skipped
1	C	14.53 % / 26.5 %	13	A	14.53 % / 38.46 %	25	C	66.67 % / 16.24 %	37	B	5.98 % / 10.26 %	49	C	66.67 % / 10.25 %
2	B	25.64 % / 34.19 %	14	C	11.97 % / 40.17 %	26	C	38.46 % / 13.68 %	38	B	82.05 % / 10.26 %	50	C	61.54 % / 7.69 %
3	B	24.79 % / 36.75 %	15	C	16.24 % / 44.44 %	27	A	23.08 % / 13.67 %	39	C	85.47 % / 9.4 %	51	C	76.92 % / 9.4 %
4	A	13.68 % / 44.44 %	16	A	16.24 % / 39.32 %	28	A	35.04 % / 10.26 %	40	C	87.18 % / 7.69 %	52	C	88.89 % / 8.55 %
5	A	13.68 % / 41.88 %	17	C	14.53 % / 44.44 %	29	A	77.78 % / 10.25 %	41	A	40.17 % / 15.39 %	53	C	70.09 % / 11.96 %
6	C	18.8 % / 43.59 %	18	B	16.24 % / 46.15 %	30	A	66.67 % / 10.25 %	42	D	53.85 % / 11.11 %	54	C	84.62 % / 8.54 %
7	B	30.77 % / 39.32 %	19	C	23.08 % / 35.89 %	31	A	69.23 % / 9.4 %	43	B	60.68 % / 11.11 %	55	D	70.09 % / 9.4 %
8	A	10.26 % / 47.0 %	20	D	14.53 % / 36.75 %	32	C	58.12 % / 9.4 %	44	C	61.54 % / 9.4 %	56	C	48.72 % / 14.53 %
9	B	18.8 % / 42.74 %	21	B	67.52 % / 13.68 %	33	B	79.49 % / 10.25 %	45	D	29.91 % / 9.41 %	57	C	38.46 % / 14.53 %
10	B	23.08 % / 43.59 %	22	A	67.52 % / 11.97 %	34	B	79.49 % / 9.4 %	46	A	80.34 % / 11.11 %	58	B	50.43 % / 11.96 %
11	D	12.82 % / 44.44 %	23	B	70.09 % / 13.67 %	35	A	73.5 % / 11.12 %	47	C	82.05 % / 9.4 %	59	C	40.17 % / 13.68 %
12	B	20.51 % / 42.74 %	24	B	11.11 % / 14.53 %	36	C	85.47 % / 8.55 %	48	A	41.03 % / 11.11 %	60	B	70.94 % / 10.26 %

//Hints and Solutions//

1. $(K-2)x^2 + 8x + K + 4 = 0$

$$x^2 + \frac{8}{(K-2)}x + \frac{K+4}{(K-2)} = 0$$

Let $f(x) = x^2 + \frac{8}{(K-2)}x + \frac{K+4}{(K-2)}$

If the equation $f(x) = 0$, has real distinct and negative roots then

$$D > 0 \,\&\, f(0) > 0 \,\&\, -\frac{B}{2A} < 0$$

(i) $D > 0$ $\dfrac{8^2}{(K-2)^2} - 4\dfrac{(K+4)}{K-2} > 0$

$64 - 4(K^2 + 2K - 8) > 0$

$-K^2 - 2K + 24 < 0$ $K^2 + 2K - 24 < 0$

$(K+6)(K-4) < 0$

$-6 < K < 4$

(ii)

$f(0) > 0$ $\dfrac{(K+4)}{(K-2)} > 0$

$\Rightarrow K < -4$ or $K > 2$

(iii) $-\dfrac{B}{2A} < 0$ $-\dfrac{8}{2(K-2)} < 0$ $\dfrac{4}{(K-2)} > 0$

$K - 2 > 0$

$K > 2$

$\therefore D > 0$ $8f(0) > 0$ 8

$-\dfrac{B}{2A} < 0$

$-6 < K < 4 \,\&\, (K < -4 \text{ or } K > 2) \,\&\, K > 2$

$-6 < K < 4 \,\&\, K < -4 \,\&\, K > 2)$ or $(K > 2 \,\&\, K > 2)$

$-6 < K < 4 \,\&\, \quad (K \in \phi \text{ or } K > 2)$

$2 < K < 4$

$K \in (2,4)$

Among the given options 3 lies in the given range. Hence $K = 3$

Hence, the correct option is (C).

2. (a) since $\log_a a = 1$, so $\log_{10} 10 = 1$

(b) $\log(2+3) = \log 5$ and $\log(2 \times 3) = \log 6 = \log 2 + \log 3$

$\therefore \log(2+3) \neq \log(2 \times 3)$

(c) since $\log_a 1 = 0$, so $\log_{10} 1 = 0$

(d) $\log(1+2+3) = \log 6 = \log(1 \times 2 \times 3) = \log 1 + \log 2 + \log 3$

So, (b) is incorrect.

Hence, the correct option is (B).

3. $B = -A^{-1} BA$

$AB = A\,(-A^{-1}BA)$

$AB = (AA^{-1})(BA)$

$AB = -BA$

$AB + BA = 0$

Now, $(A + B)^2 = A^2 + B^2 + AB + BA$

$(A + B)^2 = A^2 + B^2$, $(\because AB + BA = 0)$

Hence, the correct option is (B).

4. Let $\dfrac{1+i}{2} = x$ Hence the given series S is $S = (1+x)(1+x^2)|^4_{1+x^4} \cdot \left(1 + x^{2^n}\right)$

$S(1-x) = 1 - x^{2^{n+1}}$

$S = \dfrac{1 - x^{2^{n+1}}}{1-x} = \dfrac{1 - x^{2^{n+1}}}{1 - \frac{1+i}{2}}$

$= \dfrac{1 - \left(\frac{1+i}{\sqrt{2}} \cdot \frac{\sqrt{2}}{2}\right)^{2^{n+1}}}{\left(\frac{1-i}{2}\right)} = \dfrac{1 - \left(\frac{1+i}{\sqrt{2}}\right)^{2^{n+1}} \left(\frac{\sqrt{2}}{2}\right)^{2^{n+1}}}{\left(\frac{1-i}{2}\right)}$

$= \dfrac{2\left\{1 - \left(\frac{i\pi}{4}\right)^{2^{n+1}} \left(\frac{1}{\sqrt{2}}\right)^{2 \times 2^n}\right\}}{\frac{(1-1)(1+i)}{(1+i)}} = \dfrac{2(1+i)\left\{1 - \left(e^{i*}\right)^{2-1}\left(\frac{1}{2}\right)^2\right\}}{2}$

$= \left(1 + i\left(1 - 2^{-2^n}\right)\right)\left(\because n \geq 2 \Rightarrow (-1)^{2^{n-1}} = 1\right)$

Hence, the correct option is (A).

5. If possible let $z = re^{i\theta}$ be a root which lies inside $|z| = \dfrac{2}{3}$.

Hence $0 \leq r < 2/3$ Hence $a_1\left(re^{i\theta}\right)^3 + a_2\left(re^{i\theta}\right)^2 + a_3\left(re^{i\theta}\right) + a_4 = 3$

Comparing real parts we get $a_1 r^3 \cos 3\theta + a_2 r^2 \cos 2\theta + a_3 r \cos\theta + a_4 = 3$

but $(r^3 a_1 \cos 3\theta + r^2 a_2 \cos 2\theta + r a_3 \cos\theta + a_4)$

$$\leq r^3 + r^2 + r + 1$$

(Q)a$| \leq 18$ so also $\cos 3 €_1 \cos 2\theta \,\&\, \cos\theta)$

$$3 \leq r^3 + r^2 + r + 1$$

$$\frac{r^4 - 1}{r - 1} \geq 3$$

$$\frac{1-r^4}{1-r} \geq 3$$

$$\frac{1}{1-r} \geq 3$$

$$1 - r \leq \frac{1}{3}$$

$$1 - \frac{1}{3} \leq$$

$$r \geq 2/3$$

Which is a contradiction to the assumption $0 \leq r < 2/3$ Hence no root of the given equation can lie inside the circle

$$|z| = \frac{2}{3}$$

Hence the roots lie outside or on the circle.

Hence, the correct option is (A).

6. The general term of the expansion of $\left(\frac{3}{2}x^2 - \frac{1}{3x}\right)^9$

$$T_{r+1} = {}^9 C_r \left(\frac{3}{2}x^2\right)^{9-r} \left(-\frac{1}{3x}\right)^r$$

$$= {}^9 C_f \left(\frac{3}{2}\right)^{9-\tau} \left(-\frac{1}{3x}\right)^r$$

The coefficient of independent of x in the expansion of $(1 + x + 2x^3)$

$\left(\frac{3}{2}x^2 - \frac{1}{3x}\right)^9 =$ sum of coefficient of $x^0, x^{-1}2x^{-3}$ in

expansion of $\left(\frac{3}{2}x^2 - \frac{1}{3x}\right)^9$

(i) For coefficient of x^0: $18 - 3r = 0.$, according to (1): $rr =$

6. Put in (i) $T_7 = {}^9 C_6 \left(\frac{3}{2}\right)^{9-6} \left(-\frac{1}{3}\right)^6 = {}^9 C_3 \left(\frac{3}{2}\right)^3 \cdot \left(\frac{1}{3}\right)^6$

$$= {}^9 c_3 \frac{1}{6^3} = \frac{7}{18}$$

(ii) For Coefficient of x^{-3}: $18 - 3r = -1$ or, $r - 19/3$ fraction. No such term exists

(iii) For coefficient of $2x^{-3}$: $18 - 3r - -3$ or $r = 7$. Put in

(1) $\tau_8 = 2\left[9c_7 \left(\frac{3}{2}\right)^{9-7} \left(-\frac{1}{3}\right)^7\right]$

$$= ({}^9C_2)\left(2\left(\frac{3}{2}\right)^2 (-1)\left(\frac{1}{3}\right)^7\right) = -\frac{2}{27}$$

Sum of coefficients $-\frac{7}{18} - \frac{2}{27} = \frac{17}{54}$

Hence, the correct option is (C).

7. We have

$$\frac{a+b+\frac{c}{2}+\frac{c}{2}}{4} \geq \sqrt[4]{ab - \frac{c}{2} \cdot \frac{c}{2}}$$

or $\dfrac{a+b+c}{4} \geq \sqrt{\dfrac{abc^2}{4}}$

$$\therefore \left(\frac{a+b+c}{4}\right)^4 \geq \frac{abc^2}{4}$$

Or $abc^2 \leq \frac{1}{64}(a + b + c)^4$

the greatest value of $abc^2 = \frac{1}{64}(a + b + c)^4$ Also for the

greatest value of abc ^{2} the numbers have to be equal, ie $a = b - \frac{c}{2}$ Also given that maximum value $= \frac{1}{64}$

$50, a + b + c = 1$

ie. $a = b = \frac{1}{4} \cdot c = \frac{1}{2}$

Hence, the correct option is (B).

8. $f(x) = x + \frac{1}{x} f(x^3) = x^3 + \frac{1}{x^3}$

$$f(x) = x + \frac{1}{x} = f\left(\frac{1}{x}\right) = \frac{1}{x} + xf(x) = f\left(\frac{1}{x}\right)$$

$$\therefore f^3(x) = \left(x + \frac{1}{x}\right)^3$$

$$= \left(x^3 + \frac{1}{x^3}\right) + 3x \cdot \frac{1}{x}\left(x + \frac{1}{x}\right)$$

$$= \left(x^3 + \frac{1}{x^3}\right) + 3\left(x + \frac{1}{x}\right)$$

$$= f(x^3) + 3f(x)$$

$$= f(x^3) + 3f\left(\frac{1}{x}\right), \left[\because f(x) = f\left(\frac{1}{x}\right)\right]$$

Hence, the correct option is (A).

9. Substitute $(x - 1) = t.$ Hence $x \to 1(x - 1) \to 0t \to 0$

Hence given limit is:

$$\lim_{x \to 1} \frac{3^{x-1}-9}{4^{2x+1}-64} = \lim_{i \to 0} \frac{3^{1+2}-9}{4^{2[1+1+1+1}-64}$$

$$= \lim_{t \to 0} \frac{3^t 2^2 - 3^2}{4^2 \cdot t^3 - 4^3} = \lim_{t \to 0} \frac{9(3^t-1)}{64(4^2-1)}$$

$$= \lim_{t \to 0} \frac{9}{04} \frac{\left(\frac{x-1}{t}\right) \cdot t}{\frac{s^2-1}{2t}} = \lim_{t \to 0} \frac{9}{64} \cdot \frac{ta33}{\ln 4} \cdot \frac{1}{2} = \frac{9\ln 3}{128\ln 4}$$

Hence, the correct option is (B).

10.

$$\frac{d\theta}{dt} = 2° \text{ per second}$$

$$= 2 \times \frac{\pi}{180} rad/sec$$

$= \dfrac{\pi}{90} rad/sec$

$\theta = 30° = \dfrac{\pi}{6} radian$

Let θ be the semi-vertical angle and r be the base

radius of the cone at time t. Then, $r = 20\tan\theta$

$\dfrac{dr}{dt} = 20\sec^2\theta \dfrac{d\theta}{dt}$

$\dfrac{dr}{dt}\bigg|_{\theta=\frac{\pi}{6}} = \left(20\sec^2\dfrac{\pi}{6}\right) \times \dfrac{\pi}{90}$

$\dfrac{dr}{dt}\bigg|_{\theta=\frac{\pi}{6}} = 20 \times \dfrac{4}{3} \times \dfrac{\pi}{90} = \dfrac{8\pi}{27} cm/sec$

Hence, the correct option is (B).

11. $\dfrac{x^2+x+2}{x^2+5x+6} \leq 0 x^2 + 5x + 6 < 0 - 3 < x < -2$

$(\because x^2 + x + 2 > 0 \forall x \in R)$

$y = 1 + a^2x - x^3$

$y = a^2 - 3x^2$

$y'' = -6x$

$\therefore y' = 0 a^2 - 3x^2 = 0 x = \pm\dfrac{a}{\sqrt{3}}$

(i) Let $a > 0$:

Hence $y'' > 0$ for $x = -\dfrac{a}{\sqrt{3}}$. Hence y has minima at $x = -\dfrac{a}{\sqrt{3}}$ for $a > 0$

$\therefore 3 < -\dfrac{a}{\sqrt{3}} < -2 2\sqrt{3} < 2 < 3\sqrt{3}$

(ii) Let $a < 0$ Hence $y'' > 0$ for $x = \dfrac{a}{\sqrt{3}}$. Hence y has

minima at $x = \dfrac{a}{\sqrt{3}}$ for $a < 0$

$-3 < \dfrac{a}{\sqrt{3}} < -2 - 3\sqrt{3} < 2 < -2\sqrt{3}$

From (i) $\&(\|)a \in \left(-3\sqrt{3}, -2\sqrt{3}\right) \cup \left(2\sqrt{3}, 3\sqrt{3}\right)$

Hence, the correct option is (D).

12. Let $I = \int_0^2 \dfrac{1}{1+e^{f(x)}} dx$

$I = \int_0^a \dfrac{1}{1+e^{f(a-x)}} dx$

$I = \int_0^2 \dfrac{1}{1+e^{-f(x)}} dx [\because f(a-x) + f(x) = 0]$

$I = \int_0^a \dfrac{e^{f(x)}}{e^{f(x)}+1} dx$

Adding (i) and (il):

$L = \int_0^a \dfrac{e^{f(x)}+1}{e^{f(x)}+1} dx = \int_0^a 1\, dx = aI = \dfrac{a}{2}$

Hence, the correct option is (B).

13. $f(x) = \int_0^x \log\left(t + \sqrt{1+t^2}\right) dt$

$f(-x) = \int_0^{-5} \log\left(t + \sqrt{1+t^2}\right) dt$, put $t = -2$

$f(-x) = \int_0^x \log\left(-z + \sqrt{1+z^2}\right) - dz)$

$f(-x) = -\int_0^x \log\dfrac{\sqrt{1+z^2}-z}{\sqrt{(1+z^2)+z}} dz$

$f(-x) = -\int_0^x \log\left(\dfrac{1}{\sqrt{1+z^2}+z}\right) dz$

$f(-x) = \int_0^x \log\left(z + \sqrt{1+z^2}\right) dz f(-x) = f(x)$

$f(x)$ is an even function.

Note: Inteqration of every even function is odd.

Hence, the correct option is (A).

14. 1. Area bounded by curve y = f(x), x =1 and x = b is

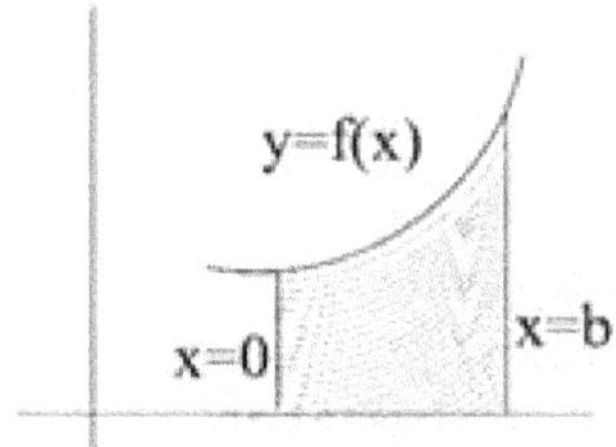

$\int f(x)dx = (b-1)\sin(3b+4)$

an

Now differentiating both sides with respect to b

we get

$fB. = \sin(3b+4) + 3(b-1)\cos(3b+4)$

$f(x) = \sin(3x+4) + 3(x-1)\cos(3x+4)$

Hence, the correct option is (C).

15. $a^{-2} + b^{-2} = c^{-2} \Rightarrow \dfrac{b^2+a^2}{a^2b^2} = \dfrac{1}{c^2} \Rightarrow a^2 + b^2 = \dfrac{a^2b^2}{c^2}$

$\dfrac{x}{a} + \dfrac{y}{b} = 1 bx + ay - ab = 0$

The foot of perpendicular to the above line from $O(0,0)$ is given by:

$\dfrac{x-0}{b} = \dfrac{y-0}{a} = -\left(\dfrac{b\times0+a\times0-ab}{b^2+a^2}\right)$

$\dfrac{x}{b} = \dfrac{y}{a} = \dfrac{ab}{a^2+b^2} x = \dfrac{ab^2}{a^2+b^2}, y = \dfrac{a^2b}{a^2+b^2}$

$x = \dfrac{ab^2}{a^2b^2}, y = \dfrac{a^2b}{a^2b^2}, \left(\because a^2 + b^2 = \dfrac{a^2b^2}{c^2}\right)$

$x = \dfrac{c^2}{a}, y = \dfrac{c^2}{b} a = \dfrac{c^2}{x}, b = \dfrac{c^2}{y}$

Using $a^{-2} + b^{-2} = c^{-2}$

$$\left(\frac{c^2}{x}\right)^{-2} + \left(\frac{c^2}{y}\right)^{-2} = c^{-2}$$
$$x^2 c^{-4} + y^2 c^{-4} = c^{-2}$$
$$x^2 + y^2 = c^2$$

Hence, the correct option is (B).

16. Equation of line joining $A(1,0)$ and $B(3,0)$ is $y = 0$.

Equation of family of circles passing through A and B is:
$$(x - 1)(x - 3) + (y - 0)(y - 0) + \lambda y = 0$$
$$x^2 + y^2 - 4x + \lambda y + 3 = 0$$

If above circle touches y-axis then $x = 0$ is a tangent.

Substituting $x = 0$: $y^2 + \lambda y + 3 = 0$

Discriminant of above quadratic must be zero. $\lambda^2 - 12 = 0$

$$2 - \pm 2\sqrt{3}$$

Hence the circles are:
$$x^2 + y^2 - 4x + 2\sqrt{3}y + 3 = 0$$
$$x^2 + y^2 - 4x - 2\sqrt{3}y + 3 = 0$$

Thus, the coordinates of C_1 and C_2 are $\left(2, -\sqrt{3}\right)$ and $\left(2\sqrt{3}\right)$ respectively. Also the radil of each of the circles is $r_1 = r_2 = 2$

We know that the angle of intersection of two circles of radius r,

and ra is given by $\cos\theta - \dfrac{\pi^2 + tg^2 - \theta^2}{2\pi 2}$ where dis the distance

between their centers $\cos\theta - \dfrac{4+4-12}{2\times2\times2} - -\dfrac{1}{2}\theta = \dfrac{27}{3}$

since between two lines whenever there is angle θ there is

always the angle $n - \theta$, therefore $\theta - \dfrac{2\pi}{3}, \dfrac{\pi}{3}$, Hence

$$\cos\theta - \frac{1}{2} \text{ or } -\frac{1}{2}$$

Alternative:

Equation of line joining $A(1,0)$ and $B(3,0)$ is $y = 0$.

Equation of family of circles passing through A and B is:
$$(x - 1)(x - 3) + (y - 0)(y - 0) + \lambda y = 0$$
$$x^2 + y^2 - 4x + \lambda y + 3 = 0$$

If above circle touches y-axis then $x = 0$ is a tangent.

Substituting $x = 0$ $y^2 + \lambda y + 3 = 0$

Discriminant of above quadratic must be zero $\lambda^2 - 12 = 0$

$$2 = \pm 2\sqrt{3}$$

Hence the circles are:
$$x^2 + y^2 - 4x + 2\sqrt{3}y + 3 = 0$$
$$x^2 + y^2 - 4x - 2\sqrt{3}y + 3 = 0$$

Clearly above circles intersect each other at (1,0) and $(3,0)$.

Also angle of intersection θ at (1,0) is same as at (3,0) . Let us find equations of tangents to the circles at (1,0) . Hence $x(1) =$
$$y(0) - 2(x + 1) + \sqrt{3}(y + 0) + 3 = 0$$
$$-x + \sqrt{3}y + 1 = 0x - \sqrt{3}y - 1 = 0$$
$$x(1) + y(0) - 2(x + 1) - \sqrt{3}(y + 0) + 3 = 0$$
$$-x - \sqrt{3}y + 1 = 0x + \sqrt{3}y - 1 = 0$$
$$m_1 = \frac{1}{\sqrt{3}}, m_2 = -\frac{1}{\sqrt{3}}$$

$$\therefore \tan\theta = \left|\frac{\frac{1}{\sqrt{3}} + \frac{1}{\sqrt{3}}}{1 + \frac{1}{\sqrt{3}} \times \frac{-1}{\sqrt{3}}}\right| = \sqrt{3}$$

$$\therefore \cos\theta = \frac{1}{2}$$

Also whenever θ is angle between two lines $(n - \theta)$ is also the angle between the lines. Hence $\cos\theta = \dfrac{1}{2}$ or $-\dfrac{1}{2}$

Hence, the correct option is (A).

17. Equation of any tangent to parabola $y^2 = 4x$ is $y = mx + \dfrac{1}{m}$

$$\Rightarrow mx - y + \frac{1}{m} = 0$$

If the tangent to parabola is also tangent to the circle
$$(x - 3)^2 + y^2 - 9$$

then:

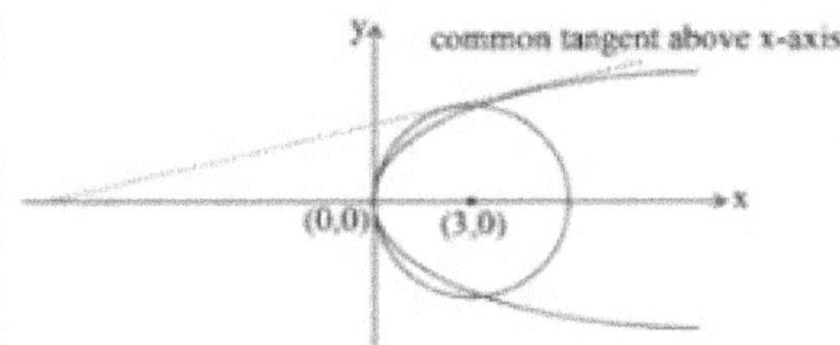

$$\left|\frac{3m - 0 + \frac{1}{m}}{\sqrt{m^2+1}}\right| = 3 \Rightarrow \left|\frac{3m + \frac{1}{m}}{\sqrt{m^2+1}}\right| = 3$$

$$\left(3m + \frac{1}{m}\right)^2 = 9m^2 + 1$$

$$(3m^2 + 1)^2 = 9m^2(m^2 + 1)$$

$$9m^4 + 6m^2 + 1 = 9m^4 + gm^2$$

$$3m^2 - 1 = 0$$

$$m = \frac{1}{0}, \frac{-1}{\sqrt{3}}, \frac{1}{\sqrt{3}}$$

From the figure it is evident that for the tangent above x-axis $m = \dfrac{1}{\sqrt{3}}$. Hence equation of required common tangent is:

$$y = \frac{x}{\sqrt{3}} + \sqrt{3}$$

$$\sqrt{3}y = x + 3$$

Hence, the correct option is (C).

18. Equation of the tangent to $\dfrac{x^2}{18} + \dfrac{y^2}{32} = 1$ whose slope $m = -\dfrac{4}{3}$ is:

$$y = \left(-\frac{4}{3}\right)x \pm \sqrt{18x\left(-\frac{4}{3}\right)^2 + 32}$$

$$y = -\frac{4x}{3} \pm \sqrt{64} \quad y = \left(-\frac{4}{3}\right)x \pm 8$$

From symmetry of ellipse it is obvious that area of the triangle ABC will be same with respect either tangent. Let us consider

$$y = \left(-\frac{4}{3}\right)x + 8 = \frac{x}{6} + \frac{y}{8} = 1$$

$$\therefore A = (6,0) \text{ and } B \equiv (0,8)$$

Hence area Δ of the triangle ABC is:

$$\Delta = \frac{1}{2} \times OB \times OA = \frac{1}{2} \times 8 \times 6 = 24 \text{ sq. units}$$

Hence, the correct option is (B).

19. Length of latus rectum of hyperbola = Length of the transverse axis

Length of latus rectum of hyperbola = Length of the transverse axis $\dfrac{2b^2}{a} = \dfrac{1}{2}(2a)$

$$\frac{2b^2}{a} = a$$

$$2b^2 - a^2$$

$$2a^2(e^2 - 1) = a^2, \quad : \quad : \quad b^2 = a^2|e^2 - 1$$

$$2e^2 - 1| = 1$$

$$e = \sqrt{\frac{3}{2}}$$

Hence, the correct option is (C).

20. We may have (3 men and 2 women) or (4 men and 1 woman) or (5 men only)

$\therefore$ Required number of ways $= (^7C_3 \times ^6C_2) + (^7C_4 \times ^6C_1) + (^7C_5)$

$$= \left(\frac{7 \times 6 \times 5}{3 \times 2 \times 1} \times \frac{6 \times 5}{2 \times 1}\right) + \left(7C_3 \times \overset{6}{C_1}\right) + (7C_2)$$
$$= 525 + \left(\frac{7 \times 6 \times 5}{3 \times 2 \times 1} \times 6\right) + \left(\frac{7 \times 6}{2 \times 1}\right)$$
$$= (525 + 210 + 21)$$
$$= 756$$

We may have (3 men and 2 women) or (4 men and 1 woman) or (5 men only)

$\therefore$ Required number of ways $= (^7C_3 \times ^6C_2) + (^7C_4 \times ^6C_1) + (^7C_5)$

$$= \left(\frac{7 \times 6 \times 5}{3 \times 2 \times 1} \times \frac{6 \times 5}{2 \times 1}\right) + \left(7C_3 \times \overset{6}{C_1}\right) + (7C_2)$$
$$= 525 + \left(\frac{7 \times 6 \times 5}{3 \times 2 \times 1} \times 6\right) + \left(\frac{7 \times 6}{2 \times 1}\right)$$
$$= (525 + 210 + 21)$$
$$= 756$$

Hence, the correct option is (D).

21.

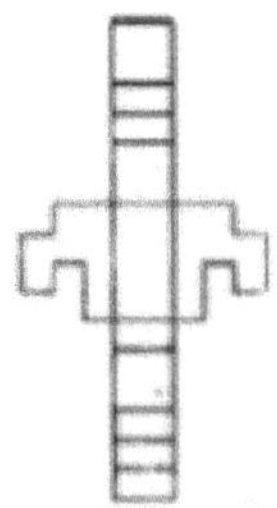

Hence, the correct option is (B).

22.

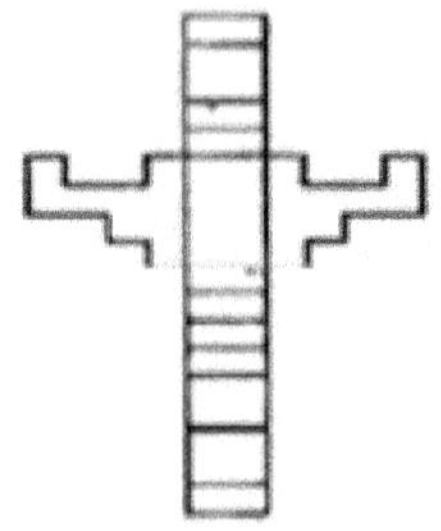

Hence, the correct option is (A).

23.

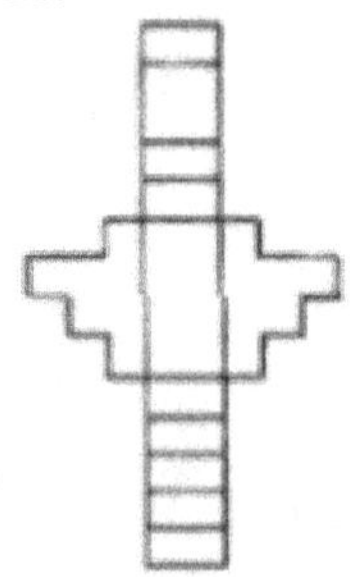

Hence, the correct option is (B).

24.

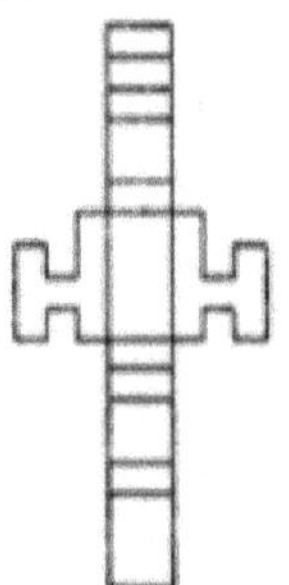

Hence, the correct option is (B).

25.

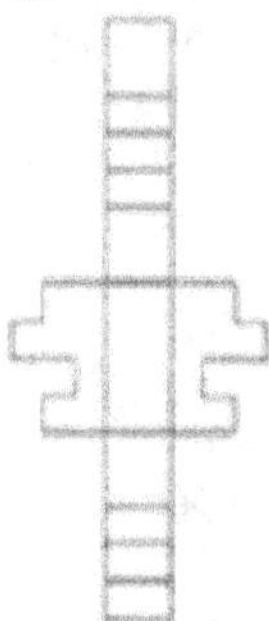

Hence, the correct option is (C).

26. Fraud increased 30 percent overall in Q3 2019 and bot-driven account registration fraud is up 70 percent as cybercriminals test stolen credentials in advance of the holiday retail season.

Hence, the correct option is (C).

27. Given-

AGM, BHN, CIO, ?

In the letter series, every letter of the set changes to its next letter.

A changes to B and B changes to C.

G changes to H and H changes to I.

M changes to N and N changes to O.

On following the same pattern we have,

C changing to D.

I changing to J.

O changing to P.

DJP comes in place of ?.

Hence, the correct option is (A).

28. Given-

$$7 : 48 :: 12 : ?$$

The logic followed is-

$$7^2 - 1 = 48$$

Similarly,

$$12^2 - 1 = ?$$

$$? = 143$$

143 will come in place of ' ?'.

Hence, the correct option is (A).

29. Given-

$$11 : 1330 :: 9 : ?$$

The logic followed is-

$$11^3 - 1 = 1330$$

Similarly,

$$9^3 - 1 = ?$$

$$? = 728$$

728 will come in place of ' ?'.

Hence, the correct option is (A).

30.

Hence, the correct option is (A).

31.

Hence, the correct option is (A).

32.

Hence, the correct option is (C).

33.

Hence, the correct option is (B).

34.

Hence, the correct option is (B).

35.

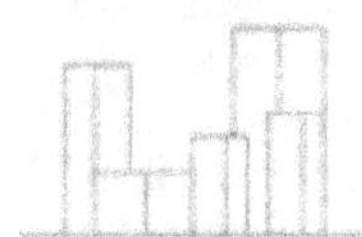

Hence, the correct option is (A).

36.

Hence, the correct option is (C).

37.

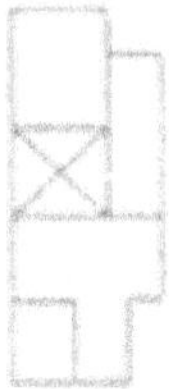

Hence, the correct option is (B).

38.

Hence, the correct option is (B).

39.

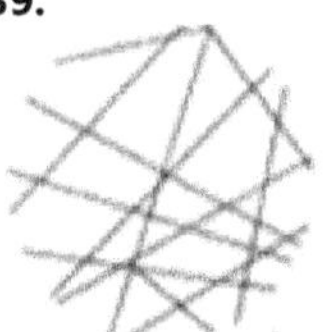

Hence, the correct option is (C).

40.

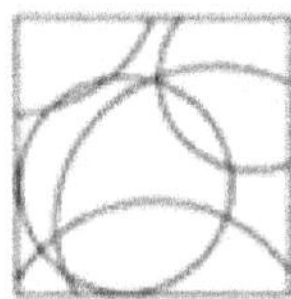

Hence, the correct option is (C).

41. The Battle of Plassey, 23 June 1757, was a decisive British East India Company victory over the Nawab of Bengal and his French allies, establishing Company rule in South Asia which expanded over much of the Indies for the next 190 years. The battle took place at Palashi, Bengal, on the river banks of the Bhagirathi River, about 150 km north of Calcutta, near Murshidabad, then capital of undivided Bengal. The belligerents were Siraj-ud-daulah, the last independent Nawab of Bengal, and the British East India Company.

Hence, the correct option is (A).

42. Akshardham or Swaminarayan Akshardham complex is a Hindu temple, and a spiritual-cultural campus in Delhi, India. Also referred to as Akshardham Temple or Swaminarayan Akshardham, the complex displays millennia of traditional Hindu and Indian culture, spirituality, and architecture.

Hence, the correct option is (D).

43. The grid plan, grid street plan, or gridiron plan is a type of city plan in which streets run at right angles to each other, forming a grid. The infrastructure cost for regular grid patterns is generally higher than for patterns with discontinuous streets.

Hence, the correct option is (B).

44. The Egyptian pyramids are ancient pyramid-shaped masonry structures located in Egypt. As of November 2008, sources cite either 118 or 138 as the number of identified Egyptian pyramids. Most were built as tombs for the country's pharaohs and their consorts during the Old and Middle Kingdom periods.

Hence, the correct option is (C).

45. Fly ash brick is a building material, specifically masonry units, containing class C or class F fly ash and water. Compressed at 28 MPa and cured for 24 hours in a 66 °C steam bath, then toughened with an air entrainment agent, the bricks last for more than 100 freeze-thaw cycles.

Hence, the correct option is (D).

46. The ozone layer or ozone shield is a region of Earth's stratosphere that absorbs most of the Sun's ultraviolet radiation. It contains high concentration of ozone (O_3) in relation to other parts of the atmosphere, although still small in relation to other gases in the stratosphere.

Hence, the correct option is (A).

47. The Taj Mahal is an ivory-white marble mausoleum on the south bank of the Yamuna river in the Indian city of Agra. It was commissioned in 1632 by the Mughal emperor, Shah Jahan (reigned from 1628 to 1658), to house the tomb of his favourite wife, Mumtaz Mahal.

Hence, the correct option is (C).

48. Here, in the northern hemisphere, the sun is always to our south. That means that whichever wall is facing south will receive the most sunlight.

Hence, the correct option is (A).

49. Pondicherry (or Puducherry), a French colonial settlement in India until 1954, is now a Union Territory town bounded by the southeastern Tamil Nadu state. Its French legacy is preserved in its French Quarter, with tree-lined streets, mustard-colored colonial villas and chic boutiques. A seaside promenade runs along the Bay of Bengal and passes several statues, including a 4m-high Gandhi Memorial.

Hence, the correct option is (C).

50. Steel frame is a building technique with a "skeleton frame" of vertical steel columns and horizontal I-beams, constructed in a rectangular grid to support the floors, roof and walls of a building

which are all attached to the frame. The development of this technique made the construction of the skyscraper possible.

Hence, the correct option is (C).

51. A tsunami is a large ocean wave that is caused by sudden motion on the ocean floor. This sudden motion could be an earthquake, a powerful volcanic eruption, or an underwater landslide. Tsunamis travel across the open ocean at great speeds and build into large deadly waves in the shallow water of a shoreline.

Hence, the correct option is (C).

52. The Eiffel Toweris a wrought-iron lattice tower on the Champ de Mars in Paris, France. It is named after the engineer Gustave Eiffel, whose company designed and built the tower.

Hence, the correct option is (C).

53. Of total **freshwater**, over 68 percent is locked up in ice and glaciers. Another 30 percent of **freshwater** is in the ground. Rivers are the source of most **of the fresh** surface **water** people use, but they only constitute about 509 mi^3 (2,120 km^3), about 1/10,000th of one percent of total **water**.

Hence, the correct option is (C).

54. The Burj Khalifa, known as the Burj Dubai prior to its inauguration in 2010, is a skyscraper in Dubai, United Arab Emirates. With a total height of 829.8 m and a roof height of 828 m, the Burj Khalifa has been the tallest structure and building in the world since its topping out in 2009.

Hence, the correct option is (C).

55. Concrete slab water proofed and covered with a roof garden roof will provide maximum protection from heat radiation in a building.

Hence, the correct option is (D).

56. The Centre for Cellular and Molecular Biology or CCMB is an Indian Biotechnology research establishment of the Council of Scientific and Industrial Research located in Hyderabad, India, and a designated Center of Excellence for Global Molecular and Cell Biology Network, UNESCO.

Hence, the correct option is (C).

57. The National Academy of Indian Railways, Vadodara formerly Railway Staff College is a Centralised Training Institute for Group A and B Officers of Indian Railways, headed by a Director General and manned by an faculty of experienced Railway Managers and Experts.

Hence, the correct option is (C).

58. The Dilwara Temples are located about 2½ kilometres from Mount Abu, Rajasthan's only hill station. These Jain temples were built by Vimal Shah and designed by Vastupala-Tejpal, Jain ministers of Dholka, between the 11th and 13th centuries AD and are famous for their use of marble and intricate marble carvings.

Hence, the correct option is (B).

59. Dehradun is an autonomous research institute for the study of Geology of the Himalaya under the Department of Science and Technology, Ministry of Science and Technology, Govt. of India. It was established in June, 1968 in the Botany Department, Delhi University, the Institute was shifted to Dehradun, Uttrakhand during April, 1976.

Hence, the correct option is (C).

60. Varanasi also known as Benares, Banaras   or Kashi , is a city on the banks of the river Ganga in Uttar Pradesh, (India), 320 kilometres (200 mi) south-east of the state capital, Lucknow, and 121 kilometres (75 mi) east of Allahabad. A major religious hub in India.

Hence, the correct option is (B).

Mathematics

Q.1 If sin 5x + sin 3 x + sin x = 0, then the value of x other than zero, lying between 0 is-

A. $\frac{\pi}{6}$ B. $\frac{\pi}{12}$ C. $\frac{\pi}{3}$ D. $\frac{\pi}{4}$

Q.2 Sum of the series

1 + 3 + 6 + 10 + 15 + ...n terms is-

A. $\frac{1}{6}n(n-1)(n+2)$

B. $\frac{1}{6}n(n+1)(n-2)$

C. $\frac{1}{6}n(n+1)(n+2)$

D. $\frac{1}{6}n(n-1)(n-2)$

Q.3 In an experiment with 15 observations on X, the following results where available: $\sum X^2 = 2830 \sum X = 170$. One observation that was 20 was found to be wrong and was replaced by the correct value 30. The corrected variance is-

A. 8.33   B. 78.00   C. 18866   D. 177.33

Q.4 There are two balls in an urn whose colours are not known (each ball can be either white or black). A white ball is put into the urn. A ball is drawn from the urn. The probability that it is white is:-

A. $\frac{1}{4}$ B. $\frac{1}{3}$ C. $\frac{2}{3}$ D. $\frac{1}{6}$

Q.5 The number of ways in which a mixed double game can be arranged from amongst 9 married couples if no husband and wife play in the same game is-

A. 756   B. 1512

C. 3024   D. none of these

Q.6 If $\vec{a}, \vec{b}$ are unit vectors such that the vector $\vec{a} + 3\vec{b}$ is perpendicular to $7\vec{a} - 5\vec{b}$ and $\vec{a} - 4\vec{b}$ is perpendicular to $7\vec{a} - 2\vec{b}$, then the angle between $\vec{a}$ and $\vec{b}$ is-

A. $\frac{\pi}{6}$

B. $\frac{\pi}{2}$

C. $\frac{\pi}{2}$

D. such $\underset{A}{\to}, \underset{B}{\to}$ are non existent

Q.7 Let $a = 2i + 3j - \hat{k} \& b = \hat{i} - 2\hat{j} + 3\hat{k}$. Then, the value of λ for which the vector

$\vec{c} = \lambda\dot{i} + j + (2\lambda - 1)\Bbbk$

is parallel to the plane containing $\bar{z} \& \bar{b}$

is-

A. 1   B. 0   C. -1   D. 2

Q.8 The plane passing through the point (−2, −2, 2) and containing the line joining the points (1, 1, 1) and (1, −1, 2)

makes intercepts on the coordinates axes the sum of whose lengths is-

A. 3   B. $\frac{4}{3}$ C. 4   D. $\frac{16}{3}$

Q.9 All the values of x satisfying the

equation $\begin{vmatrix} x+1 & x+2 & 1 \\ x+2 & x+4 & 2 \\ x+3 & x+6 & 3 \end{vmatrix} = 0$ are given by-

A. x = 0, 1   B. x = −1 or 1

C. $x \in (-\infty, \infty)$ D. none of these

Q.10 The solution of the equation (2x + y + 1) dx + (4x + 2y − 1) dy = 0 is-

A. log (2x + y − 1) = C + x + y

B. log (4x + 2y − 1) = C + 2x + y

C. log (2x + y + 1) + x + y = C

D. log (2x + y − 1) + x + 2y = C

Q.11 Suppose a, b, c are in AP and a^2, b^2, c^2 are in GP. If $a < b < c \& a + b + c = \frac{3}{2}$, then the value of a is-

A. $\frac{1}{2} - \frac{1}{\sqrt{2}}$ B. $\frac{1}{2} + \frac{1}{\sqrt{2}}$

C. $\frac{1}{2}$ D. None of these

Q.12 Sum of n terms of series 12+16+24+10........... will be-

A. $2(2^n - 1) + 8n$ B. $2(2^n - 1) + 6n$

C. $3(2^n - 1) + 8n$ D. $4(2^n - 1) + 8n$

Q.13 If $\vec{a} \cdot \vec{b} = \frac{15}{2}, \left|\vec{a}\right| = 3$ and $\left|\vec{b}\right| = 5$. Find the angle between the vectors $\vec{a}$ and $\vec{b}$.

A. $\frac{\pi}{2}$ B. $\frac{\pi}{4}$ C. $\frac{\pi}{3}$ D. $\frac{\pi}{2}$

Q.14 The length of the longer diagonal of the parallelogram constructed on $5^2 + 2b$ and $\vec{a} - 3\vec{b}$, if it is given that $|a| = 2\sqrt{2}, \left|\vec{b}\right| = 3$ and angle between a $\& b$ is $\frac{\pi}{4}$, is:

A. 15   B. $\sqrt{113}$ C. $\sqrt{593}$ D. $\sqrt{369}$

Q.15 The projection of the line joining the points (3,4,5) and (4,6,3) on the line joining the points (-1,2,4) and (1,0,5) is

A. $\frac{4}{3}$ B. $\frac{2}{3}$ C. $\frac{1}{3}$ D. $\frac{1}{2}$

Q.16 From the bottom of pole of height h, the angle of elevation of the top of a tower is α. The pole subtends an angle β at the top of the tower. Then the height of the tower is:

A. $h\sin\alpha\cos\beta\cos(\alpha - \beta)$

B. $h\sin\alpha\csc\beta\cos(\alpha - \beta)$

C. $h\csc\alpha\sin\beta\cos(\alpha - \beta)$

D. none of these

Q.17 In a triangle ABC, the angle B is greater than angle A . If the values of the angle A and B satisfy the equation $3\sin x - 4\sin^3 x - k = 0, 0 < k < 1,$ then value of C is-

A. $\frac{\pi}{3}$ **B.** $\frac{\pi}{2}$ **C.** $\frac{2\pi}{2}$ **D.** $\frac{5\pi}{2}$

Q.18 Coordinates of the orthocentre of the triangle whose sides are $x = 3, y = 4$ and $3x + 4y = 6$, will be:

A. (0,0)   **B.** (3,0)   **C.** (0,4)   **D.** (3,4)

Q.19 The area bounded by the curves $x + 2|y| = 1$ and $x = 0$ is:

A. $\frac{1}{3}$ **B.** $\frac{1}{2}$ **C.** 2   **D.** 3

Q.20 Consider the following statements regarding the events E, A, B and C .

(i) Event E can take place due to the occurrence of any of the events A, B, C.

(ii) Events A, B and C are equiprobable, mutually exclusive and exhaustive.

(iii) Probability of occurrence of event E is $\frac{5}{12}$.

(iv) $P\left(\frac{E}{A}\right) = \frac{3}{8}$ and $P\left(\frac{E}{B}\right) = \frac{1}{4}$

Considering above data the value of $P(E/C)$ is:

A. $\frac{3}{4}$ **B.** $\frac{3}{8}$ **C.** $\frac{4}{5}$ **D.** $\frac{5}{8}$

General Aptitude

Q.21 Identify the type of staircase

A. spiral staircase
B. helical staircase
C. dogglegged staircase
D. none of these

Q.22 Resins are-
A. not soluble in water
B. soluble in spirit
C. used in varnishes
D. left behind on evaporation of oil

Q.23 Refractory bricks are used for-
A. retaining walls
B. columns
C. piers
D. combustion chambers.

Q.24 Expanded metal is-

A. manufactured from steel sheets
B. used for reinforced concrete in road pavements
C. measured in term of SWM (shortway mesh) and LWM (long way mesh)
D. all the above.

Q.25 The rock generally used for roofing, is-
A. Granite   **B.** Basalt   **C.** Slate   **D.** Pumice

Q.26 Every one of the following questions consists of a related pair of words, followed by four pairs of words. Choose the pair that best represents a similar relationship to the one expressed in the original pair of words.

COTTON : BALE
A. Butter : churn   **B.** Wine : ferment
C. Grain : shock   **D.** Curd : cheese

Q.27 Every one of the following questions consists of a related pair of words, followed by four pairs of words. Choose the pair that best represents a similar relationship to the one expressed in the original pair of words.

ELEPHANT : PACHYDERM
A. Mantis : rodent
B. Podle : feline
C. Kangaroo : marsupial
D. Zebra : horse

Q.28 Every one of the following questions consists of a related pair of words, followed by four pairs of words. Choose the pair that best represents a similar relationship to the one expressed in the original pair of words.

PSYCHOLOGIST : NEUROSIS
A. Ophthalmologist : cataract
B. Dermatologist : fracture
C. Infant : pediatrician
D. Rash : orthopedist

Q.29 Every one of the following questions consists of a related pair of words, followed by four pairs of words. Choose the pair that best represents a similar relationship to the one expressed in the original pair of words.

PASTORAL : RURAL
A. Metropolitan : urban
B. Harvest : autumn
C. Agrarian : benevolent
D. Sleepy : nocturnal

Q.30 Every one of the following questions consists of a related pair of words, followed by four pairs of words. Choose the pair that best represents a similar relationship to the one expressed in the original pair of words.

TAILOR : SUIT
A. Scheme : agent   **B.** Edit : manuscript
C. Revise : writer   **D.** Mention : opinion

Q.31 Find out which of the figures (a), (b), (c) and (d) can be formed from the pieces given in figure (X).

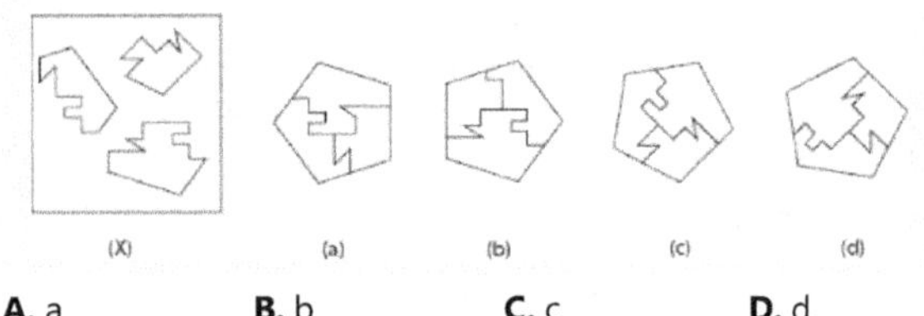

A. a **B.** b **C.** c **D.** d

Q.32 The below question consists of problem figures and followed by four answer figures (A), (B), (C) and (D). Find out the figure from the answer figures which will continue the given series.

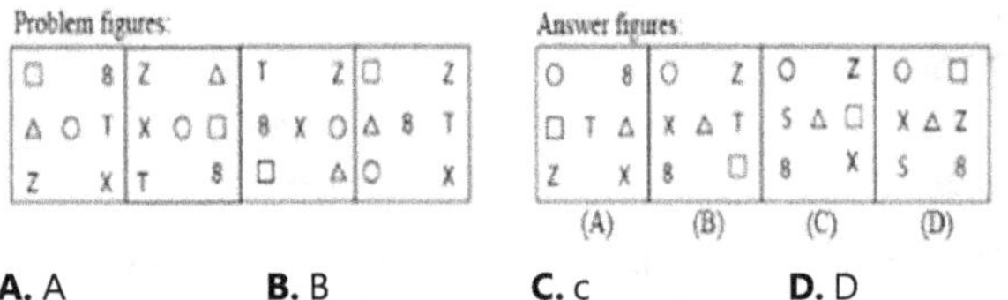

A. A **B.** B **C.** c **D.** D

Q.33 The below question consists of a set of three figures K, L and M showing a sequence of folding of a piece of paper. Figure M shows the manner in which the folded paper has been cut. These three figures are followed by four figures (1), (2), (3) and (4) from which you have to choose a figure which would most closely resemble the unfolded form of figure M.

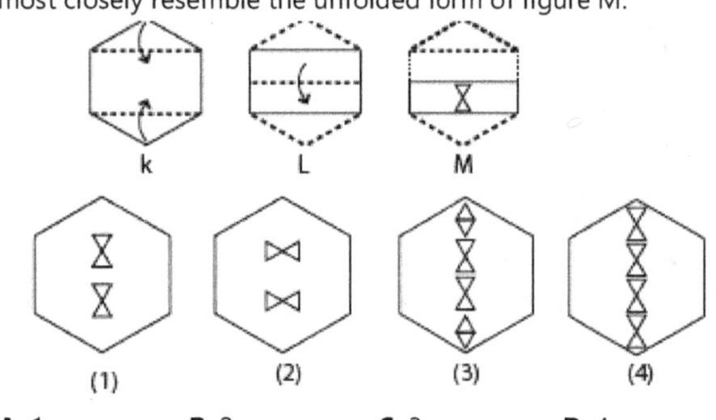

A. 1 **B.** 2 **C.** 3 **D.** 4

Q.34 For the below question, group the given figures into different classes on the basis of their orientation, shape etc.

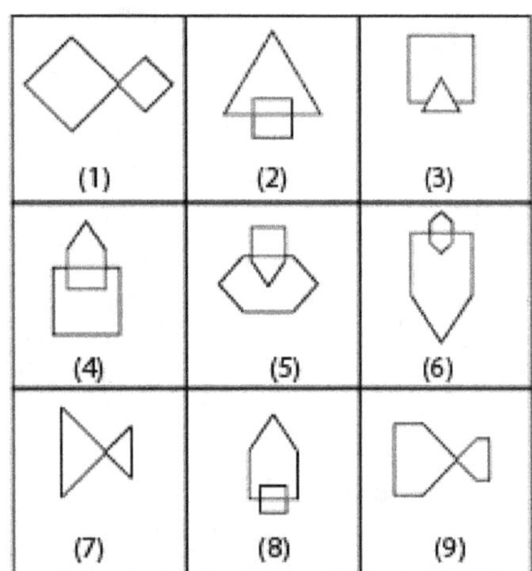

A. (179), (234), (568) **B.** (179), (236), (458)
C. (134), (278), (569) **D.** (179), (246), (358)

Q.35 The below question consists of four figures a, b, c and d and followed by answer figures marked as (A), (B), (C) and (D) each consisting of two figures marked a and d. Select a figure from the answer sets which suitable in the problem figure such that c is related to figure d and in the same way figure a is related to figure b.

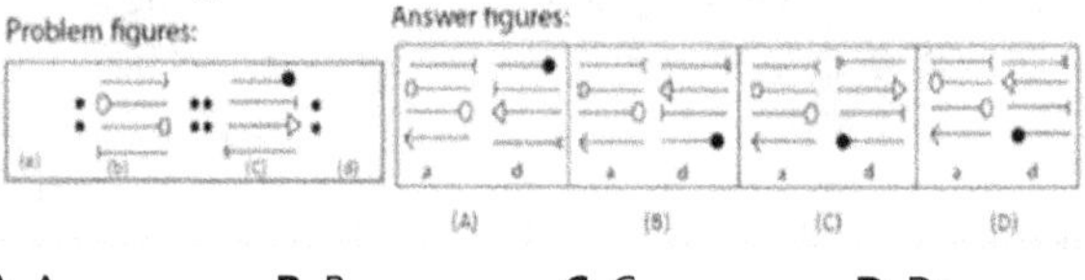

A. A **B.** B **C.** C **D.** D

Q.36 In the below question, element (b) is related to element (a) in a particular way in three pairs of figures out of the given four. Find out the pair of figures in which the element (b) is not related to element (a).

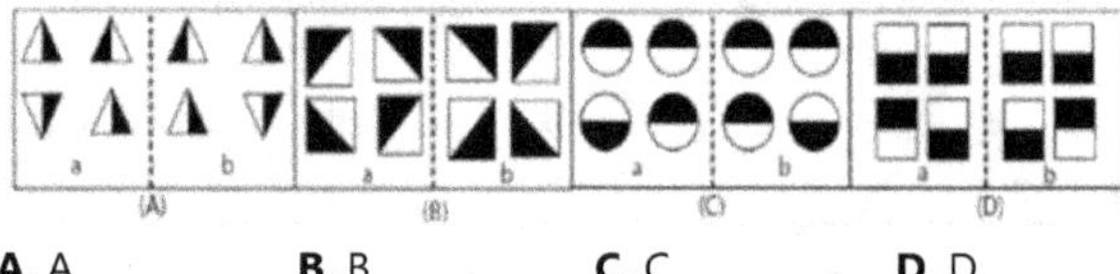

A. A **B.** B **C.** C **D.** D

Q.37 The below question consists of a question figure and followed by four figures (a), (b), (c) and (d). Choose one out of these four figures that can replace '?' to complete the question figure.

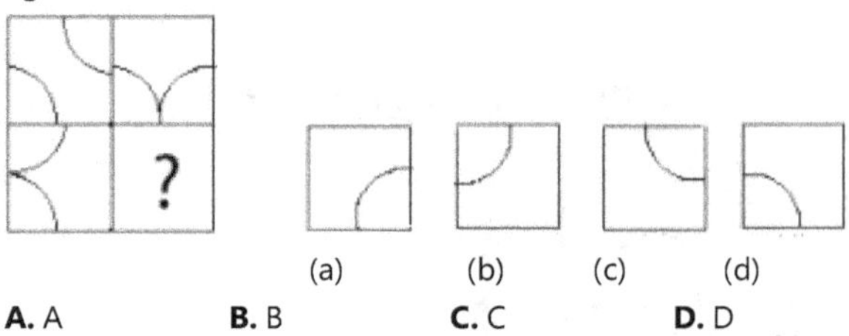

A. A **B.** B **C.** C **D.** D

Q.38

| Which number is on the face opposite to 6? |

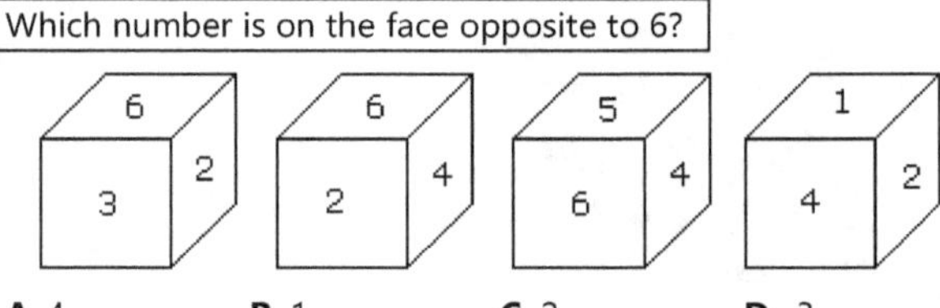

A. 4 **B.** 1 **C.** 2 **D.** 3

Q.39 The below question consists of a unfolded dice in the left side and four choices (a), (b), (c) and (d) are given in the form of complete dices in the right side. You are required to select the correct answer choice which is formed by folding the unfolded dice.

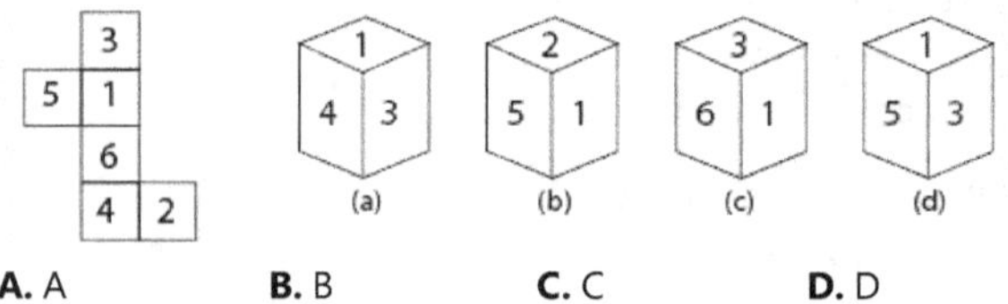

A. A **B.** B **C.** C **D.** D

Q.40 In the below question, one or more dots are placed in the problem figure (X) followed by four alternatives (a), (b), (c) and (d). One out of these four alternatives contain region(s) common to the circle, square, triangle and rectangle similar to that marked by the dot in figure (X).

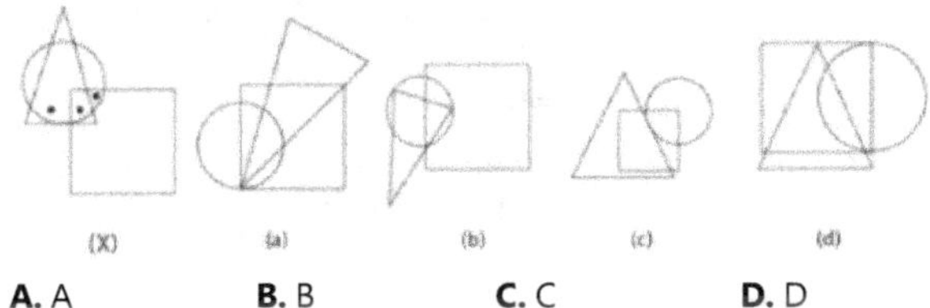

A. A   **B.** B   **C.** C   **D.** D

Q.41 The below question consists of figure (Y) and followed by four alternatives (1), (2), (3) and (4). Choose the correct alternative among the four alternatives such that the pattern would appear like when the figure (Y) is folded at the dotted line.

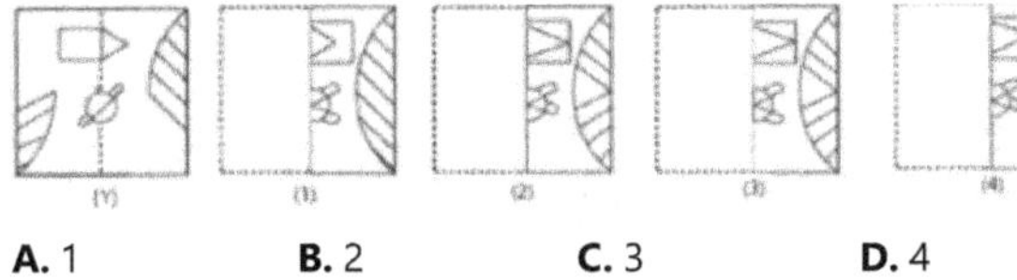

A. 1   **B.** 2   **C.** 3   **D.** 4

Q.42 Choose the correct mirror image for the given figure among the four alternatives (1), (2), (3) and (4). The mirror is represented by a line AB

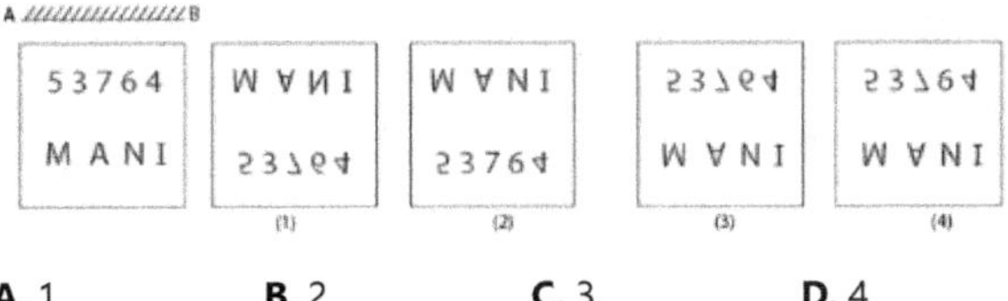

A. 1   **B.** 2   **C.** 3   **D.** 4

Q.43 Find the number of squares in the given figure-

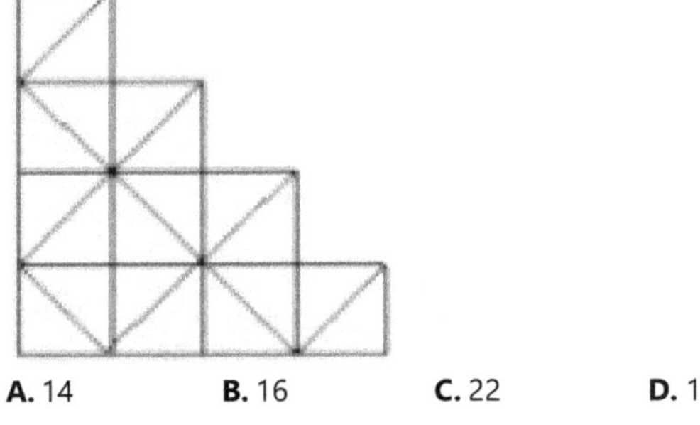

A. 14   **B.** 16   **C.** 22   **D.** 12

Q.44 The below question consists of a problem figure (X) followed by four other alternative figures marked (a), (b), (c) and (d). Select a figure from the alternative figures which exactly fit into figure(X) to form a complete square.

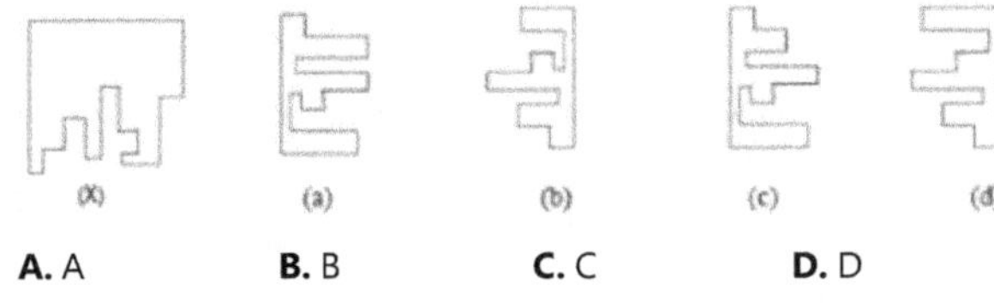

A. A   **B.** B   **C.** C   **D.** D

Q.45 The below question consists of a figure matrix with one or more missing terms and followed by four answer figures (1), (2), (3) and (4). Find the correct answer figure that will replace '?'

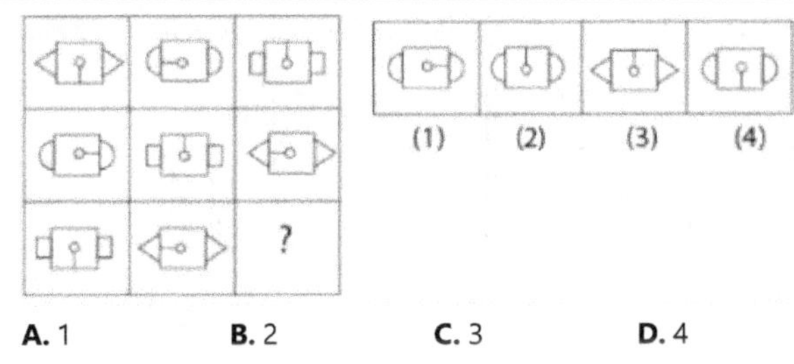

A. 1   **B.** 2   **C.** 3   **D.** 4

Q.46 Which one of the given set of figures violates the given rule?

Rule: Second figure is mirror image of first figure and third figure is water image of first figure.

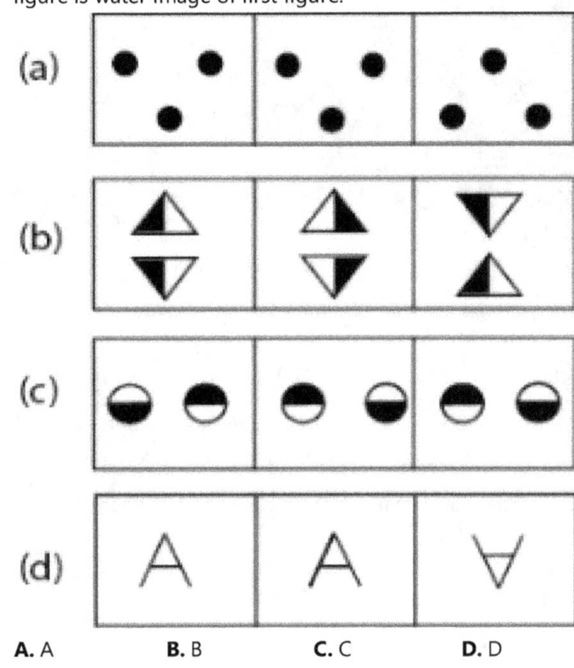

A. A   **B.** B   **C.** C   **D.** D

Q.47 The below question consists of a figure matrix with one or more missing terms and followed by five answer figures (1), (2), (3), (4) and (5). Find the correct answer figure that will replace the blanks.

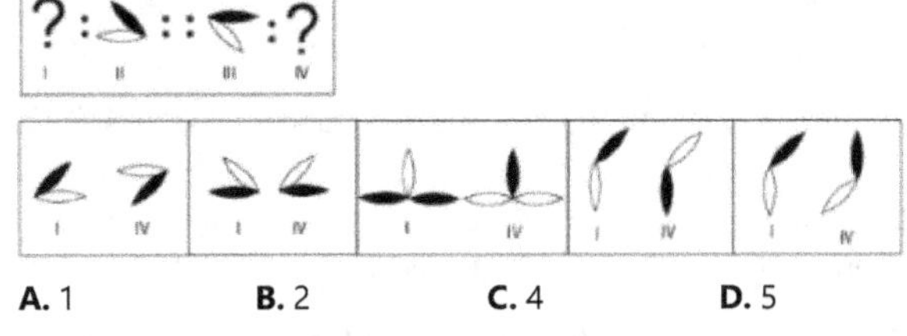

A. 1   **B.** 2   **C.** 4   **D.** 5

Q.48 The below question consists of two problems figures and followed by answer figure marked as (1), (2), (3) and (4). The two problem figures have some common characteristics. Select the answer figure which has the same characteristics as that of the problem figure.

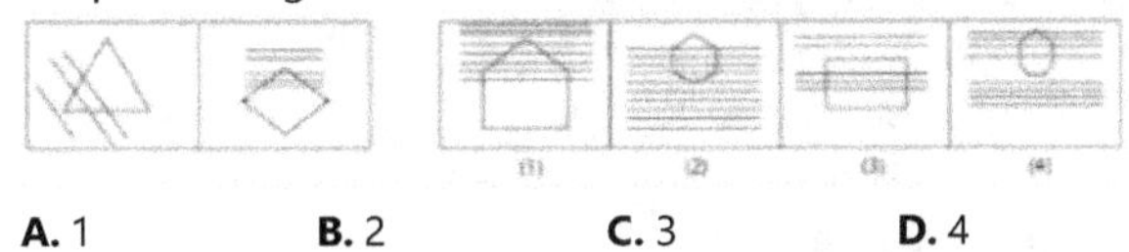

A. 1   **B.** 2   **C.** 3   **D.** 4

Q.49 Choose the correct alternative which contains figure (X) as its part.

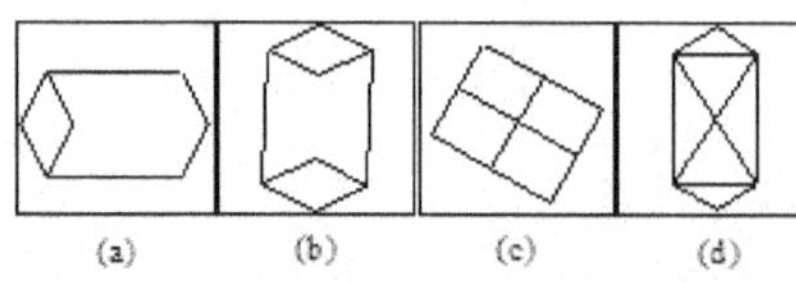

A. A   **B.** B   **C.** C   **D.** D

Q.50 Identify the given type of brick bonding

A. English bond   **B.** Flemish bond
C. Rat trap Bond   **D.** Dutch bond

Q.51 The 'Char Minar' is in-
A. Ahmedabad   **B.** Hyderabad
C. Delhi   **D.** Sikri

Q.52 Where is the National Institute of Virology situated?
A. Pune   **B.** Delhi   **C.** Kolkata   **D.** Madras

Q.53 The 'satellite freight city' is being developed near which of the following cities?
A. New Delhi   **B.** Orissa
C. Gurgaon   **D.** Kolkata

Q.54 Central Arid Zone Research Institute is located in-
A. Bihar   **B.** Gujarat
C. Rajasthan   **D.** Madhya Pradesh

Q.55 National Institute of Nutrition is located in which of the following place?
A. Bangalore   **B.** Kerala
C. Gandhinagar   **D.** Hyderabad

Q.56 National Institute of Aeronautical Engineering is located at-
A. Dehradun   **B.** Lucknow
C. Bangalore   **D.** Delhi

Q.57 The world famous 'Khajuraho' sculptures are located in-
A. Gujarat   **B.** Madhya Pradesh
C. Orissa   **D.** Maharashtra

Q.58 'Kandla' is situated on the Gulf of Kachh is well known for which of the following?
A. Export Processing Zone
B. Centre for Marine Food products
C. Cutting and Polishing of diamonds
D. Ship breaking industry

Q.59 National Police Academy is located at-
A. Bangalore   **B.** Hyderabad
C. Abu Road   **D.** Dehradun

Q.60 National Archives is located at-
A. Calcutta   **B.** Dehradun
C. Bombay   **D.** New Delhi

// Smart Answer Sheet //

Correct — Percentage of students who answered correctly. **Skipped** — Percentage of students who skipped.

Q.	Ans.	Correct / Skipped
1	C	21.05 % / 30.53 %
2	C	30.53 % / 35.79 %
3	B	22.11 % / 36.84 %
4	C	26.32 % / 35.79 %
5	B	22.11 % / 37.89 %
6	C	12.63 % / 38.95 %
7	B	14.74 % / 41.05 %
8	D	11.58 % / 41.05 %
9	C	14.74 % / 38.94 %
10	D	11.58 % / 36.84 %
11	A	15.79 % / 38.95 %
12	D	16.84 % / 41.05 %

Q.	Ans.	Correct / Skipped
13	C	23.16 % / 35.79 %
14	C	21.05 % / 37.9 %
15	A	14.74 % / 38.94 %
16	D	10.53 % / 35.79 %
17	C	18.95 % / 38.94 %
18	D	17.89 % / 40.0 %
19	B	41.05 % / 29.48 %
20	D	8.42 % / 36.84 %
21	A	73.68 % / 11.58 %
22	C	38.95 % / 14.73 %
23	D	40.0 % / 13.68 %
24	D	57.89 % / 14.74 %

Q.	Ans.	Correct / Skipped
25	C	53.68 % / 14.74 %
26	C	16.84 % / 18.95 %
27	C	53.68 % / 16.85 %
28	A	33.68 % / 18.95 %
29	A	55.79 % / 20.0 %
30	B	32.63 % / 15.79 %
31	B	25.26 % / 16.85 %
32	B	26.32 % / 18.94 %
33	D	61.05 % / 15.79 %
34	D	36.84 % / 16.84 %
35	B	27.37 % / 22.1 %
36	B	62.11 % / 16.84 %

Q.	Ans.	Correct / Skipped
37	D	16.84 % / 14.74 %
38	B	56.84 % / 16.84 %
39	D	64.21 % / 16.84 %
40	B	52.63 % / 15.79 %
41	A	61.05 % / 13.69 %
42	A	57.89 % / 13.69 %
43	A	71.58 % / 16.84 %
44	C	60.0 % / 14.74 %
45	B	65.26 % / 15.79 %
46	B	44.21 % / 20.0 %
47	D	24.21 % / 16.84 %
48	D	14.74 % / 15.79 %

Q.	Ans.	Correct / Skipped
49	B	73.68 % / 16.85 %
50	C	52.63 % / 12.63 %
51	B	71.58 % / 12.63 %
52	A	46.32 % / 14.73 %
53	C	51.58 % / 14.74 %
54	C	47.37 % / 15.79 %
55	D	27.37 % / 16.84 %
56	D	25.26 % / 13.69 %
57	B	62.11 % / 11.57 %
58	A	38.95 % / 17.89 %
59	B	45.26 % / 15.79 %
60	D	33.68 % / 16.85 %

//Hints and Solutions//

1. 1. $\sin 5x + \sin x + \sin 3x = 0$

$2\sin 3x \cdot \cos 2x + \sin 3x = 0$

$\sin 3x(2\cos 2x + 1) = 0, 0 \le x \le \dfrac{\pi}{2}$

(i) $\sin 3x = 0$ $3x = n\pi x = \dfrac{n\pi}{3}$

(ii) $\cos 2x = \dfrac{-1}{2} = \cos \dfrac{2\pi}{3} 2x = 2k\pi \pm \dfrac{2\pi}{3}$

$x = kx \pm \dfrac{\pi}{3}$

From both $x = \dfrac{\pi}{3}$ (other than 0).

Hence, the correct option is (C).

2. $S = 1 + 3 + 6 + 10 + 15 + \cdots + t_{2-1} + t_2$

$S = 1 + 3 + 6 + 10 + \cdots + t_2 = 1 + t_2$

$0 = 1 + [2 + 3 + 4 + .. (n-1) \text{ terms}] - t_n$

$t_n = 1 + [2 + 3 + 4 + \cdots + n]$

$S_n = \sum_{n=1}^{n} t_n = \dfrac{1}{6}n(n+1)(n+2)$

Hence, the correct option is (C).

3. Let ΣX^2 and $\Sigma X'$ denotes correct value of sum of squares and sum of the given data.

$\Sigma X' = \Sigma X - 20 + 30 = 170 - 20 + 30 = 180$

$\sum X^2 = \sum X^2 - 20^2 + 30^2 = 2830 - 400 + 900 = 3330$

Variance $= \dfrac{1}{n}\Sigma X'^2 - \left(\dfrac{1}{n}\Sigma X'\right)^2$

$= \dfrac{1}{15}3330 - \left(\dfrac{1}{15}180\right)^2 = 222 - 144 = 78$

Hence, the correct option is (B).

4. Let $E_1(0 \le i \le 2)$ denote the event that urn contains " white and $'(2-i)$ ' black balls.
Let A denote the event that a white ball is drawn from the urn.

We have $P(E_i) = \dfrac{1}{3}$ for $i = 0, 1, 2$

$P(A \mid E_1) = \dfrac{1}{3}, P(A \mid E_2) = \dfrac{2}{3}, P(A \mid E_3) = 1$

By the total probability rule,

$P(A) = P(E_1)P(A \mid E_1) + P(E_2)P(A \mid E_2) + P(E_3)P(A \mid E_3)$

$-\dfrac{1}{3}\left[\dfrac{1}{3} + \dfrac{2}{3} + 1\right] = \dfrac{2}{3}$

Hence, the correct option is (C).

5. 1. We can choose two men out of 9 in 9C2 ways. Since no husband and wife are to play in the same game, two women out of the remaining 7 can be chosen in 72 two women out of the remaining 7 can be chosen in 7C2 ways. If M1, M2, W1 & W2 are chosen, then a team may consist of M1 and W1 or M1and W2. Thus, the number of ways of arranging the game is

$(9c_2)^7C_2(2) = \dfrac{9\times 8}{2} \times \dfrac{7\times 6}{2} \times 2 = 1512.$

Hence, the correct option is (B).

6. Let θ be the angle between $\vec{a} \& \vec{b}$

$(a + 3b) \perp (7a - 5b)$

$\left(\vec{a} + 3\vec{b}\right) \cdot \left(7\vec{a} - 5\vec{b}\right) = 0$

$7|a|^2 + 16|a \cdot b| - 15|b|^2 = 0$

$7 + 16\cos\theta - 15 = 0$

$\cos\theta = \dfrac{1}{2}$

$\theta = \dfrac{\pi}{3}$

$And, [a - 4b)|\left(7a - 2\vec{b}\right)$

$\left(\vec{a} - 4\vec{b}\right) \cdot (7a - 2b) = 0$

$7|a|^2 + 8|b|^2 - 30\left|\vec{a} \cdot b\right| = 0$

$15 - 30\cos\theta = 0\cos\theta = \dfrac{1}{2}\theta = \dfrac{\pi}{3}$

Hence, the correct option is (C).

7. We are given that z is paralilel to the plane containing $arax$ i The plane containing vectors a and b can be

$$\Rightarrow [\vec{a}\vec{b}\vec{c}] = 0$$

$\left(\vec{a} \times \vec{b}\right)$. Then, $\vec{c} \cdot \left(\vec{a} \times \vec{b}\right) = 0$ $\Rightarrow$

$\begin{vmatrix} 2 & 3 & -1 \\ 1 & -2 & 3 \\ \lambda & 1 & 2\lambda - 1 \end{vmatrix} = 0$

$\Rightarrow 2(-4\lambda+2-3)-3(2\lambda-1-3\lambda)-1(1+2\lambda)=0$

$\Rightarrow 2(-4\lambda-1)-3(-\lambda-1)-1-2\lambda=0$

$\Rightarrow -8\lambda-2+3\lambda+3-1-2\lambda=0$

$\Rightarrow -7\lambda=0$

$\Rightarrow \lambda=0$

Hence, the correct option is (B).

8. Equation of any plane passing through (-2,-2,2) is

$a(x + 2) + b(y + 2) + c(z - 2) = 0$

since it contains the line joining the points (1,1,1) and (1,-1,2) , it contains these points as well
so that

$3a + 3b - c = 0$

and $3a + b + 0 = 0$

Solving we get

$$\frac{a}{1} = \frac{b}{-3} = \frac{c}{0}$$

and thus the equation of the plane is is

$$(x + 2) - 3(y + 2) = 0$$
$$x + 3y - 4 = 0$$
$$\frac{x}{4} + \frac{y}{\frac{4}{3}} = 1$$

Intercepts on axes $= 4, \frac{4}{3}$

The required sum $= 4 + \frac{4}{3} = \frac{16}{3}$

Hence, the correct option is (D).

9. Using $C_2 \to C_2 - C_1$ we get $\begin{vmatrix} x+1 & 1 & 1 \\ x+2 & 2 & 2 \\ x+3 & 3 & 3 \end{vmatrix} = 0$

If any two columns of the determinant is identical, then the determinant is always zero.

Thus, all real values of x are possible.

Hence, the correct option is (C).

10. Put $2x + y = x \Rightarrow 2 + \frac{dy}{dx} = \frac{dX}{dx}$. Therefore, the given equation is reduced to

$$\frac{dX}{dx} - 2 = -\frac{X+1}{2X-1} = \frac{dX}{dx} = \frac{3(X-1)}{2X-1} \Rightarrow \frac{2X-1}{3(X-1)}dX =$$
$$dx \Rightarrow \frac{1}{3}\left[2 + \frac{1}{X-1}\right]dX = dx$$

$$\frac{1}{3}[2X + \log(X - 1)] = x + \text{constant}$$

$2(2x + y) + \log (2x + y - 1) = 3x + \text{constant}$

$x + 2y + \log (2x + y - 1) = C$

Hence, the correct option is (D).

11. a, b, c are in $AP \Rightarrow 2b = a + c$

Also, $\frac{3}{2}a + b + c = 3/2 \Rightarrow 3b = 3/2$

$\frac{1}{2} \Rightarrow b = 1/2$

$$\Rightarrow a + c = 1$$

Next, a^2, b^2, c^2 are in GP.

$$\Rightarrow b^2 = \sqrt{a^2 c^2} \Rightarrow b^2 = \pm ac$$
$$\Rightarrow ac = 1/4 \quad - (2)$$

or

$$\frac{1}{4}ac = -1/4$$

From (1)&(2) a &c are roots of a quadratic $x^2 - (a + c)x + ac = 0$

$$\Rightarrow x^2 - x + (1/4) = 0$$

$$\Rightarrow \left(x - \frac{1}{2}\right)^2 = 0$$

Thus, the equation has roots $a = c = \frac{1}{2}$

since, a sbec, the above results are not satisfied.

If we consider ac=$-\frac{1}{4}$, then

$$x^2 - x - (1/4) = 0$$

$$x = \frac{1 \pm \sqrt{2}}{2}$$

$$= \frac{1}{2} \pm \frac{1}{\sqrt{2}}$$

since, $a < b < c$, then $a = \frac{1}{2} - \frac{1}{\sqrt{2}}$

and

$$c = \frac{1}{2} + \frac{1}{\sqrt{2}}$$

Hence, the correct option is (A).

12. $S_n = 12 + 16 + 24 + 40 + \cdots \ldots \ldots + t_n$

$S_n = 0 + 12 + 16 + 24 + \cdots \ldots \ldots t_{n-1} + t_n$

On Subtracting, $0 = 12 + 4 + 8 + 16 + \cdots +$
$(t_n - t_{n-1}) - t_n$

Or

$t_n = 12 + [4 + 8 + 16 + \cdots (n - 1) \text{ terms }]$

$= 12 + \frac{4(2^{n-1}-1)}{2-1} = 12 + 2^{n-1+2} - 4$ or,

$t_n = 8 + 2^{n+1} = 8 + 2.2^n S_n = \sum_{n=1}^{n} t_n = \sum_{n=1}^{n}$
$(8 + 2.2^n) = 8n + 2\left[\frac{2 \cdot (2^n - 1)}{2-1}\right]$

$= 8n + 4(2^n - 1)$ as $\sum 2.2^n = 2\sum 2^n = 2(2 + 2^2 + 2^3 + \cdots)$

Hence, the correct option is (D).

13. Given:

$$\vec{a} \cdot \vec{b} = \frac{15}{2}, |\vec{a}| = 3 \text{ and } |\vec{b}| = 5$$

We know that,

If $\vec{a}$ and $\vec{b}$ are two vectors, then the scalar product between the given vectors is given by:

$$\vec{a} \cdot \vec{b} = |\vec{a}| \times |\vec{b}| \times \cos\theta$$

$\Rightarrow \cos\theta = \dfrac{\vec{a}\cdot\vec{b}}{|\vec{a}|\times|\vec{b}|}$

$\Rightarrow \cos\theta = \dfrac{\frac{15}{2}}{3\times5}$

$\Rightarrow \cos\theta = \dfrac{1}{2}$

$\Rightarrow \theta = \cos^{-1}\left(\dfrac{1}{2}\right)$

$\Rightarrow \theta = \dfrac{\pi}{3}$

Hence, the correct option is (C).

14. $\alpha = p + q, p - q = \beta$

where $p = 5a + 2b, q = a - 3b$, then $\alpha = p + q = 6a - b$

$\alpha^2 = (6a - b)^2 = 36a^2 + b^2 - 12a \cdot b$

$= 36(8) + 9 - 12(2\sqrt{2})(3)\cos\left(\dfrac{\pi}{4}\right) = (15)^2$

$\beta^2 = (\vec{p} - \vec{q})^2 = (4\vec{a} + 5\vec{b})^2 = 16a^2 + 25b^2 + 40\vec{a}\cdot\vec{b}$
$= 16(8) + 25(9) + 40(2\sqrt{2})(3)\cos\left(\frac{\pi}{4}\right) = 593$

$\therefore \alpha = 15, \beta = \sqrt{593}, \beta > \alpha$

$\therefore \beta = \sqrt{593}$ is required length. (c)

Hence, the correct option is (C).

15. The direction ratios of the line joining $P(-1,2,4)$ and $Q(1,0,5)$ are proportional to 2,-2,1

$\therefore$ Its direction cosines are $\dfrac{2}{3}, -\dfrac{2}{3}, \dfrac{1}{3}$

Thus, the projection of the line joining $A(3,4,5)$ and $B(4,6,3)$ on PQ is given by

$= \left|(4 - 3)\times\dfrac{2}{3} + (6 - 4)\times-\dfrac{2}{3} + (3 - 5)\times\dfrac{1}{3}\right|$

$= \left|\dfrac{2}{3} - \dfrac{4}{3} - \dfrac{2}{3}\right| = \dfrac{4}{3}$

Hence, the correct option is (A).

16.

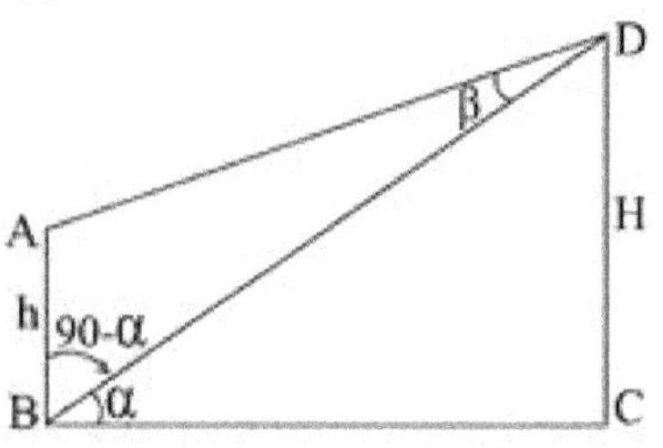

Let AB be the pole and CD be the tower. Then as given in the question. $AB = h, \angle DBC = \alpha, \angle ADB = \beta$ Let $CD = H$

$\ln \Delta BCD, \sin\alpha = \dfrac{H}{BD}$

$\Rightarrow BD = \dfrac{H}{\sin\alpha} = H\cosec\alpha$

$\angle ABD = 90° - \alpha$

$\angle BAD = 180° - (90° - \alpha + \beta) = 90° + \alpha - \beta$

in $\triangle ABD$ applying sine Rule, we have

$\dfrac{\sin\beta}{h} = \dfrac{\sin(\angle BAD)}{BD}$

$\Rightarrow \dfrac{\sin\beta}{h} = \dfrac{\sin(90°+\alpha-\beta)}{H\cosec\alpha} \Rightarrow \dfrac{\sin\beta}{h} = \dfrac{\cos(\alpha-\beta)}{H\cosec\alpha}$

$\Rightarrow H = \dfrac{h\cos(\alpha-\beta)}{\sin\beta\cosec\alpha}$

$\Rightarrow H = h\cosec\beta\sin\alpha\cos(\alpha - \beta)$

Hence, the correct option is (D).

17. $\sin 3x = k$ is satisfied by $A\&B \Rightarrow \sin 3A = k\&\sin 3B = k$

$\Rightarrow \sin 3A = \sin 3B \Rightarrow 3A = 3B$ or $3A = \pi - 3B$

But $3A = 3B$ rejected $(QB > A)$

$\Rightarrow 3A = \pi - 3B \Rightarrow A + B = \dfrac{\pi}{3} \Rightarrow C = \dfrac{2\pi}{3}$

Hence, the correct option is (C).

18. Sides of a triangle ABC are given by $x = 3, y = 4, 3x + 4y = 6$. It forms a right angle triangle ABC with $B(3,4)$ as right angle.

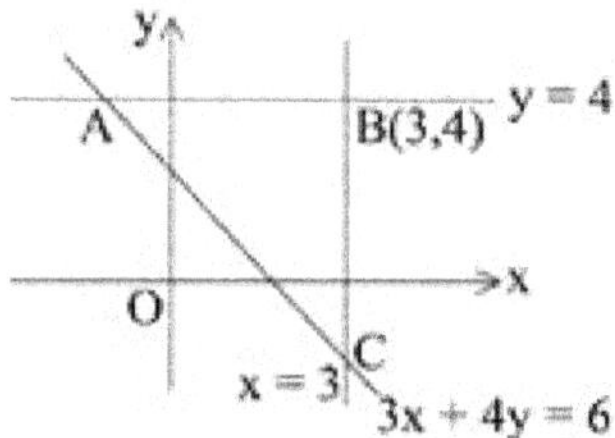

Hence B is the orthocentre as perpendiculars drawn from A and C meet at B.

Hence, the correct option is (D).

19. $x + 2|y| = 1 \Rightarrow x + 2y = 1, x - 2y = 1 \Rightarrow \dfrac{x}{1} + \dfrac{y}{\left(\frac{1}{2}\right)} = 1$ and $\dfrac{x}{1} + \dfrac{y}{\left(-\frac{1}{2}\right)} = 1$ Clearly $BC = \dfrac{1}{2} + \dfrac{1}{2} = 1, OA = 1$

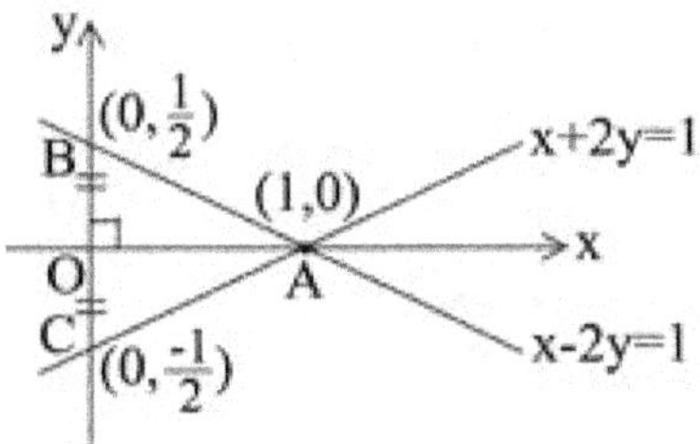

Area of $ABC = \dfrac{OA.BC}{2} = \dfrac{1 \times 1}{2} = \dfrac{1}{2}$

Hence, the correct option is (B).

20. A, B, C are equiprobable $\Rightarrow P(A) = P(B) = P(C)$

A, B, C are mutually exclusive and exhaustive

$\Rightarrow P(A) + P(B) + P(C) = 1$

$\therefore (i)$ and $(ii) \Rightarrow P(A) = P(B) = P(C) = \dfrac{1}{3}$

Using the law of total probability:

$$P(E) = P(A)P\left(\dfrac{E}{A}\right) + P(B)P\left(\dfrac{E}{B}\right) + P(C)P\left(\dfrac{E}{C}\right)$$

$$\Rightarrow \dfrac{5}{12} = \dfrac{1}{3}\dfrac{3}{8} + \dfrac{1}{3}\dfrac{1}{4} + \dfrac{1}{3}P\left(\dfrac{E}{C}\right)$$

$$\Rightarrow \dfrac{5}{12} = \dfrac{3+2}{24} + \dfrac{1}{3}P\left(\dfrac{E}{C}\right)$$

$$\Rightarrow \dfrac{1}{3}P\left(\dfrac{E}{C}\right) = \dfrac{5}{12} - \dfrac{5}{24} = \dfrac{10-5}{24} = \dfrac{5}{24}$$

$$\Rightarrow P\left(\dfrac{E}{C}\right) = \dfrac{5}{8}$$

Hence, the correct option is (D).

21. Spiral stairs have a wide range of benefits depending upon your space and style. Hence, the correct option is (A).

22. Many different kinds of resins may be used to create a varnish. Natural resins used for varnish include amber, kauri gum, dammar, copal, rosin (pine resin), sandarac, balsam, elemi, mastic, and shellac. Varnish may also be created from synthetic resins such as acrylic, alkyd, or polyurethane.

Hence, the correct option is (C).

23. A fire brick, firebrick, or refractory brick is a block of refractory ceramic material used in lining furnaces, kilns, fireboxes, and fireplaces. A refractory brick is built primarily to withstand high temperature, but will also usually have a low thermal conductivity for greater energy efficiency.

Hence, the correct option is (D).

24. Expanded metal is a type of sheet metal which has been cut and stretched to form a regular pattern (often diamond-shaped) of metal mesh-like material. It is commonly used for fences and grates, and as metallic lath to support plaster or stucco.

Hence, the correct option is (D).

25. Slate is a fine-grained, foliated metamorphic rock that is created by the alteration of shale or mudstone by low-grade regional metamorphism. It is popular for a wide variety of uses such as roofing, flooring, and flagging because of its durability and attractive appearance.

Hence, the correct option is (D).

26. Upon harvesting, cotton is gathered into bales similarly grain is gathered into shocks. Hence, the correct option is (C).

27. An elephant is a pachyderm similarly a kangaroo is a marsupial. Hence, the correct option is (C).

28. A psychologist treats a neurosis similarly an ophthalmologist treats a cataract. Hence, the correct option is (A).

29. Pastoral describes rural areas similarly metropolitan describes urban areas. Hence, the correct option is (A).

30. To tailor a suit is to alter it similarly to edit a manuscript is to alter it. Hence, the correct option is (B).

31.

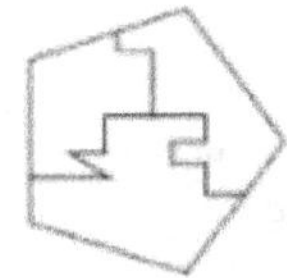

Hence, the correct option is (B).

32.

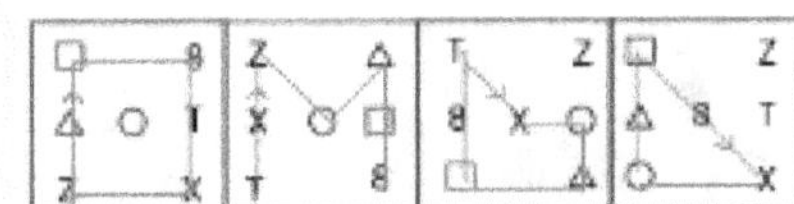

Hence, the correct option is (B).

33.

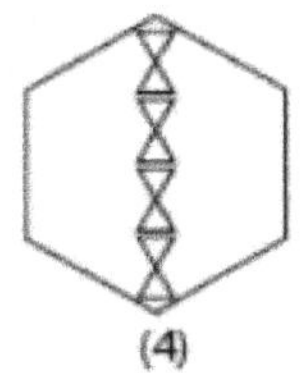

(4)

Hence, the correct option is (D).

34.

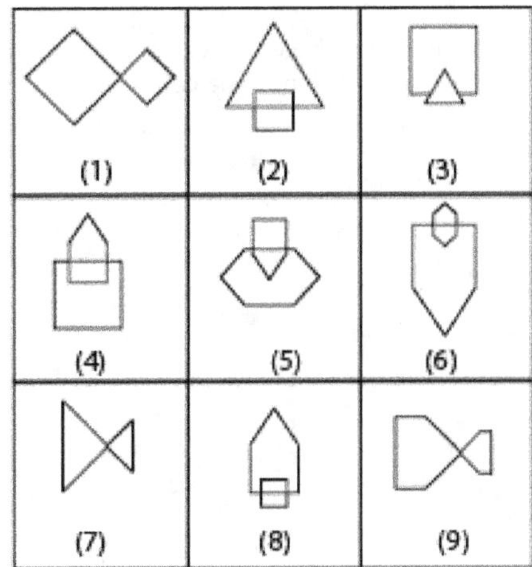

Hence, the correct option is (D).

35. Solution From figure a to figure b: The entire series rotates in clockwise direction by 1 step and each element rotated by 180 degree.

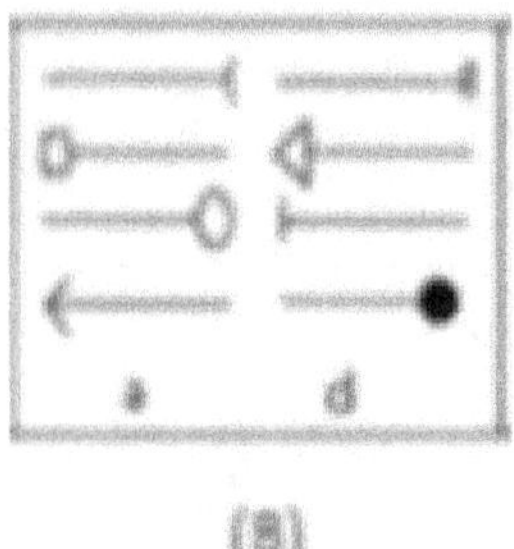

(B)

Hence, the correct option is (B).

36. Solution The upper two elements reflect mirror images, whereas the lower two elements reflect water images.

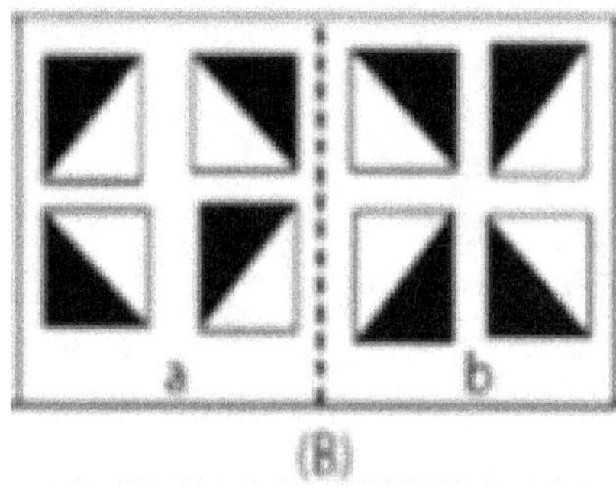

(B)

Hence, the correct option is (B).

37.

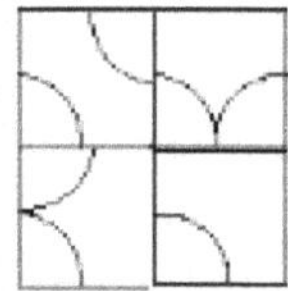

Hence, the correct option is (D).

38. As the numbers 2, 3, 4 and 5 are adjacent to 6. Hence the number on the face opposite to 6 is 1.Hence, the correct option is (B).

39.

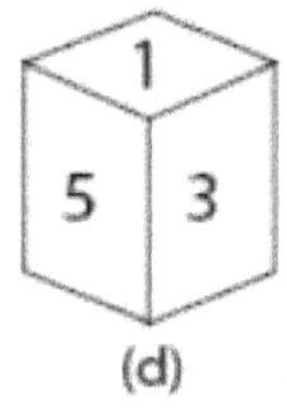

(d)

Hence, the correct option is (D).

40.

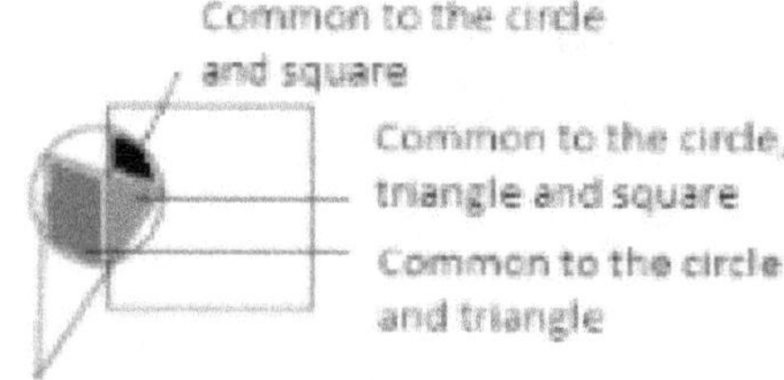

Hence, the correct option is (B).

41.

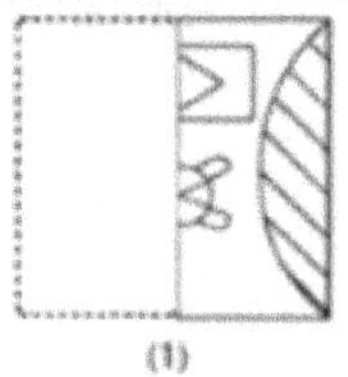

(1)

Hence, the correct option is (A).

42.

Hence, the correct option is (A).

43.

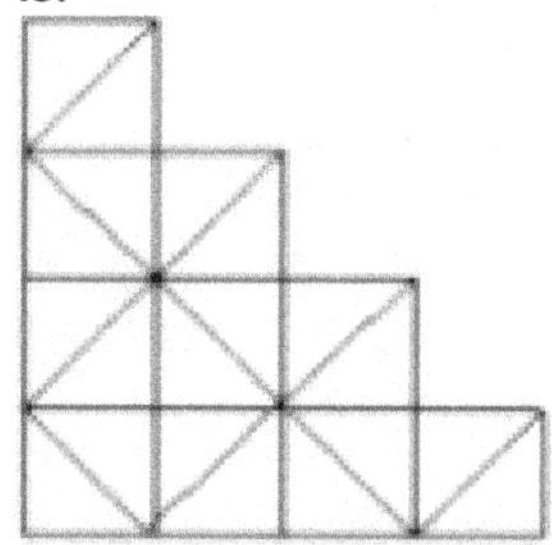

14 squares in the given figure.Hence, the correct option is (A).

44.

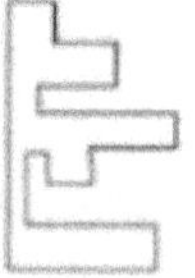

Hence, the correct option is (C).

45.

Hence, the correct option is (B).

46.

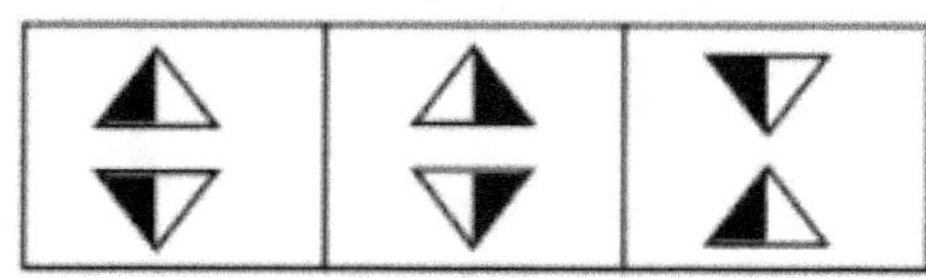

Hence, the correct option is (B).

47. The white leaf of figure (1) rotates

90° CW and the black leaf of figure (1) rotates

90° ACW to form figure (2).

Hence, the correct option is (D).

48. The number of lines touching the figure = Number of sides − 1 and number of lines without touching the figure = Number of sides − 2.

Hence, the correct option is (D).

49.

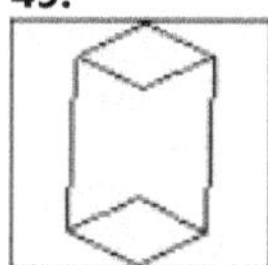

Hence, the correct option is (B).

50. A "Rat-Trap Bond" is a type of wall brick masonry bond in which bricks are laid on edge (The height of each course in case of a brick size 230x110x75 mm, will be 110 mm plus mortar thickness) such that the shinner and rowlock are visible on the face of masonry .

Hence, the correct option is (C).

51. The Charminar is a monument in Hyderabad, India. The structure was built in 1591 AD. It is the most famous building of Hyderabad and also one of the most famous buildings in India. It was built by Muhammad Quli Qutb Shahi to celebrate the end of a deadly plague.

Hence, the correct option is (B).

52. The National Institute of Virology is one of the major Institutes of the Indian Council of Medical Research (ICMR). It was established at Pune, Maharashtra State in 1952 as Virus Research Centre (VRC) under the auspices of the ICMR and the Rockefeller Foundation (RF), USA.

Hence, the correct option is (A).

53. A satellite town or satellite city is a concept in urban planning that refers essentially to smaller metropolitan areas which are located somewhat near to, but are mostly independent of larger metropolitan areas.

Hence, the correct option is (C).

54. This was later expanded into Desert Afforestation and Soil Conservation Station in 1957, and finally upgraded to Central Arid Zone Research Institute (CAZRI) in 1959 under Indian Council of Agricultural Research, New Delhi. The CAZRI operates through Six Divisions, located at the headquarters in Jodhpur.

Hence, the correct option is (C).

55. The National Institute of Nutrition (NIN) is an Indian Public health, Nutrition and Translational research center located in Hyderabad, India. The institute is one of the oldest research centers in India, and the largest center, under the Indian Council of Medical Research, located in the vicinity of Osmania University. The institute has associated clinical and pediatric nutrition research wards at various hospitals such as the Niloufer Hospital for Women and Children, the Government Maternity Hospital, the Gandhi Medical College and the Osmania General Hospital in Hyderabad.

Hence, the correct option is (D).

56. The Indian **Institute of Aeronautical Engineering** is a college of **engineering** at Dehradun, Uttarakhand, northern India. It was founded in 1992 at 15/1, Kalidas Road, Dehradun. In 1995 it moved to 179 Kalidas Road, and in 2006 relocated near Jolly Grant Airport.

Hence, the correct option is (D).

57. The Khajuraho Group of Monuments in Khajuraho, a town in the Indian state of Madhya Pradesh, located in Chhatarpur District, about 620 kilometres (385 mi) southeast of New Delhi, are one of the most popular tourist destinations in India.

Hence, the correct option is (B).

58. Kandla, also known as the Kandla Port Trust or Deendayal Port is a seaport in Kutch District of Gujarat state in western India, near the city of Gandhidham. Located on the Gulf of Kutch, it is one of major ports on west coast. Kandla was constructed in the 1950s as the chief seaport serving western India, after the partition of India and Pakistan left the port of Karachi in Pakistan.

The Port of Kandla is located on the Gulf of Kutch on the northwestern coast of India, some 256 nautical miles southeast of the Port of Karachi in Pakistan and over 430 nautical miles north-northwest of the Port of Mumbai (Bombay). It is the largest port of India by volume of cargo handled. Kandla Port Trust, India's busiest major port in recent years, is gearing to add substantial cargo handling capacity with private sector participation. The west coast port handled 72,225 million tonnes of cargo in 2008-09, over 11% more than the 64,920 million tonnes handled in 2007-08.

Even as much of this growth has come from handling of crude oil imports, mainly for Essar Oil's Vadinar refinery in Gujarat, the port is also taking measures to boost non-POL cargo. Last fiscal, POL traffic accounted for 63 per cent of the total cargo handled at Kandla Port, as against 59% in 2007-08.

Hence, the correct option is (A).

59. Sardhar Vallabhbhai Patel National Police Academy (SVPNPA) is located in Hyderabad, the capital of the Telengana state in India and spread over 275 acres of land.

Hence, the correct option is (B).

60. The National Archives of **India** is located at the intersection of **Rajpath** and Janpath.Originally established as the Imperial Record Department in 1891, in Calcutta, the capital of British India, the NAI is situated at the intersection of Janpath and

Rajpath, in Delhi. It functions as an Attached Office of the Department of Culture under the Ministry of Culture, Government of India.

Hence, the correct option is (D).

Mathematics

Q.1 The equation of a circle C1 is x2+y2−4x−2y−11=0. A circle C2 of radius 1 unit rolls on the outside of the circle C1 touching it externally. The locus of the centre of C2 has the equation-

A. x2 + y2 − 4x − 2y − 20 = 0

B. x2 + y2 + 4x + 2y − 20 = 0

C. x2+ y2− 3x − 2y − 11 = 0

D. None of these

Q.2 Let PQ and RS be tangents at the extremities of the diameter PR of a circle of radius r. If PS and RQ intersect at a point X on the circumference of the circle, then 2r is equal to-

A. $\sqrt{PQ.RS}$

B. $\dfrac{PQ+RS}{2}$

C. $\dfrac{2PQ\cdot RS}{PQ+RS}$

D. $\sqrt{\dfrac{PQ^2+RS^2}{2}}$

Q.3 If the fourth term of $\left(\sqrt{x^{\left(\frac{1}{1+\log_{10}x}\right)}} + \sqrt[12]{x}\right)^6$ is equal to 200 and $x > 1$, then x is equal to-

A. $10\sqrt{2}$

B. 10^4

C. 100

D. 10

Q.4 If for a ΔABC, cot A·cot B·cot C>0 then the triangle is-

A. Right angled

B. Acute angled

C. Obtuse angled

D. All these options are possible

Q.5 If $\vec{a}$ and $\vec{b}$ be two perpendicular unit vectors such that $\vec{x} = \vec{b} - \left(\vec{a} \times \vec{x}\right)$, then $\left|\vec{x}\right|$ is equal to-

A. 1

B. $\sqrt{2}$

C. $\dfrac{1}{\sqrt{2}}$

D. $\sqrt{3}$

Q.6 The least positive integral value of m, if $\left(\dfrac{1+i}{1-i}\right)^m = 1$ (where $i = \sqrt{-1}$ is)-

A. 4

B. 6

C. 2

D. 1

Q.7 The equation of the smallest circle passing through the intersection of the line x + y = 1 and the circle x2 + y2= 9 is-

A. x2 + y2 + x + y − 8 = 0

B. x2 + y2 − x − y − 8 = 0

C. x2 + y2 − x + y − 8 = 0

D. None of these

Q.8 If $a^3 + b^6 = 2$, then the maximum value of the term independent of x in the expansion of $\left(ax^{1/3} + bx^{-1/6}\right)^9$ $(a > 0, b > 0)$ is-

A. 42

B. 68

C. 148

D. 84

Q.9 If $\tan\theta = \tan30° \cdot \tan60°$ and θ is an acute angle,then 2θ is equal to:

A. 30°

B. 45°

C. 90°

D. 0°

Q.10 The function f(x) = x3 + λx2 + 5x + sin 2x will be an invertible function if λ belongs to the set -

A. $[-\infty,-3]$

B. $[-3,3]$

C. $[3,\infty]$

D. None of these

Q.11 If the tangent and the normal to x2− y2= 4 at a point cut off intercepts a1, a2on the x-axis respectively and b1, b2on the y-axis respectively then the value of a1a2+ b1b2 is-

A. 1

B. -1

C. 0

D. 4

Q.12 The number of real values of k for which the lines $\dfrac{x-k}{4} = \dfrac{y-1}{2} = \dfrac{z+1}{1}$ and $\dfrac{x-(k+1)}{1} = \dfrac{y}{-1} = \dfrac{z-1}{2}$ are intersecting, is-

A. 0

B. 2

C. 1

D. Infinite

Q.13 A line makes angles of 45° and 60° with the positive directions of x and y axes respectively. An angle, which the line can make with the positive direction of z-axis is:

A. 60°

B. 40°

C. 80°

D. 100°

Q.14 The co-ordinates of the point which divides the line segment joining the points (5,4, 2) and (−1,−2, 4) in the ratio 2 : 3 externally is-

A. (17, 16,−2)

B. (15, 12,−3)

C. (14, 10,−2)

D. (11, 13,−4)

Q.15 The third vertex of the triangle whose centroid is (7,−2, 5) and whose other two vertices are (2, 6, −4) and (4,−2, 3) is-

A. (15,−10, 16)

B. (10,−12, 16)

C. (13,−14, 11)

D. (6,−11, 10)

Q.16 The vertices of a triangle are A(x1, x1tan α), B (x2, x2tan β) and C(x3, x3 tan γ) . If the circumcentre of ΔABC coincides with the origin and H (a,b) be its orthocentre, then a/b is equal to: (Here α, β and γ are acute angles)-

A. $\dfrac{\tan\alpha+\tan\beta+\tan\lambda}{\tan\alpha\,\tan\beta\,\tan\lambda}$

B. $\dfrac{\sin\alpha+\sin\beta+\sin\lambda}{\sin\alpha\,\sin\beta\,\sin\lambda}$

C. $\dfrac{\tan\alpha+\tan\beta+\tan\gamma}{\tan\alpha\tan\beta\tan\gamma}$

D. $\dfrac{\cos\alpha+\cos\beta+\cos\gamma}{\sin\alpha+\sin\beta+\sin\gamma}$

Q.17 The area of an expanding rectangle is increasing at the rate of 48 cm2/sec. The length of the rectangle is always equal to the square of the breadth. At the instant when the breadth is 4.5 cm, The length is increasing at the rate of-

A. 7.11

B. 8.11

C. 6.11

D. 5.11

Q.18 If ln(x + y) = 2xy, theny' (0) is equal to-

A. 1

B. -1

C. 2

D. 0

Q.19 Two vertices of a triangle are (3, -2) and (-2, 3) and its orthocentre is (- 6, 1). The coordinates of its third vertex are-

A. (1, 6)

B. (-1, 6)

C. (1, -6)　　　　　　**D.** None of these

Q.20 If nPr = 1680 andnCr = 70, then 69 n + r! is equal to-
A. 128　　　**B.** 256　　　**C.** 576　　　**D.** 625

General Aptitude

Q.21 Which letter replaces the question mark?

A. Y　　　**B.** K　　　**C.** M　　　**D.** N

Q.22 The Indian state which is called as "Bamboo Queen" is __
A. Assam　　　　　　**B.** Mizoram
C. Kerala　　　　　　**D.** West Bengal

Q.23 Identify the given Material image-

A. Cement blocks　　　　**B.** Granite blocks
C. Concrete blocks　　　**D.** Sandstone blocks

Q.24 When was the Earth Day celebrated?
A. 22nd April　　　　　**B.** 12th January
C. 25th March　　　　　**D.** 23rd February

Q.25 Answer the correct TOP view for the given 3 D object:

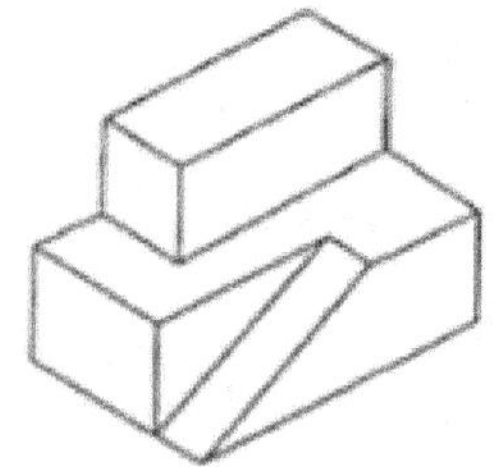

(A)

(B)

(C)

(D)

A. D　　　**B.** C　　　**C.** B　　　**D.** A

Q.26 Which number replaces the question mark?

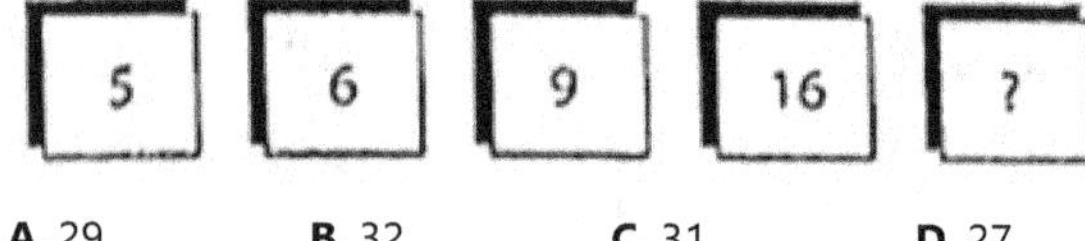

A. 29　　　**B.** 32　　　**C.** 31　　　**D.** 27

Q.27 Let Z denote the set of all integers. If a relation R is defined on Z as follows (x, y)∈R if an only if x is multiple of y, then R is-
A. Reflexive, symmetric but not transitive
B. Symmetric, transitive but not reflexive
C. Neither reflexive nor transitive but symmetric
D. Reflexive, transitive but not symmetric

Q.28 Which of the following composition best fits hierarchy?

(A)

(B)

(C)

(D)

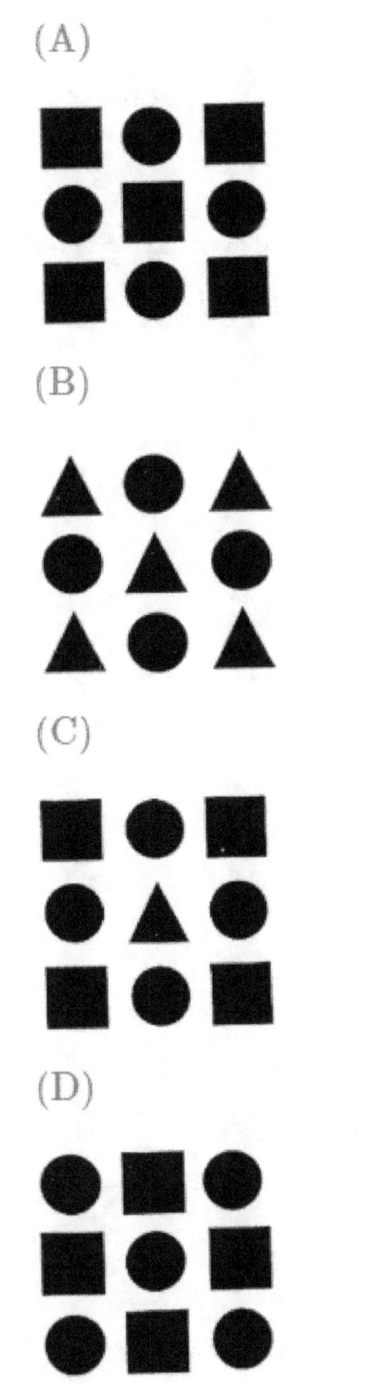

A. C   **B.** A   **C.** D   **D.** B

Q.29 Which Indian city ranks in World Heritage list 2017?
A. Ahmedabad   **B.** Kanchipuram
C. Chandigarh   **D.** Kolkata

Q.30 Which composition best fits variety?

A. D   **B.** B   **C.** C   **D.** A

Q.31 Find the odd figure in the problem.

(A)

(B)

(C)

(D)

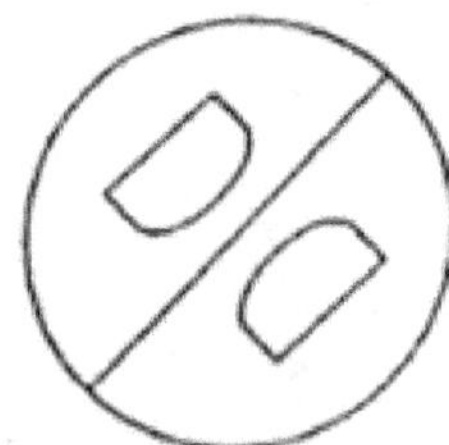

A. C   **B.** A   **C.** D   **D.** B

Q.32 Which of these is not a structural part of a building?
A. Foundation
B. Doors and windows
C. Roof Framing structure
D. Column and Beam

Q.33 Which of the following diagrams indicates the best relation between Paris, France, Italy and World?

(A)

(B)

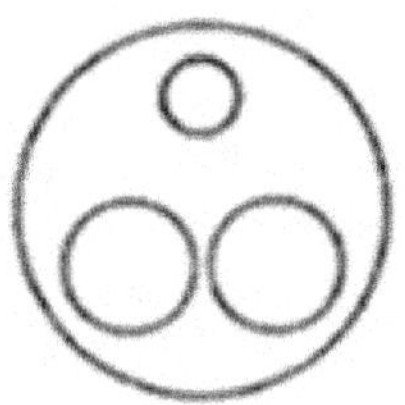

(C)

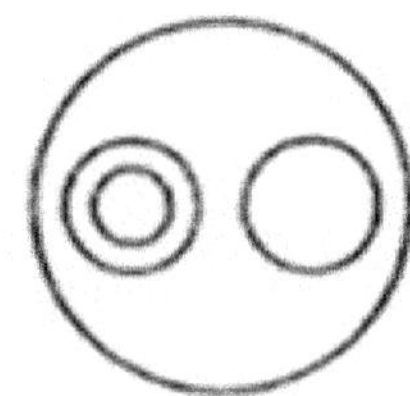

(D)

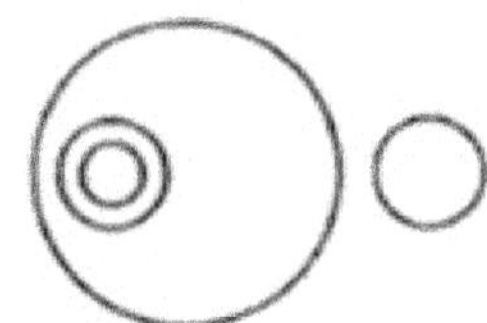

A. D   **B.** B   **C.** A   **D.** C

Q.34 Find the odd figure in the problem

(A)

(B)

(C)

(D)

A. D   **B.** B   **C.** C   **D.** A

Q.35 Which of the following best illustrates a colonnade?

(A)

(B)

(C)

(D)

A. A   **B.** D   **C.** C   **D.** B

Q.36 Where is the given building located?

A. Tamil Nadu   **B.** Andhra Pradesh
C. Karnataka   **D.** Kerala

Q.37 Paris Summit discusses which of the following issues?
A. Climate change
B. Migration
C. Natural conservation
D. Built heritage

Q.38 Find the odd figure in the problem

(A)

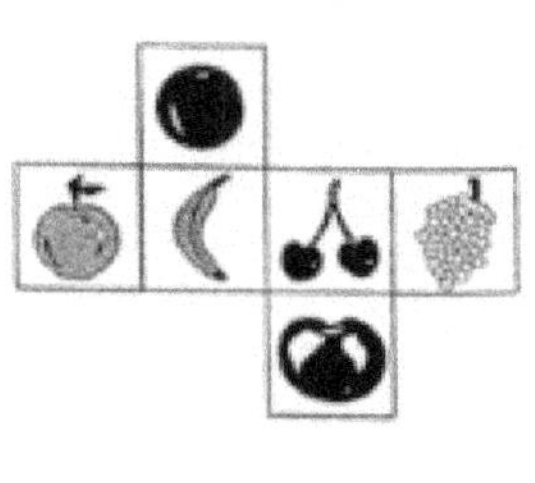

(B)

(C)

(D)

A. D   **B.** A   **C.** B   **D.** C

Q.39 Which picture cube does the unfolded shape make?

(A)

(B)

(C)

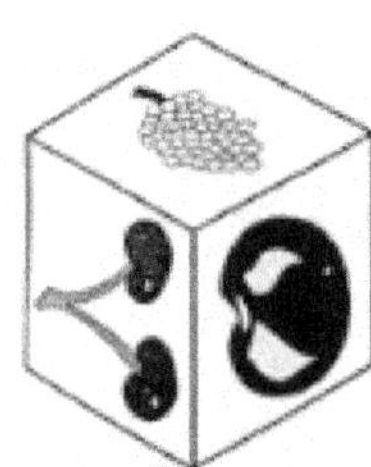

(D)

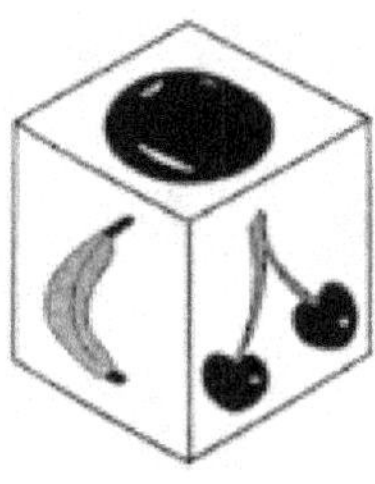

A. B   **B.** A   **C.** D   **D.** C

Q.40 The internal angle formed by the edges of a cube in isometric projection is-

A. 120 degree   **B.** 60 degree
C. 45 degree   **D.** 90 degree

Q.41 A truncated (horizontally cut in mid-way) hexagonal pyramid has following number of surfaces, edges and vertices respectively.

A. 8, 16, 12   **B.** 6, 12, 10   **C.** 6, 16, 10   **D.** 8, 18, 12

Q.42 A circle is inscribed within an equilateral triangle of area $\sqrt{3}$ m². The circumference of the circle is:

A. $\frac{\pi}{\sqrt{3}}m$ **B.** $\sqrt{3}$ m   **C.** $\frac{2\pi}{\sqrt{3}}m$ **D.** $\frac{2\pi}{3}m$

Q.43 The linear scale of a map is 1 cm=2 m. The drawing dimensions of an on-site rectangular plot measuring 25 m×40 m will be-

A. 50 cm ×80 cm   **B.** 25 cm×40 cm
C. 12.5 cm×20 cm   **D.** 5 cm×8 cm

Q.44 When a clock is seen through a mirror, the hour arm and minute arm are seen at 99 and 44 respectively, so that the time seen is 9:20. What will be the actual time after 15min ?

A. 2:35   **B.** 3:35   **C.** 3:55   **D.** 2:55

Q.45 Length of a solid diagonal of a cube is 6 cm. The volume of the cube is-

A. 24√3 cm³   **B.** 8 cm³
C. 12√3cm³   **D.** 27 cm³

Q.46 How many surfaces are there in the model? Consider all seen and unseen surfaces.

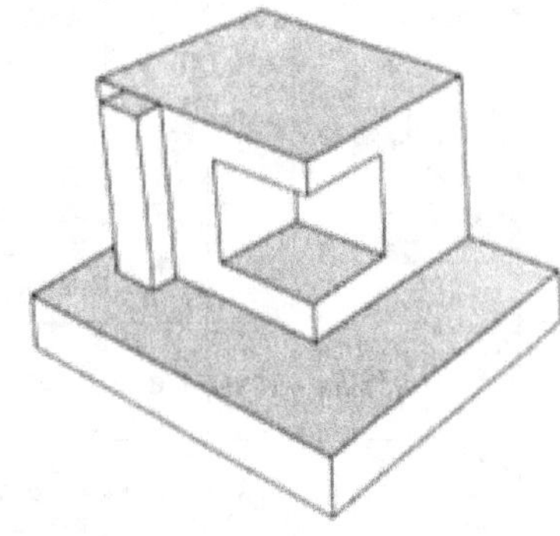

A. 21   **B.** 17   **C.** 12   **D.** 15

Q.47 A horizonal supporting crosspiece over an opening is called-

A. Lattice   **B.** Leader   **C.** Lancet   **D.** Lintel

Q.48 What secondary colour is obtained by mixing blue and red colours?

A. Pink   **B.** Brown   **C.** Orange   **D.** Purple

Q.49 What is Texture?

A. Solid colour
B. Type of shape
C. Lines drawn in colour
D. The way a surface looks and feels

Q.50 World Environment Day is observed on __

A. February 14   **B.** May 01
C. June 05   **D.** August 06

Q.51 Gypsum is a __

A. mechanically formed sedimentary rock.
B. igneous rock.
C. chemically precipitated sedimentary rock.
D. metamorphic rock.

Q.52 Which of the following is a scalar quantity?

A. Energy   **B.** Momentum
C. Torque   **D.** Impulse

Q.53 A heavy ladder resting in the floor and against a vertical wall may not be in equilibrium if-

A. floor is smooth and wall is rough.
B. floor is rough and wall is smooth.
C. both floor and wall are rough.
D. both floor and wall are smooth.

Q.54 The type of roof suitable in plains where rainfall is meagre and temperature is high is-

A. pitched and slope.   **B.** flat
C. vault   **D.** shell

Q.55 The angle which an inclined plane makes with the horizonal when a body placed on it is about to slide down is known as angle of-

A. limiting friction.   **B.** inclination.
C. repose   **D.** overturning

Q.56 Which one of the following consumes least amount of electricity?

A. Tungsten bulb
B. Fluorescent tube
C. Light Emitting Diodes (LED)
D. Compact Fluorescent Lamp (CFL)

Q.57 Green Architecture is promoted these days because-

A. it costs less initially.
B. it is environment friendly.
C. it lasts longer.
D. it uses good colours.

Q.58 Building acoustics concerns-

A. Water related issues.
B. Sound related issues.
C. Ventilation related issues.
D. Daylight related issues.

Q.59 Fly ash is a waste product from which of the following:

A. Nuclear installation
B. Coal mine
C. Thermal power plant
D. Iron ore conversion

Q.60 French influence in architecture is found at __

A. Kerala   **B.** Sikkim
C. Goa   **D.** Puducherry

// Smart Answer Sheet //

Correct — Percentage of students who answered correctly. **Skipped** — Percentage of students who skipped.

Q.	Ans.	Correct / Skipped
1	A	18.07 % / 33.74 %
2	A	18.07 % / 45.79 %
3	D	8.43 % / 39.76 %
4	B	22.89 % / 40.97 %
5	C	25.3 % / 38.56 %
6	A	18.07 % / 44.58 %
7	B	26.51 % / 40.96 %
8	D	9.64 % / 45.78 %
9	C	16.87 % / 44.58 %
10	B	19.28 % / 44.58 %
11	C	21.69 % / 38.55 %
12	D	16.87 % / 43.37 %
13	A	25.3 % / 38.56 %
14	A	24.1 % / 39.76 %
15	A	24.1 % / 39.76 %
16	D	13.25 % / 39.76 %
17	A	20.48 % / 43.38 %
18	A	10.84 % / 43.38 %
19	B	30.12 % / 34.94 %
20	C	25.3 % / 36.15 %
21	C	53.01 % / 14.46 %
22	B	48.19 % / 12.05 %
23	A	28.92 % / 10.84 %
24	A	63.86 % / 14.45 %
25	D	78.31 % / 13.26 %
26	C	22.89 % / 15.66 %
27	D	26.51 % / 19.27 %
28	C	56.63 % / 14.45 %
29	A	44.58 % / 14.46 %
30	C	63.86 % / 14.45 %
31	C	81.93 % / 12.05 %
32	B	59.04 % / 10.84 %
33	D	55.42 % / 15.66 %
34	B	31.33 % / 12.04 %
35	D	42.17 % / 15.66 %
36	C	55.42 % / 12.05 %
37	A	44.58 % / 14.46 %
38	A	25.3 % / 16.87 %
39	D	22.89 % / 9.64 %
40	A	28.92 % / 14.45 %
41	D	28.92 % / 16.86 %
42	C	39.76 % / 15.66 %
43	C	54.22 % / 14.45 %
44	D	20.48 % / 19.28 %
45	A	39.76 % / 16.87 %
46	B	50.6 % / 14.46 %
47	D	60.24 % / 14.46 %
48	D	72.29 % / 12.05 %
49	D	72.29 % / 12.05 %
50	C	71.08 % / 10.85 %
51	C	50.6 % / 13.26 %
52	A	54.22 % / 12.05 %
53	D	60.24 % / 10.84 %
54	B	51.81 % / 12.05 %
55	C	32.53 % / 13.25 %
56	C	77.11 % / 10.84 %
57	B	80.72 % / 12.05 %
58	B	53.01 % / 12.05 %
59	B	43.37 % / 13.26 %
60	D	68.67 % / 12.05 %

//Hints and Solutions//

1. The centre of $C_1 = (2,1)$ and the radius $= \sqrt{2^2 + 1^2 + 11} = 4$

If (α, β) be the centre of C_2, $\sqrt{(\alpha - 2)^2 + (\beta - 1)^2} = 4 + 1$

$\Rightarrow \alpha^2 + \beta^2 - 4\alpha - 2\beta - 20 = 0$

Hence locus is $x^2 + y^2 - 4x - 2y - 20 = 0$

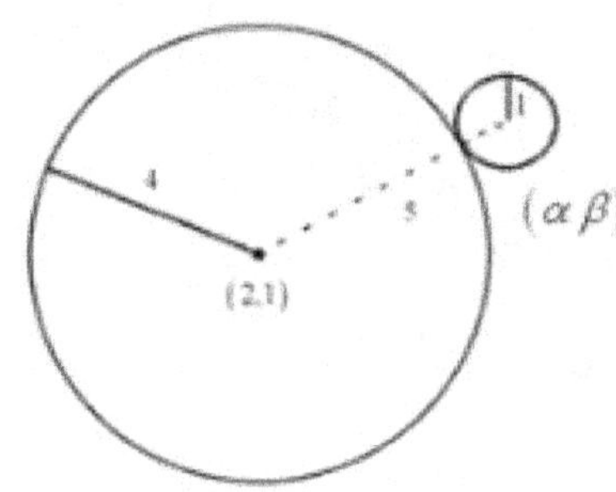

Hence, the correct option is (A).

2. From figure it is clear that ΔPRQ and ΔRSP are similar

$\therefore \dfrac{PR}{RS} = \dfrac{PQ}{RP}$

$\Rightarrow PR^2 = PQ \cdot RS$

$\Rightarrow PR = \sqrt{PQ \cdot RS}$

$\Rightarrow 2r = \sqrt{PQ \cdot RS}$

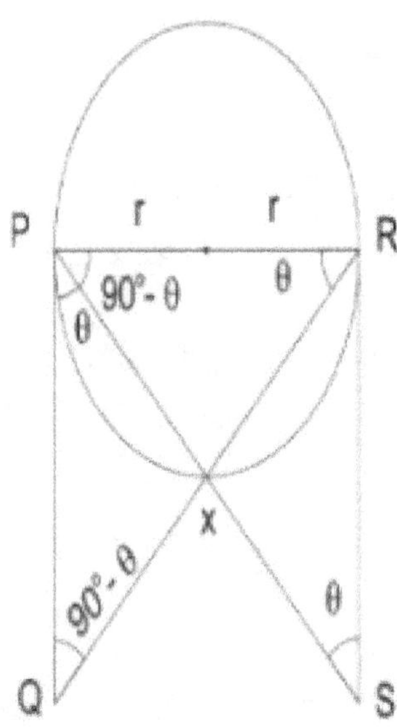

Hence, the correct option is (A).

3. since, fourtht

$$\left(\sqrt{x^{\left(\frac{1}{1+k_{10}ax}\right)}} + \sqrt[12]{x} \right)^6 = 200$$

$$\sqrt[6]{a_3}\left(\sqrt{x^{\left(\frac{1}{1+k_{18}ax}\right)}} \right)^3 \left(\sqrt[3]{x}\right)^3 = 200$$

$$\Rightarrow \frac{654}{123} \cdot x^{\frac{3}{2}\left(\frac{1}{1+k_{800}}\right)} \cdot x^{1/4} = 200$$

$$\Rightarrow x^{\frac{3}{2}\left(\frac{1}{1+\log_{10}x}\right)+\frac{1}{4}} = 10$$

Taking logarithm on both sides

$$\Rightarrow \left[\frac{3}{2}\left(\frac{1}{1+\log_{10}x}\right) + \frac{1}{4}\right]\log_{10}x = 1$$

Let $\log_{10}x = t$

$\therefore \quad \left\{\dfrac{3}{2(1+t)} + \dfrac{1}{4}\right\}t = 1$

$\Rightarrow \quad \left\{\dfrac{6+1+t}{4(1+t)}\right\}t = 1$

$\Rightarrow \quad t^2 + 7t = 4t + 4$

$t^2 + 3t - 4 = 0$

$\quad (t + 4)(t - 1) = 0$

$t = -4, 1$

$\qquad \log_{10}x = -4, 1$

$x = 10^{-4}, 10^1$

Hence, the correct option is (D).

4. cot A·cot B·cot C>0$\Rightarrow$cot A>0, cot B>0, cot C > 0

Because two or more of cot A, cot B, cot C cannot be negative at the same time in a triangle, as no two angle could be more then 90 degree.

Hence, the correct option is (B).

5. We have, $\vec{x} = \vec{b} - \left(\vec{a} \times \vec{x}\right)$

Taking dot product with $\vec{a}$ on both sides

$\vec{x} \cdot \vec{a} = \vec{b} \cdot \vec{a} - \left(\vec{a} \times \vec{x}\right) \cdot \vec{a}$

$= \vec{b} \cdot \vec{a}$

$= 0 \left(\because \vec{a} \perp \vec{b} \text{ given}\right)$

$\vec{x} = \vec{b} + \left(\vec{x} \times \vec{a}\right)$

$\vec{x} \times \vec{a} = \vec{b} \times \vec{a} + \left(\vec{x} \times \vec{a}\right) \times \vec{a}$

$$\vec{x} \times \vec{a} = \vec{b} \times \vec{a} + \left(\vec{x} \cdot \vec{a}\right)\vec{a} - \left(\vec{a} \cdot \vec{a}\right)\vec{x}$$

$$\vec{x} \times \vec{a} = \vec{b} \times \vec{a} - \vec{x}$$

Now $\vec{x} - \vec{b} = \vec{b} \times \vec{a} - \vec{x}$

$$\Rightarrow 2\vec{x} = \vec{b} + \vec{b} \times \vec{a}$$

$$\Rightarrow \left|2\vec{x}\right| = \left|\vec{b} + \vec{b} \times \vec{a}\right|$$

$$= \sqrt{\left|\vec{b}\right|^2 + \left|\vec{b} \times \vec{a}\right|^2}$$

$$= \sqrt{1^2 + (1.1 \cdot \sin 90°)^2}$$

$$= \sqrt{2}$$

$$\Rightarrow \left|\vec{x}\right| = \frac{1}{\sqrt{2}}$$

Hence, the correct option is (C).

6. We have: $\dfrac{1+i}{1-i} = \dfrac{1+i}{1-i} \times \dfrac{1+i}{1+i} = \dfrac{(1+i)^2}{1-i^2}$

$$= \dfrac{1+2i+i^2}{1-i^2}$$

$$= \dfrac{1+2i-1}{1+1} = \dfrac{2i}{2} = i$$

$$\therefore \left(\dfrac{1+i}{1-i}\right)^m = 1 \Rightarrow i^m = 1$$

$\Rightarrow m$ is a multiple of 4

Hence the smallest positive value of m is 4

Hence, the correct option is (A).

7. The equation of the circle passing through the intersection of the line $x + y = 1$ and the circle $x^2 + y^2 = 9$ is $x^2 + y^2 - 9 + k(x + y - 1) = 0$

$$\Rightarrow x^2 + y^2 + kx + ky - 9 - k = 0$$

radius $= \sqrt{\dfrac{k^2}{4} + \dfrac{k^2}{4} + 9 + k} = \dfrac{1}{2}\sqrt{(k+1)^2 + 17}$

radius is minimum when $k = -1$

Equation of circle is $x^2 + y^2 - x - y - 8 = 0$

Hence, the correct option is (B).

8. Let $(r + 1)$ th term be independent of x, then

$$T_{r+1} \overset{9}{=} C_r \left(ax^{\frac{1}{3}}\right)^{9-r} \left(bx^{-1/6}\right)^r$$

$$\overset{9}{=} C_r a^{9-r} \cdot b^r \cdot x^{3 - \frac{r}{3} - \frac{r}{6}}$$

As T_{r+1} is independent of x

$$\therefore \quad 3 - \frac{r}{3} - \frac{r}{6} = 0$$

$$\Rightarrow r = 6$$

$$\therefore \quad T_{6+1} = {}^9C_6 a^3 b^6 = {}^9C_3 a^3 b^6 = 84 a^3 b^6$$

$$\because AM \geq GM$$

$$\therefore \quad \frac{a^3 + b^6}{2} \geq \sqrt{a^3 b^6}$$

$$\Rightarrow \quad \frac{2}{2} \geq \sqrt{a^3 b^6}$$

$$\Rightarrow \quad a^3 b^6 \leq 1$$

or $84 a^3 b^6 \leq 84$

or $T_7 \leq 84$

$$\therefore \quad \text{Maximum value} = 84$$

Hence, the correct option is (D).

9. Given:

$$\tan\theta = \tan 30° \cdot \tan 60°$$

$$\Rightarrow \tan\theta = \frac{1}{\sqrt{3}} \times \sqrt{3}$$

$$\Rightarrow \tan\theta = 1$$

$$\Rightarrow \tan\theta = \tan 45°$$

$$\Rightarrow \theta = 45°$$

So,

$$2\theta = 2 \times 45°$$

$$\Rightarrow 2\theta = 90°$$

Hence, the correct option is (C).

10. For given function $f(x)$

$$f'(x) = 3x^2 + 2\lambda x + 5 + 2\cos 2x$$

since $\cos 2x \in [-1, 1]$

$$\Rightarrow 3x^2 + 2\lambda x + 3 \leq f'(x) \leq 3x^2 + 2\lambda x + 7$$

But $3x^2 + 2\lambda x + 7 \leq 0$ is not possible for all $x \in R$ for any λ

$\therefore f'(x) \geq 3x^2 + 2\lambda x + 3 \geq 0$ for all $x \Rightarrow D \leq 0$, i.e. $4\lambda^2 - 4 \cdot 3 \cdot 3 \leq 0$

or $\lambda^2 - 9 \leq 0 \Rightarrow -3 \leq \lambda \leq 3$

$\therefore$ if $-3 \leq \lambda \leq 3$, $f(x)$ is strictly $m.$ i. and so $f(x)$ is invertible.

Hence, the correct option is (B).

11. Consider a general point $P(\theta) \equiv (2\sec\theta, 2\tan\theta)$ On the given hyperbola

The tangent at $(2\sec\phi, 2\tan\phi)$ is $x\sec\phi - y\tan\phi = 2$

$\therefore a_1 = 2\cos\phi, b_1 = -2\cot\phi$

The normal at $(2\sec\phi, 2\tan\phi)$ is $x\cos\phi + y\cot\phi = 4$

$\therefore a_2 = 4\sec\phi, b_2 = 4\tan\phi$

$\therefore a_1a_2 + b_1b_2 = 8\cos\phi\sec\phi + (-2\cot\phi)(4\tan\phi)$
$= 8 - 8 = 0$

Hence, the correct option is (C).

12. Any point on the first line is $(4r + k, 2r + 1, r - 1)$, and any point on the second line is $(r' + k + 1, -r', 2r' + 1)$. The lines are intersecting if these two points coincide i.e

$4r + k = r' + k + 1, 2r + 1 = -r', r - 1 = 2r' + 1$ for some r and r'

$\Rightarrow 4r - r' = 1, 2r + r' = -1, r - 2r' = 2$

Now, $4r - r' = 1, 2r + r' = -1 \Rightarrow r = 0, r' = -1$ which satisfy $r - 2r' = 2$

$\Rightarrow$ The given lines are intersecting for all real values of 'k'

Hence, the correct option is (D).

13. Let α, β, γ be the angles, which the line makes with the positive directions of x -axis, y -axis and z-axis respectively.

$\therefore \quad \cos\alpha = \cos45° = \dfrac{1}{\sqrt{2}}, \cos\beta = \cos60° = \dfrac{1}{2}$

since $\cos^2\alpha + \cos^2\beta + \cos^2\gamma = 1$

$\therefore \quad \dfrac{1}{2} + \dfrac{1}{4} + \cos^2\gamma = 1$

$\Rightarrow \quad \cos^2\gamma = \dfrac{1}{4}$

$\Rightarrow \quad \cos\gamma = \pm\dfrac{1}{2}$

$\Rightarrow \quad \gamma = 60°$ or $120°$

Hence the line makes an angle of $60°$ with the positive direction of z-axis.

Hence, the correct option is (A).

14. Let $A(5,4,2)$ and $B(-1,-2,4)$ be the given points

Let $P(x, y, z)$ be the point, which divides the line segment $[AB]$ in the ratio -2: 3

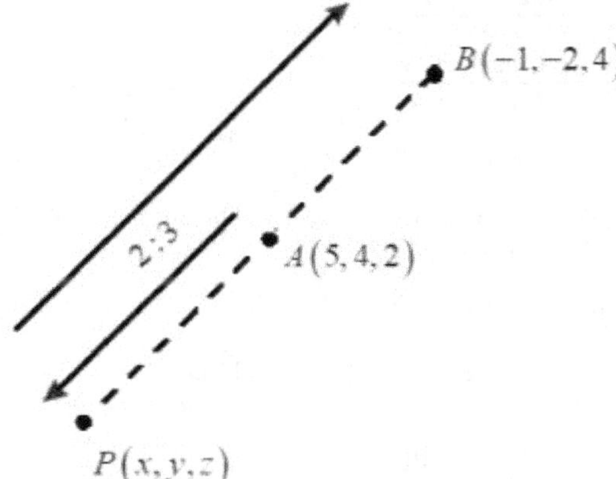

$\therefore$ The co-ordinates of P are

$\left(\dfrac{(-2)(-1)+3(5)}{-2+3}, \dfrac{(-2)(-2)+3(4)}{-2+3}, \dfrac{(-2)(4)+3(2)}{-2+3}\right)$

$= \left(\dfrac{2+15}{1}, \dfrac{4+12}{1}, \dfrac{-8+6}{1}\right) = (17,16,-2)$

Hence, the correct option is (A).

15. Let $A(2,6,-4)$ and $B(4,-2,3)$ be the two given vertices of the triangle. Let $C(\alpha, \beta, \gamma)$ be the third verte since $G(7,-2,5)$ is the centroid of ΔABC

$\therefore 7 = \dfrac{2+4+a}{3}, -2 = \dfrac{6-2+\beta}{3}$

$$5 = \dfrac{-4 + 3 + \gamma}{3}$$

$\Rightarrow \quad 6 + \alpha = 21, 4 + \beta = -6, -1 + \gamma = 15$
$\Rightarrow \quad \alpha = 15, \beta = -10, \gamma = 16$

Hence $C(15,-10,16)$ is the third vertex

Hence, the correct option is (A).

16. Let R be the radius of the circumcircle and 0 be the origin,
$\Rightarrow \quad R = x_1\sec\alpha$
$\Rightarrow \quad x_1 = R\cos\alpha$
Similarly, $x_2 = R\cos\beta$ and $x_3 = R\cos\gamma$
So, the coordinates of vertices are
$A(R\cos\alpha, R\sin\alpha), B(R\cos\beta, R\sin\beta), C(R\cos\gamma, R\sin\gamma)$
Hence, the coordinates of centroid G are

$$\left(\dfrac{\sum R\cos\alpha}{3}, \dfrac{\sum R\sin\alpha}{3}\right)$$

since, the orthocentre $H(a,b)$, circumcentre $O(0,0)$ and the centroid G are collinear therefore, slope of $OH =$ slope of OG

$$\Rightarrow \frac{b}{a} = \frac{R(\sin\alpha+\sin\beta+\sin\gamma)}{R(\cos\alpha+\cos\beta+\cos\gamma)}$$

$$\therefore \quad \frac{d}{b} = \frac{\cos\alpha+\cos\beta+\cos\gamma}{\sin\alpha+\sin\beta+\sin\gamma}$$

Hence, the correct option is (D).

17. Let $'l'(= b^2)$ and 'b' be the length and breadth respectively of the rectangle.

$\therefore A$, the area $= l \times b = b^2 \times b = b^3$

$\therefore \frac{dA}{dt} = 3b^2\frac{db}{dt} \Rightarrow 48 = 3b^2\frac{db}{dt} \quad \ldots (1)[\text{By the question}]$

But $l = b^2 \Rightarrow \frac{dl}{dt} = 2b\frac{db}{dt}$

$$\Rightarrow \frac{d\ell}{dt} = 2b \cdot \frac{1}{3b^2}\frac{dA}{dt}$$

$$= \frac{2}{3b}\frac{dA}{dt}$$

$$\Rightarrow \frac{dl}{dt}\bigg|_{b-4.5} = \frac{2\times48}{3\times45} = 7.11 cm/sec$$

Hence, the correct option is (A).

18. Given equation is $\ln(x + y) = 2xy$

For $x = 0$

$\ln(0 + y) = 2.0. y = 0$

$\Rightarrow \ln y = 0$

$\Rightarrow y = 1$

Now, differentiating (1), we get

$$\frac{1}{(x+y)}\left(1 + \frac{dy}{dx}\right) = 2y + 2x\frac{dy}{dx}$$

$\Rightarrow$ At point $(0,1)$

$$\left(\frac{1}{0+1}\right)\left(1 + \frac{dy}{dx}\right) = 2(1) + 2.0 \cdot \left(\frac{dy}{dx}\right)$$

$$\Rightarrow 1 + \frac{dy}{dx} = 2$$

$$\Rightarrow \frac{dy}{dx} = 1 = y'(0)$$

Hence, the correct option is (A).

19. Using the diagram, $OA \perp BC$

$\Rightarrow$ Slope of OA x slope of $BC = -1$

$$\frac{\beta-1}{\alpha+6} \times \frac{3+2}{-2-3} = -1$$

$$\Rightarrow \quad \beta - 1 = \alpha + 6$$

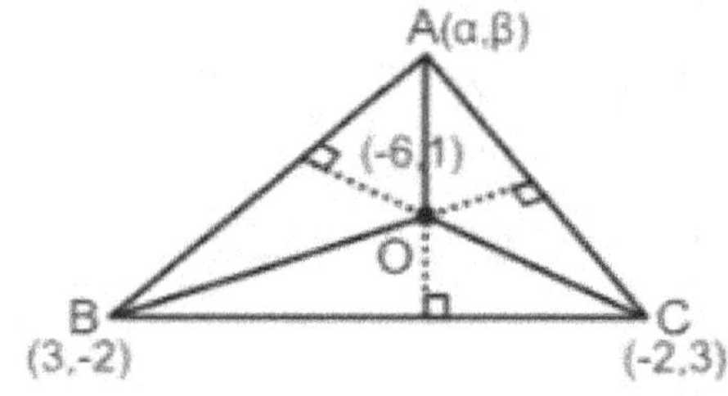

$$\therefore \quad \alpha - \beta + 7 = 0$$

Similarly $OB \perp AC$

$\Rightarrow$ Slope of OBx slope of $AC = -1$

$$\Rightarrow \quad \frac{-2-1}{3+6} \times \frac{\beta-3}{\alpha+2} = -1$$

$$\frac{\beta-3}{\alpha+2} = 3$$

$$\beta - 3 = 3\alpha + 6$$

$$\Rightarrow \quad 3\alpha - \beta + 9 = 0$$

Solving Eqs. (i) and (ii), we get

$$\alpha = -1, \beta = 6$$

$\therefore$ Third vertex is (-1,6)

Hence, the correct option is (B).

20. $\because {}^n P_r = 1680$

$$\Rightarrow \frac{n!}{(n-r)!} = 1680$$

and ${}^n C_r = 70$

$$\Rightarrow \frac{n!}{(n-r)!r!} = 70$$

From equation (i) and (ii), we get

$$r! = \frac{1680}{70} = 24 = 4! \Rightarrow r = 4$$

On putting the value of r in equation (i), we get $\frac{n!}{(n-4)!} = 1680$

$$\Rightarrow n(n - 1)(n - 2)(n - 3) = 1680$$

$$\Rightarrow n(n - 1)(n - 2)(n - 3) = 8(8 - 1)(8 - 2)(8 - 3)$$

$$\Rightarrow n = 8$$

$$\therefore 69n + r! = 69 \times 8 + 24 = 576$$

Hence, the correct option is (C).

21. Considering each column of circles, take the sum of the numbers. The sum number decides the position of the letter starting from A at being 1st position and Z at being 26th position. So,

1st column: 3+2+1+4=10 gives 10th position alphabet J.

2nd column: 5+9+4+6=24 gives the 24th position alphabet X.

3rd column: 2+1+3+3=9 gives 9th position alphabet I.

4th column: 8+4+9+5=26 gives 26th position alphabet Z.

5th column: 7+3+1+2=13 gives 13th position alphabet M.

Hence, the correct option is (C).

22. Mizoram is called "Bamboo Queen" because the maximum percentage of its geographical area is under bamboo forests as compared to other states of the country. It is the largest bamboo producing state in India.

Hence, the correct option is (B).

23. Cement blocks

A concrete masonry unit (CMU) is a standard size rectangular block used in building construction. CMUs are some of the most versatile building products available because of the wide variety of appearances that can be achieved using concrete masonry units.

Hence, the correct option is (A).

24. Earth day is celebrated worldwide on 22nd April to support environmental protection.Hence, the correct option is (A).

25. Viewing from the top, three surfaces will be visible, namely 1,2 and 3

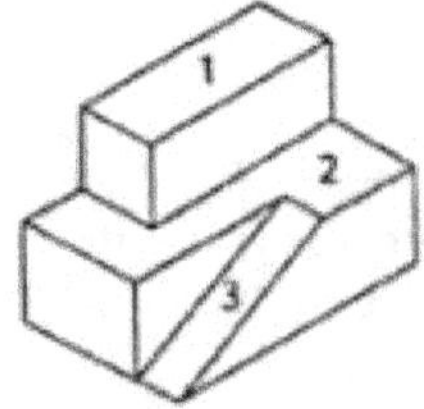

All given figures have three visible surfaces, namely 1,2 and 3:

(A)

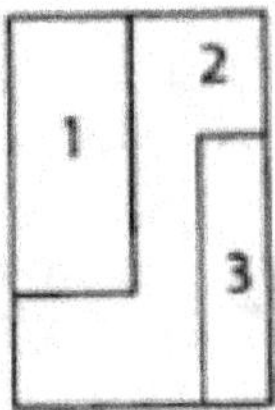

(B)

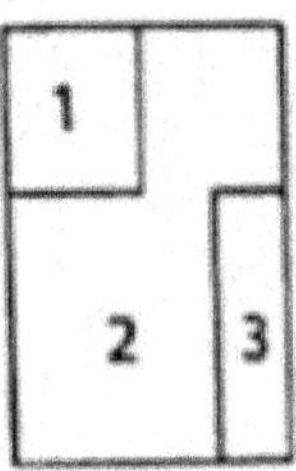

(C)

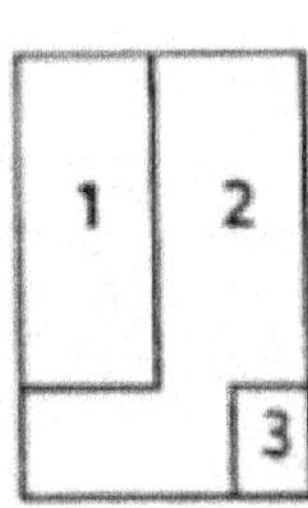

(D)

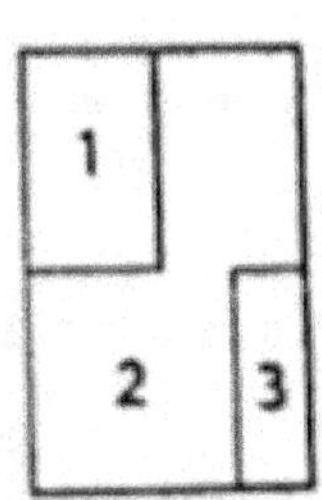

In figure B, surface 1 is not matching with given $3D$ figure.

In figure C, surface 3 is not matching with given $3D$ figure.

In figure D, surface 1 and 3 are not matching with given $3D$ figure

Figure A, is identical with the given $3D$ figure.

Hence, the correct option is (D).

26. The sequence follows this pattern:

$5 \times 2 - 4 = 6$

$6 \times 2 - 3 = 9$

$9 \times 2 - 2 = 16$

$16 \times 2 - 1 = \mathbf{31}$

Hence, the correct option is (C).

27. Given set Z of all integers, relation R as $(x, y) \in R$ if an if only if x is multiple of y.

The set is reflexive if every element of set is related to itself. Here, $\forall x \in Z : xRx; \forall y \in Z : yRy$. Hence set Z is reflexive set

The set is transitive if whenever an element x is related to an element y and x is related to an element w then x is also related to w. Here, or all $x, y, w \in Z$, if αxRy and yRw, then xRw. Hence set Z is transitive.

But set Z is not symmetric

Hence, the correct option is (D).

28. Hierarchy means objects, names, ranks, values, categories, etc., at different levels constituting a system. Here, the circles in figure D composition are of different sizes and placed systematically.

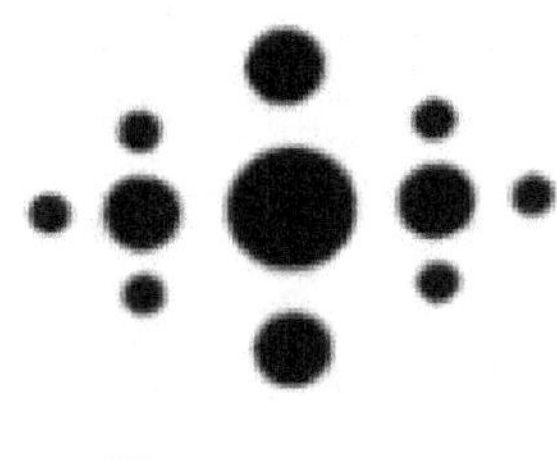

(D)

Hence, the correct option is (C).

29. In its 41st session on July 12, the **World Heritage** Committee inscribed 21 new **sites** in its **UNESCO world heritage list** which features the **Indian city** of Ahmedabad. Founded by Sultan Ahmad Shah in the 15th century, the ancient walled **city** of Ahmadabad has been marked as a **UNESCO world heritage** spot.

Hence, the correct option is (A).

30. The figure C compositon best fits variety because it includes shapes: squares, circles and a triangle, while all other compositions just include two of these shapes.

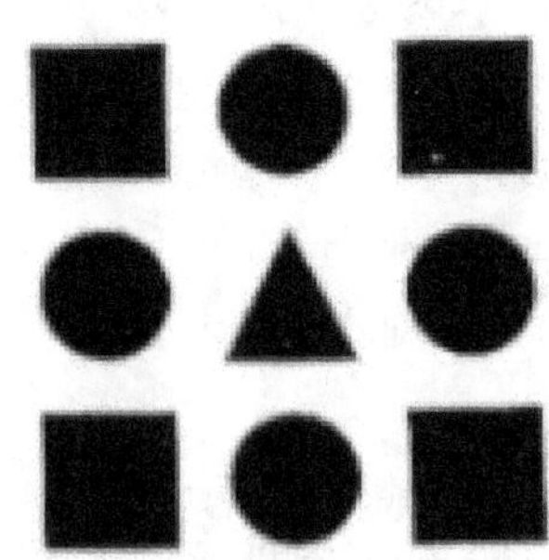

Hence, the correct option is (C).

31. Figure D is the odd figure as all other figures have their inner shapes aligned with the outer shapes, but in figure D the inner semicircles are misaligned with respect to the outer semicircles.

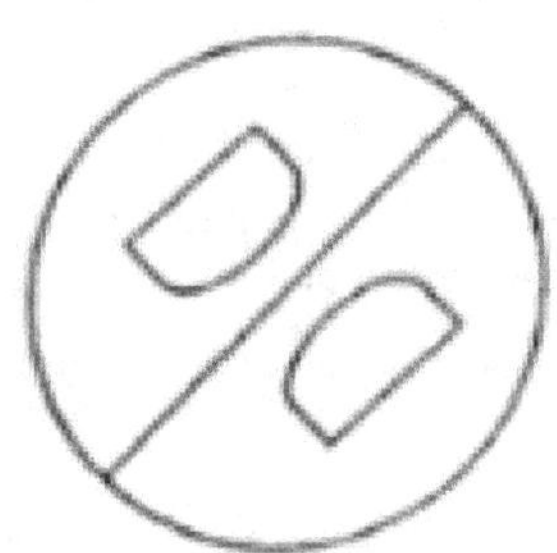

Hence, the correct option is (C).

32. During the construction of a building, foundation, roof framing structure, and column and beam constitute the structural parts of a building, and spaces are left in the design to incorporate doors and windows later.

Hence, the correct option is (B).

33. Paris is the capital of France. France and Italy are the two countries of the world. Hence, the best relation would be described by Figure C.

Hence, the correct option is (D).

34. The lines of symmetry for pentagon (Figure A), equilateral triangle (Figure C) and right-angled triangle (Figure D) pass through the vertex and the mid-point of the side opposite to that vertex. This line divides the polygon into two polygons having equal areas. But trapezium (Figure B) does not have a symmetrical line passing through vertex (although it is having a symmetrical line passing through the mid-points of parallel sides).

Hence, the correct option is (B).

35. Figure B best illustrates a colonnade as a row of evenly spaced columns supporting a roof, and entablature, or arches.

Hence, the correct option is (D).

36. Karnataka is a state in the south western region of India. The state covers an area of 191,976 square kilometres (74,122 sq mi), or 5.83 percent of the total geographical area of India.

Hence, the correct option is (C).

37. The Paris Agreement builds upon the Convention and for the first time brings all nations into a common cause to undertake ambitious efforts to combat climate change and adapt to its effects, with enhanced support to assist developing countries to do so. As such, it charts a new course in the global climate effort.

The Paris Agreement central aim is to strengthen the global response to the threat of climate change by keeping a global temperature rise this century well below 2 degrees Celsius above pre-industrial levels and to pursue efforts to limit the temperature increase even further to 1.5 degrees Celsius. Additionally, the agreement aims to strengthen the ability of countries to deal with the impacts of climate change. To reach these ambitious goals, appropriate financial flows, a new technology framework and an enhanced capacity building framework will be put in place, thus supporting action by developing countries and the most vulnerable countries, in line with their own national objectives. The Agreement also provides for enhanced transparency of action and support through a more robust transparency framework. Further information on key aspects of the Agreement can be found here.

Hence, the correct option is (A).

38.

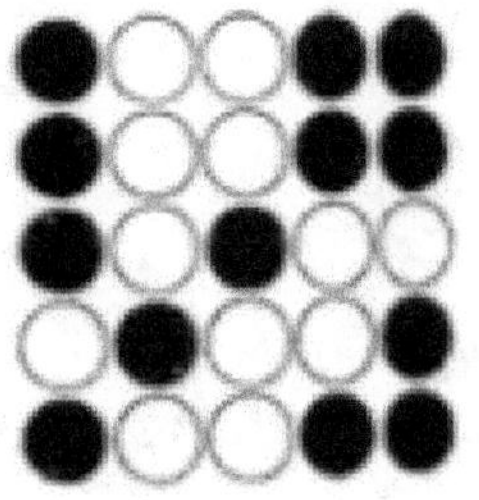

Hence, the correct option is (A).

39.

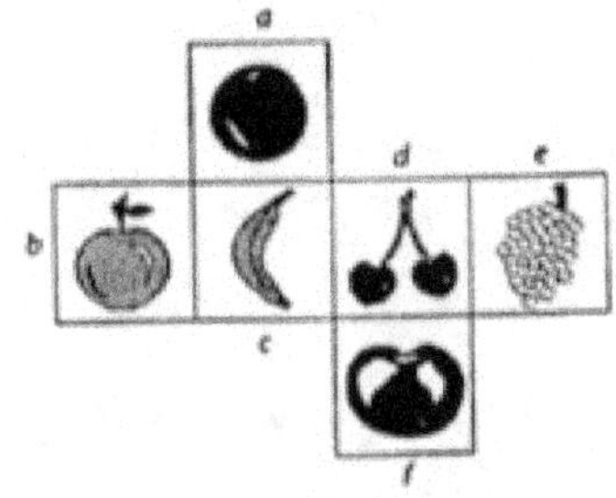

For cube A : Fruit a and fruit f should be on opposite faces, but they are adjacent. So, it is wrong.

For cube B. Fruit a is rotated by $90°$ when cube B is formed, which cannot happen. So, it is wrong.

For cube C : Fruit d, e and f are adjacent as they should be and their orientation is also correct. So, it is right.

For cube D : Fruit a is rotated by $90°$ when cube D is formed, which cannot happen. So, it is wrong.

Hence, the correct option is (D).

40. In isometric projection, three dimensional objects are represented in two dimensions. The three coordinate axes are drawn with the angle between any two of them as 120°.

Hence, the correct option is (A).

41. A hexagonal pyramid has 7 number of surfaces, 12 edges and 7 vertices. When it is cut horizontally in midway, then,

Number of surfaces $=8$

Number of edges $=18$

Number of vertices $=12$

Hence, the correct option is (D).

42. Let the sides of the equilateral triangle be a.

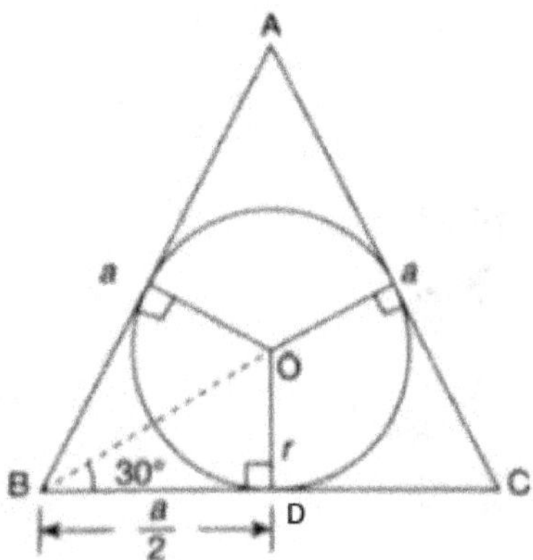

Area of equilateral triangle $= \sqrt{3}m^2$

$\Rightarrow \dfrac{\sqrt{3}}{4}a^2 = \sqrt{3}$

$\Rightarrow a^2 = 4$

$\Rightarrow a = 2$

So, in triangle BOD,

$\tan30° = \dfrac{r}{a/2}$

$\Rightarrow r = \dfrac{a}{2\sqrt{3}}$

$\Rightarrow r = \dfrac{1}{\sqrt{3}}$

Therefore, circumference $= 2\pi r = \dfrac{2\pi}{\sqrt{3}}m$

Hence, the correct option is (C).

43. 1 cm=2 m

25 m×40 m=12.5 cm×20 cm

Hence, the correct option is (C).

44. Given time =9:20

9:20 is corresponding to 2:40

After 15 min:

2:40+0:15=2:55

Hence, the correct option is (D).

45. Given

Diagonal of cube $= 6$

$\Rightarrow \sqrt{3}a = 6$

$\Rightarrow a = 2\sqrt{3}$

Therefore,

Volume of cube $= a^3 = \left(2\sqrt{3}\right)^3 = 24\sqrt{3}cm^3$

Hence, the correct option is (A).

46. Surfaces 1,2,3,4,5,6,7,8,9,10,11 and 12 are visible from the front Surtace 13 is the hidden surface opposite to Surface 7. Surtace 14 is the hidden surface of groove opposite to Surface 6. Surface 15 is the hidden bottom surface of the main block Surtaces 16 and 17 are the hidden side surfaces of the main block

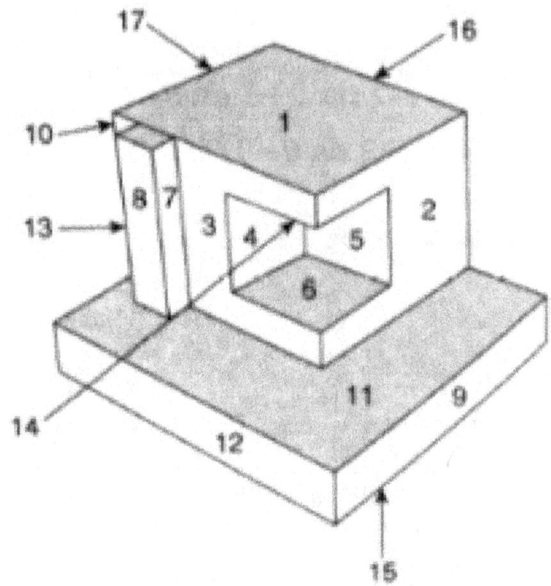

Hence, the correct option is (B).

47. Lintel is a horizontal support of timber, stone, concrete, or steel across the top of a door or window.Hence, the correct option is (D).

48. Commonly people think about pigment and in that case the color you get when mixing blue and red would be purple or violet. However, if you are referring to additive color (light), then the result of mixing red and blue light would be magenta.

Hence, the correct option is (D).

49. Texture refers to the way an object feels to the touch or looks as it may feel if it were touched. Texture is one of the seven elements of art. Understanding it fully will lead to stronger drawings and paintings. . Texture - element of art that refers to the way an object feels to the touch or looks as it may feel.

Hence, the correct option is (D).

50. World environment day is observed every year on 5 June, and it is the United Nation's principal vehicle for encouraging worldwide awareness and action for the protection of our environment.

Hence, the correct option is (C).

51. Gypsum is a chemically precipitated sedimentary rock formed by the evaporation of seawater and the precipitation of halite.

Hence, the correct option is (C).

52. Momentum, torque and impulse all have magnitude as well as direction, whereas energy only has magnitude. So, it is a scalar quantity.

Hence, the correct option is (A).

53. If both the floor and wall are smooth, then any heavy ladder resting on the floor and against a vertical wall may not be in equilibrium.

Hence, the correct option is (D).

54. The flat roof is such a roof, whose top finished surface has a slight slope to drain off rainwater. The construction of flat roof is similar to that of upper floors except that the top surface is made slightly sloping and also they are given such a treatment that they do not leak even in heavy rains. Flat roots may be constructed in RCC, flagstone, bricks, tiles, etc. Therefore, flat type of roofs is suitable in plains, where rainfall is meagre and temperature is high.

Hence, the correct option is (B).

55. The minimum angle that an inclined plane makes with the horizontal when a body placed on it just begins to slide down is called. Angle of repose is the minimum angle that an inclined plane makes with the horizontal when a body placed on it just begins to slide down.

Hence, the correct option is (C).

56. LED consumes least amount of energy. It is a special kind of diode that glows when electricity passes through it. Most LEDs are made from a semiconducting material.

Hence, the correct option is (C).

57. Green architecture is promoted these days because it is environment friendly and does not harm nature.Environmentally, green architecture helps in reducing pollution, conserve natural resources and prevent environmental degradation. ... Green architecture is growing exponentially. With increasing awareness among buyers, these days developers are trying to build their projects with green architecture concept.

Hence, the correct option is (B).

58. Architectural and building acoustics is concerned with improving the sound in rooms.Acoustics in buildings concerns controlling the quality and amount of sound inside a building. It is used to allow for pleasant sound in a concert hall and to reduce echoes and noise within an office building. Acoustics also concerns suppressing sound coming from outside the building, such as in apartments.

Hence, the correct option is (B).

59. Fly ash or flue ash, also known as pulverised fuel ash, it is a coal combustion product that is composed of the particulates (fine particles of burned fuel) that are driven out of coal-fired boilers together with the flue gases.

Hence, the correct option is (B).

60. Pondicherry was below the **influence** of the **French** for the longest of time , hence it is marked as the **French**. It is one of the important seen in it and is one of the union territory but it has

fresh vibe which start to explain the core existence in a fine manner.

Hence, the correct option is (D).

Mathematics

Q.1 The line x = c cuts the triangle with corners (0, 0), (1, 1) and (9, 1) into two regions. For the area of the two regions to be the same c must be equal to :

A. $\frac{5}{2}$ **B.** 3 **C.** $\frac{7}{2}$ **D.** 15 or 3

Q.2 The projection of any line on co-ordinate axes be respectively 3, 4, 5 then its length is:

A. 12 **B.** 50 **C.** $5\sqrt{2}$ **D.** 25

Q.3 A function y =f(x) has a second order derivative f"=6(x-1). If its graph passes through the point(2,1) and at that point the tangent to the graph is y =3x -5, then the function is :

A. $(x-1)^2$ **B.** $(x-1)^3$ **C.** $(x+1)^2$ **D.** $(x+1)^3$

Q.4 A bag contains 3 white, 3 black and 2 red balls. One by one, three balls are drawn without replacing them. Then the probability that the third ball is red , is given by:

A. $\frac{5}{24}$ **B.** $\frac{1}{12}$ **C.** $\frac{1}{4}$ **D.** $\frac{1}{2}$

Q.5 A five digit number is formed with digits 0. 1. 2. 3. 4 without repetition. A number is selected at random, then the probability that it is divisible by 4 is:

A. $\frac{1}{3}$ **B.** $\frac{5}{16}$ **C.** $\frac{1}{4}$ **D.** $\frac{4}{15}$

Q.6 A bag contains 'a' white and 'b' black balls. Two players A and B alternately draw a ball from the bag, replacing the ball each time after the draw. A begins the game. If the probability of A winning (that is drawing a white ball) is twice the probability of B winning, then the ratio a : b is equal to:

A. 1 : 2 **B.** 2 : 1 **C.** 1 : 1 **D.** 1 : 3

Q.7 The value of $\cos^{-1}(\cos 12) - \sin^{-1}(\sin 14)$ is:

A. -2 **B.** $8\pi-26$

C. $4\pi+2$ **D.** one of these

Q.8 Total number of positive integral value of 'n' such that the equations $\cos^{-1}x + (\sin^{-1}y)^2 = \frac{n\pi^2}{4}$ and $(\sin^{-1}y)^2 - \cos^{-1}x = \frac{\pi^2}{16}$ are consistent, is equal to :

A. 1 **B.** 4 **C.** 3 **D.** 2

Q.9 If A=(1,3,-5) and B=(3,5,-3), then the vector equation of the plane passing through the midpoint of AB and perpendicular to AB is :

A. (^i+^j+^k)=2 **B.** (^i+^j−^k)=2
C. (^i−^j+^k)=2 **D.** None

Q.10 If 5a + 4b + 20c = t, then the value of t for which the line ax + by + c - 1 = 0 always passes through a fixed point is :

A. 0 **B.** 20
C. 30 **D.** None of these

Q.11 The equation of the pair of straight lines parallel to the y - axis and which are tangents to the circle x2+ y2- 6x - 4y - 12 = 0 is :

A. x^2 - 4x - 21 = 0 **B.** x^2 - 5x + 6 = 0
C. x^2 - 6x - 16 = 0 **D.** None of these

Q.12 If the perpendicular distance of a point other than the origin from the plane x+y+z=p is equal to the distance of the plane from the origin, then the coordinates of the point are:

A. (p, 2 p, 0) **B.** (0, 2p, -p)
C. (2p, p, -p) **D.** (2p, -p, 2p)

Q.13 What is the equation of the tangent to the parabola y2- 2x-6y+5=0 at the point (-2,3)? How can I find it?

A. -2 **B.** 3 **C.** 4 **D.** 5

Q.14 The equations of the tangents of the parabola y^2 = 12x, which passes through the point (2,5).

A. 2y = 3x + 4, y = x + 3
B. 2y = 3x − 4, y = x + 3
C. y = 3x + 4, y = x − 3
D. 2y = 3x − 4, y = x − 3

Q.15 The approximate value of square root of 25.2 is :

A. 5.01 **B.** 5.02 **C.** 5.03 **D.** 5.04

Q.16 If the lines $\frac{x-1}{2} = \frac{y1}{3} = \frac{z-1}{4}$ and $\frac{x-3}{1} = \frac{y-k}{2} = \frac{z}{1}$ intersect, then the value ofk is:

A. $\frac{3}{2}$ **B.** $\frac{9}{2}$ **C.** $-\frac{2}{9}$ **D.** $-\frac{3}{2}$

Q.17 With reference to a universal set, the inclusion of a subset in another, is relation, which is:

A. Symmetric only
B. Equivalence relation
C. Reflexive only
D. None of these

Q.18 Let f (x) = sinx + ax + b. Then f(x) = 0 has:

A. only one real root which is positive i a > 1, b <0
B. only one real root which is negative if a > 1, b <0
C. only one real root which is negative if a < - 1, b >0
D. Can't say anything

Q.19 If $f: R \to R, g: R \to R$ and $h: R \to R$ are such that $f(x) = x^2, g(x) = \tan x$ and $h(x) = \log x$, then the value of (ho (gof)) (x) if $x = \sqrt{\frac{\pi}{4}}$ will be:

A. 0 **B.** 1 **C.** -1 **D.** π

Q.20 If x = 9 is the chord of contact of the hyperbola $x^2 - y^2 = 9$, then the equation of the corresponding pair of tangents is:

A. $9x^2 - 8y^2 18x - 9 = 0$
B. $9x^2 - 8y^2 - 18x + 9 = 0$
C. $9x^2 - 8y^2 - 18x - 9 = 0$
D. $9x^2 - 8y^2 18x9 = 0$

General Aptitude

Q.21 National Archives is located at?
A. Calcutta   **B.** Dehradun
C. Bombay   **D.** New Delhi

Q.22 Which is known as 'Garden City of India'?
A. Trivandram   **B.** Imphal
C. Simla   **D.** Bangalore

Q.23 The Central Rice Research institute is located at:
A. Rajamundry   **B.** Madra
C. Cuttack   **D.** Cochin

Q.24 Where is the 'National Remote Sensing Agency' situated?
A. Shadnagar   **B.** Bangalore
C. Chennai   **D.** Dehradun

Q.25 Badrinath is situated on the bank of river:
A. Ganga   **B.** Yamuna
C. Alaknanda   **D.** Saraswathi

Q.26 Indian Cancer Research institute is located at:
A. New Delhi   **B.** Calcutta
C. Chennai   **D.** Mumbai

Q.27 Ajanta-Ellora caves are situated near:
A. Ajmer   **B.** Jaipur
C. Patna   **D.** Aurangabad

Q.28 Identify the structure-

A. Rashtrapati Bhavan   **B.** Parliament House
C. Red Fort   **D.** Taj mahal

Q.29 A 3-D problem figure is given below. Identify the correct top view from the options-

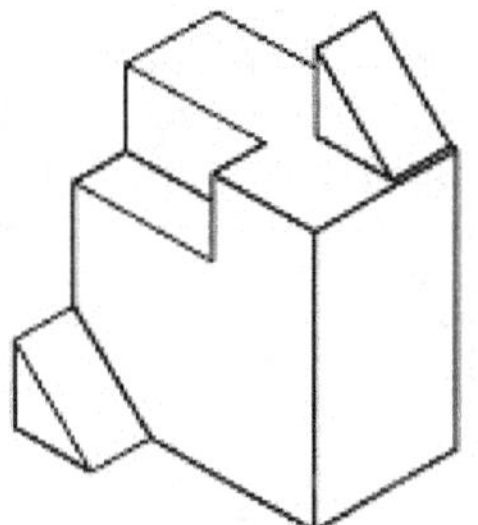

A.

B.
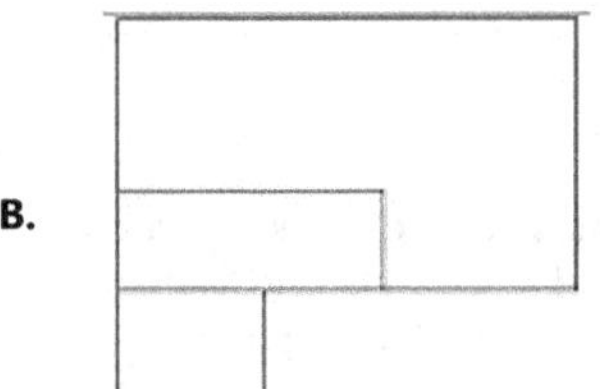

C.
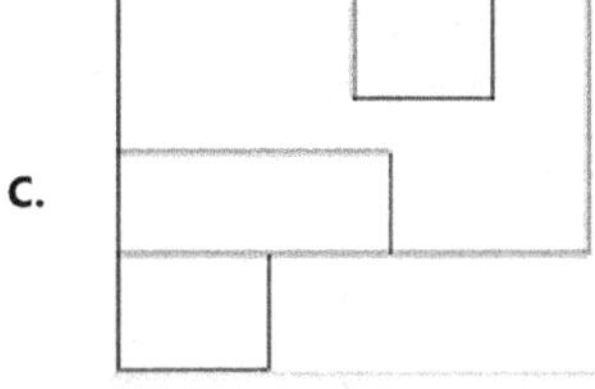

D.
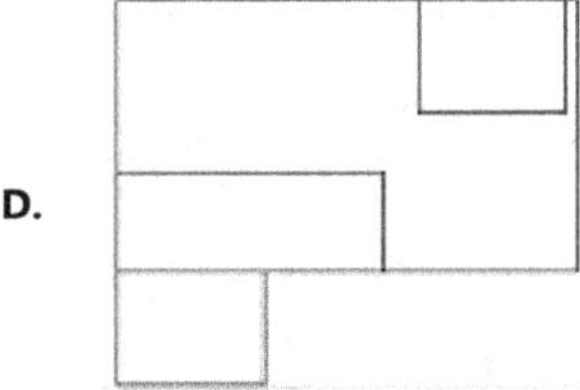

Q.30 Identify the structure-

A. Colossus of Rhodes
B. Statue of liberty
C. Pharos of Alexandria
D. Pharos of Alexandria

Q.31 The below question consists of problem figures and followed by four answer figures (A), (B), (C) and (D). Find out the figure from the answer figures which will continue the given series.

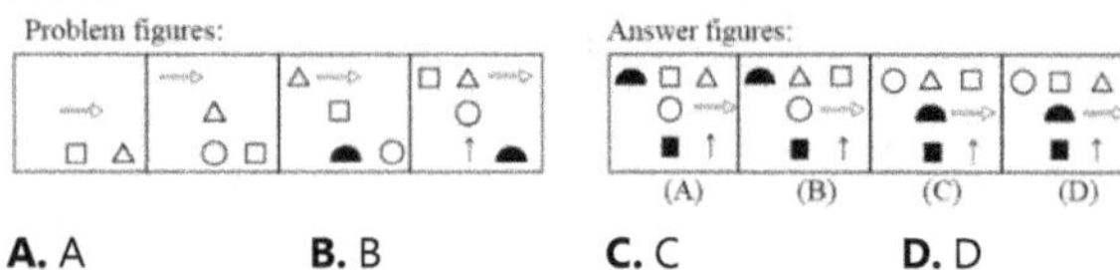

A. A   **B.** B   **C.** C   **D.** D

Q.32 The below question consists of problem figures and followed by four answer figures (A), (B), (C) and (D). Find out the figure from the answer figures which will continue the given series.

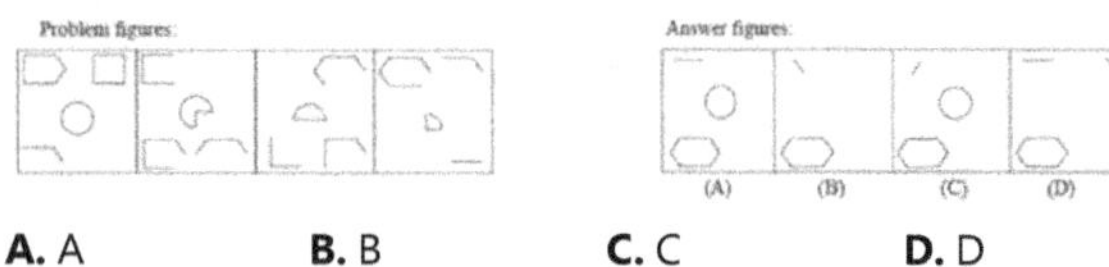

A. A   **B.** B   **C.** C   **D.** D

Q.33 The below question consists of a set of three figures K, L and M showing a sequence of folding of a piece of paper. Figure M shows the manner in which the folded paper has been cut. These three figures are followed by four figures (1), (2), (3) and (4) from which you have to choose a figure which would most closely resemble the unfolded form of figure M.

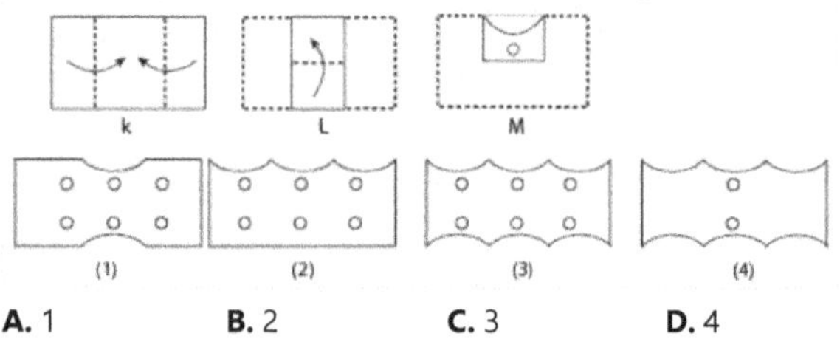

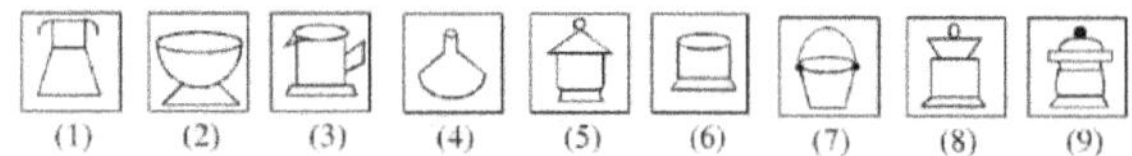

A. 1   **B.** 2   **C.** 3   **D.** 4

Q.34 A series of figures is given which can be grouped into classes. Select the group into which the figures can be classified from the given responses.

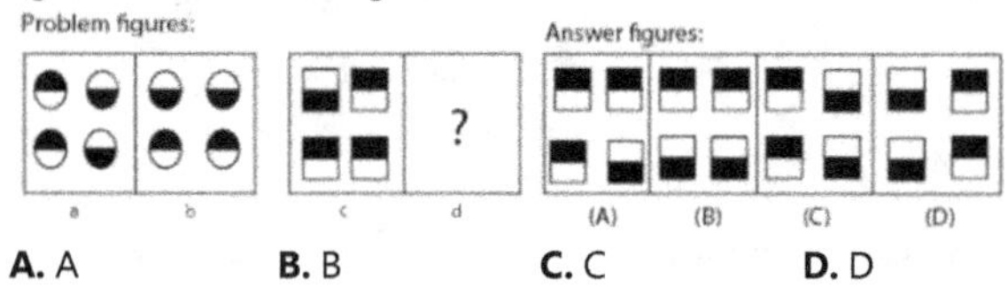

A. 1, 4, 7, 2, 5, 9, 3, 8, 6
B. 2, 6, 9, 1, 4, 7, 5, 8, 3
C. 1, 4, 7, 2, 3, 6, 5, 8, 9
D. 3, 5, 1, 4, 7, 8, 6, 2, 9

Q.35 The below question consists of two pairs of figures a, b and c,d are given as problem figures and followed by four answer figures as (A), (B),(C) and (D). Select the answer figure that will replace figure 'd' of problem figures, so that relation is established between figure 'c' and 'd' similar to the relation that figure 'a' holds with figure 'b'.

A. A   **B.** B   **C.** C   **D.** D

Q.36 The below question consists of a problem figures and followed by answer figures marked as (A), (B), (C) and (D). You have to select that figure from the set of answer figures which would come in the place of question mark (?) in the problem figure.

Problem Figure

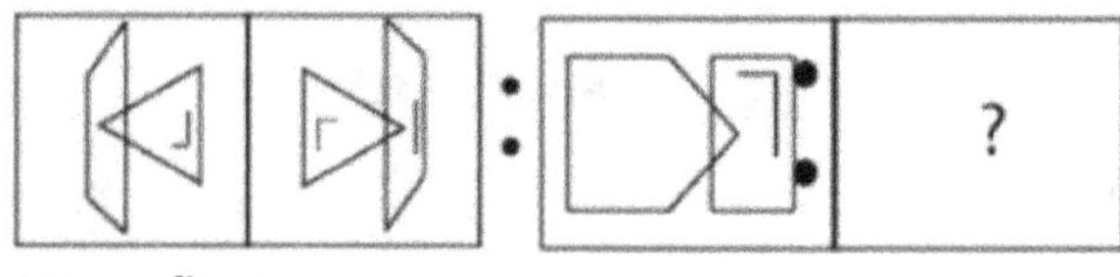

Answer figure

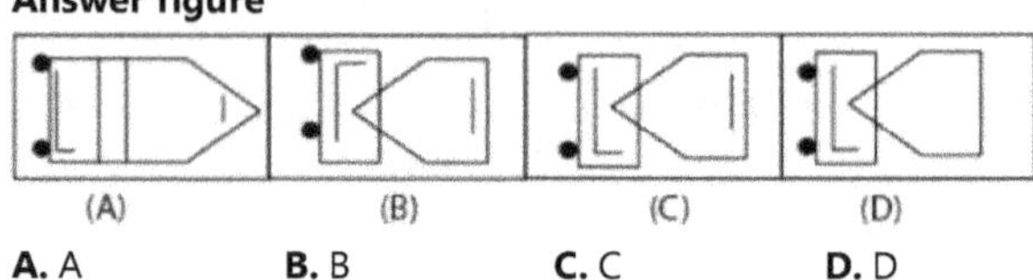

A. A   **B.** B   **C.** C   **D.** D

Q.37 The below question consists of a question figure and followed by four figures (1), (2), (3) and (4), which show the possible water images of the question figure. Choose one out of these four figures which shows the correct water image of the question figure.

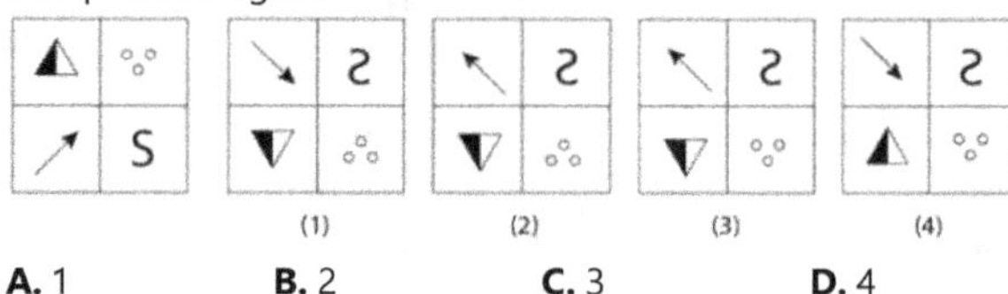

A. 1   **B.** 2   **C.** 3   **D.** 4

Q.38 The below question consists of a question figure and followed by four figures (a), (b), (c) and (d). Choose one out of these four figures that can replace '?' to complete the question figure.

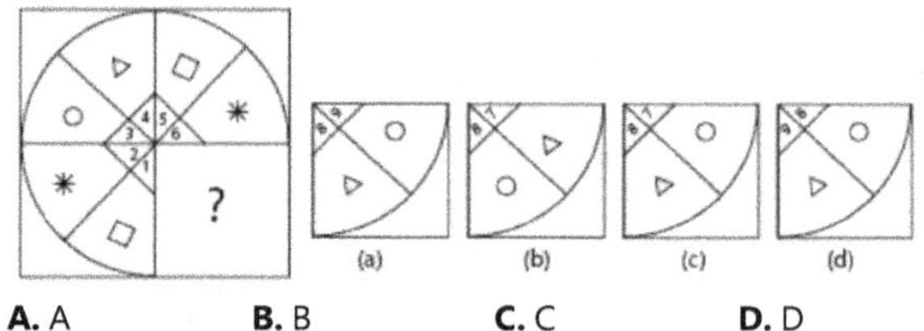

A. A   **B.** B   **C.** C   **D.** D

Q.39 Identify the type of dome in the given image

A. Circular dome   **B.** Onion dome
C. Spherical dome   **D.** None of the above

Q.40 Direction: The sheet of paper shown in figure A given on the leftmost side, in each question, is folded to form a box. Choose from amongst the alternatives 1, 2, 3, and 4, the boxes that are similar to the box that will be formed.

Which option has boxes that are similar to the box made from the given sheet of paper A?

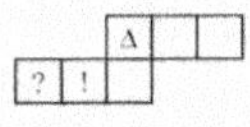 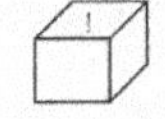 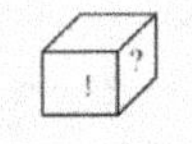 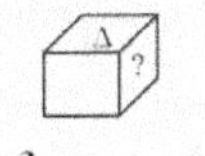 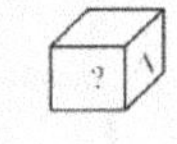

A   1   2   3   4

A. 2 & 3 only

B. 1, 2 & 3 only

C. 1, 2, 3 & 4

D. 1 only

Q.41 Find out the correct alternative that looks like figure (X) after rotation.

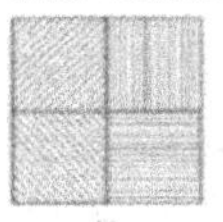 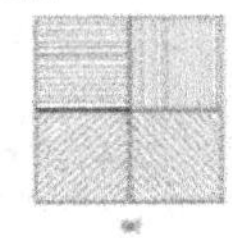 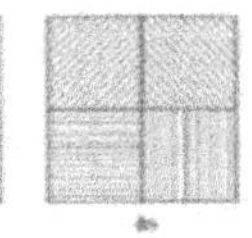 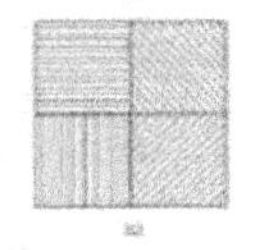 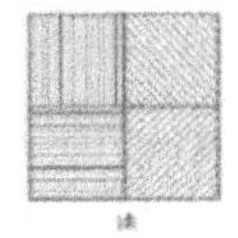

A. A   **B.** B   **C.** C   **D.** D

Q.42 In the below question, one or more dots are placed in the problem figure (X) followed by four alternatives (a), (b), (c) and (d). One out of these four alternatives contain region(s) common to the circle, square, triangle and rectangle similar to that marked by the dot in figure (X).

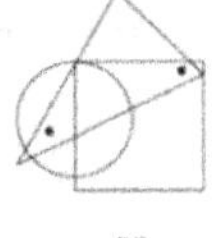 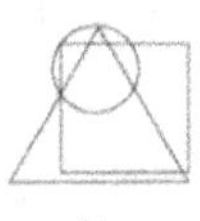 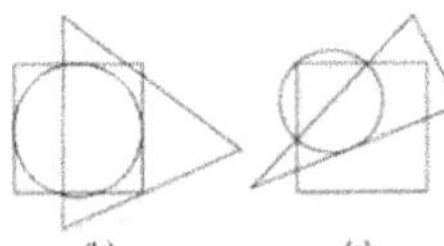 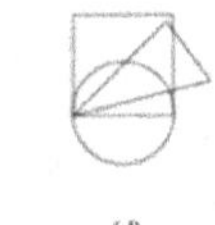

(X)   (a)   (b)   (c)   (d)

A. A   **B.** B   **C.** C   **D.** D

Q.43 The below question consists of figure (Y) and followed by four alternatives (1), (2), (3) and (4). Choose the correct alternative among the four alternatives such that the pattern would appear like when the figure (Y) is folded at the do tted line.

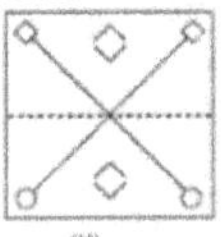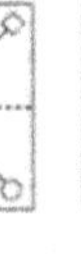 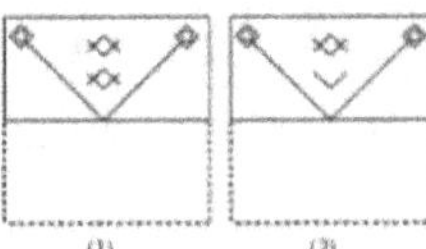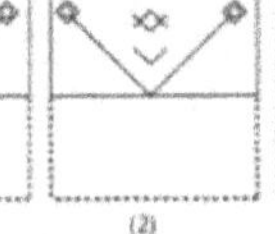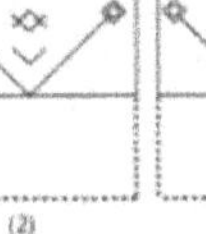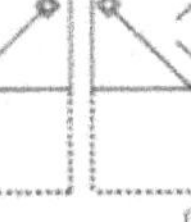 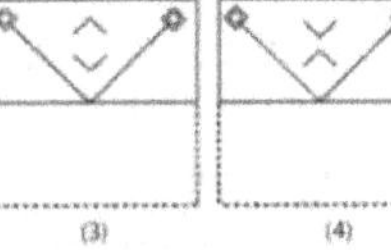

(Y)   (1)   (2)   (3)   (4)

A. 1   **B.** 2   **C.** 3   **D.** 4

Q.44 The below question consists of a combination of alphabets and numbers followed by four alternatives (a), (b), (c) and (d). Choose the alternative which is closely resembles the mirror image of the given combination.

t e s t 5 a n d

(a) t ɘ ƨ t ʮ ƨ ɒ n b   (c) q n ɒ ƨ t ƨ ɘ t

(b) t ɘ ƨ t 5 ɒ n q   (d) b n ɒ ʮ t ƨ ɘ t

A. A   **B.** B   **C.** C   **D.** D

Q.45 What is the minimum number of different colours required to paint the given figure such that no two adjacent regions have the same colour?

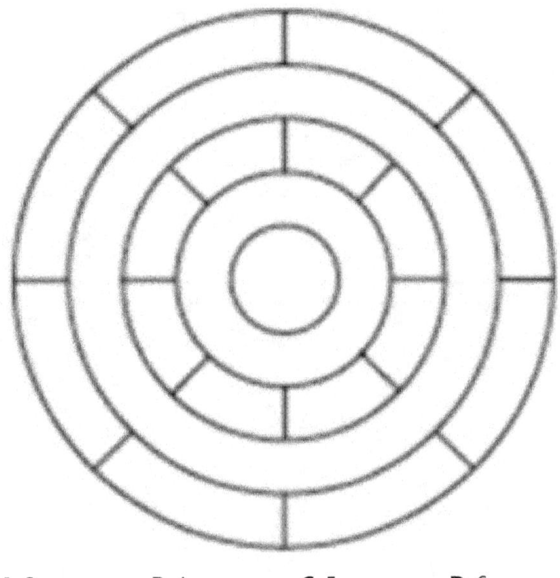

A. 3   **B.** 4   **C.** 5   **D.** 6

Q.46 Two different positions of unbiased dice are shown in the figure below. Which digit should appear on the face opposite to the face with the digit 4?

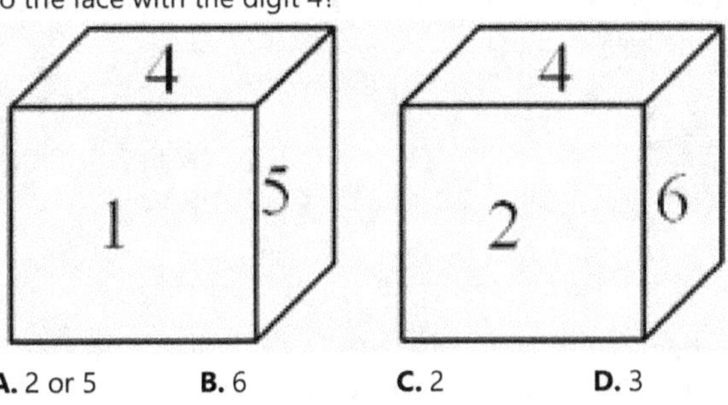

A. 2 or 5   **B.** 6   **C.** 2   **D.** 3

Q.47 The below question consists of a four figures. Three are similar in a certain way and so form a group. Find out which one of the figures does not belong to that group.

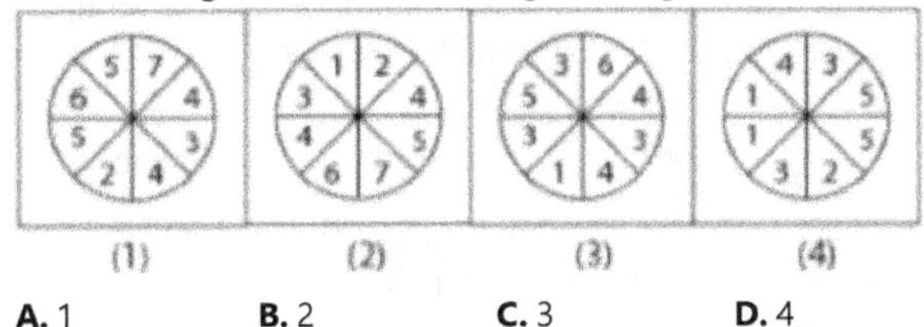

(1)   (2)   (3)   (4)

A. 1   **B.** 2   **C.** 3   **D.** 4

Q.48 Choose the correct alternative which contains figure (X) as its part.

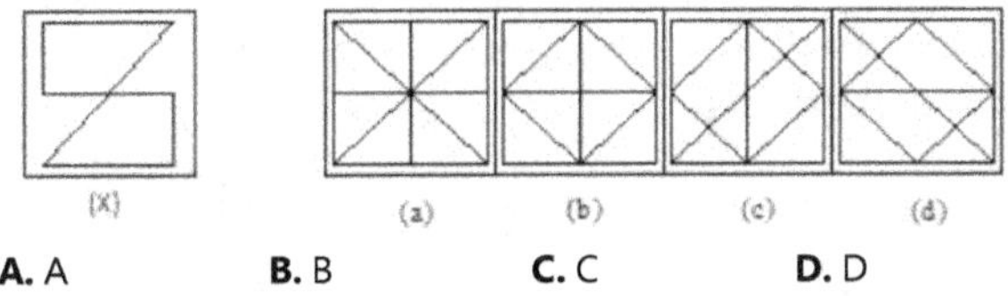

(X)   (a)   (b)   (c)   (d)

A. A   **B.** B   **C.** C   **D.** D

Q.49 Which one of the given set of figures violates the given rule?

Rule: A new bigger element is added to the previous elements.

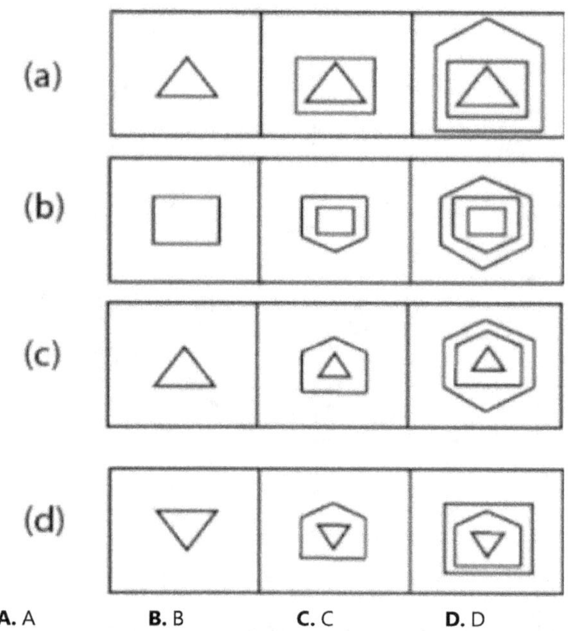

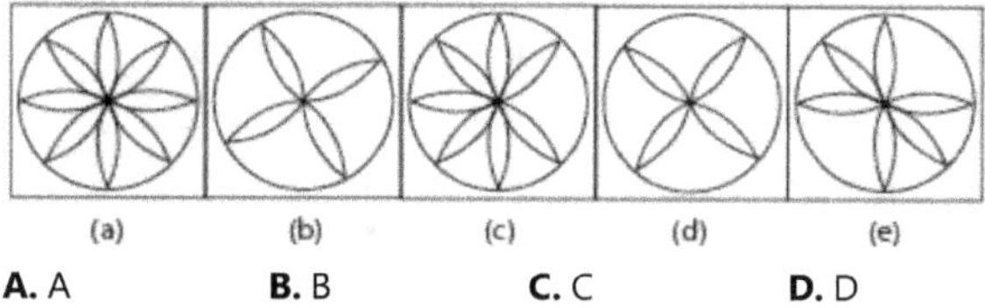

A. A   B. B   C. C   D. D

Q.50 The below question consists of a five figures. Four are similar in a certain way and so form a group. Find out which one of the figures does not belong to that group.

A. A   B. B   C. C   D. D

Q.51 Direction : In each of the following questions, select the related word/letters/number from the given alternatives.

CEIM :DGLQ : : FGIO : ?

A. GILS   **B.** GMSI   **C.** GMIS   **D.** GLIS

Q.52 Direction : In each of the following questions, select the related word/letters/number from the given alternatives.

G - 12 : Canada :: G - 5 :

A. France   **B.** Japan   **C.** Mexico   **D.** Belgium

Q.53 Which one set of letter when sequentially placed at the gaps in the given series will be complete it.

m_no mm_n_m_nno_

A. mnoon   **B.** mnomo   **C.** mnoom   **D.** monom

Q.54 From the given alternative words, select the word which cannot be formed using the letters of the given word:

TITATORNTEATUIAL

A. TUTION   **B.** TEAR
C. TYRE   **D.** TATA

Q.55 Select the number which can be placed at the sign of the question mark (?) from the given alternatives.

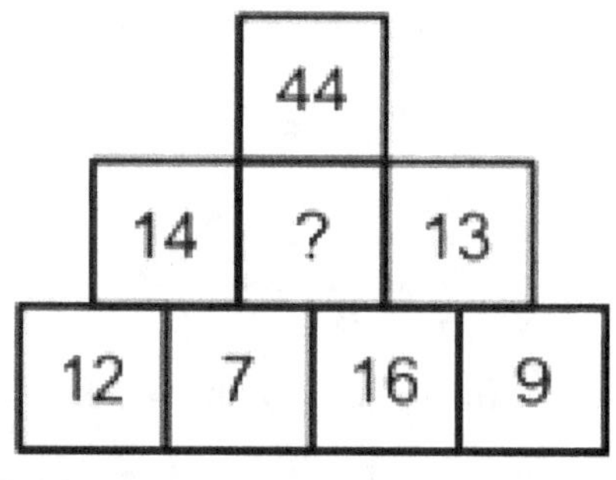

A. 17   **B.** 12   **C.** 16   **D.** 11

Q.56 In a certain code language, 'sky' means 'red', 'red' means 'tomato', 'tomato' means 'milk', 'milk' means 'soil' and 'soil' means 'white'. In the given code language where does a plant grow?

A. Soil   **B.** White   **C.** Red   **D.** Tomato

Q.57 In this Question consists of a set three figures X, Y and Z showing a sequence of folding of a piece of paper. Figure (Z) shows the manner which the folded paper has been cut. These three figures are followed by four answer figures from which you have to choose a figure which would most closely resemble the unfolded form of figure (Z).

Question Figure:

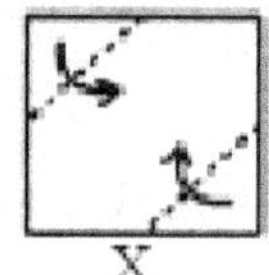 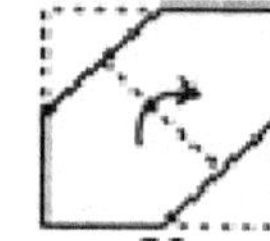 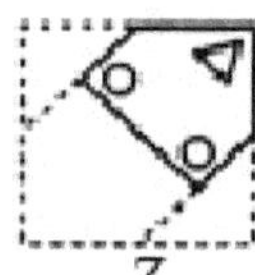

X   Y   Z

Answer Figures:

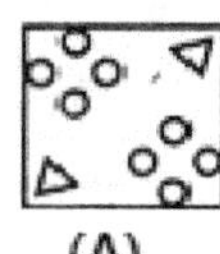 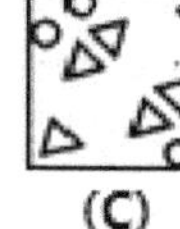 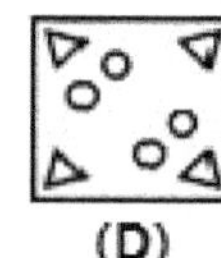

(A)   (B)   (C)   (D)

A. A   B. B   C. C   D. D

Q.58 T is the sister of U. U is the son of M. M is husband of A. N is the husband of T. On the basis of the information, find out how is N related to A?

A. Son-in -Law   **B.** Brother
C. Father   **D.** Sister

Q.59 House, bedroom and bathroom are best represented by which venn diagram?

 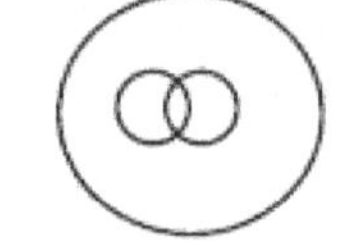

A. A   B. B   C. C   D. D

Q.60 What will be the mirror image of given figure?

Question figure

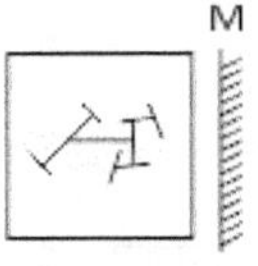

Answer figure

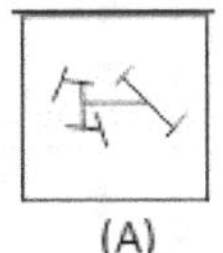

(A)

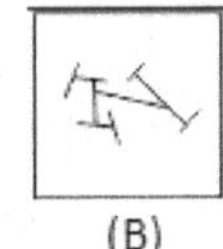

(B)

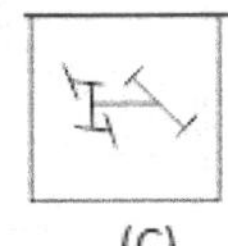

(C)

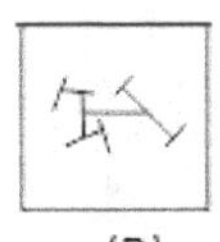

(D)

A. A	**B.** B	**C.** C	**D.** D

// Smart Answer Sheet //

Correct — Percentage of students who answered correctly. **Skipped** — Percentage of students who skipped.

Q.	Ans.	Correct / Skipped	Q.	Ans.	Correct / Skipped	Q.	Ans.	Correct / Skipped	Q.	Ans.	Correct / Skipped	Q.	Ans.	Correct / Skipped
1	B	21.21 % / 39.4 %	13	A	19.7 % / 45.45 %	25	C	34.85 % / 15.15 %	37	A	66.67 % / 15.15 %	49	D	54.55 % / 16.66 %
2	C	16.67 % / 40.91 %	14	A	19.7 % / 45.45 %	26	D	45.45 % / 18.19 %	38	C	72.73 % / 15.15 %	50	C	56.06 % / 13.64 %
3	B	27.27 % / 43.94 %	15	B	21.21 % / 42.43 %	27	D	75.76 % / 13.63 %	39	B	66.67 % / 13.63 %	51	A	68.18 % / 16.67 %
4	C	19.7 % / 48.48 %	16	B	19.7 % / 48.48 %	28	A	83.33 % / 13.64 %	40	C	22.73 % / 27.27 %	52	C	37.88 % / 16.67 %
5	B	27.27 % / 42.43 %	17	D	10.61 % / 42.42 %	29	D	74.24 % / 15.15 %	41	C	46.97 % / 15.15 %	53	B	48.48 % / 15.16 %
6	C	18.18 % / 48.49 %	18	A	13.64 % / 51.51 %	30	B	84.85 % / 13.63 %	42	A	39.39 % / 16.67 %	54	C	74.24 % / 15.15 %
7	D	12.12 % / 43.94 %	19	A	21.21 % / 46.97 %	31	D	54.55 % / 18.18 %	43	C	57.58 % / 16.66 %	55	A	27.27 % / 13.64 %
8	A	15.15 % / 54.55 %	20	B	22.73 % / 42.42 %	32	B	34.85 % / 16.67 %	44	D	63.64 % / 15.15 %	56	B	62.12 % / 18.18 %
9	A	27.27 % / 43.94 %	21	D	51.52 % / 18.18 %	33	C	72.73 % / 16.66 %	45	A	51.52 % / 13.63 %	57	A	66.67 % / 16.66 %
10	B	24.24 % / 50.0 %	22	D	56.06 % / 15.15 %	34	C	69.7 % / 15.15 %	46	D	27.27 % / 28.79 %	58	A	69.7 % / 16.66 %
11	C	27.27 % / 48.49 %	23	C	40.91 % / 18.18 %	35	A	56.06 % / 18.18 %	47	C	37.88 % / 18.18 %	59	C	60.61 % / 13.63 %
12	C	24.24 % / 43.94 %	24	A	30.3 % / 16.67 %	36	C	54.55 % / 16.66 %	48	A	81.82 % / 15.15 %	60	A	71.21 % / 15.15 %

//Hints and Solutions//

1. Equation $OB: y - 1 = \frac{2}{x} - 5)$

$\Rightarrow 9y = x$

$\Rightarrow E\left(c, \frac{c}{5}\right)$

Area of $\triangle OAB = \frac{1}{2} \times h \times AB = \frac{1}{2} \times 1 \times 8 = 4$

$\Rightarrow$ Area of BDE $= \frac{4}{2} = 2$

$\Rightarrow \frac{1}{2}\begin{vmatrix} C & 1 & 1 \\ 9 & 1 & 1 \\ C & \frac{C}{5} & 1 \end{vmatrix} R_1 \to R_1 - R_2 \Rightarrow \frac{1}{2}\begin{vmatrix} C-9 & 0 & 1 \\ 9 & 1 & 1 \\ C & \frac{C}{5} & 1 \end{vmatrix}$

$= \left| \frac{1}{2}(C - 5) \right.$

$\left(1 - \frac{C}{5}\right| = 2 \Rightarrow |(C-9)(5-C)| = 36 \Rightarrow$

$-(C-9)^2 = 36 \Rightarrow (C-9)^2 = 36 \Rightarrow C - 9 = \pm 6$

$\Rightarrow C = 15 \quad$ or $\qquad\qquad 3$

Hence, the correct option is (B).

2. Solution Let the line segment be AB, then as given

$AB\cos\alpha = 3, AB\cos\beta = 4, AB\cos\gamma = 5$

$\Rightarrow AB^2(\cos^2\alpha + \cos^2\beta + \cos^2\gamma) = 3^2 + 4^2 + 5^2$

$$AB = \sqrt{9 + 16 + 25} = 5\sqrt{2}$$

where α, β and γ are the angles made by the line with the axes.

Hence, the correct option is (C).

3. Solution since $f''(x) = 6(x - 1)$

$\Rightarrow f'(x) = 3(x - 1)^2 + c$ (integrating)

Also, at the point (2,1) , the tangent to the graph is $y = 3x - 5$ and slope of thetangent $= 3 \Rightarrow f'(2) = 3$

$3(2 - 1)^3 + c = 3[$ from eq (i)

$\Rightarrow 3 + c = 3 \Rightarrow c = 0$

From Eq (i) we have $f'(x) = 3(x - 1)^2$

$\Rightarrow f(x) = (x - 1)^3 + k$ (Integrating)

$\therefore 1 = (2 - 1)^3 + k \Rightarrow k = 0$

Hence the equation of the function is $f(x) = (x - 1)^3$

Hence, the correct option is (B).

4. Solution Number of white balls $= 3$, black balls $= 3$ red balls $= 2$ since drawn balls are not replaced, for third ball to red, we have following

patterns:

$E_1 = WWR, BBR, E_2 = BWR, WBR$; and $E_3 = RBR, RWR, BRR, WRR$

$P(E_1) = 2 \times \frac{3}{8} \times \frac{2}{7} \times \frac{2}{6}, P(E_2) = 2 \times \frac{3}{8} \times \frac{3}{7} \times \frac{2}{6}, P(E_3) = \frac{4\times2\times3\times1}{8.7.6}$

Required probability $= P(E_1) + P(E_2) + P(E_3) = \frac{1}{4}$

Hence, the correct option is (C).

5. Solution The number formed is divisible by 4 if the last two digits are 04,40,34,32,20,12.

Therefore total number of favorable ways = 3! + 3! +4 + 4+ 3! + 4 = 30 (This is the sum of number of ways in which the first two digits can be formed)

Total numbers that can be formed = 5! – 4! = 96 (Number of ways of arranging 5 digits - Number of ways in which zero comes as the first digit)

Therefore required probability

$= \frac{30}{96} = \frac{5}{16}.$

Hence, the correct option is (B).

6. Solution Let the event when a white ball is draw be W and for black

ball let it be B. So A wins when we get sequence of the form Wor WBW or WBBBW or WBBBBBW.....

Probability of getting W is a/a+b. So we get

$P(A) = \frac{a}{a+b} + \left(\frac{b}{a+b}\right)^2 \frac{a}{a+b} + \left(\frac{b}{a+b}\right)^4 \frac{a}{a+b} + \dots \infty = \frac{a+b}{a+2b}$

Similarly we get $P(B) = \frac{b}{a+b} \cdot \frac{a}{a+b} + \left(\frac{b}{a+b}\right)^3 \frac{a}{a+b} + \dots \infty = \frac{b}{a+2b}$

$P(A) = 2P(B) \Rightarrow a + b = 2b \Rightarrow a = b$

Hence, the correct option is (C).

7. $\cos^{-1}(\cos 12) - \sin^{-1}(\sin 14) \Rightarrow 4\pi - 12 + 5\pi - 14 = 9\pi - 26$

Hence, the correct option is (D).

8. Solution $(\sin^{-1}y)^2 + \cos^{-1}x = \frac{n\pi^2}{4}$

$(\sin^{-1}y)^2 - \cos^{-1}x = \frac{\pi^2}{16}$

$\Rightarrow (\sin^{-1}y)^2 = \frac{(4n+1)\pi^2}{32}, \cos^{-1}x = \frac{\pi^2(4n-1)}{32}$

$\Rightarrow 0 \leq \frac{(4n+1)}{32}\pi^2 \leq \frac{\pi^2}{4}, 0 \leq \frac{(4n-1)}{32}\pi^2 \leq \pi$

$\Rightarrow -\frac{1}{4} \leq n \leq \frac{7}{4}, \frac{1}{4}, \leq n \leq \frac{8}{\pi} + \frac{1}{4}$

Hence, the correct option is (A).

$$\overrightarrow{AB} = \overrightarrow{OB} - \overrightarrow{OA} = (3\hat{i} + 5\hat{j} - 3\hat{k}) - (\hat{i} + 3\hat{j} - 5\hat{k})$$

9. $= 2\hat{i} + 2\hat{j} + 2\hat{k}$

Midpoint of AB is (2,4,-4) Vector equation of the plane is $[r - (2\hat{i} + 4\hat{j} - 4\hat{k})] \cdot (2\hat{i} + 2\hat{j} + 2\hat{k}) = 0$

$$\Rightarrow r \cdot (\hat{i} + \hat{j} + \hat{k}) = 2 + 4 - 4 \Rightarrow r \cdot (\hat{i} + \hat{j} + \hat{k}) = 2$$

Hence, the correct option is (A).

10. Equation of given line is $axbyc - 1 = 0$

$$\Rightarrow 20ax + 20by + 20c - 20 = 0$$

From given relation, substuting value of c

$$20ax + 20by + t - 5a - 4b - 20 = 0$$

$$\Rightarrow 20a(x - 14) + 20b(y - 15) + (t - 20) = 0$$

Clearly for $t = 20$, the given line will pass through the point $\left(\frac{1}{4}, \frac{1}{5}\right)$ for all values of a $\&b$

Hence, the correct option is (B).

11. Given circle is $x^2 y^2 - 6x - 4y - 12 = 0$

$$\Rightarrow (x - 3)^2 + (y - 2)^2 = 25 = 5^2$$

Centre $= (3,2)$ radius $= 5$

If a line parallel to y-axis, $x = \lambda$ touches the given circle, then

$$\Rightarrow 3 - \lambda 1 = \pm 5 \quad (\text{radius})$$

$$\Rightarrow 3 - \lambda = \pm 5$$

$$\lambda = 3 \pm 5 = -2,8$$

Pair of lines $\quad (x) + 2 \quad x - 8 = 0$

$$\Rightarrow$$

$$x^2 - 6x - 16 = 0$$

Hence, the correct option is (C).

12. Solution The perpendicular distance of the origin (0,0,0) from the plane $x + y + z = p$ is $\left|\frac{-p}{\sqrt{1+1+1}}\right| = \frac{|p|}{\sqrt{3}}$

If the coordinates of P are (x, y, z), then we must have $\left|\frac{x+y+z-p}{\sqrt{3}}\right| = \frac{|p|}{\sqrt{3}}$

$$\Rightarrow |x + y + z - p| = |p|$$

Which is satisfied by (c)

Hence, the correct option is (C).

13. We want to find out the equation of the tangent to the parabola $y^2 - 2x - 6y + 5 = 0$ at the point (-2,3)
The equation of the parabola is $y^2 - 2x - 6y + 5 = 0$

$$\Rightarrow \quad 2y\frac{dy}{dx} - 2 - 6\frac{dy}{dx} = 0 \quad \Rightarrow \quad \frac{dy}{dx} = \frac{1}{y-3}$$

$$\Rightarrow$$

At any point (x, y) on the parabola, the slope of the tangent is $\frac{dy}{dx} = \frac{1}{y-3}$

The tangent that we require passes through the point (-2,3).
It can be seen that the point (-2,3) lies on the parabola since

$$(3)^2 - 2(-2) - 6(3) + 5 = 0$$

$$\Rightarrow$$

The slope of the parabola at the point (-2,3) is $\frac{1}{3-3}$, which is not defined.

$$\Rightarrow$$

The inclination of the slope of the parabola at the point (-2,3) is $90°$.

$$\Rightarrow$$

The equation of the tangent to the parabola at the point (-2,3) is $x = -2$

Hence, the correct option is (A).

14. y2 = 12 x

4a

= 12 $(\because$ y2=4ax)

$\Rightarrow$ a = 3

Equation of tangent in slope form is

$$y = mx\frac{3}{m}$$

It passes through (2,5)

$\Rightarrow$5=2m+3m

$\Rightarrow$ 5m=2m2+3

$\Rightarrow$2m2-5m+3=0

$\Rightarrow$m-12m-3=0

$\Rightarrow$ m=1,32

So equation of tangents are

y = x + 3

and

$$y = \frac{3}{2}x2$$

or

2y = 3x + 4

Hence, the correct option is (A).

15. Let $f(x) = \sqrt{x}$

Now, $f(x + \delta x) - f(x) = f'(x).\delta x = \frac{\delta x}{2\sqrt{x}}$

We may write, $25.2 = 25 + 0.2$ Taking $x = 25$ and $\delta x = 0.2$ We have $f(25.2) - f(25) = \frac{0.2}{2\sqrt{25}} = 0.02$

$$\therefore f(25.2) = f(25) + 0.02$$

$$= \sqrt{25} + 0.02 = 5.02$$

$$\Rightarrow \sqrt{(25.2)} = 5.02$$

Hence, the correct option is (B).

16. A point on L1x–12=y13=z–14=λ is

x=2λ1

y=3λ–1

z=4λ1

Similarly a point on L2x–31=y–k2=z–01=μ is

⇒x=μ+3

y=2μk

z=μ

For these two points to coincide (intersection point of lines)

2λ1=μ3

3λ–1=2μk

4λ1=μ

Solving (1) and (3)

λ=–32

μ=–32×4+1

=–5

Now, from (2)

3λ–1=2μk

$$\Rightarrow -\frac{9}{2} - 1 = -10 + k \Rightarrow k = \frac{9}{2}$$

Hence, the correct option is (B).

17. Solution since $A \subseteq A$

$\therefore$ Relation $'\subseteq'$ is reflexive. since $A \subseteq B, B \subseteq C \Rightarrow A \subseteq C$

$\therefore$ Relation $'\subseteq'$ is transitive. But If $A \subseteq B$, Doesn't imply $B \subseteq A$

$\therefore$ Relation is not symmetric.

Hence, the correct option is (D).

18. f'(x) = - cosx + a, if a > 1,then f(x) entirely increasing. So f(x) =0 has only one real root, which is positive if f(0) < 0 and negative if f(0) > 0.

Similarly when a <

-1. Then f(x) entirely decreasing. So f(x) has only one real root which is negative if f(0) < 0 and positive if f(0) > 0

Hence, the correct option is (A).

19. $= h\{\tan x^2\} = \log\{\tan x^2\}$

$\therefore At x = \sqrt{\dfrac{\pi}{4}} \Rightarrow (ho(gof))(x) = \log\tan\dfrac{\pi}{4}$

$= \log 1 = 0$

Hence, the correct option is (A).

20. Let (h, k) be point whose chord of contact with respect to hyperbola $x^2 - y^2 = 9$ is $x = 9$

We know that, chord of contact of (h, k) with respect to hyperbola $x^2 - y^2 = 9$ is $T = 0$

$\Rightarrow h \cdot x + k - y - 9 = 0$

$\therefore hx - ky - 9 = 0$

But it is the equation of the line $x = 9$.

This is possible when $h = 1, k = 0$ (by comparing both equations).

Again equation of pair of tangents is $T^2 = SS_1$

$$(x - 9)^2 = (x^2 - y^2 - 9)(1^2 - 0^2 - 9)$$
$$x^2 - 18x + 81 = (x^2 - y^2 - 9)(-8)$$
$$x^2 - 18x + 81 = -8x^2 + 8y^2 + 72$$
$$9x^2 - 8y^2 - 18x + 9 = 0$$

Hence, the correct option is (B).

21. The National Archives of India is a repository of the non-current records of the Government of India and is holding them in trust for the use of administrators and scholars. The National Archives is situated at the Inter-section of Janpath and Rajpath, in Delhi.

Shri K.R. Narayanan, Hon'ble President of India, declared open the "Museum of the National Archives" to the general public on 6 July 1998. This Museum is a representative overview of the multifarious holdings of the National Archives, promotes a common man's interest in archival holdings.

Hence, the correct option is (D).

22. Bangalore is famous for its neat lawns, parks and gardens all over the city. So it got the name as Garden City. Its also having other names such as Silicon Valley, Electronic city, Pensioner's Paradise etc.

Hence, the correct option is (D).

23. Cuttack is the second largest city around 22 kilometers from Bhubaneswar which is the capital city of ODISHA.

Cuttack is famous for silver work and Dahi Vada Aloo dum.

The State High Court is also present in Cuttack and it was the first capital of Odisha. It is surrounded by two rivers namely the Mahanadi and the Kathjodi.

Hence, the correct option is (C).

24. Shadnagar is a town and assembly constituency in the Mahbubnagar district in Telangana, India. Recently it turned into municipality. Shadnagar also known as Farooqnagar.

Hence, the correct option is (A).

25. At Alakanada's origin, Lake Satopanth is a triangular lake, located at a height of 4402 meters above the sea level and named after the Hindu trinity Lord Brahma, Lord Vishnu, Lord Shiva.Badrinath, one of the holy destinations for Hindus in India is located near to the bank of the Alaknanda River. This place is surrounded by two mountain ranges of Nar and Narayan and Neelkanth peak is located at the back side.

Hence, the correct option is (C).

26. The origins of the Advanced Centre for Treatment, Research and Education in Cancer (ACTREC) are rooted in the Indian Cancer Research Centre (ICRC), which was established in 1952 in **Parel**, **Mumbai**, under the purview of the Ministry of Health, Government of India.

Hence, the correct option is (D).

27. Aurangabad is a city which was ruled by Aurangzeb. Except Ajanta-Ellora may other historical monuments are also situated there.

Hence, the correct option is (D).

28. The Rashtrapati Bhavan is the official home of the President of India located at the Western end of Rajpath in New Delhi, India.

Hence, the correct option is (A).

29.

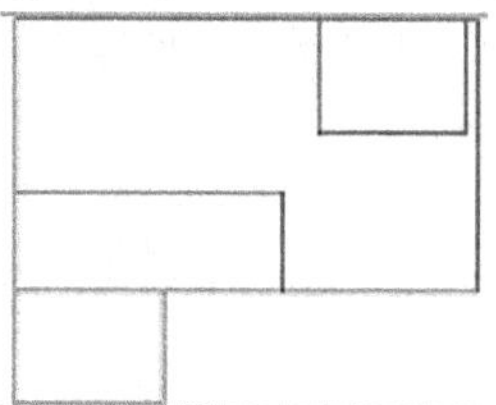

Hence, the correct option is (D).

30. The Statue of Liberty is a colossal neoclassical sculpture on Liberty Island in New York Harbor in New York, in the United States.

The copper statue, a gift from the people of France to the people of the United States, was designed by French sculptor Frédéric Auguste Bartholdi and its metal framework was built by Gustave Eiffel. The statue was dedicated on October 28, 1886.

Hence, the correct option is (B).

31.

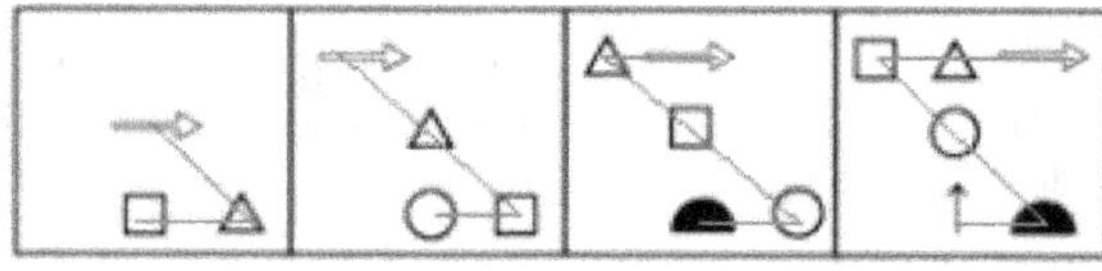

Hence, the correct option is (D).

32.

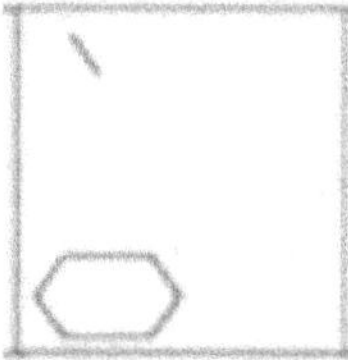

Hence, the correct option is (B).

33.

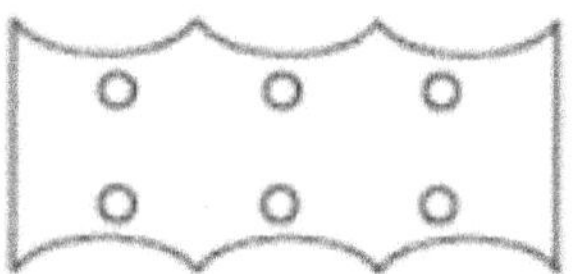

Hence, the correct option is (C).

34. Figures (1), (4) and (7) : Different types of pots
Figures (2), (3) and (6) : Pot with base and without lid
Figures (5), (8) and (9) : Pot with Lid

Hence, the correct option is (C).

35. Solution The elements in (1,1) and (2,2) have changed their positions, whereas the other elements are still the same.

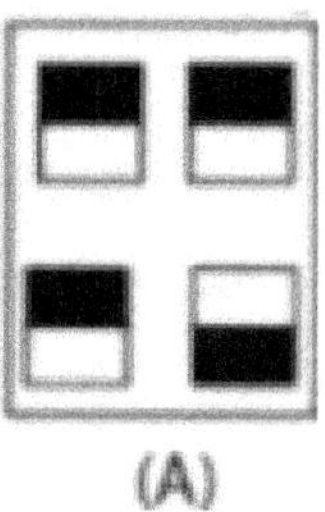

(A)

Hence, the correct option is (A).

36. Solution There are three changes observed:

i) The second element is the mirror image of the first.,

ii) One small mark has appeared just inside the rightmost boundary of the elements.

iii) The L symbol in the result figure is rotated through 180° in the clockwise direction of the problem figure.

Hence, the correct option is (C).

37.

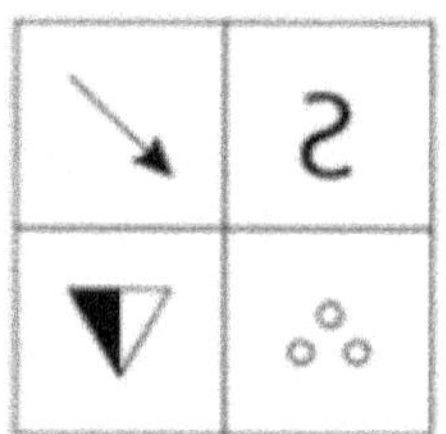

Hence, the correct option is (A).

38.

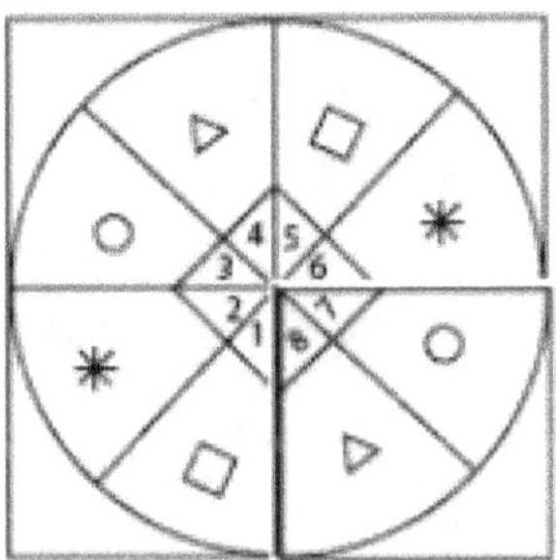

Hence, the correct option is (C).

39. An onion dome is a dome whose shape resembles an onion and is usually associated with Russian architectural style. Such domes are often larger in diameter than the tholobate upon which they sit, and their height usually exceeds their width. These bulbous structures taper smoothly to a point.

Hence, the correct option is (B).

40. When the sheet in figure A is folded to form a hollow box, then the face that features '?' is opposite to the face which is blank, another blank face is opposite to the face that features with a '!' sign, and the third blank face is opposite to the face with a triangle on it.

Therefore, all the hollow cubes shown in all four figures are possible.

Hence, the correct option is (C).

41.

Hence, the correct option is (C).

42.

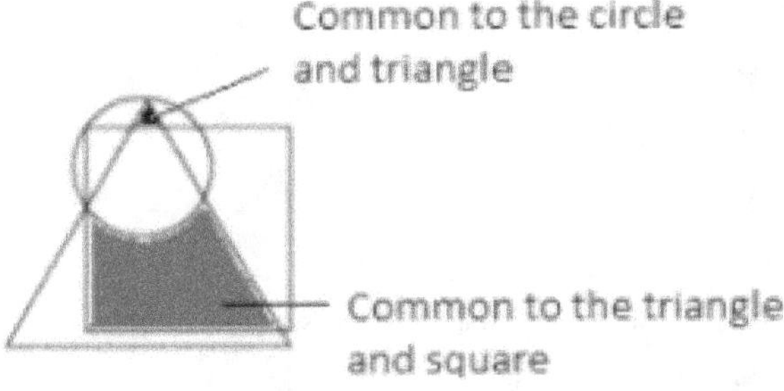

Hence, the correct option is (A).

43.

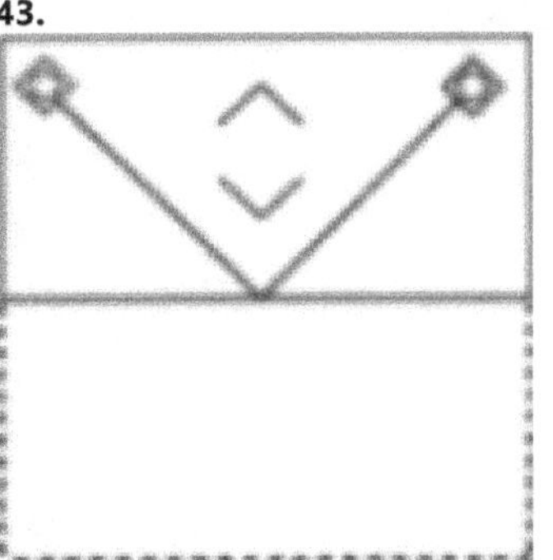

Hence, the correct option is (C).

44.

Hence, the correct option is (D).

45. Minimum number of colours required is 3

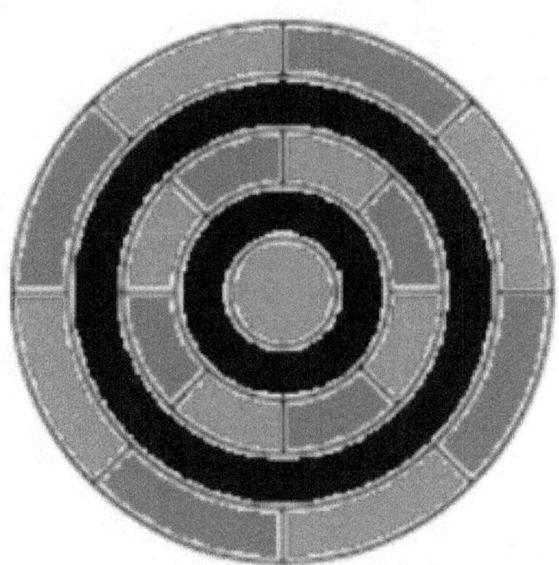

Hence, the correct option is (A).

46. In this case, it is very obvious to see that 1, 2, 5 & 6 are adjacent to the digit 4. So the only number that can be opposite to 4 is 3.

Hence, the correct option is (D).

47. In all figures, the summation of opposite side numbers are same except in third figure

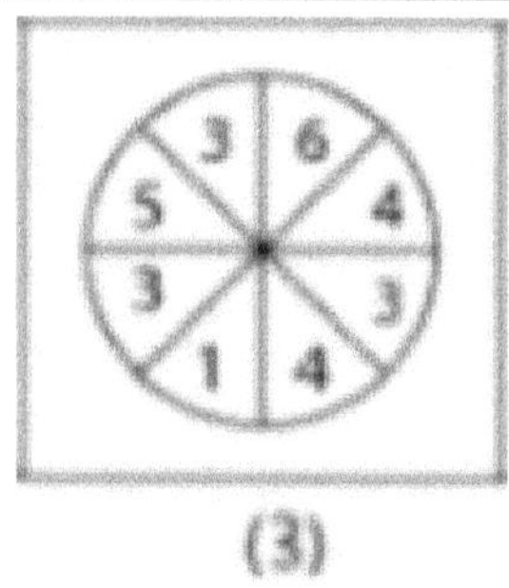

(3)

.

Hence, the correct option is (C).

48.

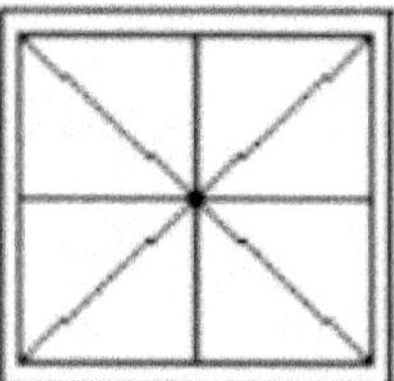

Hence, the correct option is (A).

49.

Hence, the correct option is (D).

50. Solution Except figure (c) all other figures contain even number of leaves.

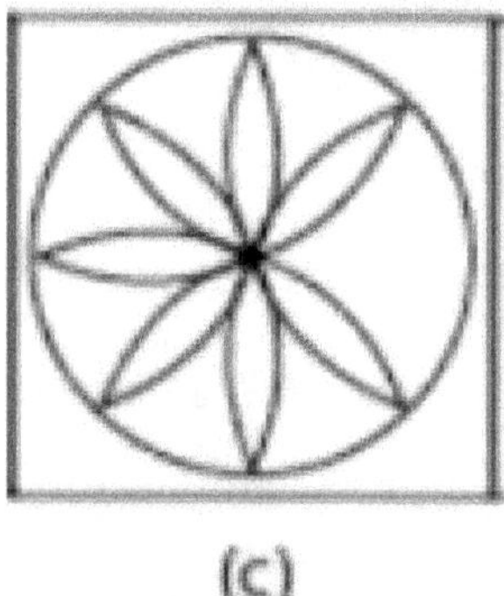

(c)

Hence, the correct option is (C).

51. As,C + 1 = D

E + 2 = G

I + 3 = L

M + 4 = Q

Similarly,

F + 1 = G

G +2 = I

I + 3 = L

O + 4= S

Hence, the correct option is (A).

52. Mexico is a member of G-5 countries. All other countries are member of G-12 countries.

Group 5 countries:

Brazil.

China.

India.

Mexico.

South Africa.

Hence, the correct option is (C).

53. m m n o / m m n n o / m m n n o o

Hence, the correct option is (B).

54. The word 'TYRE' cannot be formed from the given word. Because the letter 'Y' is not present in the word 'TITATORNTEATUIAL'

Hence, the correct option is (C).

55. The pattern followed is:

12 + 7 + 16 + 9 = 44

Similarly,

14 + ? + 13 = 44

⇒ ? = 44 – 27

⇒ ? = 17

Therefore, 17 is the missing number.

Hence, the correct option is (A).

56. The words are coded as -

'sky' means 'red'

'red' means 'tomato'

'tomato' means 'milk'

'milk' means 'soil'

'soil' means 'white'.

The plant grows in soil and soil is coded as white.

Hence, the correct option is (B).

57.

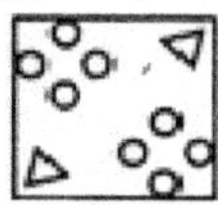

Hence, the correct option is (A).

58.

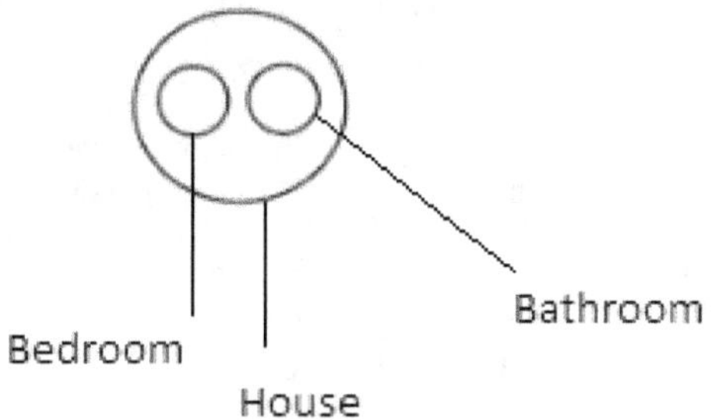

| (-) -- Female |
| (+) -- Male |

It is clear from the diagram, that N is son in-law of A.

Hence, the correct option is (A).

59.

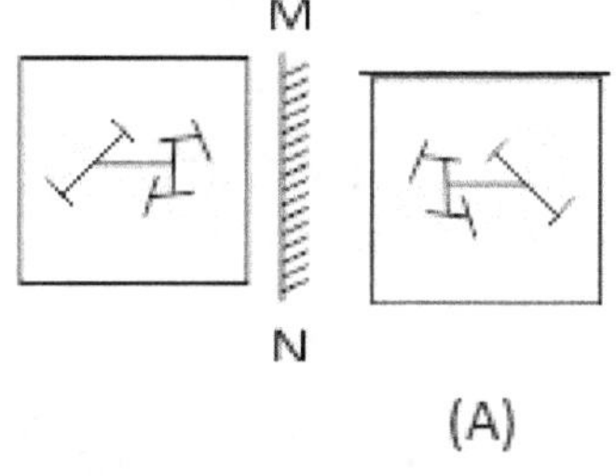

Hence, the correct option is (C).

60.

Hence, the correct option is (A).

Mathematics

Q.1 A five digit number divisible by 3 has to be formed using the numerals 0, 1, 2, 3, 4 and 5 without repetition. The total number of ways in which this can be done?

A. 216   **B.** 40   **C.** 600   **D.** 3125

Q.2 sin 20°sin 40°sin 60°sin 80°=

A. $-\frac{3}{16}$ **B.** $\frac{5}{16}$ **C.** $\frac{3}{16}$ **D.** $-\frac{5}{16}$

Q.3 The general solution of the differential equation $\frac{dy}{dx} = y\tan x - y^2 \sec x$ is:

A. tan x = (c + sec x)y   **B.** sec y = (c + tan y)x
C. sec x = (c + tan x)y   **D.** None of these

Q.4 If two vertices of a triangle are (5, -1), (-2, 3) and the orthocentre of the triangle lies at the origin, then the third vertex is:

A. (4, 7)   **B.** (-4, -7)   **C.** (4, -7)   **D.** (-4, 7)

Q.5 Find the sum of the series : $C_0 - 3C_1 + 5C_2 + ... + (-1)^n (2n + 1) C_n$ for n > 1?

A. 1   **B.** 2   **C.** 3   **D.** 0

Q.6 There are unlimited number of identical balls of four different colours. How many arrangements of at most 8 balls in row can be made by using them?

A. 97380   **B.** 87380   **C.** 87370   **D.** 87480

Q.7 The number of ways in which the letters of the word ARRANGE can be arranged such that both R do not come together is-

A. 360   **B.** 900   **C.** 1260   **D.** 1620

Q.8 How many three-digit numbers can be formed without using the digits 0, 2, 3, 4, 5 and 6 ?

A. 64   **B.** 63   **C.** 62   **D.** 60

Q.9 The equation $x^3 - 3x + [a] = 0$, will have three real and distinct roots if –

(where [ ] denotes the greatest integer function).

A. $a \in (-\infty, 2)$
B. $a \in (0,2)$
C. $a \in (-\infty, -2) \cup (0, \infty)$
D. $a \in [-1, 2)$

Q.10 If the progressions 3, 10, 17, ... and 63, 65, 67, ... are such that their n^{th} terms are equal, then n is equal to-

A. 13   **B.** 15   **C.** 19   **D.** 18

Q.11 Ten different letters of an alphabet are given. Words with five letters are formed from these given letters. Then the number of words which have at least one letter repeated is-

A. 69760   **B.** 30240

C. 99784   **D.** none of these

Q.12 The odds in favour of A solving a problem are 3 to 4 and the odds against B solving the same problem are 5 to 7. If they both try the problem, the probability that the problem is solved is:

A. $\frac{41}{84}$ **B.** $\frac{16}{21}$ **C.** $\frac{5}{21}$ **D.** $\frac{1}{4}$

Q.13 Events A. B. C are mutually exclusive events such that $P(A) = \frac{3x+1}{3}, P(B) = \frac{1-x}{4}$, and $P(C) = \frac{1-2x}{2}$.

Then set of possible values of x are in the interval?

A. $[\frac{1}{3}, \frac{2}{3}]$ **B.** $[\frac{1}{3}, \frac{13}{3}]$ **C.** [0, 1]   **D.** $[\frac{1}{3}, \frac{1}{2}]$

Q.14 The equation of the plane through the line of intersection of planes x + y + z + 3 = 0 and 2x − y + 3z + 1 =0 and parallel to the line $\frac{X}{1} = \frac{Y}{2} = \frac{Z}{3}$ is-

A. x – 5y + 3z = 7   **B.** x – 5y + 3z = – 7
C. x + 5y + 3z = 7   **D.** none of these

Q.15 If g[f(x)] = |sin x| and f[g(x)] = (sin√x)² then,

A. f(x) = sin² x, g(x) = √x
B. f(x) = sin x, g(x) = |x|
C. f(x) = x² , g(x) = sin √x
D. f and g cannot be determined

Q.16 A box contains 24 identical balls of which 12 are white and 12 black. The balls are drawn at random from the box one at a time with replacement. The probability that a white ball is drawn for the 4th time on the 7th draw is:

A. $\frac{5}{64}$ **B.** $\frac{27}{32}$ **C.** $\frac{5}{32}$ **D.** $\frac{1}{2}$

Q.17 Which of the following is logically equivalent to ~ (~p ⇒ q) ?

A. p ∨ q   **B.** p ∨ q
C. ~p ∨ q   **D.** ~p ∨ ~q

Q.18 If the mean of a binomial distribution is 25, then its standard deviation lies in the interval of,

A. (0, 5)   **B.** (0, 5)   **C.** (0, 25)   **D.** (0, 25)

Q.19 A coin whose faces marked 2 and 3 is thrown 5 times, then chance of obtaining a total of 12 is:

A. $\frac{5}{16}$ **B.** $\frac{5}{8}$ **C.** $\frac{5}{32}$ **D.** $\frac{5}{64}$

Q.20 If sin (sin⁻¹ 1/7 + cos⁻¹x) =1, then x is equal to-

A. 1   **B.** 0   **C.** $\frac{6}{7}$ **D.** $\frac{1}{7}$

General Aptitude

Q.21 The below question consists of problem figures and followed by four answer figures (A), (B), (C) and (D). Find out the figure from the answer figures which will continue the given series.

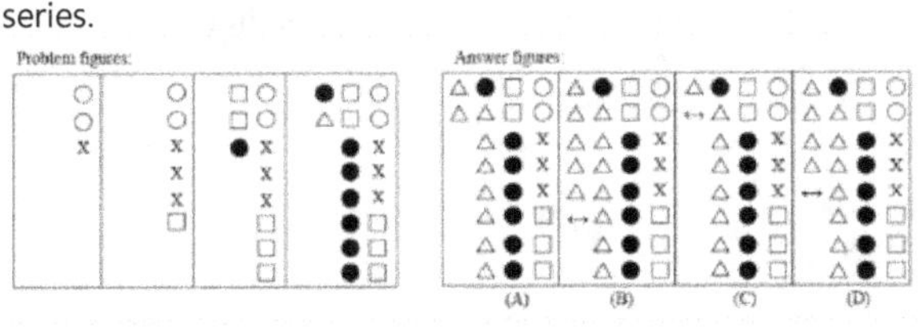

A. A   **B.** B   **C.** C   **D.** D

Q.22 The below question consists of problem figures and followed by four answer figures (A), (B), (C) and (D). Find out the figure from the answer figures which will continue the given series.

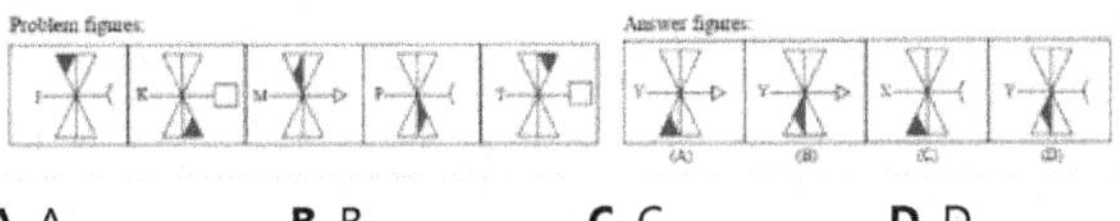

A. A   **B.** B   **C.** C   **D.** D

Q.23 The below question consists of a set of three figures K, L and M showing a sequence of folding of a piece of paper. Figure M shows the manner in which the folded paper has been cut. These three figures are followed by four figures (1), (2), (3) and (4) from which you have to choose a figure which would most closely resemble the unfolded form of figure M.

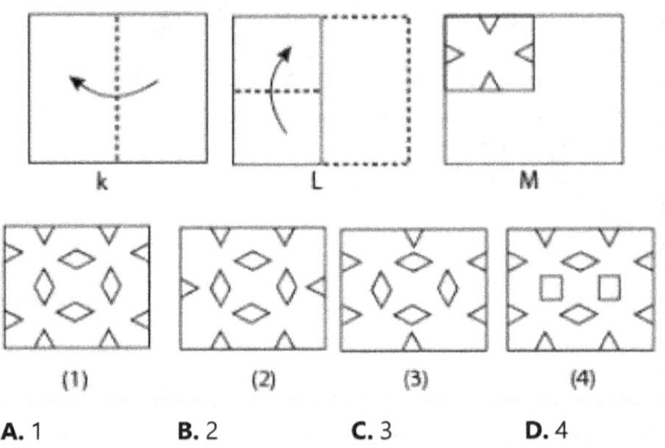

A. 1   **B.** 2   **C.** 3   **D.** 4

Q.24 Which one of the given set of figures violates the given rule?

Rule: Second figure is at an angle of 90⁰ to the first figure and third figure is at an angle of 45⁰ to the first figure.

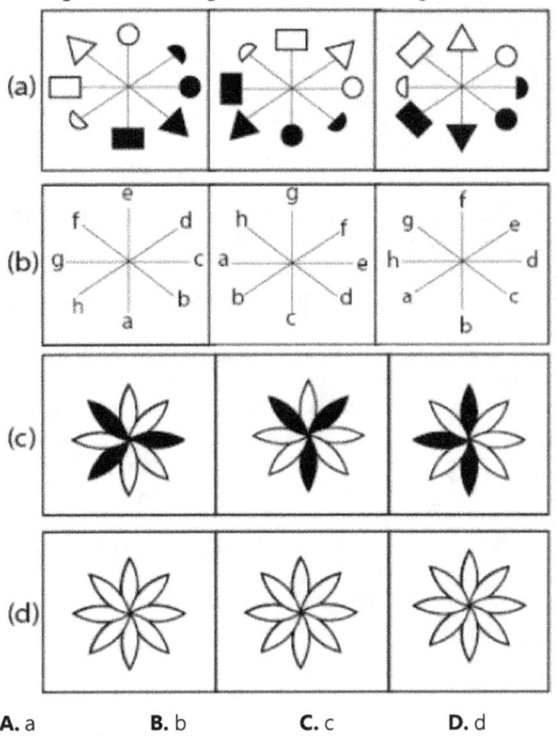

A. a   **B.** b   **C.** c   **D.** d

Q.25 Identify the type of roof

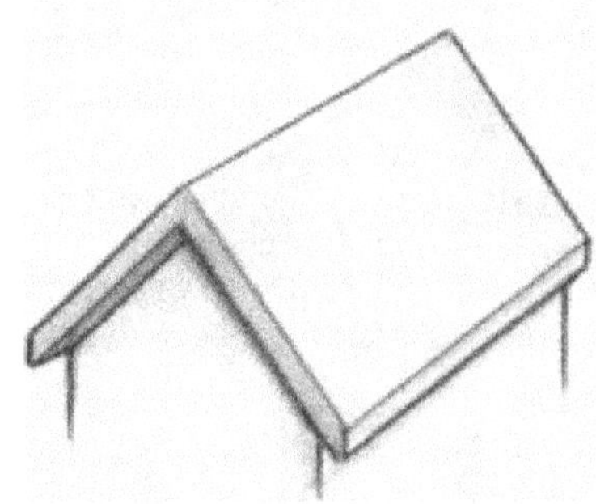

A. Pointed roof   **B.** Shed roof
C. Hipped roof   **D.** Gable roof

Q.26 In the below question, one or more dots are placed in the problem figure (X) followed by four alternatives (a), (b), (c) and (d). One out of these four alternatives contain region(s) common to the circle, square, triangle and rectangle similar to that marked by the dot in figure (X).

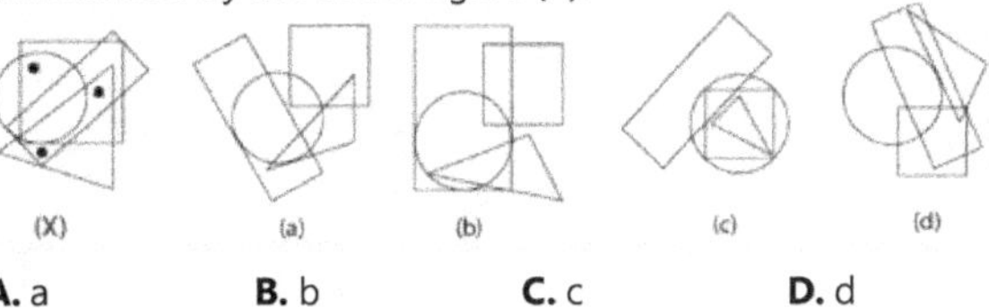

A. a   **B.** b   **C.** c   **D.** d

Q.27 The below question consists of a question figure and followed by four figures (a), (b), (c) and (d). Choose one out of these four figures that can replace '?' to complete the question figure.

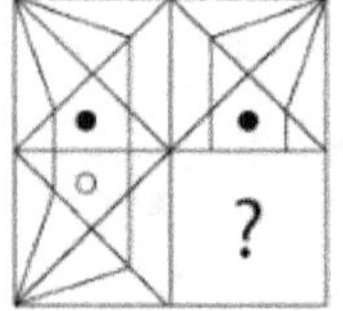
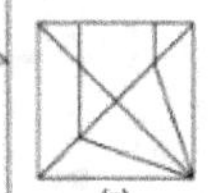
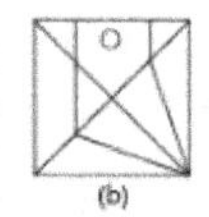
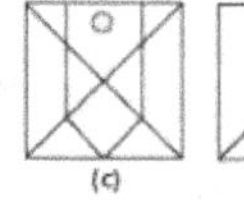
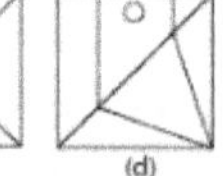

A. a   **B.** b   **C.** c   **D.** d

Q.28 The below question consists of a unfolded dice in the left side and four choices (a), (b), (c) and (d) are given in the form of complete dices in the right side. You are required to select the correct answer choice which is formed by folding the unfolded dice.

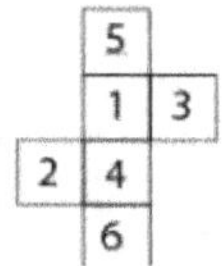
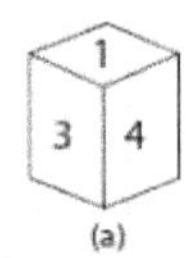
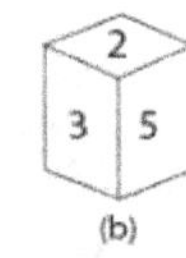
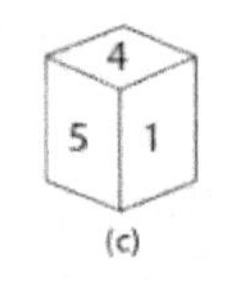
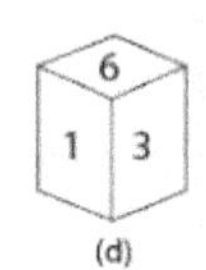

A. a   **B.** b   **C.** c   **D.** d

Q.29 The below question consists of a unfolded dice in the left side and four choices (a), (b), (c) and (d) are given in the form of complete dices in the right side. You are required to select the correct answer choice which is formed by folding the unfolded dice.

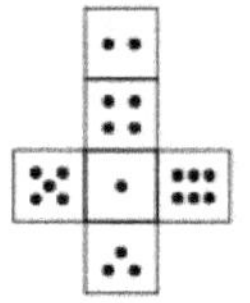
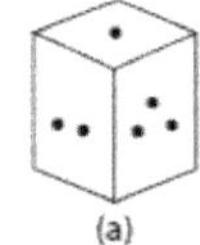
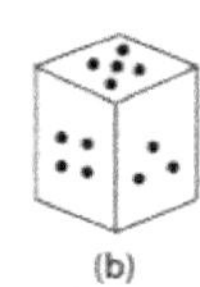
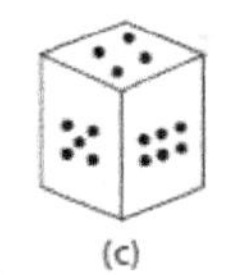
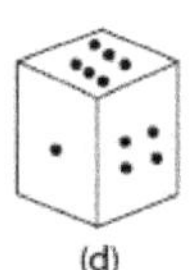

A. a   **B.** b   **C.** c   **D.** d

Q.30 The below question consists of figure (Y) and followed by four alternatives (1), (2), (3) and (4). Choose the correct alternative among the four alternatives such that the pattern would appear like when the figure (Y) is folded at the dotted line.

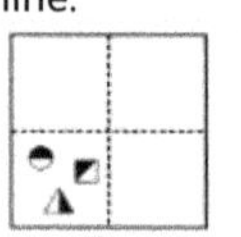
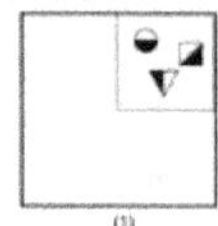
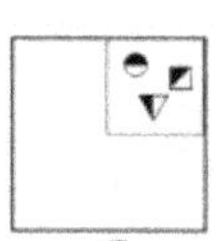
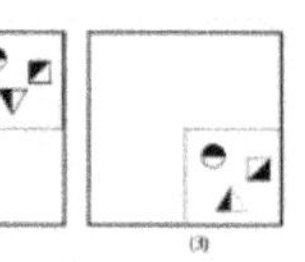

A. 1   **B.** 2   **C.** 3   **D.** 4

Q.31 Choose the correct mirror image for the given figure among the four alternatives (1), (2), (3) and (4). The mirror is represented by a line AB.

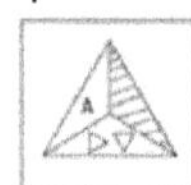
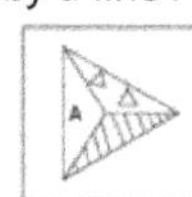
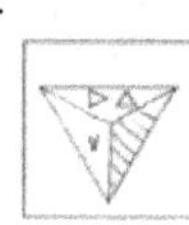

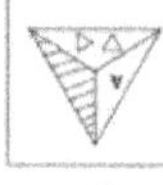

A. 1   **B.** 2   **C.** 3   **D.** 4

Q.32 Find the number of triangles in the given figure.

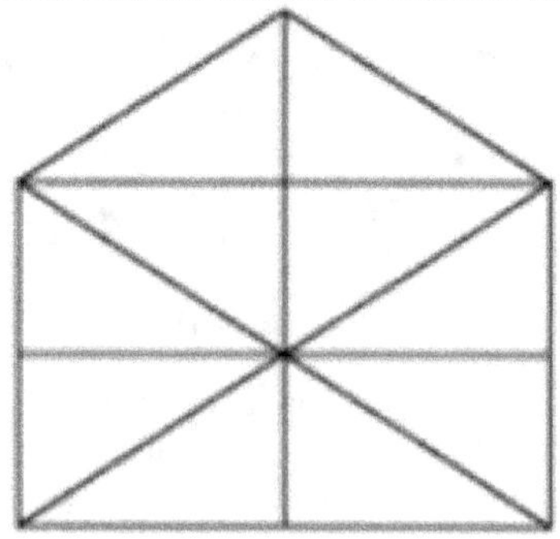

A. 10   **B.** 19   **C.** 21   **D.** 23

Q.33 The below question consists of four figures a, b, c and d followed by a set of four alternatives A, B, C and D. Which of the combinations given below when fitted into each other would form a complete circle?

A. abc   **B.** acd   **C.** abd   **D.** bcd

Q.34 The below question consists of figure (Y) and followed by four alternatives (1), (2), (3) and (4). Choose the correct alternative among the four alternatives such that the pattern would appear like when the figure (Y) is folded at the dotted line.

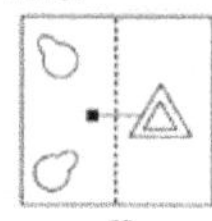
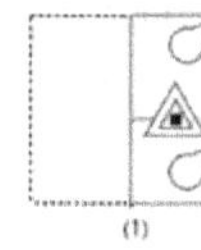
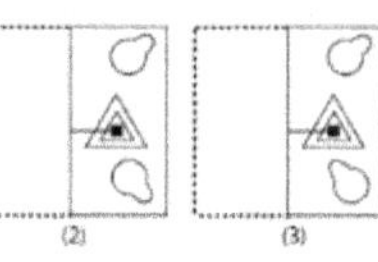
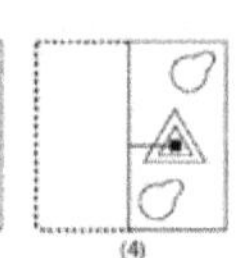

A. 1   **B.** 2   **C.** 3   **D.** 4

Q.35 The below question consists of a figure matrix with one or more missing terms and followed by four answer figures (1), (2), (3) and (4). Find the correct answer figure that will replace '?'

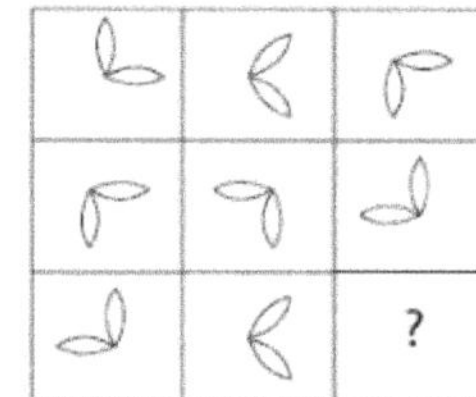

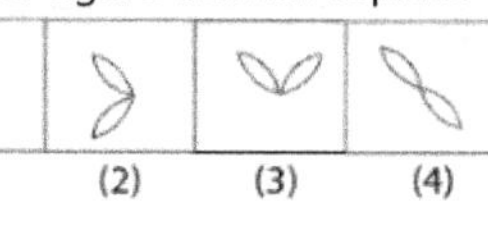

A. 1   **B.** 2   **C.** 3   **D.** 4

Q.36 The below question consists of a four figures. Three are similar in a certain way and so form a group. Find out which one of the figures does not belong to that group.

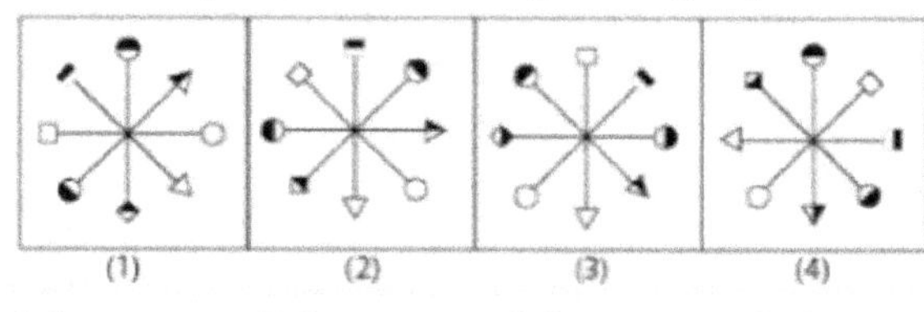

A. 1   **B.** 2   **C.** 3   **D.** 4

Q.37 Identify the given material

A. Pvc pipes   **B.** Steel pipes
C. Steel rod   **D.** Rubber pipes

Q.38 The below question consists of a problem figures and followed by answer figures marked as (A), (B), (C) and (D). You have to select that figure from the set of answer figures which would come in the place of question mark (?) in the problem figure.

Problem figures:

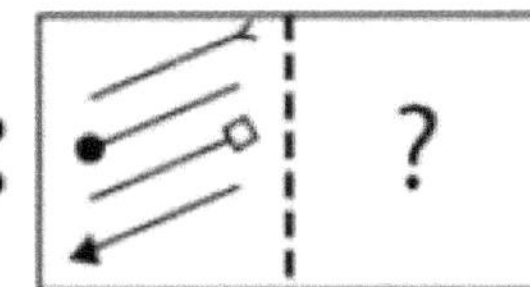

Answer figures:

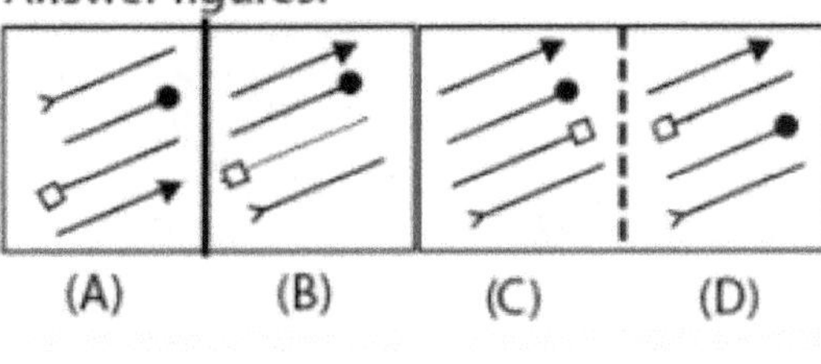

(A)   (B)   (C)   (D)

A. A   **B.** B   **C.** C   **D.** D

Q.39 The below question consists of problem figures followed by answer figures marked as (1), (2), (3), (4) and (5). You have to select that figure from the set of answer figures which would come in the place of question mark (?) in the problem figure.

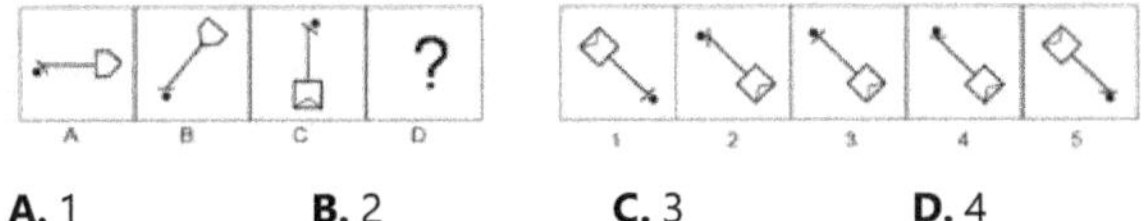

A. 1   **B.** 2   **C.** 3   **D.** 4

Q.40 Choose the correct alternative in which only specified components of the key figure (X) are found.

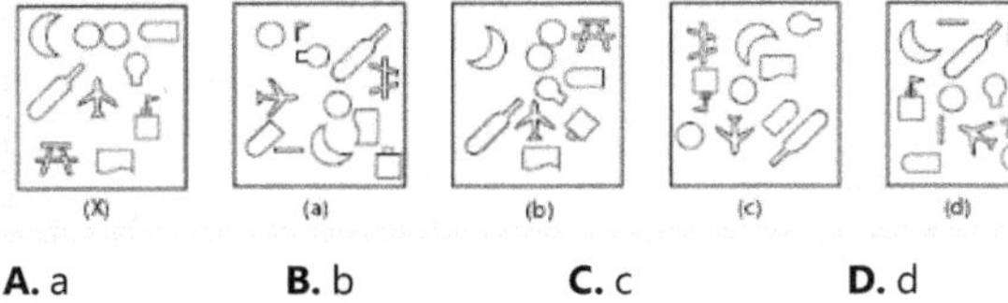

A. a   **B.** b   **C.** c   **D.** d

Q.41 Vikram Sarabhai Space Centre is located at-
A. Pune
B. Ahmedabad
C. Sriharikota
D. Thiruvananthapuram

Q.42 'Mandi House' is a-
A. the office of the P.M.
B. the office of Director General of Doordarshan
C. the office of NFDC
D. the Doordarshan C.P.C

Q.43 The National Institute of Community Development is located at-
A. Chennai   **B.** Pant Nagar
C. Hyderabad   **D.** Bangalore

Q.44 The famous Rock Garden is located in which city?
A. Jaipur   **B.** Lucknow
C. Simla   **D.** Chandigarh

Q.45 Sanchi Stupa is located near-
A. Gaya   **B.** Bhopal   **C.** Varanasi   **D.** Bijapur

Q.46 National Science Centre is located at-
A. Bangalore   **B.** Bombay
C. Kolkata   **D.** Delhi

Q.47 Central Road Research Institute is in-
A. Delhi   **B.** Bangalore
C. Roorkee   **D.** Hyderabad

Q.48 The world famous Ajanta caves are situated in-
A. Orissa   **B.** Andhra Pradesh
C. Kerala   **D.** Maharashtra

Q.49 Where is Chitrakut situated?
A. Maharashtra   **B.** Uttar Pradesh
C. Bihar   **D.** Madhya Pradesh

Q.50 Which city is called 'White City' of Rajasthan?
A. Bihar   **B.** Jaipur   **C.** Udaipur   **D.** Jodhpur

Q.51 SCD, TEF, UGH, ____, WKL.
A. CMN   **B.** UJI   **C.** VIJ   **D.** IJT

Q.52 FAG, GAF, HAI, IAH, ____.
A. JAK   **B.** HAL   **C.** HAK   **D.** JAI

Q.53 ELFA, GLHA, ILJA, ____, MLNA.
A. OLPA   **B.** KLMA   **C.** LLMA   **D.** KLLA

Q.54 CMM, EOO, GQQ, ____, KUU.
A. GRR   **B.** GSS   **C.** ISS   **D.** ITT

Q.55 B_2CD, ____, BCD_4, B_5CD, BC_6D.
A. B_2C_2D **B.** BC_3D **C.** B_2C_3D **D.** BCD_7

Q.56 Odometer is to mileage as compass is to-
A. speed   **B.** hiking   **C.** needle   **D.** direction

Q.57 Look at this series: 22, 21, 23, 22, 24, 23, ... What number should come next?
A. 22   **B.** 24   **C.** 25   **D.** 26

Q.58 Look at this series: 53, 53, 40, 40, 27, 27, ... What number should come next?

A. 12   **B.** 14   **C.** 27   **D.** 53

Q.59 Identify the given image below?

A.   Auroville (Pondicherry)
B.   Golgumbas
C.   Toronto
D.   Sanchi stupa

Q.60 Identify the given image below ?

A.   sun temple Gwalior
B.   sun temple konark
C.   sun temple modhera
D.   sun temple orrisa

// Smart Answer Sheet //

Correct — Percentage of students who answered correctly.   **Skipped** — Percentage of students who skipped.

Q.	Ans.	Correct / Skipped	Q.	Ans.	Correct / Skipped	Q.	Ans.	Correct / Skipped	Q.	Ans.	Correct / Skipped	Q.	Ans.	Correct / Skipped
1	A	36.84 % / 24.56 %	13	D	8.77 % / 35.09 %	25	A	29.82 % / 8.78 %	37	A	47.37 % / 7.02 %	49	D	40.35 % / 12.28 %
2	C	29.82 % / 33.34 %	14	A	21.05 % / 36.84 %	26	D	49.12 % / 14.04 %	38	D	66.67 % / 15.79 %	50	C	71.93 % / 7.02 %
3	C	21.05 % / 36.84 %	15	A	24.56 % / 35.09 %	27	B	84.21 % / 8.77 %	39	D	40.35 % / 14.04 %	51	C	84.21 % / 10.53 %
4	B	21.05 % / 36.84 %	16	C	29.82 % / 35.09 %	28	A	59.65 % / 10.53 %	40	A	29.82 % / 8.78 %	52	A	78.95 % / 10.52 %
5	D	19.3 % / 33.33 %	17	D	21.05 % / 36.84 %	29	D	63.16 % / 12.28 %	41	D	42.11 % / 8.77 %	53	D	70.18 % / 10.52 %
6	B	28.07 % / 38.6 %	18	A	10.53 % / 38.59 %	30	A	49.12 % / 14.04 %	42	B	54.39 % / 10.52 %	54	C	78.95 % / 10.52 %
7	B	26.32 % / 35.08 %	19	A	19.3 % / 24.56 %	31	B	64.91 % / 8.77 %	43	C	57.89 % / 10.53 %	55	B	77.19 % / 10.53 %
8	A	29.82 % / 33.34 %	20	D	28.07 % / 33.33 %	32	C	43.86 % / 7.02 %	44	D	63.16 % / 7.02 %	56	D	56.14 % / 7.02 %
9	D	12.28 % / 36.84 %	21	D	38.6 % / 10.52 %	33	B	57.89 % / 12.29 %	45	B	52.63 % / 8.77 %	57	C	71.93 % / 8.77 %
10	A	35.09 % / 36.84 %	22	A	56.14 % / 10.53 %	34	C	82.46 % / 10.52 %	46	D	35.09 % / 12.28 %	58	B	78.95 % / 12.28 %
11	A	21.05 % / 35.09 %	23	A	73.68 % / 10.53 %	35	A	61.4 % / 12.28 %	47	A	54.39 % / 12.28 %	59	A	70.18 % / 8.77 %
12	B	26.32 % / 36.84 %	24	C	43.86 % / 10.53 %	36	C	75.44 % / 10.52 %	48	D	84.21 % / 5.26 %	60	A	42.11 % / 10.52 %

//Hints and Solutions//

1. We know that a five digit number is divisible by 3 , if and only if sum of its digits $(= 15)$ is divisible by 3 , therefore we should not use 0 or 3 while forming the five digit numbers.

Now,

(i) In case we do not use 0 the five digit number can be formed (from the digit $1,2,3,4,5$) in $^5P_5$ ways

(ii) In case we do not use 3 , the five digit number can be formed (from the digit $0,1,2,4,5$) in $^5P_5 - {}^4P_4 = 5! - 4! = 120 - 24 = 96$ ways

The total number of such 5 digit number $= {}^5P_5 + (^5P_5 - {}^4P_4) = 120 + 96 = 216$

Hence, the correct option is (A).

2. $\sin20°\sin40°\sin60°\sin80°$

$= \frac{1}{2}\sin20°\sin60°(2\sin40°\sin80°)$

$= \frac{1}{2}\sin20°\sin60°(\cos40° - \cos120°)$

$= \frac{1}{2} \cdot \frac{\sqrt{3}}{2}\sin20° \left(1 - 2\sin^2 20° + \frac{1}{2}\right)$

$= \frac{\sqrt{3}}{4}\sin20° \left(\frac{3}{2} - 2\sin^2 20°\right)$

$= \frac{\sqrt{3}}{8}(3\sin20° - 4\sin^3 20°)$

$= \frac{\sqrt{3}}{8}\sin60° = \frac{\sqrt{3}}{8} \cdot \frac{\sqrt{3}}{2} = \frac{3}{16}$

Hence, the correct option is (C).

3. Solution We have $\frac{dy}{dx} = y\tan x - y^2\sec x$

$$\Rightarrow \frac{1}{y^2}\frac{dy}{dx} - \frac{1}{y}\tan x = -\sec x$$

Putting $\frac{1}{y} = v \Rightarrow \frac{-1}{y^2}\frac{dy}{dx} = \frac{dv}{dx'}$ we obtain

$\frac{dv}{dx} + \tan x . v = \sec x$ which is linear

$I.F = e^{\int \tan x dx} = e^{\log \sec x} = \sec x$

$\therefore$ The solution is

$v\sec x = \int \sec^2 x dx + c \Rightarrow \frac{1}{y}\sec x = \tan x + c$

$\Rightarrow \sec x = y(c + \tan x)$

Hence, the correct option is (C).

4. Let the third vertex C be (x_1, y_1) since $O(0,0)$ is the orthocenter

$m_{CO} \times m_{AB} = -1$

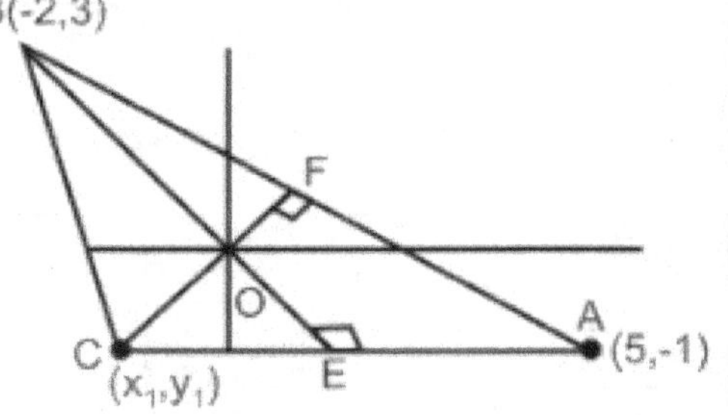

$\Rightarrow y1 - 0 \times 1 - 0 \cdot 3 - -1 - 2 - 5 = -1$
$\Rightarrow y1 \times 1 \cdot 47 - 1 \Rightarrow 7 \times 1 = 4y1$

$$y_1 = \frac{7}{4}x_1$$

$... + (i)$

Also $m_{BO} \times m_{AC} = -1$
$\Rightarrow 3 - 2 \times y1 + 1 \times 1 - 5 = -1 \Rightarrow 3y1 + 3 = 2 \times 1 - 10$
$\Rightarrow 3 \times 74 \times 1 + 3 = 2 \times 1 - 10$
$\Rightarrow x_1 = -4$
$y_1 = -7$
Hence, the third vertex is
(-4,-7)

Hence, the correct option is (B).

5. We have $(1 - x)^n = C_0 - C_1 x C_2 x^2 - \cdots C_n(-1)^n x^n$
(1)

Replacing x by x^2 in equation (i), we have

$(1 - x^2)^n = C_0 - C_1 x^2 C_2 x^4 - \cdots C_n(-1)^n x^{2n}$

Multiplying throughout by x, we have

$x1 - x2n - c0x - C1 \times 3 + C2 \times 5 - -6n - 1nx$

$$2n + 1$$

Differentiating equation (iii) w.r.tx, we have
$(1 - x^2)^n - 2nx^2(1 - x^2)^{n-1} = C_0 - 3C_1 x^{25} C_2 x^4 - \cdots (-1)^n(2n1)C_n x^{2n}$
(iv)

Putting $x = 1$ in equation (iv), we have
$C_0 - 3C_1 5C_2 - \cdots (-1)^n(2n1)C_n = 0$

Hence, the correct option is (D).

6. The number of arrangements of one ball $= 4$
because there are only four different balls
The number of arrangements of two balls
$-4 \times 4 - 4^2$, etc
$\therefore$ the required number of arrangements

$$-4 + 4^2 + 4^3 + \cdots + 4^8 = \frac{4(4^8 - 1)}{4 - 1}$$

$-4348 - 1 - 43 \times 65535 - 4 \times 21845$
$= 87380$

Hence, the correct option is (B).

7. The word ARRANGE, has AA,RR, NGE letters. That is two A' s, two R's and

N. G, E one each. The total number of arrangements
$\frac{71}{21211!11!} = 1260$ But, the number of arrangements in which
both RR are together as one unit $= \frac{6!}{2!1!+1!!1!} = 360$

The number of arrangements in which both RR do not come
together = $1260 - 360 = 900$

Hence, the correct option is (B).

8. Three-digit numbers are to be formed by using the digits 1, 7, 8 and 9.

To form a number of three digits, we are to fill up three places : the hundred's, the ten's and the unit's. The hundred's place can be filled in 4 different ways because anyone of 1, 7, 8 and 9 can fill up this place.

Similarly, ten's and unit's places can also be filled in 4 different ways each.

Accordingly, by FPC,

the no. of three-digit numbers $= 4 \times 4 \times 4 = 64$

Hence, the correct option is (A).

9. $f(x) = x^3 - 3x + |a|$

Let [a] - t (where t will be an integer)

$f(x) = x^3 - 3x + t$

$\Rightarrow f'(x) = 3x^2 - 3$

$\Rightarrow f'(x) = 0$ has two real and distinct solution which are
$x - 1$ and $x = -1$

so $f(x) = 0$ will have three distinct and real solution when
$f(1). f(-1) < 0$

Now.

$f(1) - (1)^3 - 3(1) + t - t - 2$

$f(-1) - (-1)^3 - 3(-1) + t - t + 2$

From equation (ii)

$(t - 2)(t + 2) < 0$

$\Rightarrow t \in (-2,2)$

Now t - la]

Hence lal $\in (-2,2)$

$\Rightarrow a \in [-1,2)$

Hence, the correct option is (D).

10. n^{th} term of 1st series =nth term of 2nd series

$\Rightarrow 3 + (n - 1) 7 = 63 + (n - 1) 2$

$\Rightarrow (n - 1)5 = 60$

$\Rightarrow n -1=12$

$\Rightarrow n = 13$

Hence, the correct option is (A).

11. The total number of words that can be formed is 105 and number of these words in which no letters are repeated is 10P5.

Hence the required number

= 105 – 10P5

= 100000 – 10 × 9 × 8 × 7 × 6

= 69760

Hence, the correct option is (A).

12. $P(A) = \frac{3}{7} P(B) = \frac{7}{12}$

$P(\overline{A}) = \frac{4}{7}, P(B) = \frac{5}{12}$

$P(A \cup B) = 1 - P\left(A \overline{\cup} B\right) = 1 - P(\overline{A} \cap B)$

$\therefore P(A \cup B) = 1 - \frac{4}{7} \times \frac{5}{12} = \frac{16}{21}$

Hence, the correct option is (B).

13. $0 \leq \frac{3x+1}{3} \leq 1, 0 \leq \frac{1-x}{4} \leq 1, 0 \leq \frac{1-2x}{2} \leq 1$

and $0 \leq \frac{3x+1}{3} + \frac{1-x}{4} + \frac{1-2x}{2} \leq 1$

Considering the four inequalities $-\frac{1}{3} \leq x \leq \frac{2}{3}, -3 \leq x \leq 1, -\frac{1}{2} \leq x \leq \frac{1}{2}$

and $\frac{1}{3} \leq x \leq \frac{13}{3}$, hence $\frac{1}{3} \leq x \leq \frac{1}{2}$

Hence, the correct option is (D).

14. Any plane through the given line is 2x – y + 3z + 1 + λ (x + y + z + 3) = 0 If this plane is parallel to the line then the normal to the plane is also perpendicular to the above line.

$\frac{X}{1} = \frac{Y}{2} = \frac{Z}{3}$

$\therefore (l_1 l_2 + m_1 m_2 + n_1 n_2 = 0$

$\Rightarrow (2 + \lambda) 1 + (\lambda - 1) 2 + (3 + \lambda) 3 = 0$

$\Rightarrow \lambda = -\dfrac{3}{2}$

and the required plane is

$2x - y + 3z + 1 + (-\dfrac{3}{2})(x + y + z + 3) = 0$

$\Rightarrow x - 5y + 3z - 7 = 0$

or

$x - 5y + 3z = 7$

Hence, the correct option is (A).

15. $g\big(f(x)\big) = |\sin x| = \sqrt{(\sin x)^2}$

$f\big(g(x)\big) = \left(\sin\sqrt{x}\right)^2 = \sin^2\sqrt{x}$

$\therefore f(x) = \sin^2 x$ and $g(x) = \sqrt{x}$

Hence, the correct option is (A).

16. Solution In any trail, P(getting white ball) $= \dfrac{1}{2}$ P(getting black ball) $= \dfrac{1}{2}$ Now, required event will occur if in the first six trails 3 white balls are drawn in any one of the 3 trails from six. The remaining 3 trails must be kept reserved for black balls. This can happen $\ln^6 C_3 \times^3 C_3 = 20$ ways

$= 20 \times \left(\dfrac{1}{2}\right)^3 \times \left(\dfrac{1}{2}\right)^3 \times \dfrac{1}{2} = \dfrac{5}{32}$

Hence, the correct option is (C).

17.

p	q	~p	~q	~p⇒q	~(~p⇒q)	p ∨ q	p ∨~ q	~p ∨ q	~p ∨ ~q
F	F	T	T	F	T	F	F	F	T
F	T	T	F	T	F	F	F	T	F
T	F	F	T	T	F	F	T	F	F
T	T	F	F	T	F	T	F	F	F

Hence, the correct option is (D).

18. $SD.\ \sigma = \sqrt{npq} \geq 0$

Mean, $np = 25$ and $q < 1 \therefore \sigma = \sqrt{npq} < \sqrt{np}$

$\sigma < 5$

$\Rightarrow 0 \leq \sigma < 5$

Hence, the correct option is (A).

19. Solution It is given that the coin has faces 2 and 3 , tossed five times.

To get sum 12 we need 2,2,2,3,3 in any combination.

So, in the 5 throws, there need to be 3 2 's. Automatically other 2 will be 3 's since there is no other possibility.

So, it boils down to choosing 3 from 5

Therefore P(getting sum 12) $= 5C_3 \left(\dfrac{1}{2}\right)^5 = \dfrac{5}{16°}$

Hence, the correct option is (A).

20. $\sin\left(\sin^{-1}\dfrac{1}{7} + \cos^{-1}x\right) = 1$

$\Rightarrow \sin^{-1}\dfrac{1}{7} + \cos^{-1}x = \dfrac{\pi}{2}$

$\Rightarrow \sin^{-1}\dfrac{1}{7} = \dfrac{\pi}{2} - \cos^{-1}x$

$\Rightarrow \sin^{-1}\dfrac{1}{7} = \sin^{-1}x$

$\Rightarrow x = \dfrac{1}{7}$

Hence, the correct option is (D).

21. The elements in the figures are increasing in certain pattern 2, 3, 5, 7 and 11(Prime numbers).Hence, the correct option is (D).

22.

Hence, the correct option is (A).

23.

Hence, the correct option is (A).

24.

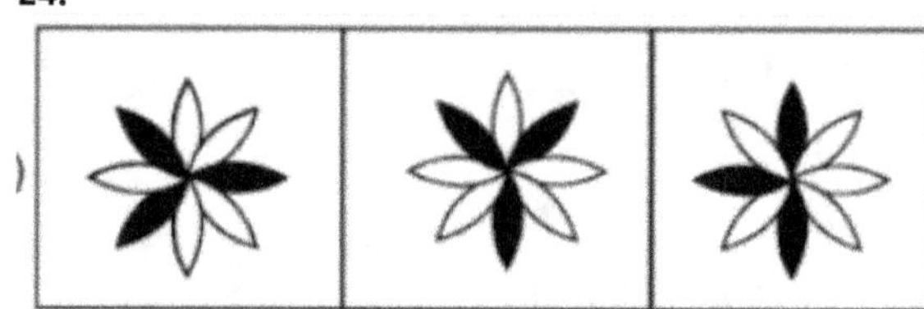

Hence, the correct option is (C).

25. A roof with two slopes that form an "A" or triangle is called a gable, or pitched, roof. This type of roof was used as early as the temples of ancient Greece and has been a staple of domestic architecture in northern Europe and the Americas for many centuries.

Hence, the correct option is (A).

26.

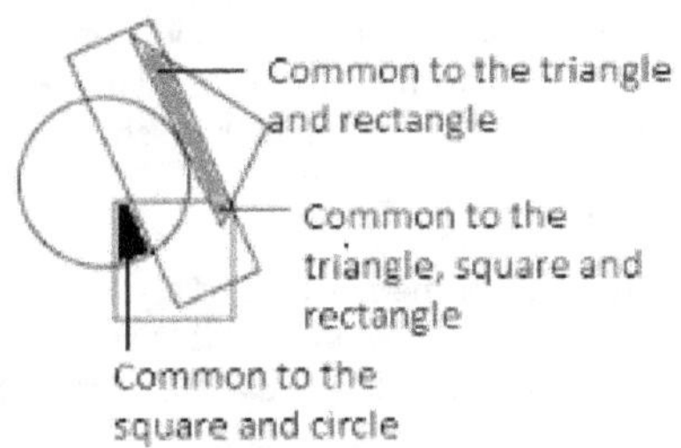

Hence, the correct option is (D).

27.

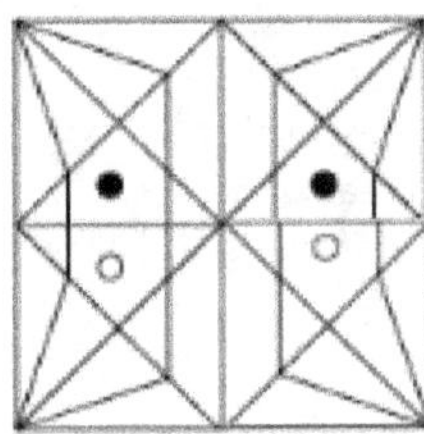

Hence, the correct option is (B).

28.

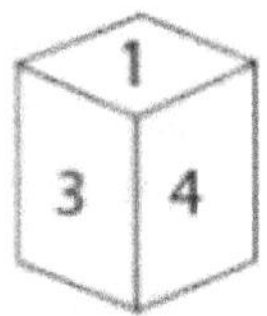

Hence, the correct option is (A).

29.

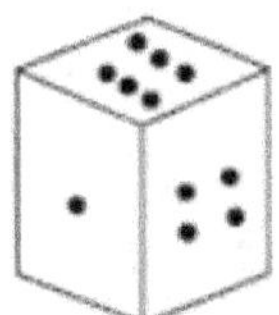

Hence, the correct option is (D).

30.

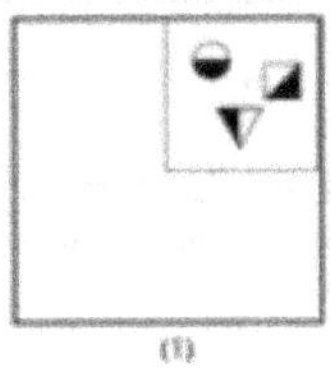

Hence, the correct option is (A).

31.

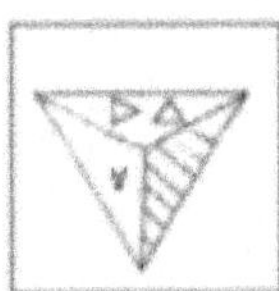

Hence, the correct option is (B).

32.

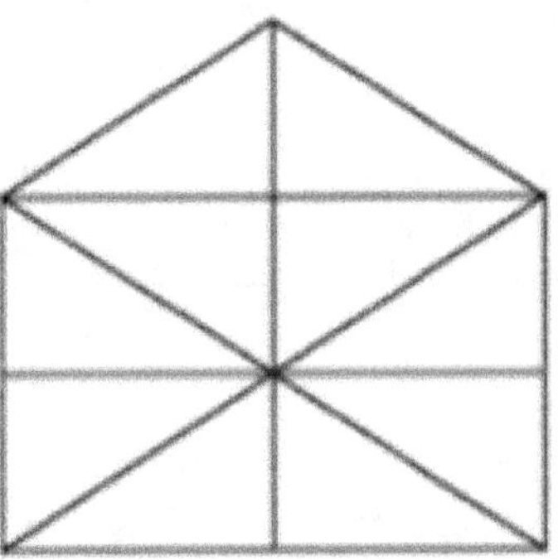

10 (small triangles) + 7 (medium triangles) + 4 (big triangles) = 21

Hence, the correct option is (C).

33.

Hence, the correct option is (B).

34.

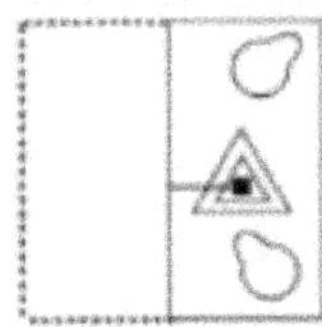

Hence, the correct option is (C).

35.

Hence, the correct option is (A).

36.

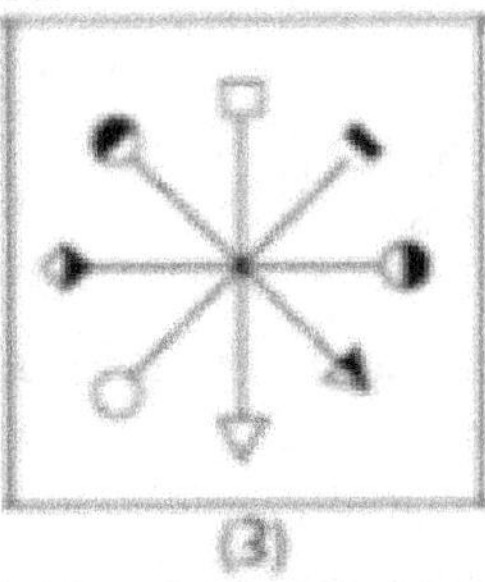

In all figures, the triangle (without shading) is first compared to the circle (without shading) except in the third figure.

Hence, the correct option is (C).

37. Polyvinyl chloride is the world's third-most widely produced synthetic plastic polymer, after polyethylene and polypropylene.

About 40 million tonnes are produced per year. PVC comes in two basic forms: rigid and flexible.

Hence, the correct option is (A).

38. The first and fourth element exchanged their positions, and were rotated through 180°, similarly the second and third elements exchanged their positions and were rotated by 180°.

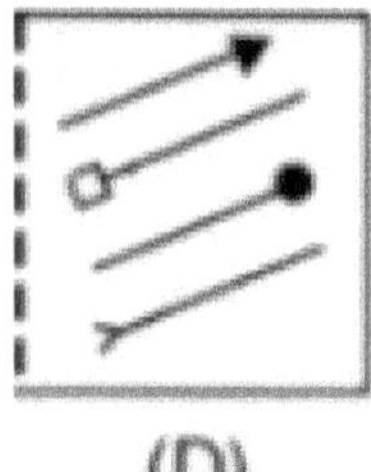

Hence, the correct option is (D).

39. The figure rotates 45° ACW and the symbol at one end of the line segment gets rotated through 180^0.

Hence, the correct option is (D).

40.

Hence, the correct option is (A).

41. The Vikram Sarabhai Space Centre (VSSC) is a major space research centre of the Indian Space Research Organisation (ISRO), focusing on rocket and space vehicles for India's satellite programme. It is located in **Thiruvananthapuram**, in the Indian state of Kerala.

Hence, the correct option is (D).

42. 'Mandi House' is the office of Director General of Doordarshan. Hence, the correct option is (B).

43. The National Institute of Community Development Institute is located in the historic city of Hyderabad in Telangana state.

Hence, the correct option is (C).

44. The Rock Garden of Chandigarh is a sculpture garden in Chandigarh, India. It is also known as Nek Chand's Rock Garden after its founder Nek Chand Saini, a government official who started the garden secretly in his spare time in 1957. Today it is spread over an area of 40 acres.

Hence, the correct option is (D).

45. Sanchi Stupa, also written Sanci, is a Buddhist complex, famous for its Great Stupa, on a hilltop at Sanchi Town in Raisen District of the State of Madhya Pradesh, India. It is located in 46 kilometres north-east of Bhopal, capital of Madhya Pradesh.

Hence, the correct option is (B).

46. The National Science Centre established in 1992, is a science museum in Delhi, India. It is part of the National Council of Science Museums, an autonomous body under India's Ministry of Culture. It stands close to Gate no 1, of Pragati Maidan overlooking the Purana Qila.

Hence, the correct option is (D).

47. Central Road Research Institute or CRRI established in 1952 is a constituent laboratory of India's Council of Scientific and Industrial Research. The CRRI is located in New Delhi and conducts research and development in the areas of design, construction, maintenance and management of roads and airport runways.

Hence, the correct option is (A).

48. The Ajanta Caves are 30 rock-cut Buddhist cave monuments which date from the 2nd century BCE to about 480 CE in Aurangabad district of Maharashtra state of India.

Hence, the correct option is (D).

49. Chitrakoot is a famous pilgrimage centre and a nagar panchayat in the Satna district in the state of Madhya Pradesh, India. It is a place of religious, cultural, historical and archaeological importance, situated in the Bundelkhand region.

Hence, the correct option is (D).

50. INDIA'S WHITE CITY. Udaipur is the southern 'big' city of Rajasthan, and also the most romantic one. Udaipur is known as the white city of India.

Hence, the correct option is (C).

51. There are two alphabetical series here. The first series is with the first letters only: STUVW. The second series involves the remaining letters: CD, EF, GH, IJ, KL.

Hence, the correct option is (C).

52. The middle letters are static, so concentrate on the first and third letters. The series involves an alphabetical order with a reversal of the letters. The first letters are in alphabetical order: F, G, H, I, J. The second and fourth segments are reversals of the first and third segments. The missing segment begins with a new letter.

Hence, the correct option is (A).

53. The second and forth letters in the series, L and A, are static. The first and third letters consist of an alphabetical order beginning with the letter E.

Hence, the correct option is (D).

54. The first letters are in alphabetical order with a letter skipped in between each segment: C, E, G, I, K. The second and third letters are repeated; they are also in order with a skipped letter: M, O, Q, S, U.

Hence, the correct option is (C).

55. Because the letters are the same, concentrate on the number series, which is a simple 2, 3, 4, 5, 6 series, and follows each letter in order.

Hence, the correct option is (B).

56. An odometer is an instrument used to measure mileage. A compass is an instrument used to determine direction. Choices a, b, and c are incorrect because none is an instrument.

Hence, the correct option is (D).

57. In this simple alternating subtraction and addition series; 1 is subtracted, then 2 is added, and so on.

22-1=21

21+2=23

23-1=22

22+2=24

24-1=23

23+2=25

Hence, the correct option is (C).

58. In this series, each number is repeated, then 13 is subtracted to arrive at the next number.

53-13=40

40-13=27

27-13=14

Hence, the correct option is (B).

59. Auroville is a universal city in the making in south-India dedicated to the ideal of human unity based on the vision of Sri Aurobindo and The Mother.

Hence, the correct option is (A).

60. The Surya Mandir or Sun Temple is one of the most spectacular shrines as well as an architectural wonder that adorns the city of Gwalior. As the name suggests, the temple is dedicated to the holy Sun God and was constructed in the year 1988 by the famous industrialist G.D. Birla. Built on the lines of legendary Sun Temple at Konark, Orissa, the Sun Temple of Gwalior is a magnificent amalgam of exquisite architecture in red sandstone and pearly white marble.

As you encounter the outer edifice, you will see the red sandstone exterior of the Sun Temple built in the manner of gradual slots that reach up to the peak of the facade. The temple sits in the midst of a lush green garden that stands in a beautiful contrast to the meticulous architecture. The interior of the temple is a serene construction in white marble and will surely fill you with a sense of calm. A splendid idol of the Sun Lord is enshrined in the temple. Although not constructed long ago, it is among the most revered shrines in the ancient city attracting tourists and devotees from all over the country in large numbers.

Hence, the correct option is (A).

Mock Test 09

Mathematics

Q.1 The eccentricity of the hyperbola $4x^2 - 9y^2 = 36$ is

A. $\frac{\sqrt{11}}{3}$ **B.** $\frac{\sqrt{15}}{3}$ **C.** $\frac{\sqrt{13}}{3}$ **D.** $\frac{\sqrt{14}}{3}$

Q.2 The length of the latus rectum of the ellipse $16x^2 + 25y^2 = 400$ is -

A. $\frac{5}{16}$ unit **B.** $\frac{32}{5}$ unit **C.** $\frac{16}{5}$ unit **D.** $\frac{5}{32}$ unit

Q.3 The locus of the middle points of all chords of the parabola $y^2 = 4ax$ passing through the vertex is -

A. a straight line
B. an ellipse
C. a parabola
D. a circle

Q.4 The coordinates of a moving point p are $(2t^2 + 4, 4t + 6)$. Then its locus will be a-

A. circle
B. straight line
C. parabola
D. ellipse

Q.5 The equation $8x^2 + 12y^2 - 4x + 4y - 1 = 0$ represents-

A. an ellipse
B. a hyperbola
C. a parabola
D. a circle

Q.6 If the straight line $y = mx$ lies outside of the circle $x^2 + y^2 - 20y + 90 = 0$, then the value of m will satisfy -

A. $m < 3$ **B.** $|m| < 3$ **C.** $m > 3$ **D.** $|m| > 3$

Q.7 The locus of the centre of a circle which passes through two variable points $(a, 0)$, $(-a, 0)$ is -

A. $x = 1$ **B.** $x + y = a$ **C.** $x + y = 2a$ **D.** $x = 0$

Q.8 The coordinates of the two points lying on $x + y = 4$ and at a unit distance from the straight line $4x + 3y = 10$ are -

A. $(-3, 1)$, $(7, 11)$
B. $(3, 1)$, $(-7, 11)$
C. $(3, 1)$, $(7, 11)$
D. $(5, 3)$, $(-1, 2)$

Q.9 The intercept on the line $y = x$ by the circle $x^2 + y^2 - 2x = 0$ is AB. Equation of the circle with AB as diameter is -

A. $x^2 + y^2 = 1$
B. $x(x - 1) + y(y - 1) = 0$
C. $x^2 + y^2 = 2$
D. $(x - 1)(x - 2) + (y - 1) + (y - 2) = 0$

Q.10 If the coordinates of one end of a diameter of the circle $x^2 + y^2 + 4x - 8y + 5 = 0$, is $(2, 1)$, the coordinates of the other end is -

A. $(-6, -7)$ **B.** $(6, 7)$ **C.** $(-6, 7)$ **D.** $(7, -6)$

Q.11 Three of six vertices of a regular hexagon are chosen at random. The probability that the triangle with these three vertices will be equilateral is-

A. $\frac{1}{10}$
B. $\frac{1}{5}$
C. $\frac{2}{15}$
D. None of these

Q.12 If $\sin$ and $\theta = \frac{2t}{1} + t^2$ lies in the second quadrant, then $\cos\theta$ is equal to-

A. $\frac{1-t^2}{1+t^2}$ **B.** $\frac{t^2-1}{1+t^2}$ **C.** $\frac{-|1-t^2|}{1+t^2}$ **D.** $\frac{1+t^2}{1-t^2}$

Q.13 The solutions set of inequation $\cos^{-1} x < \sin^{-1} x$ is-

A. $[-1, 1]$ **B.** $\left[\frac{1}{\sqrt{2}}, 1\right]$ **C.** $[0, 1]$ **D.** $\left(\frac{1}{\sqrt{2}}, 1\right]$

Q.14 The number of solutions of $2\sin x + \cos x = 3$ is:

A. 1 **B.** 2
C. infinite **D.** No solution

Q.15 Let $\tan\alpha = \frac{a}{a+1}$ and $\tan\beta = \frac{1}{2a+1}$ then $\alpha + \beta$ is

A. $\frac{\pi}{4}$ **B.** $\frac{\pi}{3}$ **C.** $\frac{\pi}{2}$ **D.** π

Q.16 If $\theta + \phi = \frac{\pi}{4}$, then $(1 + \tan\theta)(1 + \tan\phi)$ is equal to-

A. 1 **B.** 2 **C.** $\frac{5}{2}$ **D.** $\frac{1}{3}$

Q.17 If $\sin\theta$ and $\cos\theta$ are the roots of the equation $ax^2 - bx + c = 0$, then a, b and c satisfy the relation -

A. $a^2 + b^2 + 2ac = 0$
B. $a^2 - b^2 + 2ac = 0$
C. $a^2 + c^2 + 2ab = 0$
D. $a^2 - b^2 - 2ac = 0$

Q.18 If A and B are two matrices such that $A+B$ and AB are both defined, then -

A. A and B can be any matrices
B. A, B are square matrices not necessarily of the same orde
C. A, B are square matrices of the same order
D. Number of columns of A = number of rows of B

Q.19 If $A = \begin{pmatrix} 3 & x - 1 \\ 2x + 3 & x + 2 \end{pmatrix}$ is a symmetric matrix, then the value of x is:

A. 4 **B.** 3 **C.** -4 **D.** -3

Q.20 If $z = \begin{pmatrix} 1 & 1 + 2i & -5i \\ 1 - 2i & -3 & 5 + 3i \\ 5i & 5 - 3i & 7 \end{pmatrix}$ then $(i = \sqrt{-1})$:

A. z is purely
B. z is purely imaginary
C. $z + z = 0$
D. $(z - \bar{z})$ i is purely imaginary

General Aptitude

Q.21 The below question consists of problem figures and followed by four answer figures (A), (B), (C) and (D). Find out the figure from the answer figures which will continue the given series.

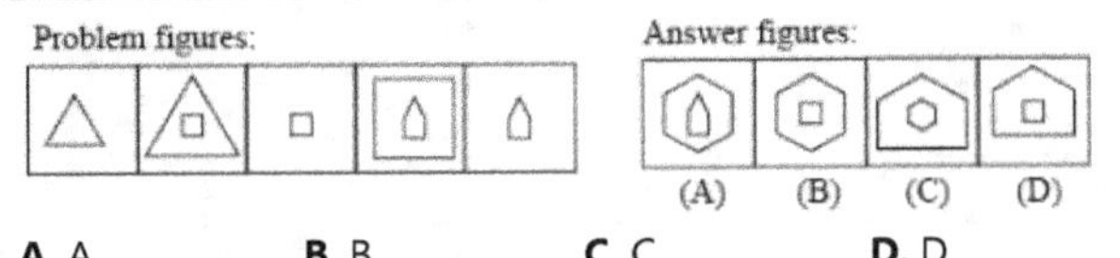

A. A   **B.** B   **C.** C   **D.** D

Q.22 The below question consists of problem figures and followed by four answer figures (A), (B), (C) and (D). Find out the figure from the answer figures which will continue the given series.

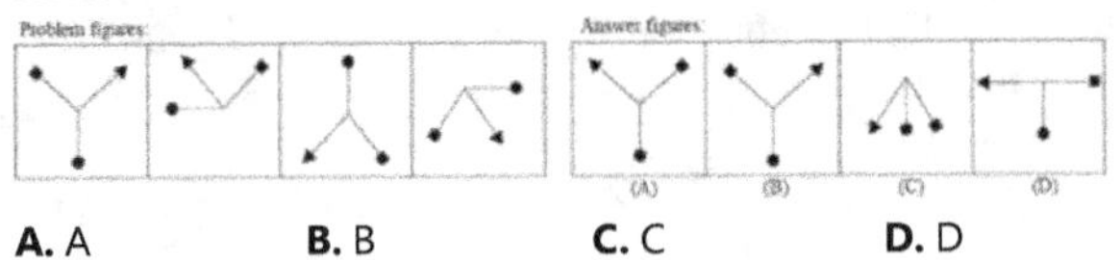

A. A   **B.** B   **C.** C   **D.** D

Q.23 Choose the correct alternative in which only specified components of the key figure (X) are found.

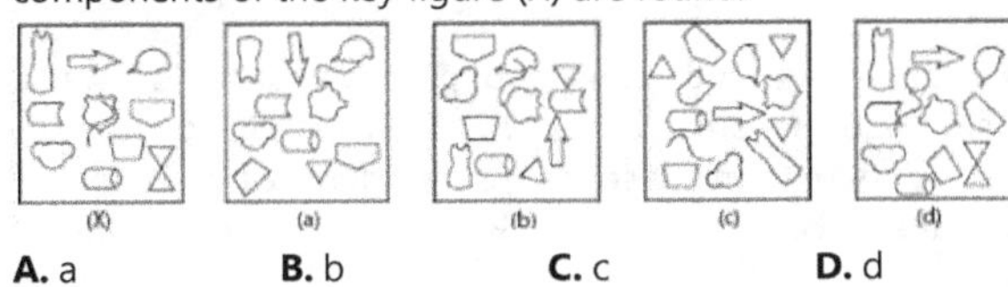

A. a   **B.** b   **C.** c   **D.** d

Q.24 Which one of the given set of figures violates the given rule?

Rule: Black elements are decreasing and white elements are increasing.

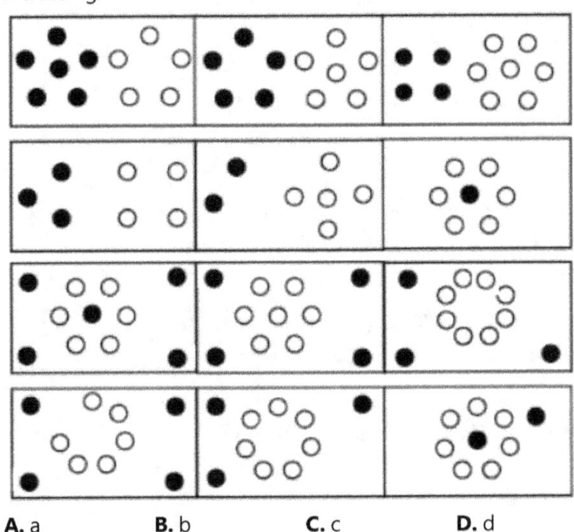

A. a   **B.** b   **C.** c   **D.** d

Q.25 The below question consists of a related pair of figures (problem pair) and followed by four answer pairs marked as (A), (B), (C) and (D). Out of these four, three have relationship similar to that in the problem pair. Only one pair of figures does not have similar relationship. You have to select that pair of figures which does not have a relationship similar to that in the problem pair.

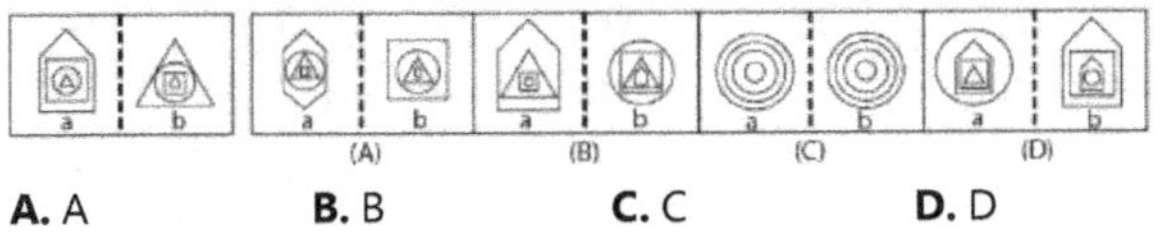

A. A   **B.** B   **C.** C   **D.** D

Q.26 By looking in a mirror, it appears that it is 6 : 30 in the clock What is the real time ?

A. 5:45   **B.** 5:30

C. 11:45   **D.** It does not exit

Q.27 The below question consists of a question figure and followed by four figures (1), (2), (3) and (4), which show the possible water images of the question figure. Choose one out of these four figures which shows the correct water image of the question figure.

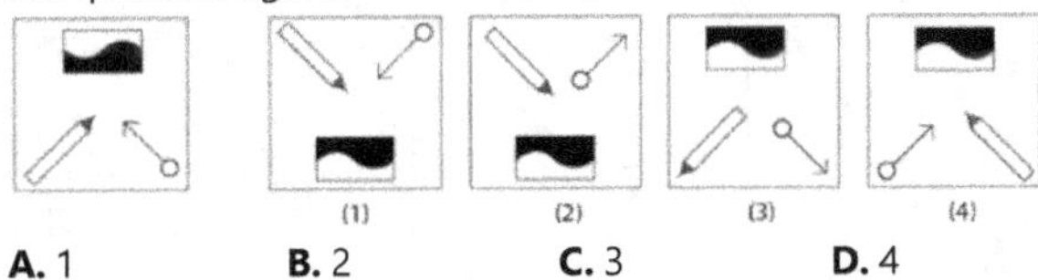

A. 1   **B.** 2   **C.** 3   **D.** 4

Q.28 The below question consists of a question figure and followed by four figures (a), (b), (c) and (d). Choose one out of these four figures that can replace '?' to complete the question figure.

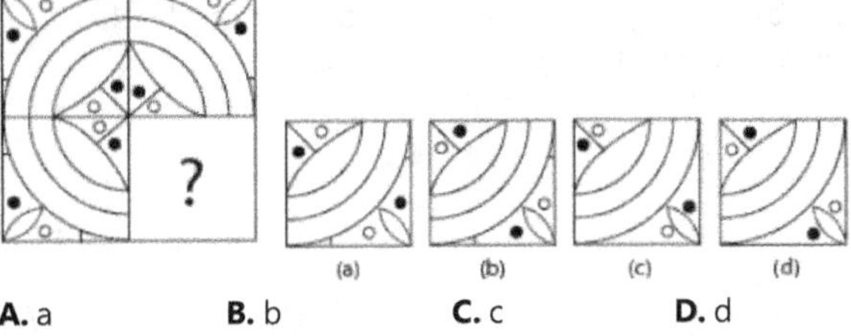

A. a   **B.** b   **C.** c   **D.** d

Q.29 In the below question, one or more dots are placed in the problem figure (X) followed by four alternatives (a), (b), (c) and (d). One out of these four alternatives contain region(s) common to the circle, square, triangle and rectangle similar to that marked by the dot in figure (X).

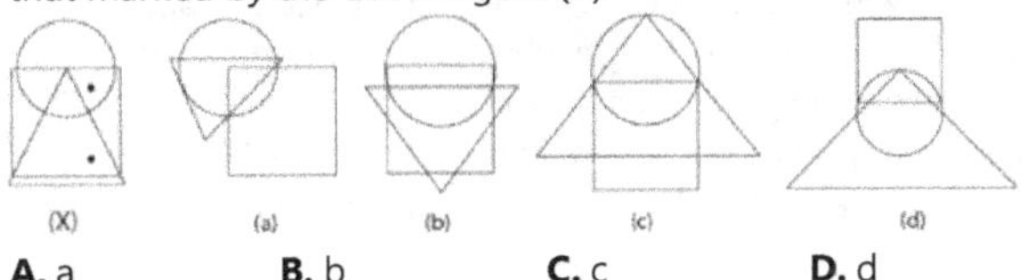

A. a   **B.** b   **C.** c   **D.** d

Q.30 The below question consists of a unfolded dice in the left side and four choices (a), (b), (c) and (d) are given in the form of complete dices in the right side. You are required to select the correct answer choice which is formed by folding the unfolded dice.

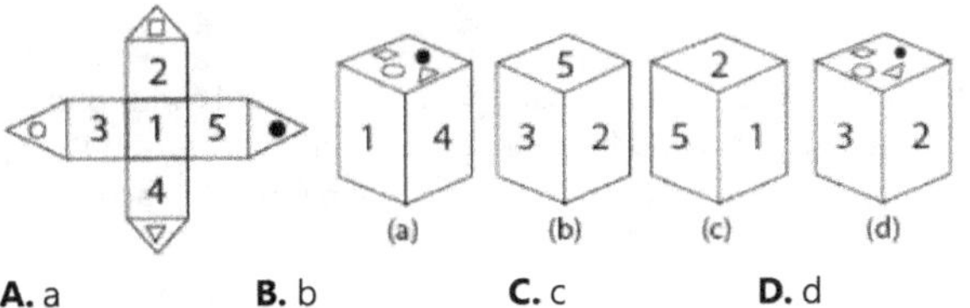

A. a   **B.** b   **C.** c   **D.** d

Q.31 A mirror is placed in front ofthe clock. The clock shows time 5:40. What will be its reflection in the mirror?

A. 6:20   **B.** 2:10

C. 2:50   **D.** It does not exist

Q.32 The below question consists of a combination of alphabets and followed by four alternatives (a), (b), (c) and (d). Choose the alternative which is closely resembles the mirror image of the given combination.

THINKANDLEARN

(a) THINKANDLEARN   (c) THINKANDLEARN

(b) THINKANDLEARN   (d) THINKANDLEARN

A. a   **B.** b   **C.** c   **D.** d

Q.33 Find the number of triangles in the given figure.

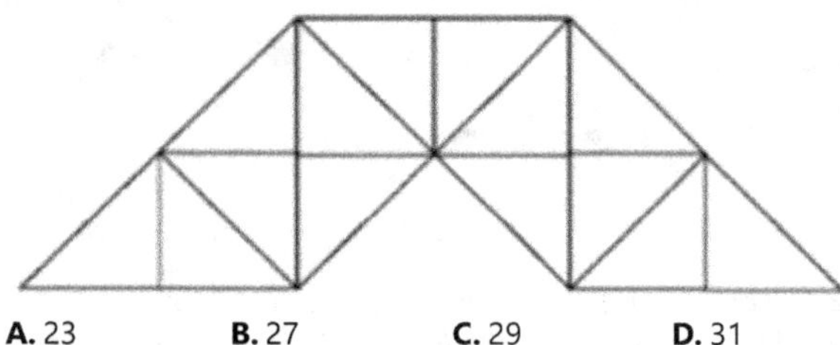

A. 23   **B.** 27   **C.** 29   **D.** 31

Q.34 The below question consists of four figures a, b, c and d followed by a set of four alternatives A, B, C and D. Which of the combinations given below when fitted into each other would form a complete square?

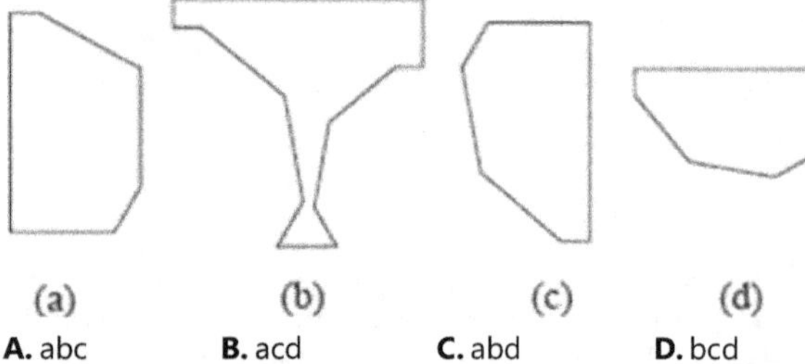

(a)   (b)   (c)   (d)

A. abc   **B.** acd   **C.** abd   **D.** bcd

Q.35 The below question consists of a set of three figures K, L and M showing a sequence of folding of a piece of paper. Figure M shows the manner in which the folded paper has been cut. These three figures are followed by four figures (1), (2), (3) and (4) from which you have to choose a figure which would most closely resemble the unfolded form of figure M.

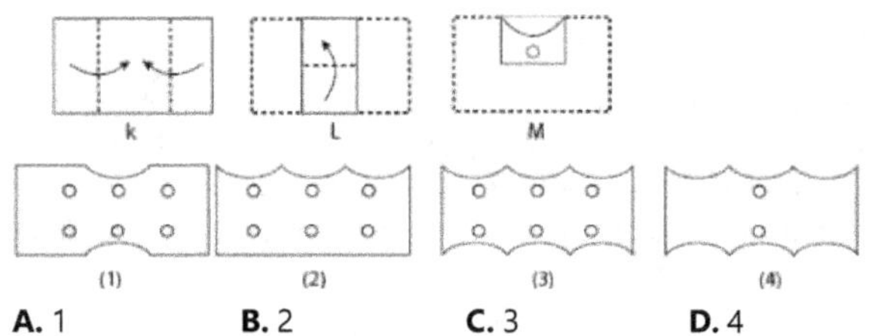

A. 1   **B.** 2   **C.** 3   **D.** 4

Q.36 The below question consists of a figure matrix with one or more missing terms and followed by four answer figures (1), (2), (3) and (4). Find the correct answer figure that will replace '?'

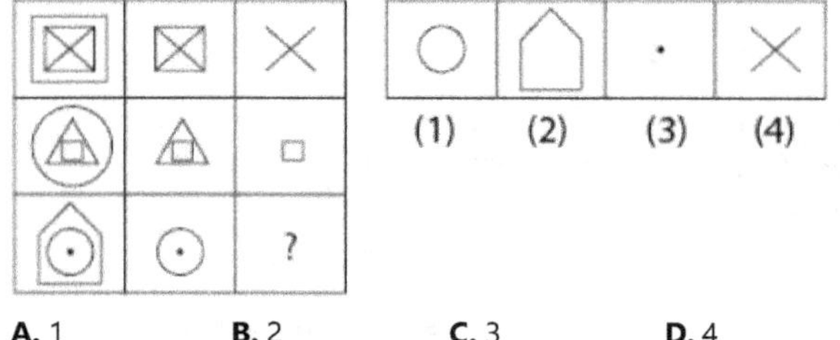

A. 1   **B.** 2   **C.** 3   **D.** 4

Q.37 The below question consists of a four figures. Three are similar in a certain way and so form a group. Find out which one of the figures does not belong to that group.

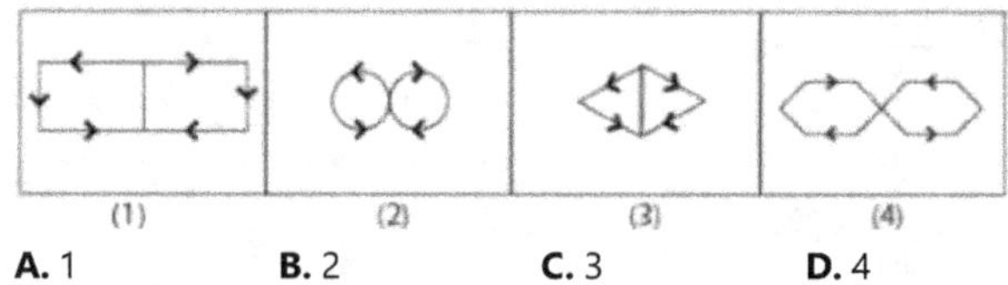

A. 1   **B.** 2   **C.** 3   **D.** 4

Q.38 The below question consists of a question figure and followed by four figures (1), (2), (3) and (4), which show the possible water images of the question figure. Choose one out of these four figures which shows the correct water image of the question figure.

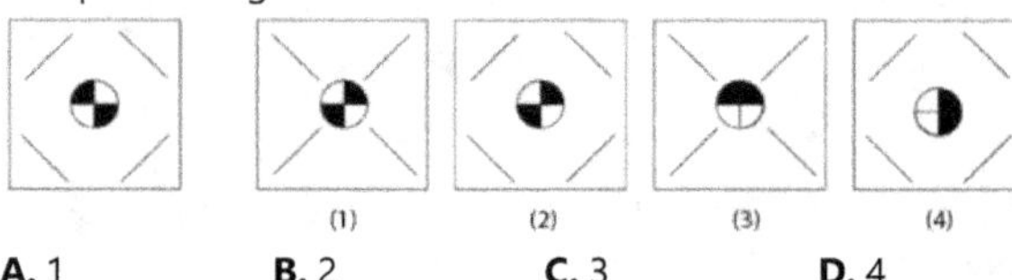

A. 1   **B.** 2   **C.** 3   **D.** 4

Q.39 The below question consists of problem figures followed by answer figures marked as (1), (2), (3), (4) and (5). You have to select that figure from the set of answer figures which would come in the place of question mark (?) in the problem figure.

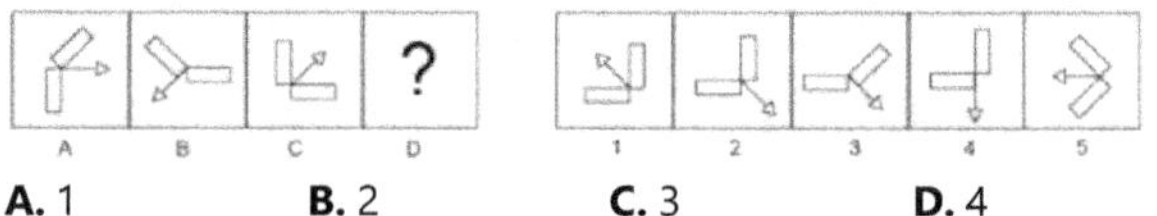

A. 1   **B.** 2   **C.** 3   **D.** 4

Q.40 Choose the correct alternative which is embedded in the question figure.

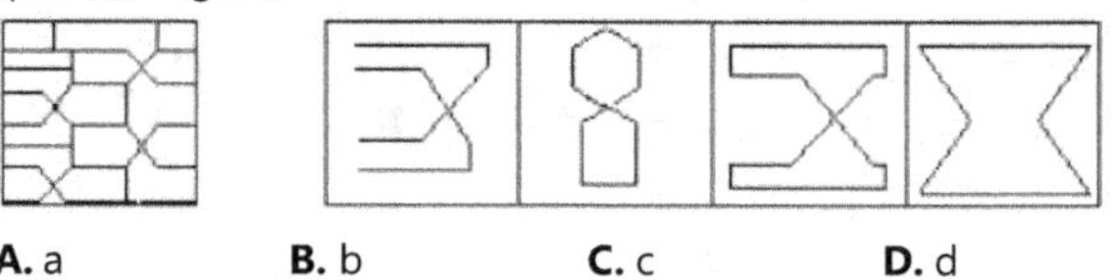

A. a   **B.** b   **C.** c   **D.** d

Q.41 Indian Cancer Research institute is located at-
A. New Delhi   **B.** Calcutta
C. Chennai   **D.** Mumbai

Q.42 Central Drug Research Institute is located at-
A. Trissur   **B.** Nagpur
C. Mysore   **D.** Lucknow

Q.43 Ajanta-Ellora caves are situated near-
A. Ajmer   **B.** Jaipur
C. Patna   **D.** Aurangabad

Q.44 National School of Mines is located in -
A. Dhanbad   **B.** Kavalpur
C. Udaipur   **D.** Hyderabad

Q.45 Sun Temple is situated at-
A. Konark   **B.** Banglore
C. Haridwar   **D.** Kerla

Q.46 The 'Golconda Fort' is in which state?
A. Telangana   **B.** Uttar Pradesh
C. Bihar   **D.** Karnataka

Q.47 Under Mother Teresa's guidance, the Missionaries of Charity built near Asansol, aleper colony is called-

A. Peace City   **B.** Sahara
C. Shanti Nagar   **D.** SOS

Q.48 'Kanchipuram' is in which of the following states?
A. Andhra Pradesh   **B.** Orissa
C. Kerala   **D.** Tamil Nadu

Q.49 The famous Meenakshi temple is located in-
A. Bihar   **B.** Madurai   **C.** Madras   **D.** Trichy

Q.50 'Tin Bhiga' lease by India to Bangladesh, was a part of-
A. West Bengal   **B.** Assam
C. Meghalaya   **D.** Tripura

Q.51 Five persons with names, P, M, U, T and X live separately in any one of the following: a palace, a hut, a fort, a house or a hotel. Each one likes one or two different colours from among the following: blue, black, red, yellow and green. U likes red and blue. T likes black. The person living in a palace does not like black or blue. P likes blue and red. M likes yellow only. X lives in a hotel. M may lives in :
A. fort   **B.** hut   **C.** palace   **D.** house

Q.52 From the given alternatives, select the word which cannot be formed using the letters of the given word.
BANGALORE
A. GARBAGE   **B.** ORANGE
C. LARGE   **D.** BANGLE

Q.53 Arrange the following in ascending order :
1. Centimeter 2. Kilometre
3. Decimetre 4. Metre
A. 3,1,2,4   **B.** 4,2,1,3,   **C.** 1,3,4,2   **D.** 2,4,3,1

Q.54 If B becomes A and P becomes O, what will K become in the English alphabet?
A. L   **B.** J   **C.** H   **D.** N

Q.55 From the given alternatives, select the word which cannot be formed using the letters of the given word.
ROTARYBLUES
A. STARY   **B.** LOUTUS
C. TABLET   **D.** BUTTER

Q.56 If you can write COLLEGE as DPMMFHF how can you write SCHOOL?
A. DITPMP   **B.** TDIPPM
C. RBGNNK   **D.** CLASS

Q.57 If 'green' is called 'white', 'white' is called 'yellow' , 'yellow' is called 'red', 'red' is called 'orange', then which of the following represents the colour of sunflower?
A. red   **B.** yellow   **C.** brown   **D.** indigo

Q.58 In a certain code language '234' means 'spark and fire', '456' means 'spark is cause' and '258' means 'fire is effect'. Which of the following numerals used for 'cause'?
A. 3   **B.** 4   **C.** 5   **D.** 6

Q.59 On 8th Feb, 2005 it was Tuesday. What was the day of the week on 8th Feb, 2004?

A. Tuesday   **B.** Monday
C. Sunday   **D.** Wednesday

Q.60 A told B,"The girl I met yesterday was the youngest daughter of the brother–in–law of my friend's mother." How is the girl related to A's friend?
A. Niece   **B.** Cousin
C. Friend   **D.** Daughter

// Smart Answer Sheet //

Correct Percentage of students who answered correctly. **Skipped** Percentage of students who skipped.

Q.	Ans.	Correct / Skipped
1	C	31.37 % / 23.53 %
2	B	27.45 % / 33.33 %
3	C	29.41 % / 33.34 %
4	C	27.45 % / 31.37 %
5	A	25.49 % / 31.37 %
6	B	33.33 % / 33.34 %
7	D	17.65 % / 33.33 %
8	B	35.29 % / 33.34 %
9	B	13.73 % / 37.25 %
10	C	25.49 % / 33.33 %
11	A	19.61 % / 35.29 %
12	C	21.57 % / 33.33 %
13	D	15.69 % / 29.41 %
14	D	21.57 % / 31.37 %
15	A	33.33 % / 33.34 %
16	B	23.53 % / 33.33 %
17	B	29.41 % / 37.26 %
18	C	23.53 % / 33.33 %
19	C	35.29 % / 27.46 %
20	A	19.61 % / 31.37 %
21	C	70.59 % / 9.8 %
22	B	58.82 % / 11.77 %
23	B	39.22 % / 9.8 %
24	D	43.14 % / 11.76 %
25	A	23.53 % / 15.69 %
26	B	29.41 % / 17.65 %
27	A	76.47 % / 11.77 %
28	A	78.43 % / 11.77 %
29	C	27.45 % / 11.77 %
30	C	49.02 % / 13.73 %
31	A	35.29 % / 9.81 %
32	D	49.02 % / 9.8 %
33	C	39.22 % / 9.8 %
34	D	39.22 % / 13.72 %
35	C	74.51 % / 11.76 %
36	C	80.39 % / 11.77 %
37	D	62.75 % / 11.76 %
38	B	76.47 % / 11.77 %
39	D	17.65 % / 11.76 %
40	A	52.94 % / 7.84 %
41	D	52.94 % / 9.81 %
42	D	49.02 % / 7.84 %
43	D	74.51 % / 7.84 %
44	A	64.71 % / 7.84 %
45	A	82.35 % / 9.81 %
46	A	49.02 % / 11.76 %
47	C	43.14 % / 9.8 %
48	D	62.75 % / 9.8 %
49	B	72.55 % / 9.8 %
50	A	68.63 % / 9.8 %
51	C	58.82 % / 11.77 %
52	A	80.39 % / 7.85 %
53	C	70.59 % / 7.84 %
54	B	80.39 % / 7.85 %
55	C	19.61 % / 15.68 %
56	B	78.43 % / 11.77 %
57	A	82.35 % / 11.77 %
58	D	62.75 % / 15.68 %
59	C	43.14 % / 9.8 %
60	B	37.25 % / 13.73 %

//Hints and Solutions//

1. $\quad \dfrac{x^2}{9} - \dfrac{y^2}{4} = 1$

$a = 3, b = 2$

$\therefore \theta = \sqrt{\dfrac{a^2+b^2}{a^2}} = \sqrt{\dfrac{13}{9}} = \dfrac{\sqrt{13}}{3}$

Hence, the correct option is (C).

2. Length of latus rectum $= 2\dfrac{b^2}{a} = \dfrac{2\times16}{5} = \dfrac{32}{5}$

$16x^2 + 25y^2 = 400$

$\dfrac{x^2}{25} + \dfrac{y^2}{16} = 1$

$a^2 = 25; b^2 = 16$

Hence, the correct option is (B).

3. 2h = x, 2k = y

y² = 4ax

K² = 2ah

y² = 2ax

Hence, the correct option is (C).

4. $x = 2t^2 + 4, y = 4t + 6, \quad y = 4t + 6 \rightarrow t = \left(\dfrac{y-6}{4}\right)$

$x = 2\left(\dfrac{y-6}{4}\right)^2 + 4 \Rightarrow \dfrac{(y-6)^2}{8} = x - 4$

$(y - 6)^2 = 4(2)(x - 4)$

Hence, the correct option is (C).

5. $ax^2 + by^2 + 2hxy + 2gx + 21y + c = 0$

represents ellipse if $h^2 - ab < 0$ $3x^2 + 12y^2 - 4x + 4y - 1 = 0$

$h = 0, a = 3, b = 12$

$h^2 - ab < 0$

Hence, the correct option is (A).

6. $x^2 + m^2x^2 - 20mx + 90$

$x^2(1 + m^2) - 20mx + 90 = 0$

$D < 0$

$400m^2 - 4 \times 90(1 + m^2) < 0$

$40m^2 < 360$

$m^2 < 9; |m| < 3$

Hence, the correct option is (B).

7.

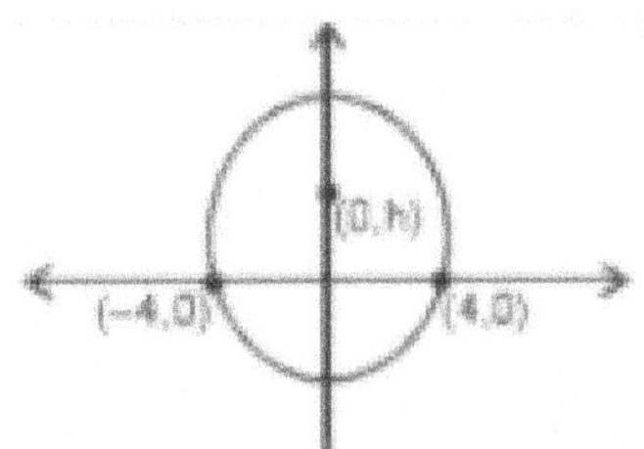

Center lies on y-axis locus x=0

Hence, the correct option is (D).

8. Let $p(h, 4 - h)$

$\left|\dfrac{4h+3(4-h)-10}{5}\right| = 1$

$|h + 2| = 5$

$h = 3, -7; p = 1,1$

$(3,1) \cdot (-7,11)$

Hence, the correct option is (B).

9. $2x^2 - 2x = 0 \quad x(x + 1) = 0 \quad x = 0,1; y = 0,1$

(0,0),(1,1) as diametric ends

$(x - 0)(x - 1) + (y + 0)(y - 1) = 0$

$x^2 + y^2 - x - y = 0$

Hence, the correct option is (B).

10.

$$x^2 + y^2 + 9x - 8y + 5 = 0$$

Centre circle (-2,4)

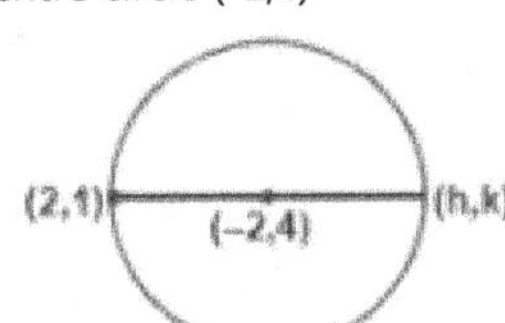

$\dfrac{h+2}{2} = -2$

$h = -4 - 2 = -6$

$\dfrac{k+1}{2} = 4 \Rightarrow k = 7$

$(h \cdot k) \rightarrow (-6.7)$

Hence, the correct option is (C).

11. Let ABCDEF be a regular hexagon.

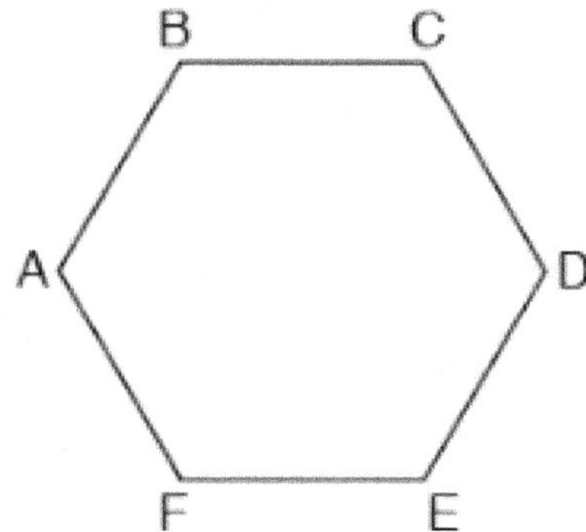

Three vertices out of its 6 vertices can be chosen in $^6C_3$ ways. Therefore, 20 triangles can be made by

joining three vertices at a time. Out of these 20 triangles, only ACE and BDF are equilateral. Hence, the required probability = $\frac{1}{10}$

$$= 1/10$$

Hence, the correct option is (A).

12. θ in 2nd quad Cos< 0

$$|\cos\theta| = \left|\frac{1-t^2}{1+t^2}\right| = \frac{|1-t^2|}{1+t^2}$$

$$\cos\theta = -\frac{|1-t^2|}{1+t^2}$$

Hence, the correct option is (C).

13. $\cos^{-1}x < \sin^{-1}x$

$$x \in \left(\frac{1}{\sqrt{2}}, 1\right], \cos^{-1}x < \sin^{-1}x$$

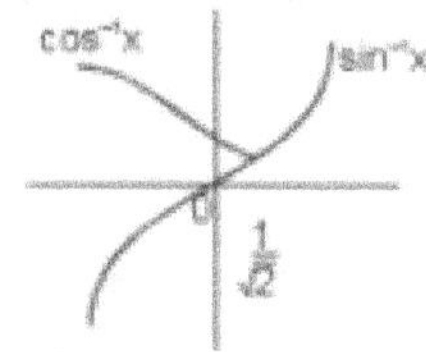

Hence, the correct option is (D).

14. Given, $2\sin x + \cos x = 3$

$$LHS = 2\sin x + \cos x$$

since, $-\sqrt{5} \le 2\sin x + \cos x \le \sqrt{5}$

But $\sqrt{5} < 3$

Hence, no solution exist.

Hence, the correct option is (D).

15. $\tan\alpha = \frac{a}{a+1}, \tan\beta = \frac{1}{2a+1}$

$$\tan(\alpha + \beta) = \frac{\frac{a}{a+1} + \frac{1}{2a+1}}{1 - \frac{a}{(a+1)(2a+1)}} = \frac{\frac{a(2a+1)+a+1}{(a+1)(2a+1)}}{\frac{(a+1)(2a+1)-a}{(a+1)(2a+1)}} = \frac{2a^2+2a+1}{2a^2+2a+1}$$

$$= 1$$

$$a + \beta = \frac{\pi}{4}$$

Hence, the correct option is (A).

16. $(1 + \tan\theta)\left(1 + \frac{(1-\tan\theta)}{1+\tan\theta}\right)$

$$= (1 + \tan\theta)\frac{2}{1+\tan\theta} = 2$$

Hence, the correct option is (B).

17.

$$\sin\theta + \cos\theta = \frac{b}{a}$$

$$\sin\theta \cdot \cos\theta = \frac{c}{a}$$

$$\left(\frac{b}{a}\right)^2 = 1 + \frac{2c}{a}$$

$$b^2 = a^2 + 2ac$$

$$a^2 - b^2 + 2ac = 0$$

Hence, the correct option is (B).

18. Addition is defined if order of A is equal to order of B

A B nxm nxm

is defined if m = n ⇒ A, B are square matrices of same order

Hence, the correct option is (C).

19. $A = A^7$

$$\begin{pmatrix} 3 & x-1 \\ 2x+3 & x+2 \end{pmatrix} = \begin{pmatrix} 3 & 2x+3 \\ x-1 & x+2 \end{pmatrix}$$

$$\Rightarrow x - 1 = 2x + 3 \text{ or } x = -4$$

Hence, the correct option is (C).

20.
$$z = \begin{matrix} 1 & 1+2i & -5i \\ 1-2i & -3 & 5+3i \\ 5i & 5-3i & 7 \end{matrix} = 1(-21-64) - 1 - 2i)(7(1+2i) + 5i(5-3i) + 5i((1+2i)(5+3i) - 15i)$$

= Real

Hence, the correct option is (A).

21.

Hence, the correct option is (C).

22. Circle and square are rotating in clockwise direction at an angle of 90°. Triangle is rotating in anticlockwise direction at an angle of 90°.

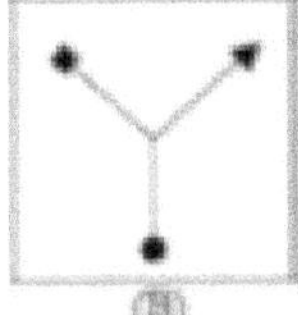

Hence, the correct option is (B).

23.

Hence, the correct option is (B).

24.

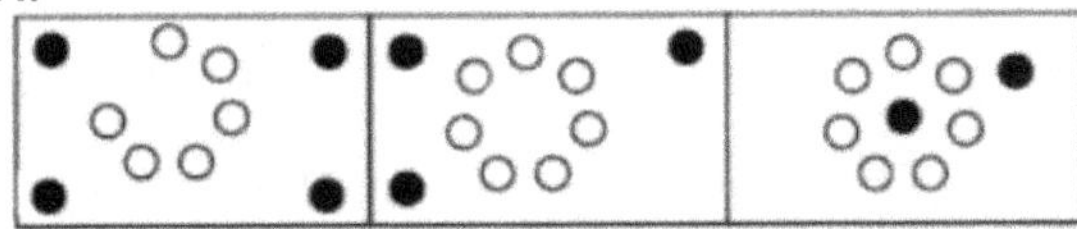

Hence, the correct option is (D).

25. The outermost element has changed its position to become the innermost element, and similarlly, all the elements have changes their respective positions.

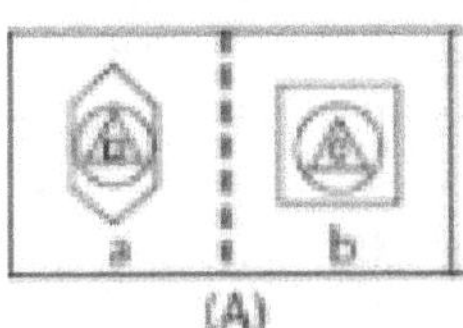

Hence, the correct option is (A).

26.

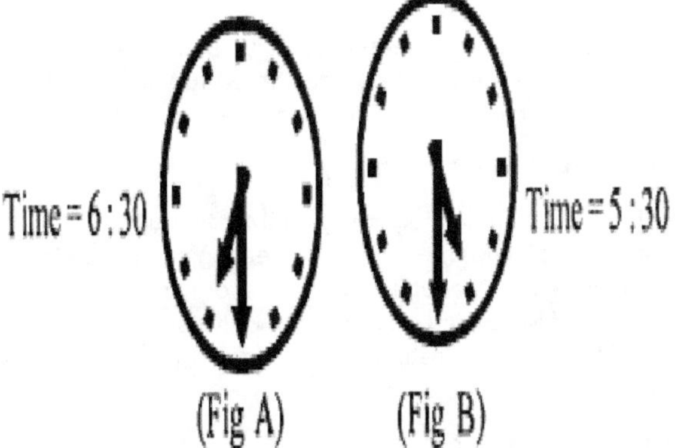

Clearly, fig (A) shows the time (6 : 30) in the clock as it appears in a mirror Then its mirror-image i.e. Fig (B) shows the actual time in the clock i.e. 5:30. You can solve it quickly if you

remember that the sum of actual time and image time is always 12 hours.

Hence, the correct option is (B).

27.

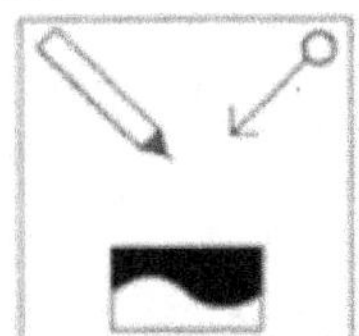

Hence, the correct option is (A).

28.

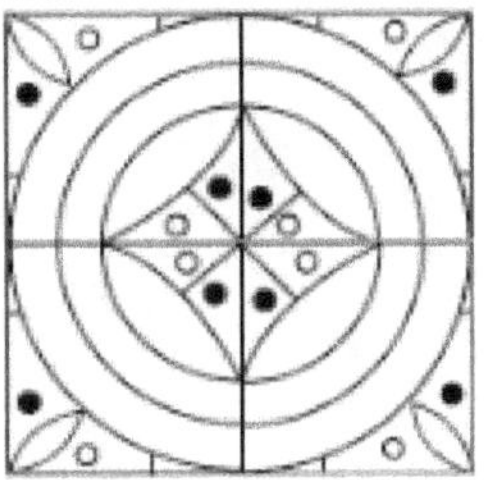

Hence, the correct option is (A).

29.

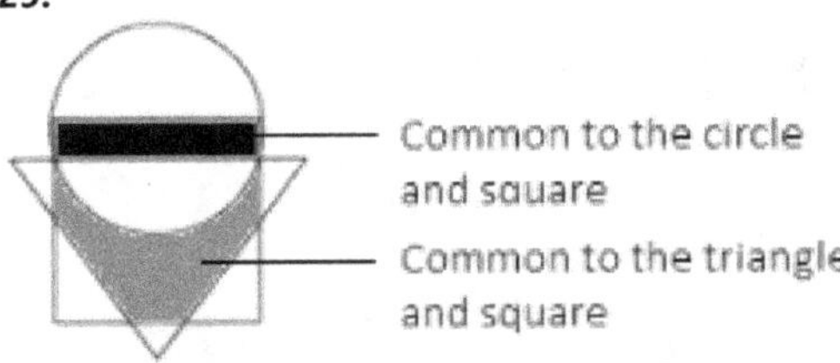

Hence, the correct option is (C).

30.

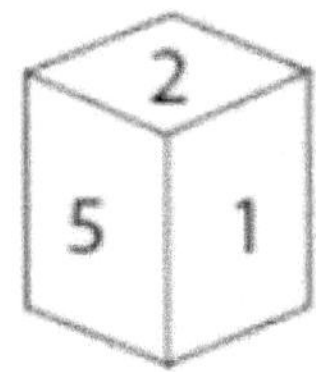

Hence, the correct option is (C).

31.

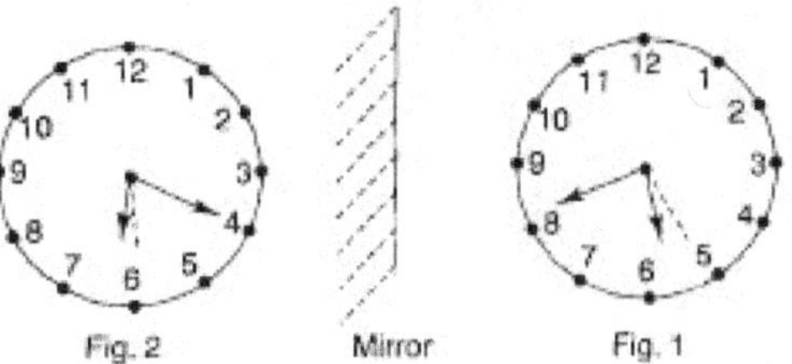

Figure 1 is the clock that shows time 5:40. On its left side, a mirror is placed and Fig. is the reflection figure of Fig.
Clearly, time seems to be 6:20. Short cut: Subtract 5:40 from 12, we get 6:20.

Hence, the correct option is (A).

32.

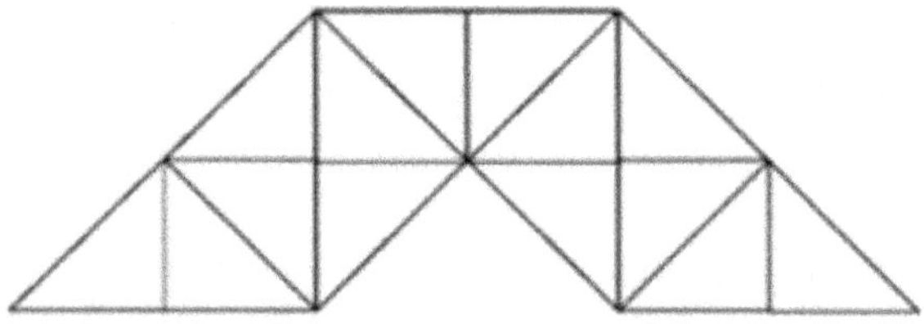

Hence, the correct option is (D).

33. 14 (small triangles) + 11(medium triangles) + 4(big triangles) = 29

Hence, the correct option is (C).

34.

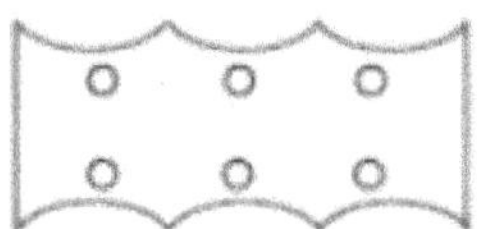

Hence, the correct option is (D).

35.

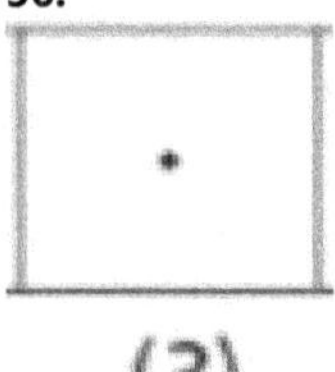

Hence, the correct option is (C).

36.

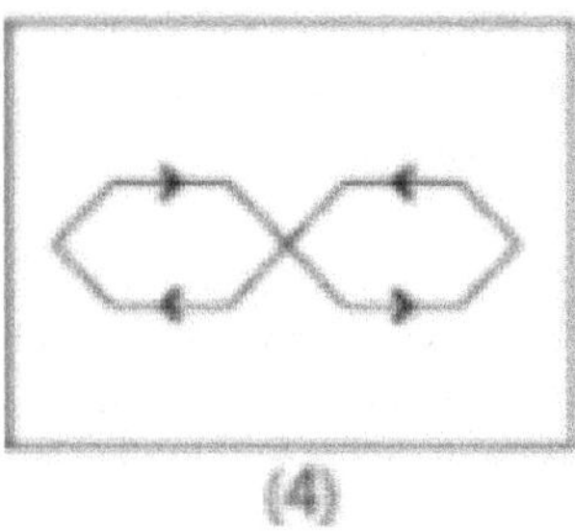

Hence, the correct option is (C).

37. In all figures, the first element is rotating in anticlockwise direction and second element is rotating in clockwise direction except in fourth figure.

Hence, the correct option is (D).

38.

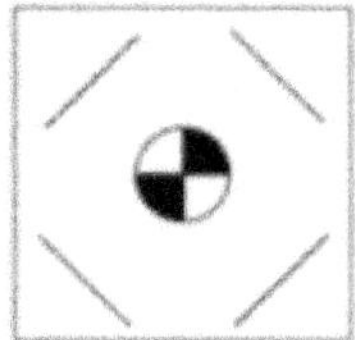

Hence, the correct option is (B).

39. The arrows rotate 135°CW and the remaining part of the figure rotates 90° ACW.

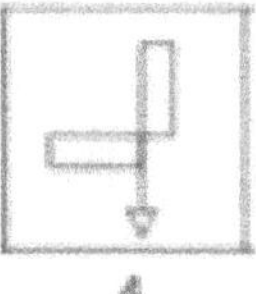

Hence, the correct option is (D).

40.

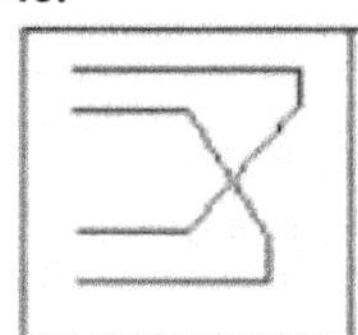

Hence, the correct option is (A).

41. The origins of the Advanced Centre for Treatment, **Research** and Education in **Cancer** (ACTREC) are rooted in the **Indian Cancer Research** Centre (ICRC), which was established in 1952 in Parel, Mumbai, under the purview of the Ministry of Health, Government of **India**.

Hence, the correct option is (D).

42. The Central Drug Research Institute is a multidisciplinary research laboratory in Lucknow, India, employing scientific personnel from various areas of biomedical sciences.

Hence, the correct option is (D).

43. The Ajanta Caves are 30 (approximately) rock-cut Buddhist cave monuments which date from the 2nd century BCE to about 480 CE in Aurangabad district of Maharashtra state of India.

Hence, the correct option is (D).

44. The Indian Institute of Technology (ISM), Dhanbad (abbreviated as IIT (ISM) is a public engineering and research institution located in Dhanbad, India. It was formerly known as Indian School of Mines and was a Central University before it was converted into an Indian Institute of Technology (IIT) and an Institute of National Importance.

Hence, the correct option is (A).

45. Konark Sun Temple is a 13th-century CE sun temple at Konark about 35 kilometres (22 mi) northeast from Puri on the coastline of Odisha, India. The temple is attributed to king Narasingha deva I of the Eastern Ganga Dynasty about 1250 CE.

Hence, the correct option is (A).

46. Golconda, also spelled Golkonda or Golkunda, historic fortress and ruined city lying 5 miles (8 km) west of Hyderabad in western Telangana state, southern India. From 1518 to 1591 it was the capital of the Quṭb Shāhī kingdom (1518–1687), one of five Muslim sultanates of the Deccan.

Hence, the correct option is (A).

47. The Missionaries of Charity (Latin: Missionariarum a Caritate) is a Roman Catholic (Latin Church) religious congregation established in 1950 by Mother Teresa, now known in the Catholic Church as Saint Teresa of Calcutta. In 2012 it consisted of over 4,500 religious sisters. Members of the order designate their affiliation using the order's initials, "M.C." A member of the congregation must adhere to the vows of chastity, poverty, obedience, and the fourth vow, to give "wholehearted free service to the poorest of the poor."Today, the order consists of both contemplative and active branches in several countries.

Missionaries care for those who include refugees, former prostitutes, the mentally ill, sick children, abandoned children, lepers, people with AIDS, the aged, and convalescent. They have schools run by volunteers to educate street children and run soup kitchens as well as other services according to the community needs. These services are provided, without charge, to people regardless of their religion or social status.

Hence, the correct option is (C).

48. Kanchipuram, also known as Kānchi or Kancheepuram, is a city in the Indian state of Tamil Nadu in Tondaimandalam region, 72 km (45 mi) from Chennai – the capital of Tamil Nadu.

Hence, the correct option is (D).

49. It is dedicated to Meenakshi, a form of Parvati, and her consort, Sundareshwar, a form of Shiva. The temple is at the center of the ancient temple city of Madurai mentioned in the Tamil Sangam literature, with the goddess temple mentioned in 6th century CE texts.

Hence, the correct option is (B).

50. The Tin (or Teen) Bigha Corridor is a strip of land belonging to India on the West Bengal–Bangladesh border which, in September 2011, was leased to Bangladesh so that it can access its Dahagram–Angarpota enclaves.

Hence, the correct option is (A).

51.

Person	Palace	Hut	Fort	House	Hotel	Blue	Black	Red	Yellow	Green
P						✓		✓		
M	✓					✕	✕		✓	
U						✓		✓		
T					✓					
X				✓						

According to the table M lives in palace.

Hence, the correct option is (C).

52. There is only one 'G' in the given word. Therefore, the word GARBAGE cannot be formed.

Hence, the correct option is (A).

53. The correct order is Centimeter (0.01 meter)-Decimeter (0.1 meter)- Meter (1 meter)-Kilometer (1000 meter). `

Hence, the correct option is (C).

54.

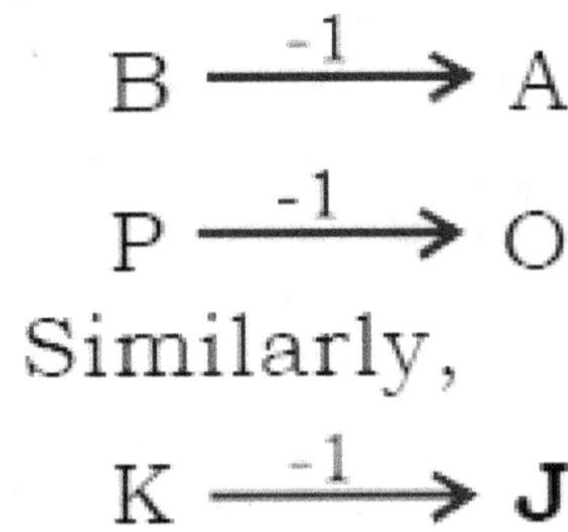

Hence, the correct option is (B).

55. there is only one 'T' in the given word. So, the word TABLET cannot be formed.

$$RO[TARY]BLUE[S] \Rightarrow STARY$$

$$R[OT]ARYB[LU]E[S] \Rightarrow LOTUS$$

R O TA ARY BLUE]S $\Rightarrow$ BUTLER

Hence, the correct option is (C).

56.

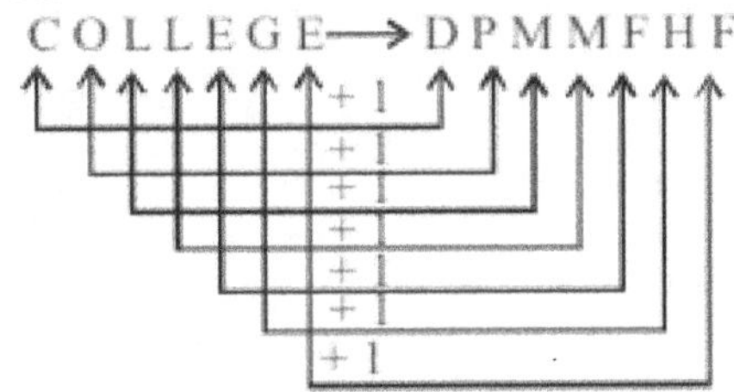

Similarly,

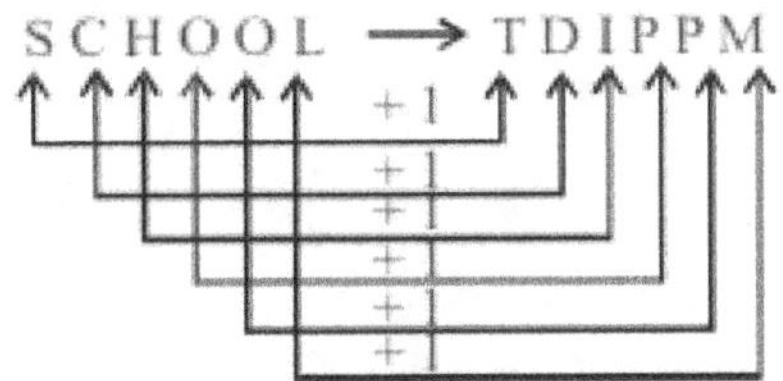

Hence, the correct option is (B).

57. The colour of sunflower is yellow and 'yellow' is called 'red'. Hence sunflower is red.

Hence, the correct option is (A).

58. In the first and second statement, the common code digit is '4' and the common word is 'spark'. So, '4' means 'spark'. In the second and third statements, the common code digit is '5' and the common word is 'is'. So, '5' means 'is'. Thus, in the second statement, '6' means 'cause'.

Hence, the correct option is (D).

59. The year 2004 is a leap year. It has 2 odd days.

∴The day on 8th Feb, 2004 is 2 days before the day on 8th

Feb, 2005. Hence, this day is Sunday.

Hence, the correct option is (C).

60. Daughter of brother-in-law — Niece; Mother's niece — Cousin.. So, the girl is the cousin of A's friend.

Hence, the correct option is (B).

Mock Test 10

Mathematics

Q.1 The value of $\dfrac{\cot x - \tan x}{\cot 2x}$ is-

A. 1   **B.** 2   **C.** -1   **D.** 4

Q.2 In how many different ways can the letters of the word 'LEADING' be arranged in such a way that the vowels always come together?

A. 360   **B.** 480   **C.** 720   **D.** 5040

Q.3 Let R be the set of real numbers and the mapping $f : R \to R$ and $g : R \to R$ be defined by $f(x) = 5 - x^2$ and $g(x) = 3x - 4$, then the value of $(fog)(-1)$ is:

A. -44   **B.** -54   **C.** -32   **D.** -64

Q.4 $A = \{1,2,3,4\}, B = \{1,2,3,4,5,6\}$ are two sets, and function $f : A \to B$ is defined by $f(x) = x + 2 \,\forall x \in A$, then the function is:

A. bijective   **B.** onto

C. one–one   **D.** many–one

Q.5 If the matrices $A = \begin{bmatrix} 2 & 1 & 3 \\ 4 & 1 & 0 \end{bmatrix}$ and $B = \begin{bmatrix} 1 & -1 \\ 0 & 2 \\ 5 & 0 \end{bmatrix}$, then AB will be:

A. $\begin{bmatrix} 17 & 0 \\ 4 & -2 \end{bmatrix}$ **B.** $\begin{bmatrix} 4 & 0 \\ 0 & 4 \end{bmatrix}$

C. $\begin{bmatrix} 17 & 4 \\ 0 & -2 \end{bmatrix}$ **D.** $\begin{bmatrix} 0 & 0 \\ 0 & 0 \end{bmatrix}$

Q.6 ω is an imaginary cube root of unity and
$$\begin{vmatrix} x + \omega^2 & \omega & 1 \\ \omega & \omega^2 & 1 + x \\ 1 & x + \omega & \omega^2 \end{vmatrix} = 0$$
then one of the values of x is:

A. 1   **B.** 0   **C.** -1   **D.** 2

Q.7 If $A = \begin{bmatrix} 1 & 2 \\ -4 & -1 \end{bmatrix}$ then A^{-1} is:

A. $\frac{1}{7}\begin{bmatrix} -1 & -2 \\ 4 & 1 \end{bmatrix}$ **B.** $\frac{1}{7}\begin{bmatrix} 1 & 2 \\ -4 & -1 \end{bmatrix}$

C. $\frac{1}{7}\begin{bmatrix} -1 & -2 \\ 4 & 1 \end{bmatrix}$ **D.** Both A and C

Q.8 The value of $\dfrac{2}{3!} + \dfrac{4}{5!} + \dfrac{6}{7!} + \cdots \cdots$ is:

A. $e^{1/2}$ **B.** e^{-1} **C.** e **D.** $e^{-1/3}$

Q.9 If sum of an infinite geometric series is $\dfrac{4}{5}$ and its 1st term is $\dfrac{3}{4}$, then its common ratio is:

A. $\dfrac{7}{16}$ **B.** $\dfrac{9}{16}$ **C.** $\dfrac{1}{9}$ **D.** $\dfrac{7}{9}$

Q.10 The number of permutations by taking all letters and keeping the vowels of the word COMBINE in the odd places is:

A. 96   **B.** 144   **C.** 512   **D.** 576

Q.11 If $^{n-1}C_3 + {}^{n-1}C_4 > {}^nC_3$, then n is just greater than integer:

A. 5   **B.** 6   **C.** 4   **D.** 7

Q.12 If in the expansion of $(a - 2b)^n$, the sum of the 5th and 6th term is zero, then the value of $\dfrac{a}{b}$ is:

A. $\dfrac{(n-4)}{5}$ **B.** $\dfrac{2(n-4)}{5}$ **C.** $\dfrac{5}{(n-4)}$ **D.** $\dfrac{5}{2(n-4)}$

Q.13 $(2^{3a} - 1)$ will be divisible by $(\forall n \in N)$-

A. 25   **B.** 8   **C.** 7   **D.** 3

Q.14 Sum of the last 30 coeffivients in the expansion of $(1 + x)^{59}$, when expanded in ascending powers of x is-

A. 2^{59} **B.** 2^{58} **C.** 2^{30} **D.** 2^{29}

Q.15 If $(1 - x + x2)n = a0 + a1x + \dots + a2n\, x2n$, then the value of $a0 + a2 + a4 + \dots + a2n$ is:

A. $3^n + \dfrac{1}{2}$ **B.** $3^n - \dfrac{1}{2}$ **C.** $\dfrac{3^n - 1}{2}$ **D.** $\dfrac{3^n + 1}{2}$

Q.16 If α, β be the roots of the quadratic equation $x2 + x + 1 = 0$ then the equation whose roots are $\alpha19, \beta7$ is:

A. $x^2 - x + 1 = 0$ **B.** $x^2 - x - 1 = 0$

C. $x^2 + x - 1 = 0$ **D.** $x^2 + x + 1 = 0$

Q.17 The roots of the quadratic equation $x^2 - 2\sqrt{3}x - 22 = 0$ are:

A. imaginry

B. real, rational and equal

C. real, irrational and unequal

D. real, rational and unequal

Q.18 The qudratic equation $x^2 + 15\,|x| + 14 = 0$ has:

A. only positive solutions

B. only negative solutions

C. no solution

D. both positive and negative solution

Q.19 If $z = \dfrac{4}{1-i}$, then $\overline{z}$ is (where $\overline{z}$ is complex conjugate of z):

A. $2(1 + i)$ **B.** $(1 + i)$ **C.** $\dfrac{2}{(1-i)}$ **D.** $\dfrac{4}{(1-i)}$

Q.20 If $-\pi < \arg(z) < -\dfrac{\pi}{2}$ then $\arg \overline{z} - \arg(-\overline{z})$ is:

A. π **B.** $-\pi$ **C.** $\dfrac{\pi}{2}$ **D.** $\dfrac{-\pi}{2}$

General Aptitude

Q.21 Select a figure from amongst the Answer Figures which will continue the same series as established by the five Problem Figures.

Problem Figures: Answer Figures:

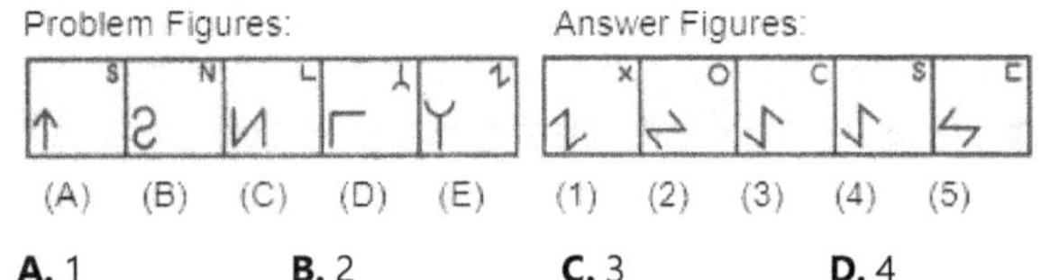

(A)   (B)   (C)   (D)   (E)   (1)   (2)   (3)   (4)   (5)

A. 1   **B.** 2   **C.** 3   **D.** 4

Q.22 Select a figure from amongst the Answer Figures which will continue the same series as established by the five Problem Figures.

Problem Figures: Answer Figures:

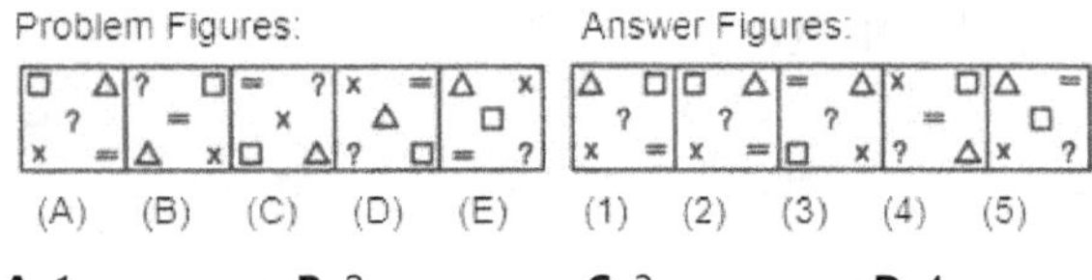

(A)   (B)   (C)   (D)   (E)   (1)   (2)   (3)   (4)   (5)

A. 1   **B.** 2   **C.** 3   **D.** 4

Q.23 Choose the figure which is different from the rest.

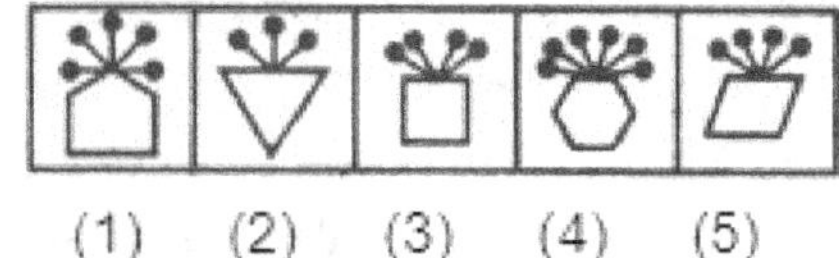

(1)   (2)   (3)   (4)   (5)

A. 1   **B.** 2   **C.** 3   **D.** 4

Q.24 Choose the figure which is different from the rest.

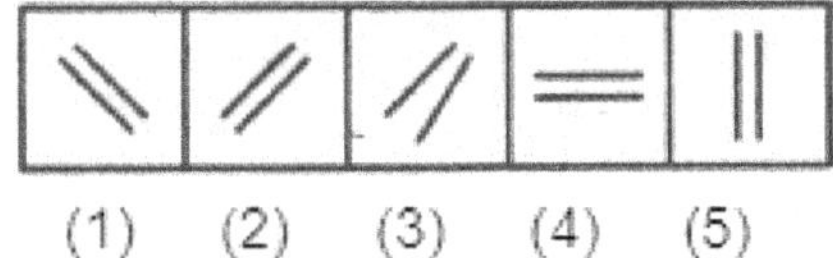

(1)   (2)   (3)   (4)   (5)

A. 1   **B.** 2   **C.** 3   **D.** 4

Q.25 Choose the alternative which is closely resembles the mirror image of the given combination.

ANS43Q12

(1) ANS43Q12
(3) SNA43Q21   (2) S1Q34SNA
(4) 1SQ43ANS

A. 1   **B.** 2   **C.** 3   **D.** 4

Q.26 Choose the alternative which is closely resembles the mirror image of the given combination.

TARAIN1014A

(1) A410INIARAT
(3) A10141TARAIN   (2) A1014INIARAT
(4) A4101NIARAT

A. 1   **B.** 2   **C.** 3   **D.** 4

Q.27 Find out the alternative figure which contains figure (X) as its part.

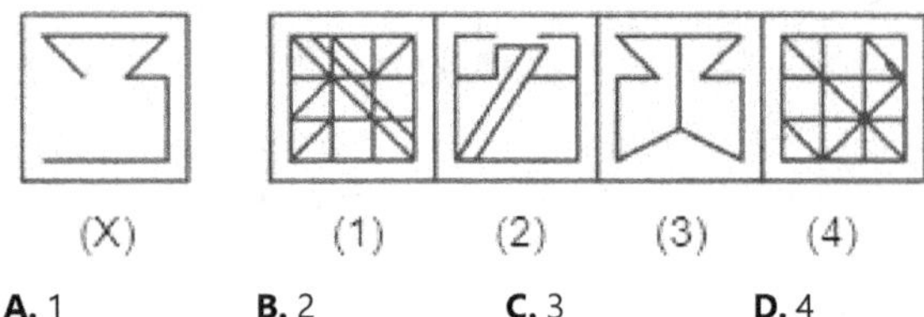

(X)   (1)   (2)   (3)   (4)

A. 1   **B.** 2   **C.** 3   **D.** 4

Q.28 Find out the alternative figure which contains figure (X) as its part.

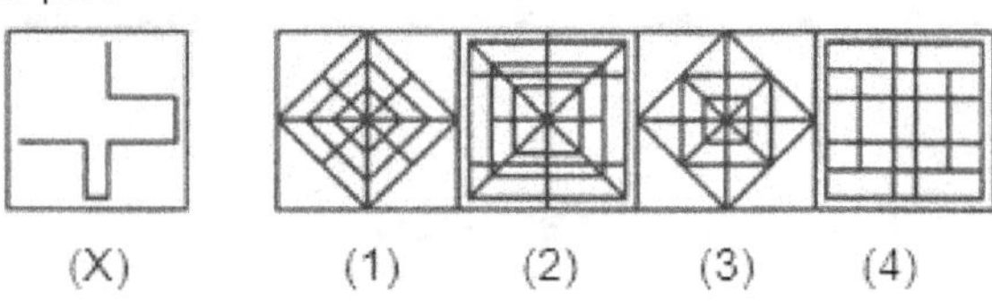

(X)   (1)   (2)   (3)   (4)

A. 1   **B.** 2   **C.** 3   **D.** 4

Q.29 Select a suitable figure from the four alternatives that would complete the figure matrix.

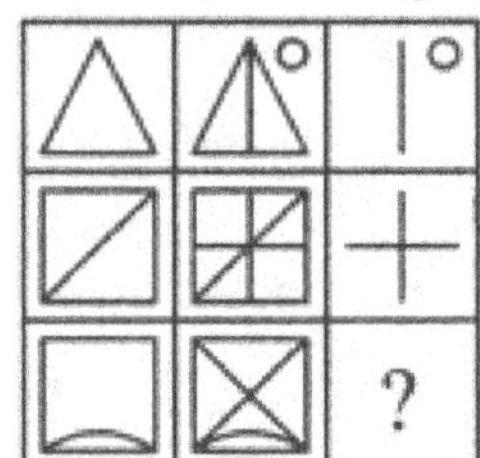

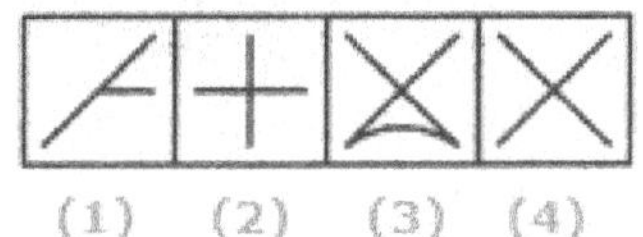

(1)   (2)   (3)   (4)

A. 1   **B.** 2   **C.** 3   **D.** 4

Q.30 Select a suitable figure from the four alternatives that would complete the figure matrix.

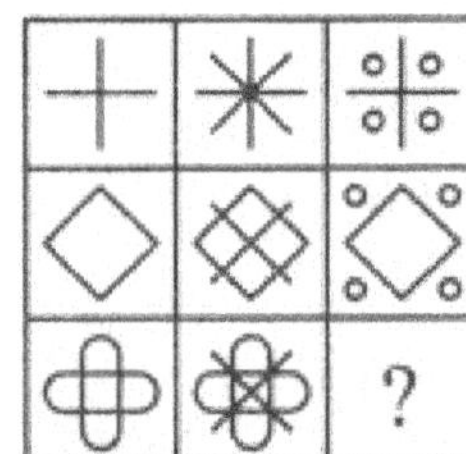

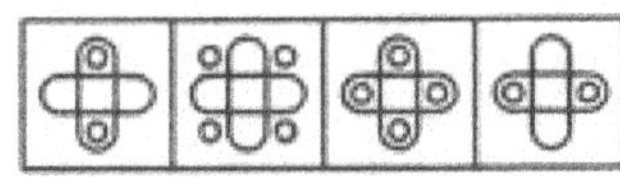

(1)   (2)   (3)   (4)

A. 1   **B.** 2   **C.** 3   **D.** 4

Q.31 Choose a figure which would most closely resemble the unfolded form of Figure (Z).

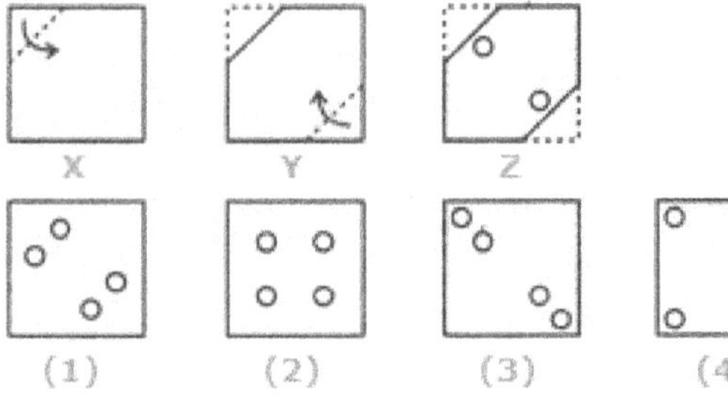

(1)   (2)   (3)   (4)

A. 1   **B.** 2   **C.** 3   **D.** 4

Q.32 Choose a figure which would most closely resemble the unfolded form of Figure (Z).

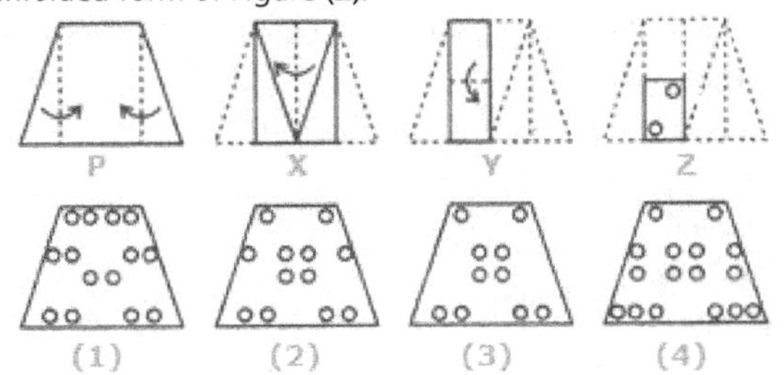

A. 1   **B.** 2   **C.** 3   **D.** 4

Q.33 Group the given figures into three classes using each figure only once.

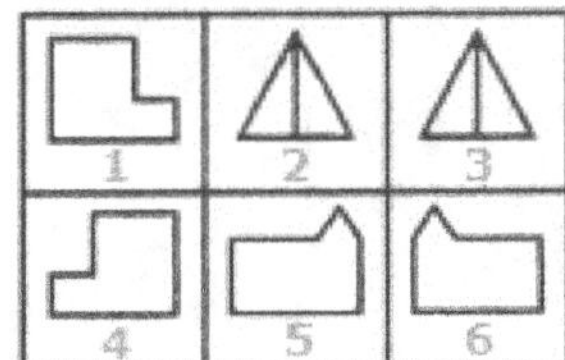

A. 1,4 ; 2,3 ; 5,6   **B.** 1,5 ; 2,6 ; 4,3
C. 1,6 ; 2,3 ; 4,5   **D.** 1,2 ; 3,6 ; 4,5

Q.34 Select the alternative which represents three out of the five alternative figures which when fitted into each other would form a complete square.

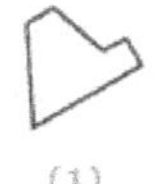   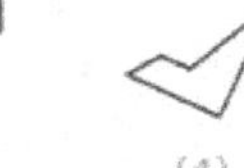 

A. 145   **B.** 245   **C.** 123   **D.** 234

Q.35 Select a suitable figure from the Answer Figures that would replace the question mark (?).

Problem Figures: Answer Figures:

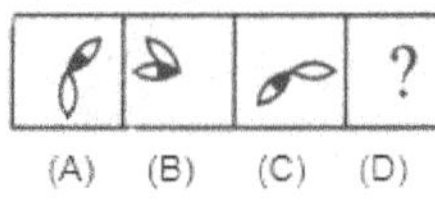 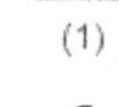 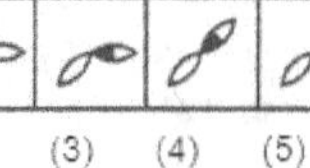

A. 1   **B.** 2   **C.** 3   **D.** 4

Q.36 Find the number of triangles in the given figure.

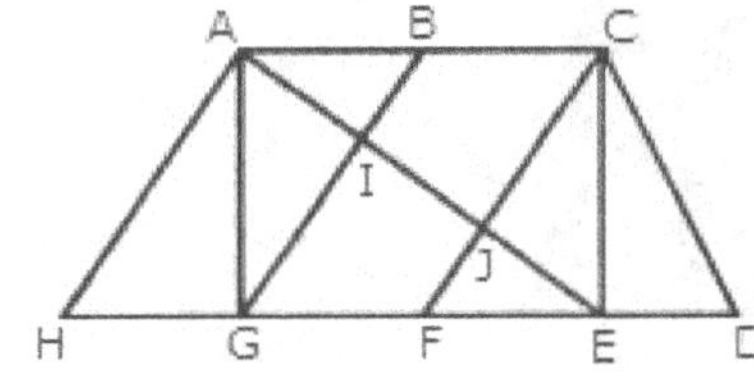

A. 8   **B.** 10   **C.** 12   **D.** 14

Q.37 Identify the figure that completes the pattern.

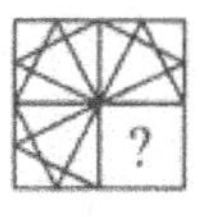     

A. 1   **B.** 2   **C.** 3   **D.** 4

Q.38 Find out from amongst the four alternatives as to how the pattern would appear when the transparent sheet is folded at the dotted line.

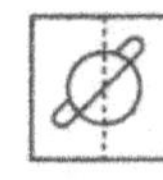 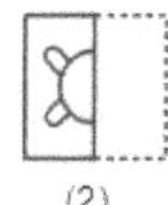 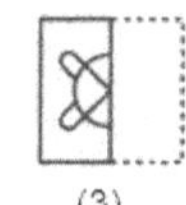 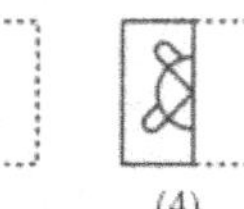

A. 1   **B.** 2   **C.** 3   **D.** 4

Q.39 Choose the set of figures which follows the given rule.
Rule: Closed figures losing their sides and open figures gaining their sides.

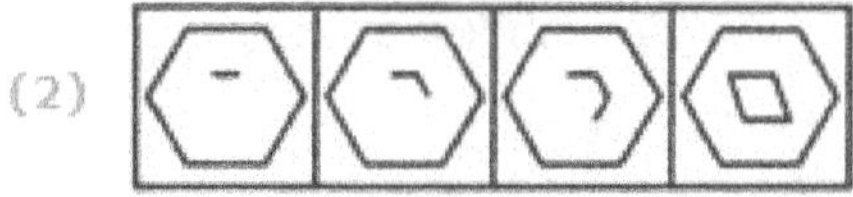
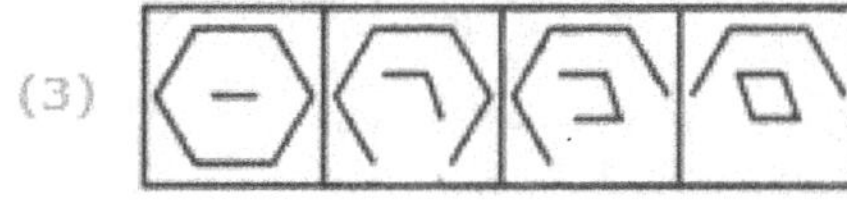
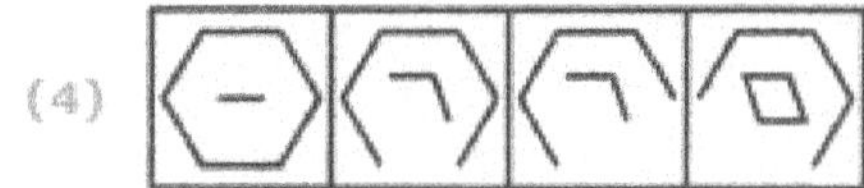

A. 1   **B.** 2   **C.** 3   **D.** 4

Q.40 Select the figure which satisfies the same conditions of placement of the dots as in Figure-X.

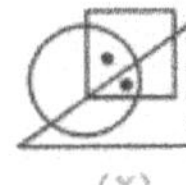  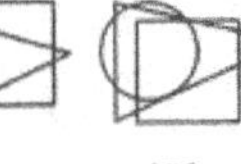  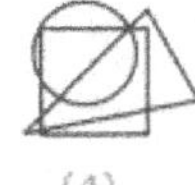

A. 1   **B.** 2   **C.** 3   **D.** 4

Q.41 The first Indian University was opened in 1857 was in-
A. Chennai   **B.** Bihar   **C.** Mumbai   **D.** Kolkata

Q.42 The largest dry rock in India is situated at:
A. Mumbai   **B.** Cochin
C. Marmugao   **D.** Kolkata

Q.43 The largest Indian State by area is-
A. Rajasthan   **B.** Maharashtra
C. Uttar Pradesh   **D.** Madhya Pradesh

Q.44 Which is the oldest monuments?
A. Qutub Minar   **B.** Ajanta Caves
C. Khajurah   **D.** Taj Mahal

Q.45 Ms. Harita Kaur has the distinction of being the first Indian Women-
A. pilot to fly an aircraft solo
B. ambassador to a foreign country
C. to be inducted into Indian Navy

D. doctor to create first test tube baby

Q.46 The largest and the oldest museum of India is located in the state/union territory of-

A. New Delhi

B. West Bengal

C. Andhra Pradesh

D. Uttar Pradesh

Q.47 The first Indian Satellite launched from Soviet Cosmodrome is?

A. Bhaskara

B. Bharat

C. Rohini

D. Aryabhatta

Q.48 The first nuclear reactor in India is:

A. Dhurva   **B.** Harsha   **C.** Vipula   **D.** Apsara

Q.49 The first person of Indian origin to be appointed as a judge in U.S. is-

A. P.A.Sangma

B. Basava Rajeswari

C. R.C.Bharadwaj

D. Ridhi Desai

Q.50 Largest Mint in India is located at-

A. Nasik

B. Kolkata

C. Hyderabad

D. Mumbai

Q.51 Arrange the given words in the sequence in which they occur in the dictionary.

1. Necrology
2. Necromancy
3. Necropolis
4. Necrophilia

A. 1243   **B.** 2314   **C.** 2431   **D.** 1234

Q.52 What will be the day of the week 15th August, 2010?

A. Thursday

B. Sunday

C. Monday

D. Saturday

Q.53 Find the wrong number in the given series.
9,11,20,31,53,82

A. 46   **B.** 521   **C.** 53   **D.** 343

Q.54 Direction : In each of the following questions, select the related word/letters/number from the given alternatives.
EV: BG::PS :?

A. CE   **B.** RT   **C.** KH   **D.** TW

Q.55 Direction : In each of the following questions, select the related word/letters/number from the given alternatives.
Cricket : LBW : : Hockey : ?

A. Breaststroke

B. Bridie

C. Checkmate

D. Stroke

Q.56 Direction : In each of the following questions, select the related word/letters/number from the given alternatives.
Cat : Kitten : : ?

A. Dog : Colt

B. Fox : Gosling

C. Lion : Cub

D. Horse : Joey

Q.57 Direction : these questions, statements are given followed by two conclusions I and II. You have to consider both the statements to be true even if they seem to be at variance from commonly known facts. You have to decide which of the given conclusions is/are definitely drawn from the given statements. Select answer as: (A) if only I follows (B) if only II follows (C) if neither I nor II follows (D) if both I and II follows

Statements :

Most clocks are fans.

Some fans are walls.

Conclusions :

I. Some walls are fans.

II. Some clocks are walls.

A. A   **B.** B   **C.** C   **D.** D

Q.58 In the following questions, select a figure from amongst the four alternatives, which when placed in the blank space of fig. (X) would complete the pattern.

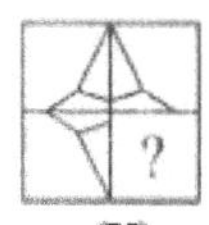   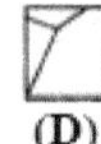

(X)   (A)   (B)   (C)   (D)

A. A   **B.** B   **C.** C   **D.** D

Q.59 Identify this building

A. Taj mahal

B. Redfort

C. Delhi railway station

D. Mumbai station

Q.60 Identify the given image

A. The Palladian bridge

B. Worker's club

C. Operahouse

D. The Parthenon

// Smart Answer Sheet //

Correct — Percentage of students who answered correctly. **Skipped** — Percentage of students who skipped.

Q.	Ans.	Correct / Skipped	Q.	Ans.	Correct / Skipped	Q.	Ans.	Correct / Skipped	Q.	Ans.	Correct / Skipped	Q.	Ans.	Correct / Skipped
1	B	26.76 % / 36.62 %	13	C	35.21 % / 40.85 %	25	B	66.2 % / 16.9 %	37	D	74.65 % / 14.08 %	49	D	40.85 % / 18.3 %
2	C	26.76 % / 42.25 %	14	B	12.68 % / 46.47 %	26	D	60.56 % / 18.31 %	38	D	63.38 % / 21.13 %	50	B	40.85 % / 14.08 %
3	A	23.94 % / 42.26 %	15	D	7.04 % / 43.66 %	27	A	70.42 % / 15.5 %	39	C	61.97 % / 15.49 %	51	A	69.01 % / 15.5 %
4	C	30.99 % / 43.66 %	16	D	8.45 % / 43.66 %	28	D	70.42 % / 21.13 %	40	D	49.3 % / 14.08 %	52	B	39.44 % / 25.35 %
5	A	32.39 % / 43.67 %	17	C	21.13 % / 43.66 %	29	D	67.61 % / 16.9 %	41	D	47.89 % / 12.67 %	53	C	28.17 % / 14.08 %
6	B	16.9 % / 45.07 %	18	C	8.45 % / 45.07 %	30	B	70.42 % / 21.13 %	42	C	56.34 % / 16.9 %	54	A	22.54 % / 25.35 %
7	D	26.76 % / 46.48 %	19	D	12.68 % / 32.39 %	31	C	76.06 % / 16.9 %	43	A	56.34 % / 14.08 %	55	D	43.66 % / 18.31 %
8	B	14.08 % / 54.93 %	20	A	15.49 % / 52.12 %	32	C	47.89 % / 18.31 %	44	B	69.01 % / 12.68 %	56	C	69.01 % / 15.5 %
9	A	18.31 % / 45.07 %	21	C	46.48 % / 12.67 %	33	A	77.46 % / 15.5 %	45	A	57.75 % / 18.31 %	57	A	14.08 % / 18.31 %
10	D	15.49 % / 46.48 %	22	B	69.01 % / 15.5 %	34	B	40.85 % / 21.12 %	46	B	49.3 % / 19.71 %	58	D	66.2 % / 18.31 %
11	D	21.13 % / 43.66 %	23	A	35.21 % / 14.09 %	35	C	38.03 % / 16.9 %	47	D	63.38 % / 15.49 %	59	D	76.06 % / 15.49 %
12	B	15.49 % / 46.48 %	24	C	81.69 % / 15.49 %	36	D	18.31 % / 15.49 %	48	D	45.07 % / 12.68 %	60	D	63.38 % / 18.31 %

//Hints and Solutions//

1. $\dfrac{\cos^2 x - \sin^2 x}{\sin x \cos x} \times \dfrac{\sin 2x}{\cos 2x} = \dfrac{2\cos 2x}{\sin 2x} \times \dfrac{\sin 2x}{\cos 2x} = 2$

Hence, the correct option is (A).

2. The word 'LEADING' has 7 different letters.

When the vowels EAI are always together, they can be supposed to form one letter.

Then, we have to arrange the letters LNDG (EAI).

Now, 5 (4 + 1 = 5) letters can be arranged in 5! = 120 ways.

The vowels (EAI) can be arranged among themselves in 3! = 6 ways.

Required number of ways = (120 x 6) = 720.

Hence, the correct option is (C).

3. $f(g(-1))$

$= f(-3-4)$

$= f(-7)$

$= 5 - 49$

$= -44$

Hence, the correct option is (A).

4. $f(x) = f(y) \rightarrow x + 2 = y + 2 \;\; x = y$

one–one

Hence, the correct option is (C).

5. $AB = \begin{bmatrix} 2 & 1 & 3 \\ 4 & 1 & 0 \end{bmatrix} \begin{bmatrix} 1 & -1 \\ 0 & 2 \\ 5 & 0 \end{bmatrix} = \begin{bmatrix} 17 & 0 \\ 4 & -2 \end{bmatrix}$

Hence, the correct option is (A).

6.
$= x \begin{vmatrix} 1 & \omega & 1 \\ 0 & \omega^2 - \omega & x \\ 0 & x & \omega^2 - 1 \end{vmatrix} = x$

$\{(\omega^2 - \omega)(\omega^2 - 1) - x^2\} = 0 \;\;\; \Rightarrow x = 0$

One value of $x = 0$

Hence, the correct option is (B).

7. $|A| = -1 + 8 = 7$

$adj(A) = \begin{bmatrix} +(-1) & -(2) \\ -(-4) & +(1) \end{bmatrix} = \begin{bmatrix} -1 & -2 \\ 4 & 1 \end{bmatrix}$

$A^{-1} = \dfrac{1}{7} \begin{bmatrix} -1 & -2 \\ 4 & 1 \end{bmatrix}$ Both $(A \text{ and } C)$

Hence, the correct option is (D).

8. $t_n = \dfrac{2n}{(2n+1)!} = \dfrac{2n+1}{(2n+1)!} - \dfrac{1}{(2n+1)!} = \dfrac{1}{(2n)!} - \dfrac{1}{(2n+1)!}$

$\sum_{n=1}^{\infty} t_n = \dfrac{1}{2!} - \dfrac{1}{3!} + \dfrac{1}{4!} - \dfrac{1}{5!} + \cdots \ldots \infty = e^{-1}$

Hence, the correct option is (B).

9. $\dfrac{a}{1-r} = \dfrac{4}{3}$

Then $\dfrac{\frac{3}{4}}{1-r} = \dfrac{4}{3} \Rightarrow r = 1 - \dfrac{9}{16} = \dfrac{7}{16}$

Hence, the correct option is (A).

10. Vowels : O, I, E

No. of Odd place : 4

No of ways = 4P3 × 4! = 576

Hence, the correct option is (D).

11. $:^{B-1}C_3 + ^{a-1}C_4 > ^{e}C_3$

$\Rightarrow ^{n}C_4 > ^{n}C_3 \Rightarrow \dfrac{n!}{4!(n-4)!} > \dfrac{n!}{3!(n-3)!} \Rightarrow \dfrac{1}{4} > \dfrac{1}{(n-3)}$

$\Rightarrow n - 3 > 4 \Rightarrow n > 7$

Hence, the correct option is (D).

12. $(a - 2b)^a = \sum_{r=0}^{n} n_r \, (a)^{n-r}(-2b)^r$

$t_s + t_6 = 0$

$\Rightarrow ^{n}C_4(a)^{a-4}(-2b)^4 + ^{n}C_s(a)^{n-5}(-2b)^5 = 0 \Rightarrow$

$\dfrac{n!}{4!(n-4)!} a^{n-4}(-2b)^4 = -\dfrac{n!}{5!(n-5)!}(a)^{n-5}(-2b)^5$

Hence, the correct option is (B).

13. $2^{3a} = (8)^n = (1+7)^e == ^{n}C_0 + ^{n}C_1 7 + ^{n}C_2 7^2 + \cdots \cdots + ^2 C_n 7^n$

$\Rightarrow 2^{3n} - 1 = 7[^{n}C_1 + ^{n}C_2 7 + \cdots \ldots + ^{n}C_n 7^{n-1}]$

$\therefore$ divisible by 7

Hence, the correct option is (C).

14. Total terms $= 60$

Sum of first 30 terms $= \dfrac{\text{Sum of all the terms}}{2} = \dfrac{2^{59}}{2} = 2^{58}$

Hence, the correct option is (B).

15. $x = 1$

$1 = a_0 + a_1 + a_2 + a_3 + \cdots \ldots \ldots + a_{2n}$

$x = -1, 3^n = a_0 - a_1 + a_2 - a_3 + \cdots \ldots \ldots + a_{2n}$

$1 + 3^2 = 2[a_0 + a_2 + a_4 + \cdots \ldots \ldots + a_{2n}]$

$\Rightarrow a_0 + a_2 + a_4 + \cdots \ldots \ldots a_{2n} = \dfrac{1+3^n}{2}$

Hence, the correct option is (D).

16. Roots are ω, ω^2 Let $\alpha = \omega, \beta = \omega^2$

$\alpha^{19} = \omega, \beta^7 = \omega^2$

$\therefore$ Equation remains same i.e. $x^2 + x + 1 = 0$

Hence, the correct option is (D).

17. $x^2 - 2\sqrt{3} - 22 = 0$

$D = 12 + (4 \times 22) > 0$

$\because$ coeffs are irrational

$x = \dfrac{2\sqrt{3} \pm \sqrt{12+88}}{2}$

$\therefore$ Roots are irrational, real, unequl.

Hence, the correct option is (C).

18.

$$x^2 + 15|x| + 14 > 0 \,\forall x$$

Hence no solution.

Hence, the correct option is (C).

19. $z = \dfrac{4}{1-i}$

$\bar{z} = \dfrac{4}{1+i}$

Hence, the correct option is (D).

20.

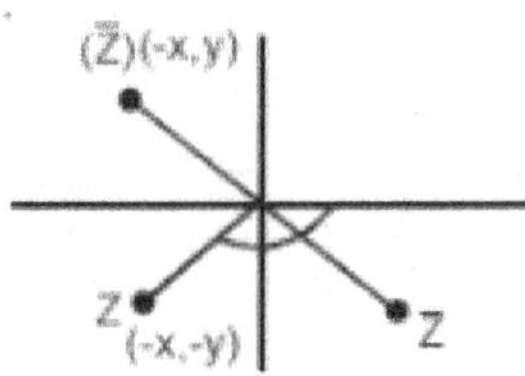

if $\arg(z) = -\pi + \theta$

$\Rightarrow \arg(\bar{z}) = \pi - \theta$

$\arg(-\bar{z}) = -\theta$

$\arg(\bar{z}) - \arg(-\bar{z}) = \pi - \theta - (-\theta) = \pi - \theta + \theta = \pi$

Hence, the correct option is (A).

21. In each step, element at the upper-right position gets enlarged, inverts vertically and reaches the lower-left corner; the existing element at the lower-left position, is lost and a new small element appears at the upper-right position.

Hence, the correct option is (C).

22. In each step, the elements move in the sequence.

Hence, the correct option is (B).

23. The pins, equal in number to the number of sides in the main figure are attached to the midpoint of a side of the main figure in case of figures (2), (3), (4) and (5). In fig. (1), these pins are attached to a vertex of the main figure.

Hence, the correct option is (A).

24. In all other figures, the two line segments are parallel to each other.

Hence, the correct option is (C).

25.

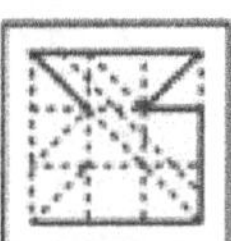

Hence, the correct option is (B).

26.

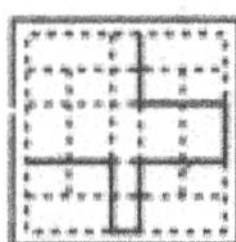

Hence, the correct option is (D).

27.

Hence, the correct option is (A).

28.

Hence, the correct option is (D).

29. The third figure in each row comprises of parts which are not common to the first two figures.

Hence, the correct option is (D).

30. In each row, the second figure is obtained from the first figure by adding two mutually perpendicular line segments at the centre and the third figure is obtained from the first figure by adding four circles outside the main figure.

Hence, the correct option is (B).

31.

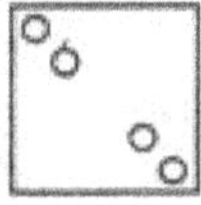

Hence, the correct option is (C).

32.

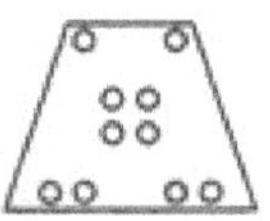

Hence, the correct option is (C).

33. (1, 4), (2, 3) and (5, 6) are three different pairs of identical figures.

Hence, the correct option is (A).

34.

Hence, the correct option is (B).

35. The half-shaded leaf rotates 135°ACW and the unshaded leaf rotates 135°CW.

Hence, the correct option is (C).

36. The figure may be labelled as shown.

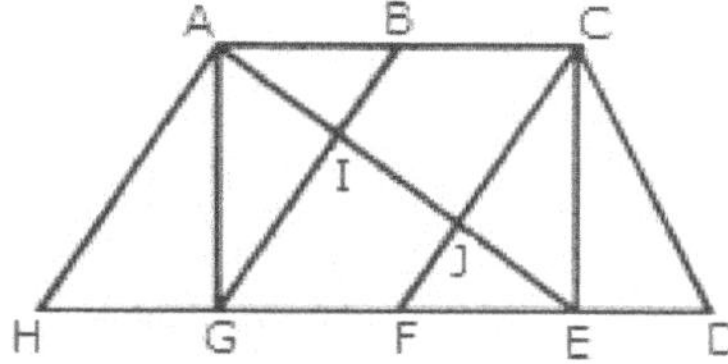

The simplest triangles are AHG, AIG, AIB, JFE, CJE and CED i.e. 6 in number.

The triangles composed of two components each are ABG, CFE, ACJ and EGI i.e. 4 in number.

The triangles composed of three components each are ACE, AGE and CFD i.e. 3 in number.

There is only one triangle i.e. AHE composed of four components.

Therefore, There are 6 + 4 + 3 + 1 = 14 triangles in the given figure.

Hence, the correct option is (D).

37.

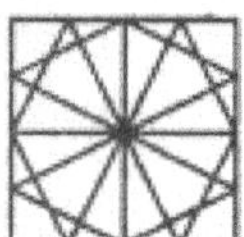

Hence, the correct option is (D).

38.

Hence, the correct option is (D).

39.

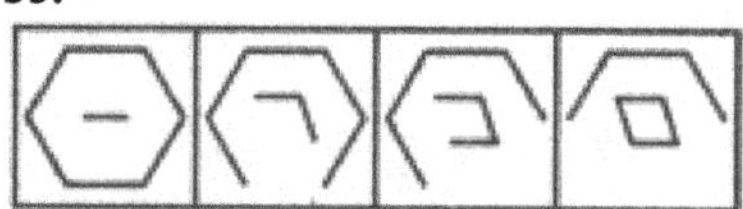

Hence, the correct option is (C).

40. In fig. (X), one of the dots lies in the region common to the circle and the square only and the other dot lies in the region common to all the three figures -the circle, the square and the triangle. In each of the alternatives (1), (2) and (3), there is no region common to the square and the circle only. Only fig. (4) consists of both the types of regions.

Hence, the correct option is (D).

41. University of Calcutta was the first university of India located in Kolkata West Bengal it was established in 24 Jan 1857. it was the first Western style University in whole Asia that time.

Hence, the correct option is (D).

42. The largest dry rock in India is situated at Marmugao.

Hence, the correct option is (C).

43. The largest Indian State by area is Rajasthan (342,239 km²,).

Hence, the correct option is (A).

44. Ajanta Caves is the oldest monuments.The Ajanta Caves are 30 (approximately) rock-cut Buddhist cave monuments which date from the 2nd century BCE to about 480 CE in Aurangabad district of Maharashtra state of India.

Hence, the correct option is (B).

45. Flight Lt. Harita Kaur Deol (10 November 1971 – 24 December 1996) was a pilot with the Indian Air Force. She was the first woman pilot to fly solo in the Indian Air Force. The flight was on 2 September 1994 in an Avro HS-748, when she was 22 years old.

Hence, the correct option is (A).

46. The largest and oldest museum in India and has rare collections of antiques, armour and ornaments, fossils, skeletons, mummies and Mughal paintings. It was founded by the Asiatic Society of Bengal in Kolkata (Calcutta), India, in 1814 C.E. The founder curator was Nathaniel Wallich, a Danish botanist.

Hence, the correct option is (B).

47.

The first Indian Satellite launched from Soviet Cosmodrome is Aryabhatta . It was launched by India on 19 April 1975.

Hence, the correct option is (D).

48. Apsara is the oldest of India's research reactors. The reactor was designed by the Bhabha Atomic Research Center (BARC) and built with assistance from the United Kingdom (which also provided the initial fuel supply consisting of 80 percent enriched uranium). Apsara first went critical on 4 August 1956.

Hence, the correct option is (D).

49. The first person of Indian origin to be appointed as a judge in U.S. is Ridhi Desai.

Hence, the correct option is (D).

50. Largest Mint in India is located at Kolkata.

Hence, the correct option is (B).

51. Arrangement of words as per order in the dictionary:

1. Necrology

2. Necromancy

4. Necrophilia

3. Necropolis

Hence, the correct option is (A).

52. 15th Aug 2010 = (2009 years + period from 1-Jan-2010 to 15-Aug-2010)

We know that number of odd days in 400 years = 0

Hence the number of odd days in 2000 years = 0 (Since 2000 is a perfect multiple of 400)

Number of odd days in the period 2001-2009 = 7normal years + 2leap year

= 7 x 1 + 2 x 2 = 11 = (11 - 7x1) odd day = 4 odd day

Days from1-Jan-2010 to15-Aug-2010 = 31 (Jan) + 28 (Feb) + 31 (Mar) + 30 (Apr) + 31(may) +

30(Jun) +31(Jul) + 15(Aug) = 227

227days = 32weeks + 3day =3 odd days

Total number of odd days = (0 + 4 + 3) = 7 odd days = 0 odd day

0 odd day = Sunday. Hence 15th August, 2010 is Sunday.

Hence, the correct option is (B).

53. The sum of any two consecutive terms of the series gives the next term.
So the wrong number in the series is 53.

Hence, the correct option is (C).

54.

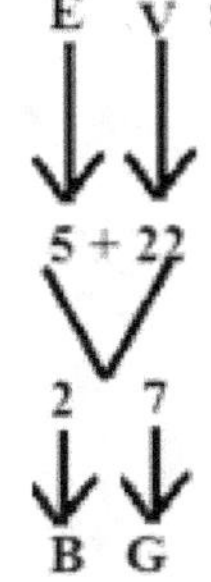
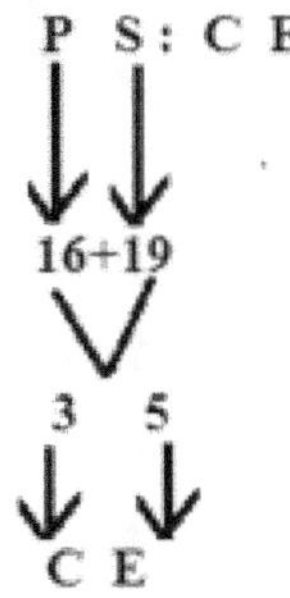

Hence, the correct option is (A).

55. LBW is a term of cricket. Similarly, 'Stroke' is a term of Hocky.

Hence, the correct option is (D).

56. Kitten Is the young one of Cat similarly cub is young one of the Lion.

Hence, the correct option is (C).

57.

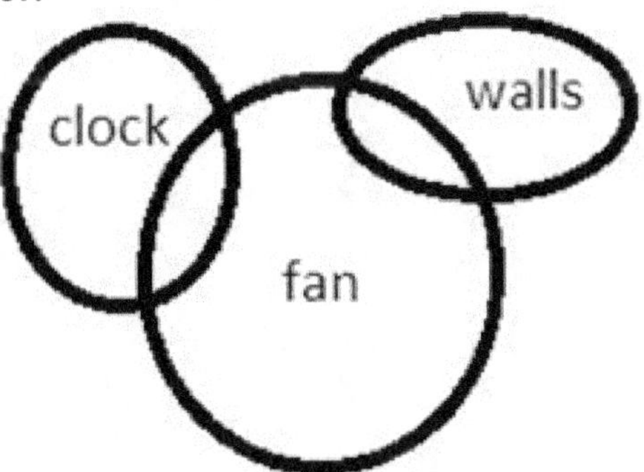

Hence, the correct option is (A).

58.

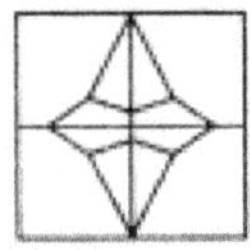

Hence, the correct option is (D).

59. Mumbai Central (formerly Bombay Central, station code: BCT) is a major railway station on the Western line, situated in Mumbai, Maharashtra in an area known by the same name.[1] Designed by British architect Claude Batley.

Hence, the correct option is (D).

60. The Parthenon is a former temple on the Athenian Acropolis, Greece, dedicated to the goddess Athena, whom the people of Athens considered their patron. Construction began in 447 BC when the Athenian Empire was at the peak of its power.

Hence, the correct option is (D).

// Notes //

// Notes //